THE
STUDY OF PALMISTRY

Comte C. de Saint-Germain,

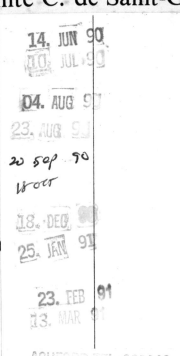

Tynron Press
Dumfriesshire

First printed 1897

This edition first published in 1989 by
Tynron Press
Stenhouse
Thornhill
Dumfriesshire DG3 4LD

ISBN: 1-871948-03-7

133-6 .

Cover by Eric C.H. Yeo
Printed by Singapore National Printers (Pte) Ltd

TABLE OF CONTENTS

TABLE OF CONTENTS

Among the tens of thousands of American readers who have given such a pleasant welcome to my syndicate articles and to my elementary work entitled *"PRACTICAL PALMISTRY,"* a large number have done me the honor of communicating with me with a view of increasing their knowledge of this most fascinating science. Many have even visited Chicago and requested me to give them personal and exhaustive instruction in Palmistry. I finally decided, a year ago, to comply with these solicitations, and have devoted a few hours, every day, to the teaching of the science rendered famous in this XIX. Century by the splendidly successful efforts of Desbarrolles and d'Arpentigny. Class after class attended my studio and received favorably whatever conscientious instruction my twenty-nine years of chirosophic studies entitled me to give them. Typewritten copies of these lessons were distributed to the pupils, and gradually modified so as to suit almost any fair grade of intellect. They have now grown to the size of a two-volume manual, and having stood well the test of actual and widely approved teaching, they are presented to the public at large with large additions, modifications and improvements and with over 1,100 illustrations, especially drawn for this work.

As a patient and painstaking instructor —and I may claim that much without fear of contradiction—I have aimed at the following results, which I failed to see realized in any book on Palmistry published to this day:

1. Clearness and absence of useless theorizing.

2. System and thoroughly logical classification.

3. Completeness. In this respect I may be allowed to state that the present book contains between two and ten times more reliable observations than any work ever published in the English tongue.

For instance, in the two largest books, of comparatively recent date, devoted to chirosophy or to the language of the hand, I find that, concerning the Line of Life and the Lines of Influence that proceed from it, one of these works contains 69 observations and the other 49. In this book, the same subject is treated in over 200 observations, all of the first importance and all illustrated by means of one separate illustration for each indication.

To this wealth of technical information I have added hundreds of actual cases from life, chosen from the untranslated works of Desbarrolles and others, or from my own stock of experiences.

An illustration accompanies each of these most interesting facts, completing the theory as fast as it is developed through the book. I soon found that in no other way can the pupil's mind be brought to grasp the intricacies of this most minute and ever varied study.

As to Clearness and Absence of theorizing or poetizing (the latter especially unbearable to the earnest student), I will say that I have strictly avoided dispersing my efforts toward imparting knowledge for the sake of ventilating some favorite doctrine, either of my own concoction or the product of a more inventive brain.

I have even played false to my beloved master, Desbarrolles, so far as to decline following him in his Astrological or Kabbalistic surmises and deductions.

Physiology I found long ago—and I find every day—sufficient to fully explain the "Mysteries of the Hand." In fact, I am ready to declare, right here, that, in my humble judgment, there are no such things as "Mysteries of the Hand" and that Chiromancy—the less explainable branch of Palmistry—is fast leaving the ranks of Occult Sciences to enter the honored family of Sciences, no longer "a poor, disdained and distant relation."

Therefore, in the Introduction, you will find Desbarrolles' admirable reasoning about the Physiological explanations of Palmistry, and this will constitute, with a very few paragraphs scattered through the book, all the theorizing to which I shall treat my readers. For this work is not to belie its title: its sole purpose is to teach you how to Read Hands accurately.

And now I will resume, for a moment, my cap and gown and, after a few necessary explanations, I shall tell my pupils —for the readers of this book all become pupils of the author—what method to follow in the study of "*THE PRACTICE OF PALMISTRY FOR PROFESSIONAL PURPOSES.*"

First, do not allow the title of the book to worry you in the least. The word professional has been inserted herein with an object, but certainly not to frighten you away. It simply means that every item of information needed to make of you a respected, refined and reliable palmist is to be found within these pages. If, after the study is over and completed, it suits your convenience to read hands for a fee, well and good: you are equipped for the task and the money paid you will be honestly earned. Should your circumstances or tastes keep you away from the profession, you will still possess a thorough knowledge of indisputable value, whose practice, among your friends, will render it daily more precious to you and to them.

Next to this first—indispensable— statement, let me make another, addressed especially to those who have never perused any work on Palmistry. I wish them to clearly understand that this book, exhaustive though it be, takes matters ab ovo, from the start, and will be just as profitable to an absolute beginner, who does not even know the name of a Mount or a Line, than to one who has dabbled in Palmistry to while away an idle hour. In fact, I truly believe that the present work will prove a great deal easier to understand and assimilate than many so-called Palmistry Primers, so much simpler in appearance. In such matters, classification is the lantern that lights the way, and, if it is thorough and based on logic, the smaller or greater number of objects (or ideas) to be classified is comparatively unimportant.

However, this allusion to beginners brings me to my third and last piece of advice, which I may entitle

How to Study this Book.

1. Read it slowly. Do not skim over parts and chapters as if the fire were in the house and you had just a minute left to reach the very last line.

2. Do not attempt to read further than Part First—"Preliminaries"—before being absolutely conversant with the Physiology of Palmistry, as laid down by Desbarrolles, and with the Map of the Hand. Let every technical term—and there are but few—be branded in your mind once for all, before attempting to interpret them.

3. In your first reading of the Book leave out the following chapters and interspersed paragraphs:

The Leading Types of Hands,

The Signatures of the Mounts,

The Cases (in smaller type) scattered through the book,

The Lines and Signs on Fingers and Thumb, and, finally,

The Palmistic Dictionary.

Reserve those for a second, leisurely reading. You will enjoy them better and it is only then that they will prove really profitable.

4. Read consecutively and refrain from looking ahead to satisfy your—or somebody else's—curiosity. This jumping from one half-digested subject to another is the surest way to get tired—if not disgusted—with the whole study. Remember that Palmistry is a language and that it has to be learned, like any other language, by gradually assimilating, first the elements—the letters—then the syllables, the words, the sentences, the paragraphs, the pages, the volumes. Fast work, in this case, is no work at all; indeed, it has destroyed the ambitions of more would-be palmists than any other mistake ever made by them.

5. Finally, when you will have decided to take this book as your Guide to Palmistry, attach yourself to it with a will, until you have mastered its contents from cover to cover. While performing this task do not open any other work on the subject; listen to no other teacher. This safeguard against a "confusion of tongues" applies just as truly to any book and any teacher you may choose instead of the present ones. There can be but one commander, when a fortress is to be stormed; but one initiator at a time into the realms of such a delicate science as Modern, Orthodox Palmistry.

To these few paragraphs of advice, warning, encouragement, there remains only for me to add my earnest wishes that you will extract from the study of *"THE PRACTICE OF PALMISTRY FOR PROFESSIONAL PURPOSES"* some of the delight—and mental profit—I have derived from my long and daily intercourse with the masterly works of d'Arpentigny and Desbarrolles, the only teachers worth listening to, the sole and direct inspirers of the present book.

Comte C. de Saint-Germain.

Chicago, November 1, 1897

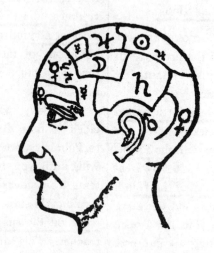

PART FIRST

Preliminaries

"From a cursory examination of the animal world, we may gather the important conclusion that from the structure of an extremity we may obtain a complete insight into the entire organism of an animal; and thus the paws furnished with sharp retractile claws of the lion indicate at once to a naturalist its strong teeth, its powerful jaws, its muscular strength of limbs; while from the cleft of the cow the complicated structure of its stomach, the definite peculiarities of its jaws and its vegetable diet may with equal certainty be predicted."—*The Hand Phrenologically Considered.*

PART FIRST

Preliminaries

THE
PRACTICE OF PALMISTRY
FOR
PROFESSIONAL PURPOSES

INTRODUCTION BY DESBARROLLES

Introducing the Introduction.

Adrien Adolphe Desbarrolles was born in Paris, August 22, 1801; or, as they used to call it then, according to the poetical calendar of the Revolution, "on the 4th of fructidor of the year IX. of the Republic, one and indivisible." He died in his beloved Paris, February 11, 1886, at the age of eighty-five, after devoting fully 50 years of his life to the study of Palmistry, or, as he preferred to call it, Chiromancy. To that favorite and absorbing occupation—which, with him, was not only theoretical, but practical, since he gave daily consultations in his apartment in the Rue d'Enfer (now Boulevard St. Michel), No. 95—he added profound researches into the kindred, semi-occult sciences of Phrenology, Physiognomy and Graphology, even going to the extent of writing an elaborate work upon this new addition to the circle of divinatory arts. Finally, he never allowed himself to doubt that in the ancient teachings of the Kabbala lay the key to all these strange manifestations that have puzzled the human brain since the dawn of civilization. According to him, from the Kabbala emanates all wisdom, all knowledge, all guidance; it reveals the existence of three worlds, the divine, the moral or mental, the material —those three elements so universally recognized by the great religions of the earth—Soul, Mind, Body.

This constantly repeated division into three component elements, Desbarrolles, logician of high degree, followed it up patiently through the various outward and inward manifestations of aspiration, action, realization. In this body of ours he recognized three forces ever at work and seldom in peaceful accord: the lowest—the material body, all instinct; the highest—the "mens" or divine projection of the body, and, between them, the connecting link so persistently searched after by the scientists of all ages—the astral body that serves as a bond between the heart and the brain, between physical and mental life.

Upon these premises, the great French chiromant built a marvelous edifice, borrowing each of its stones from the sadly neglected quarry out of which the philosophers of antiquity have drawn the grandest monuments ever conceived by human intelligence. The deepest researches of the Hindoo Brahmines, and, before them, of the Egyptian priests and Chaldean shepherds, were put to contribution, as well as Pythagoras' stupendous vision of the world and Aristotle's extraordinary divination of many of our modern problems. The Middle Age alchemists and astrologers, the profound Arabs as well as the Italian, the Dutch, the German, the French, the English savants were interrogated in the ponderous works they left behind them, for some more light upon the fate of man, before, during and after life. And, coming down to our times, the most advanced representatives of medical science as well as of natural and mental philosophy furnished their quota of demonstration and indirect approval to the theory constructed by this patient scholar, whose great common sense never allowed him to be waylaid toward the treacherous bogs of deceptive sophistry. Desbarrolles absorbed this immense knowledge; he digested it; he used the brain food thus obtained to enlighten others who had neither time nor capacity to bring to a finish such a huge enterprise. With his own tactful hands, fortified by the daily experiments of half a century, he prepared a book that would be for all times a standard work, in its special domain, and upon it has truly been founded what is becoming, every year, more universally recognized as the Science of Palmistry.

Not that the last word has been written yet upon this weighty subject, so infinitely varied in its capacity; that last word will never be penned as long as baby boys and baby girls will open their wondering eyes to the light of this world of ours.

New hands, new discoveries; the whole of Palmistry is condensed in these four words. But the principles that explain ninety per cent., or more, of these curious forms and markings offered us by hands and palms have been formulated once for all by the master-mind from whom our inspiration, as well as most of our knowledge, proceeds. To wander away from his teachings, in a fretful, childish effort toward originality, is about as silly and imprudent as would be the attempt of a village mason to erect a towering cathedral; it smacks of utter foolishness, and in the transitory period the science of Palmistry is now traversing, it is infinitely more harmful to it than the bitterest attacks of honest—if ignorant—adversaries. "From my friends preserve me, O Lord; I'll take care of my enemies," would doubtless be the first exclamation of poor Palmistry herself, if ever she appeared in propria persona to defend her cause at the bar of public opinion.

But what reverent hands are called upon to do, now that general curiosity is gradually being transformed into a serious thirst for knowledge, is to gather those teachings of the master, to strip them—for the time being—of their dazzling garb of old lore and immense learning, and to re-classify them in such a manner that the simplest minds may enjoy, and profit by, a thorough acquaintance with Desbarrolles' practical views on Palmistry in all its details.

Here and there a touch of novelty may be introduced, if really based upon repeated observations; always remembering, however, that each of the 650 cases described by Desbarrolles in his Revelations Complètes—a book never fully understood by its many English plagiarists and purloiners—rests upon the solid basis of scores and scores of similar observations and covers the ground completely enough for the average amateur or even professional palmist.

The need, really, has always been one of classification and illustration; in neither was Desbarrolles himself particularly successful; or, rather, his classification suited him to perfection and is strong and logical enough all through.

Only that logic is too deep for the average reader; he needs a whiter thread to lead him along this labyrinth wherein so many before him have pitifully lost their way.

And this white thread I have tried, by the labor of many years, to twist solid enough and to stretch with sufficiently minute care to guide the chiromants of either sex out of their discouraged meanderings to the blessed gate that opens into Daylight, Pure Air and—Truth.

A few words now, pro domo mea, in my own defense.

Of course, Adrien Desbarrolles never penned a line of this Introduction of his; he had died years before I wrote the first word of this, my third and final effort in Palmistic literature.

And yet, innocent though he be of any complicity with the author, every sentence that will be presented now over his signature expresses his inmost conviction, and expresses it in an exact translation of the very words he used. Only this Introduction represents, so to speak, the synthesis of his best thoughts, freed from many a theory the reading of which would doubtless prove most attractive—for few such masters of style ever lived—but would not be really helpful to the student. Thus the Kabbala, the ancient astrology, and the astral influences, as they were understood and presented by Desbarrolles, find no place, either in the Introduction, or in the body of this work.

As I stated in my short Preface to be Read, the object of this manual is to teach the student to interpret hands, not to fill his head with a number of theories —however ingenious, marvelous even, they may be. Thus, without desiring to belittle the superb "tout ensemble" of Desbarrolles' magnum opus, I feel that I am doing my duty in concentrating all my efforts within the scope I have already outlined and in calling upon modern science only for whatever doctrines or theory I shall think necessary to lighten the path of the reader.

With those few remarks and this ever frank declaration of principles and object, I beg leave to close my Introduction to

It is the purpose of Palmistry to teach you how to conquer the ancient art of divination by means of stated rules and not by intuition. These rules work accurately at all times and under all circumstances, while intuition comes and goes at its own sweet will, under the influence of some momentary excitement which developes, in very rare occasions, a state of true clairvoyance, never to be fully depended on.

Those fixed laws, without which no science is worthy any serious attention, have been formulated, in this XIX. Century, by two men, starting from opposite poles, but meeting on a common ground of conscientious investigation: these men were Captain d'Arpentigny and myself. The former became the creator of this ingenious and startlingly accurate system that includes, under the name of Chirognomy, all such observations as relate to the outward physiognomy of the hand, its shape, its finger tips, etc., without paying any attention to the lines or signs written on the palm. This added branch of a science as old as the world now forms part and parcel of Palmistry and is almost unrivaled in its precise revelations concerning the disposition and tendencies of body and mind. No actual events, past or future, however, does it prognosticate, while its elder sister, Chiromancy, freed by me from the heavy fetters of superstitious nonsense accumulated by the XVI. and XVII. Century palmists, emerges from its rather chaotic state to the full possession of an orderly and definite status.

But it is only since to its Kabbalitic origin has been added a full and satisfactory demonstration of its solid physiological foundation, that Palmistry has begun to be noticed and discussed in the world of thinkers and searchers. It is true that Aristotle had anticipated the modern discoveries in that direction when he wrote: "Lines have not been traced without cause in the hands of men; they evidently emanate from the influence of heaven and from human individuality." In the powerful brain of the great philosopher the germ of the present doctrine of the aura, the unexplained and imponderable atmosphere that surrounds us, had thus been deposited, to be formulated by the savants of the XIX. Century with the prudent conservatism of modern investigators.

For, indeed, there is a breath—light, heat, electricity—fluid or vibration, that gives life, and the withdrawal of which is made manifest by the state called death. All the great physicians, the renowned physiologists of our time have admitted as much, while finding no proper explanation or even definition for this mysterious primary force. So far, the nearest they have reached to the lighting up of this dark question is formulated in two words: Magnetic electricity. One of the most distinguished among them,

M. Charles Bonnet, wrote:

"Ideas are nothing but vibrations, nothing but changes occurring within us, and they are caused by some external influence transmitted through the nerves to the cerebral fibers."

Thus the existence of the vital fluid is admitted; its mode of transmission through the nerves to the brain is indicated; it will need no long reasoning to demonstate how this fluid penetrates man's body through the fingers, and, leaving its marking in the palm, runs up to the brain.

In the human body every element is combined to form a clear, distinct individuality: the features of the face, the irregularities of the skull, the length or shortness of the limbs, the bearing, the walk, the look, the words, the gestures—everything, even to the handwriting; and above all, the member that traces the writing: the hand.

Aristotle said that the hand is "the organ of organs, the instrument of instruments," and d'Arpentigny wrote in his beautiful language:

"There are hands which naturally attract us, and there are hands which excite in us repulsion. I have seen hands which seemed covered with eyes, so sagacious and so penetrating was their appearance. Some, like those of the sphinx, suggest an idea of mystery; some betray recklessness and strength, combined with activity of body; others again indicate laziness, joined to feebleness and cunning."

It is impossible to deny that the sense fo touch, concentrated in the hands and especially in the finger tips and the center of the palm, constitutes the most indispensable of the five senses and can almost take the place of the other four. The blind, the deaf, the dumb, the unfortunate one deprived of the sense of smell are still kept in communication with the world and their fellow creatures if their sense of touch is unimpaired, if their hands are still in possession of their full capabilities. This undoubted supremacy of the hand prepares us for any revelation that will demonstrate its paramount influence in the absorption and distribution of the vital fluid. In fact, it is the hand whose extreme nervous sensitiveness carries to the brain the double principle that gives birth to thought; it is the hand again which executes what the other senses have merely advised or prepared.

Besides, have not prominent physiologists stated that the fact of the palm becoming burning hot, in the advanced shape of consumption and in all diseases that arise from organic wasting away through irritation, is sufficient evidence that in the hand exists one of the centers of instinctive life? They have added that, in their opinion, this focus of instinctive life resides in the elevations (or Mounts) under the four fingers, wherein (as well as in the hollow of the hand and at the finger tips) are found, to the numbers of 250 or 300, these Pacinian Corpuscles, which are but agglomerations of nervous matter. These Corpuscles act as condensers of innervation, receiving the vital fluid through the fingers, storing it like reservoirs of electricity and endowing the hand with its surprising sensitiveness, commonly known as the <u>sense of touch</u>. Let me add to this essential statement concerning the Pacinian Corpuscles, that they do not exist in the monkey's so-called hands and are absent, or very few in number, in the hands of the congenital idiot.

So far we have stated and briefly demonstrated:

The existence of an imponderable vital fluid—known as electricity—surrounding us and the world at large; and

The paramount influence of the hand in every manifestation of human nervosity.

Let us now connect these two statements, and logically admit that from this outward, universal source of the world's instinctive life to the particular center of man's instinctive life—the brain—the vital electricity will follow the channels so admirably prepared for it, <u>the fingers,</u> and, its task performed, return over the same road to the common reservoir of physical and mental power; the operation being performed with ceaseless activity until partial or total death results from the withdrawal of the said fluid from part of the body or from the whole.

It goes without saying, or rather without useless repetition, that the complicated system of nerves acts as a network of telegraph wires in transmitting from finger tips to cerebellum the ever traveling fluid.

And it is certainly not strange that this electricity, passing ceaselessly over the palm of the hand, should leave upon this ultra-sensitive surface distinct traces of its constant action, those traces lighter or deeper according to the intensity of the nervous impression that has been undergone by the subject.

If anyone should tell you that these lines and signs in the palm have been traced by the movements of the hand, by its opening and closing, etc., answer them that those markings are found ten times more distinct and numerous in the hands of idle society women than in the palms of busy workers, and are also perfectly plain and strangely eloquent in the hands of babes but a few hours old.

And as to the existence of these lines and signs in the palm absolutely depending on the continuity of the passage of the fluid from finger tips to brain and from brain to finger tips, the inspection of a paralyzed hand will settle forever any doubt, on that score, as in that "dead" hand these markings shall have vanished, while its sister hand will remain alive and <u>lined.</u> The congenital idiots—supplied with half developed brains—display, in their hands, but a minimum of lines, just as their intelligence lacks the average amount of strength and development.

It is here that the admirable discovery of M. d'Arpentigny in reference to the shape of finger Tips and the existence of Knots (or bulging of the finger-joints) comes to the assistance of the great theory upon which Modern Palmistry has laid its strong foundations.

With Aristotle, Muller, Herder, Bichat, Humboldt, and many others among the loftiest thinkers the earth

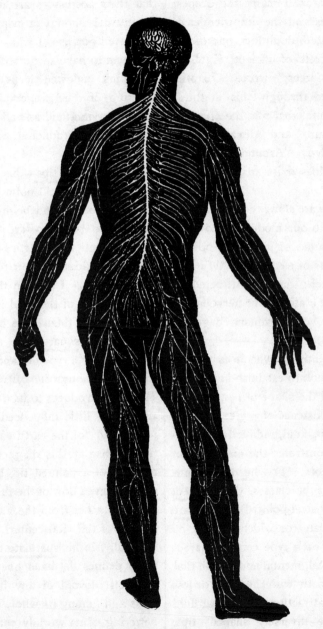

MAN'S NERVE SYSTEM.

ever produced, I have affirmed that we are surrounded with this imponderable fluid, whose nature remains the deepest of all mysteries and the knowledge of which constituted, doubtless, one of the unrevealed secrets of ancient Kabbala. "The psychic forces," wrote Aristotle, "are manifested through this slightest breath, this Aura, that fills the concavities of the brain," and Alexander von Humboldt added: "Around the human nerves there does exist an invisible atmosphere."

This fluid we are slowly conquering, as we harness it to our modern discoveries and develop some of its minor powers under the name of electricity. Of it, we know that much: that it is attracted by points and that it affects our nervous system to a most extraordinary degree—even unto death.

Now d'Arpentigny, who does not attempt in his book to establish any correlation between the shape of hand or fingers and the existence of any external or internal nervous fluid, indirectly and unwittingly demonstrates the exactness of the above theory. For he divides finger tips into four classes, the pointed, the conical (or semi-pointed), the square and the spatulate (or widened), and he bestows upon each type certain characteristics, physical, mental and moral, that correspond exactly with the more or less facility in the attraction of the vital fluid through those diversely shaped tips. Surprisingly enough, his conclusions and mine, although reached through radically different methods, culminated in identically the same results.

First, he tells us of the pointed fingers that their possessors are endowed with an unusual amount of inspiration, intuition, even genius. I add—what he does not seem to have suspected—that if they are thus endowed it is because the tapering of their fingers attracts more freely the vital fluid and allows it to perform its life-producing action quicker and better.

The conical tips—the tapering of which, although still noticeable, is much less pronounced and begins only from the middle phalanx—are characterized by d'Arpentigny as artistic fingers, but already less ideal in their tendencies and performances. I explain this by the reduced facility of the fluid in penetrating the hand and thence the brain.

With the square tips, the ingenious writer strikes a type of hand he evidently dislikes, although he calls it the useful. Here he introduces to us the hand of the utilitarian, little influenced by lofty impulses and "of the earth earthy." I feel no surprise at this diagnosis, since the absence of a pointed tip, by interfering with the even flow of the fluid, places the subject farther from the all-powerful influence of the vital center.

Finally, in his spatulate tips, d'Arpentigny defines the hand obeying material instincts, devoid of any higher aspirations and finding its whole delight in the bettering of its worldly condition. Further away from the pointed shape, it is easy for me to understand how the fluid, finding increased difficulties in penetrating the subject's organism, fails to endow him with its purest and best characteristics.

Thus have the shapes of the finger tips and their influence, as revealed in the examination of thousands of hands, affirmed the absolute truth of this axiom: that the vital fluid penetrates through the fingers because they are points—and penetrates more or less freely according to the degree of acuity of those points. Do we not read in Muller's Physiology that "the rapidity of the nervous action varies according to the nature of the individuals?" We add and we prove with d'Arpentigny: "According to the shape of their finger tips."

Another argument, just as important, in favor of the theory of the vital fluid penetrating the body through the fingers, is found in d'Arpentigny's statements concerning smooth and knotted fingers; and I repeat that he gave it to the world "by the inspiration of God," as he modestly stated to me, and certainly without attempting to connect it with the physiological fact of the vital fluid aspired through the fingers.*

Smooth fingers are distinguished from knotted fingers by the absence of knots, or visible joints, between the phalanges of the finger. D'Arpentigny declares that they give to all kinds of fingers a large amount of intuition, of instinctive, unreasoned understanding of things in general, varying of course with the degrees of pointedness of the tips. I add to this that the fact of the vital fluid traversing the length of the fingers without meeting these strong impediments named

knots must necessarily endow the subjects with the free inspiration resulting from that liberty of access of the fluid.

Knotted fingers, on the contrary, opposing barriers to the running-in of the fluid, will endow their possessors with a reasoning power, a classifying instinct which is the natural counterpart of the lightning-like intuition and decision of the smooth fingered subjects. You see how completely the statements of d'Arpentigny, left unexplained by their brilliant author, fit in with the more elaborate, thoroughly logical theory of the vital fluid entering the hand, and through it the brains by way of the finger tips.

Again, short hands, says, d'Arpentigny, are synthetical; they grasp ideas as a whole, not in their details. I add, the fluid has so little space to run over in such hands that reflection has hardly time to awaken. Long hands, on the contrary, are analytical in their tendencies, slow to decide, slow to act. Here again I call the reader's attention to the fact that the long stretch covered by the fluid has allowed reflection to interfere and to affirm itself.

And thus could the whole of d'Arpentigny's system be made strikingly stronger and clearer and logical, while standing in its entirety and its beauty as a monument of an intellect almost akin

---

*To confirm this theory of Desbarrolles—which he could honestly claim as his own splendid discovery—I beg leave to call the reader's attention to the fact that in 99 hands out of 100 the first finger—the Index—which is by excellence the Attractor of the vital fluid, the tip is always more conically inclined than that of the other fingers in the same hand. [St-G.]

to genius. By its help I have been able to demonstrate the conquering influence of the vital fluid over man's tendencies and the development of his physical, mental and moral being. I have already briefly explained how the fluid, penetrating through the finger tips, accumulating in the Pacinian Corpuscles and tracing deep channels at the surface of the palm, finally reached the brain and from it was redistributed through the whole body by means of the innumerable ramifications of nerves; finally to return to the common ocean of nature's vital fluid, this time being respired through the finger tips just as it had been aspired through them. In this aspir and respir resides the whole mystery of human life, unexplained, of course, in its deepest aspects, but fairly well followed up in some of its inward manifestations—notably in the markings it leaves in the hands.*

And thus I reach this much more bitterly contested portion of my theory, that which concerns the interpretation of these markings according to fixed, logical rules, and, these failing, according to the traditional readings left behind by the earnest chiromants of centuries past, many of them scientists of no mean degree, whose works have survived them in the memories of men.

I shall here reverse the order of arguments and speak first of those observations of the hand whose interpretation is purely traditional; i. e., based upon empiricism and not upon any logical doctrine. The word empiricism in this instance must be taken in its favorable, original meaning that of a

scientific practice depending purely on experiments, not on theories. This is, after all, and in spite of the protests of prejudiced and narrow-minded contradictors, the only method that helps us reach any degree of accuracy in the diagnosis and cure of human diseases. Now, for centuries and centuries past, the eminent scientists I spoke of in the preceding paragraph, gathered an immense number of observations concerning the lines and signs found in man's hand, and compared these with facts known to them in the lives of the subjects. Repeated coincidences between certain facts and certain lines or signs gradually convinced them that there was in these coincidences something worth patient and prolonged study. Gradually they were enabled to formulate precise statements, solely based on these experiments, and which pointed out the existence of certain chiromantic indications invariably corresponding with certain

*An interesting sketch which I reproduce herein gives a sufficiently clear idea of the connection existing—by the medium of the nerves —between the fingers and thumb and certain spots in the brain. Now, it has been proved, time and time again, that any undue pressure upon or any unhealhy condition of these particular locations in the brain that correspond more directly with the fingers or thumb immediately determines a paralysis of these members, and renders them inapt to accomplish their accustomed duties. This refers only to the muscles that set fingers and thumb in action; the general influence of the vital fluid penetrating through the fingers and pervading the entire nervous system of man is not included in this statement, which I may put down here as one universally accepted in the medical world—without taking into consideration the existence or non-existence of a vital fluid. [St-G.]

duly investigated facts. From one student to the next, the torch of light was transmitted; each one adding a new series of observations to those collected by his predecessors—until, in this XIX. Century, it became my congenial task to submit this enormous mass of documentary evidence to a thoroughly conscientious and minute shifting process that threw out the chaff and kept in the rich and nourishing grain.

During this close observation of facts, I illogical readings. Many of them I managed, through long study over an ever widening field, to gradually gather into the fold, making them part and parcel of my homogeneous system. The others I simply accepted—calling them traditional readings and ever hoping to see my way toward including them within the harmony of the whole; but I never did accept them at all, except when almost compelled to do so by the glaring evidence of their accuracy.

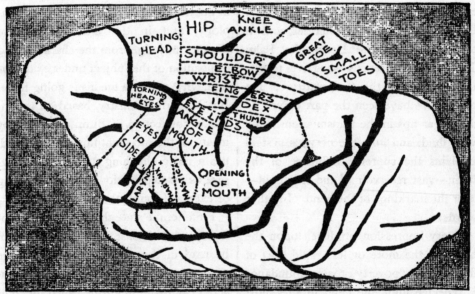

MAN'S BRAIN AND ITS CONNECTIONS WITH THE VARIOUS PARTS OF THE BODY.

met with a certain percentage--not a high one—of statements that failed to exactly fit in with my theory of the vital fluid, of its penetrating through the fingers and leaving, in the palm, traces of its constant flowing from the tips to the brain and from the brain to the tips. And yet my personal examination of thousands of hands compelled me to admit, in many cases, the exactness of these apparently

So much for traditional Palmistry; as to logical Palmistry, which I have developed by pen and picture in my principal works, its principles can be summarized as follows:

There is an outward source of vital fluid, which I earnestly believe to have been created and to be directed, even now, by a Supreme and Omnipotent Being;

This vital fluid penetrates within us through certain organs, the fingers first and foremost, and is stored principally in the cells of the brain;

It is distributed all over the body by means of the nerves, the division and classification of which would require too much space and time to belong here properly.

These nerves are richly represented in the hands, not only at the Tips, where the sense of touch is at its best, but in those elevations at the base of the fingers called the Mounts, where the Pacinian Corpuscles store it in quantities, and in this Hollow of the Hand—the Palm Proper—so extremely sensitive to the least change in the temperature of the body. We have seen the part played by the finger tips in the transmission of the vital fluid, and how the nervous system explains the supreme influence of the brain—vast reservoir of the said fluid—over the markings of the hand. In other words:

Every impression produced upon the brain by the more or less rapid flow of fluid or by its poverty or superabundance is reflected upon the hand in an almost invariably constant manner, leaving visible markings to be examined, compared, classified, interpreted.

In health matters, not only past troubles are thus revealed and remain in evidence long after their effects have vanished, but future ailments, those particularly whose incubation is a matter of months, and even years, appear in the palm as soon as the earliest germ is conceived or deposited within the brain.

As far as the life events are concerned, the same rule obtains. Every action, pleasant or otherwise, affects the brain matter, at least for a time; if the nervous system of the subject is particularly sensitive, i. e., if he is more specially under the influence of the vital fluid, that emotion will be repeated in the palm and remain in evidence long after its effects and even its memory have vanished. As to future events, they throw their shadows before and it is comparatively easy for a close student of human nature, versed in the details of Chirognomy and Phrenology, and in the meanings of the Mounts, to judge from the character and disposition of the subject under examination, what sort of a life his is going to be. But Modern Palmistry, based on the intimate connection of Brain and Palm by means of the incessant flow of vital fluid, has a more clinching argument to present as an explanation of the foretelling of events through the hands.

First, let me state that only a very limited number of past or future events can be read in the palms of those whose nervous system is comparatively inactive, and who might be called, in common parlance, cold, indifferent, stolid individuals. In their hands, the lines are so few that they have no tale to tell, and we have to pass them by unread, as if the book of their life were made up of blank

*Here I have taken the liberty to develop the ideas of the master perhaps farther than he ever attempted to do it himself; and I may lay claim to this theory of future events being imprinted in our brains—and in our palms as the registers of the brain—by presentments or persistent dreams. [St-G.]

pages. But those higher-strung organisms, that vibrate freely under emotions of a varied nature, present in their palms a multitude of lines and signs indicative of the hurried flow of fluid obeying their changeable moods. They deeply feel joy and sorrow, physical pain and material delights; and all this is written down in their palms. The past, I have explained how it is inscribed thereon. The future has also written down its facts and warnings, and this is solely due to the nervous excitability of the subject whose brain has been the battlefield of many a strong presentiment, of many a dream oft repeated, though totally forgotten on the morrow. These peculiar forebodings which come to us without our full consciousness being awakened exert at the time, a sufficiently powerful influence upon the brain to cause it to send it down, as an important message, to its recorder—the hand; and there it is inscribed in letters mysterious, not as the edict of a dark, revengeful fatality, but as precious warnings to be heeded and acted upon by our wisdom and will power.

For, and it is with this last affirmation that these pages will close, the Fatum, the Sors, the Ananke of the Ancients is not my God, it is not the arbiter of humanity, it is not its decrees that we read in the hand. Free will, influenced, it is true, by the flow of vital fluid, by its abundance or poverty, remains the proud belonging of the human race. And the knowledge of Palmistry, far from becoming a source of discouragement to those who find in their palms prognostics of an unfavorable nature, places within their reach the remedy that is known to cure most of the ailments, physical and mental, poor humanity is heir to—and that is the steadfast, reasoned exercise of our will power.

From and by

AD. DESBARROLLES.

THE MAP OF THE HAND.

Before I can begin investigating with the reader the arcana of the minute science which I have the ambition to make for him as clear as rock-crystal, I must devote a few pages, to the Technical Description of the hand, both Front and Back, requesting the student to memorize at once the few names he may not have already met with in other books on Palmistry. Without this preliminary knowledge no headway can be made toward the making of a scientific, and—at the same time—a truly practical Palmist.

First of all, I shall lay down the hand flat on the paper, the inside concealed. I have here three distinct divisions:

1. The Hand Proper; from the wrist to the lower knuckles of the fingers; it is composed—anatomically—of the five bones of the metacarpus.

2. The Fingers; four in number, each divided into three Phalanges: the first or nailed one; the second; and the third connecting with the Hand Proper.

3. The Thumb; composed of two phalanges only, as the lower portion of the thumb, attached to the wrist, is also one of the five metacarpal bones forming the Palm proper, and not a phalanx.

In the Fingers and Thumb I notice, among other characteristics, (1) the Tip or Shape of the nailed Phalanx.

This Tip is either:

Pointed, when from base to tip the finger grows more and more slender;

Conical, when from the second joint upward the finger tapers in the shape of a cone;

Square, when the breadth of the finger is practically even from base to tip;

Spatulate, when the tip broadens out in the form of that little wooden instrument called by druggists a spatula.

And (2) the Knots, or the joints between the first and second phalanges, and the second and third phalanges of the fingers whenever they are visibly bulging. They are respectively called First Knot and Second Knot; the Thumb consisting of only two phalanges, possesses only one Joint, called Knot only when quite apparent.

All these indications have to be gathered, I repeat it from the Back of the Hand; the Tips, especially, cannot be judged satisfactorily from the inside of the fingers. Neither can the length of the fingers or the relative length of the phalanges be accurately determined except from the Back of the Hand.

The Nails and the Hair on the hands are only visible, of course, by the inspection of the back of the hand; and both these elements are of the highest importance in any valuable examination.

I now turn the hand round, and I present you with what is really the Map of the Hand; for does it not contain Mounts and Rivers (The Lines) and Islands and Plains like a regular Geographical Map?

In this Map some indications given above are repeated and need, therefore, no second interpretation. Leaving the Fingers, Phalanges, Knots and Thumb aside, I reach at once the Hand proper, which is here called

The Palm—and includes the whole surface of the Hand, from the wrist up to the base of the Fingers, and from the Side of the Hand (next to the thumb) to the Percussion (the striking side of the hand), from the base of the Fourth Finger to the wrist.

It is divided into:

1. The Mounts (or elevations) at the base of each finger and around the hand, called, in the following regular order:

Mount of Jupiter,

Mount of Saturn,

Mount of the Sun,

Mount of Mercury,

Upper Mount of Mars,

Mount of the Moon.

Mount of Venus,

Lower Mount of Mars.

2. The Palm Proper—including only this portion of the Palm which is not pre-empted by the Mounts. This Palm Proper (also called the Plain of Mars) is divided into

The Quadrangle.

The Triangle,

both forming what is called, in common parlance, the Hollow of the Hand.

Over the surface of the whole Palm are found running, like rivers through a mountainous region, a number of Lines, fourteen of which, by their frequency and distinctness, have been honored with the general appellation of Main Lines.

I will insert here, after the names I have selected to be used exclusively all through this volume, other names by which several of these Main Lines have been known by the ancients and are still designated by a few of the Modern Palmists.

I will take first what I call further on the Chief Lines:

1. The Line of Life, or Vital.

2. The Line of Head, or Cerebral.

3. The Line of Heart, or Mensal.

The other Main Lines, by order of importance, are,

4. The Line of Fate, or Saturnian, or Line of Luck.

5. The Line of the Sun, or Line of Apollo, or Line of Fortune, or Line of Brilliancy.

6. The Line of Liver, or Hepatica, or Line of Health.

7. The Via Lasciva, or Milky Way.

8. The Line of Intuition, or Line of Luna.

9. The Line of Mars.

10. The Girdle of Venus, or Ring of Saturn, or Ring of Uranus.

11. The First Bracelet of the Rascette.

12. The Second Bracelet of the Rascette.

13. The Third Bracelet of the Rascette.

14. The Line (or Lines) of union, or of Marriage, or of Attachment.

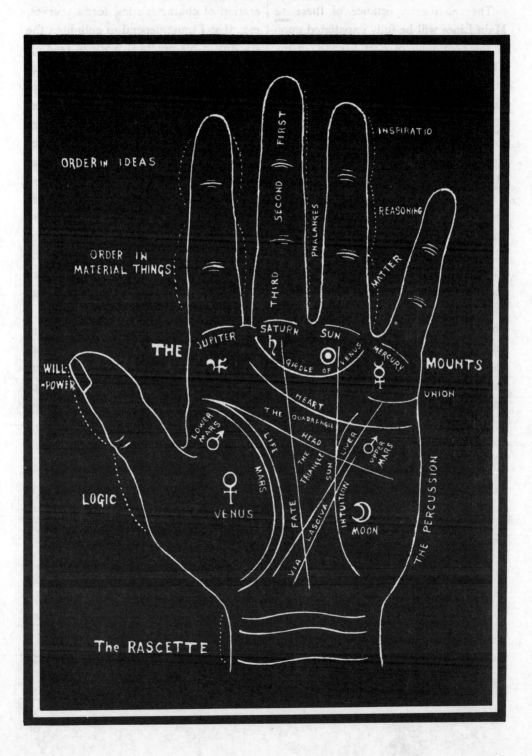

The relative importance of these 14 Main Lines will be fully expatiated upon at the beginning of Part Fourth, in my Chapter on The Lines in General. A number of Minor Lines are also discussed and read in my Chapter on Lines of Influence, finally the various Signs found in the hands are described by pen and picture in Part Third, on The Mounts. Of course, each Main Line has a chapter of its own and will be found most exhaustively studied both in text and illustration.

And yet, in spite of the systematic and minute attention paid to the various modifications in lines, signs, etc., those modifications are so infinite in number and often so extraordinary in contour and intricacy that no book would suffice to contain one-fiftieth, nay, one thousandth part of the possible amount of combinations and changes.

It is not, therefore, upon a bare enumeration of characteristics, forms, curves, etc., that I must depend to enlighten the student in his practical work of reading hands; there are happily some logical rules that may be evolved out of this apparent chaos. As I stated in my preface, the problems of lines, etc., that cannot be solved by these rules, when once well understood and digested, are comparatively few; not perhaps more than 15 per cent. of all the observations that have to be interpreted. And I take the liberty of repeating that there is no science or art, claiming to unravel the mysteries of human nature and human existence, that begins to obtain such percentage of actual results.

I had to add these few words of encouragement before taking my Telemachus by the hand and starting with him, in my self-assumed office of Mentor, toward the unknown land—yet so dark—that we are bound to explore together

PART SECOND

Chirognomic Observations

Based upon the system conceived and developed by CASIMIR STANISLAS d'ARPENTIGNY, a distinguished French cavalry officer and a scholar, born in Normandy, March 13, 1798. Served under Napoleon in 1814 at the siege of Dantzic; entered the service of King Louis XVIII., 1815; appointed to the Royal Body Guard, 1820, he had reached the rank of a captain when he retired in 1844. Attracted to the study of occult sciences, he neglected ancient Chiromancy and gave his whole attention to the outward aspect—the Physiognomy, so to speak—of the human hand. In 1839, the result of his investigations appeared under the title of *La Chirognomonie*. In 1865 a third edition of this great book came out under the title of *La Science de la Main*. Modified and improved by Desbarrolles, the knowledge of the d'Arpentigny system of Chirognomy forms the first and indispensable step toward a complete logical knowledge of the Hand.

THE HAND AS A WHOLE.

The Hand Proper, the Palm, the Palm Proper and the Nails.

As I stated in a preceding chapter, I call

Hand as a whole, the Back of the hand, from Wrist to Finger Tips;

Hand proper, the Back of the Hand from the Wrist to the Knuckles at the base of the Fingers;

Palm, the Inside of the Hand, from the Wrist to the base of the Fingers—which, by the way—does not correspond at all with the base of the Fingers as seen from the back; and

Palm Proper, the Inside of the Hand, less the space occupied by the Mounts.

I shall review now such observations as refer:

First: To the Skeleton of the Hand.

Second: To the Hand as a whole.

Third: To the Hand Proper, by itself, or in comparison of length with the Fingers.

Fourth: To the Hand Proper and the Palm examined together, to judge of the Thickness and Consistency of the Hand.

Fifth: To the Palm by itself;

Sixth: To the Palm Proper.

To follow precedents in which I find but little logic I shall include in this chapter all the indications referring, Seventh: To the Nails, although they belong altogether to the Finger Division of the Hand. My only excuse for doing so is that it is really customary to ex-amine the Nails before turning one's attention to the Fingers and Thumb.

I. The Skeleton of the Hand.

The Eight small bones at the base form the Wrist and their anatomical name is the Carpial Bones or the Carpus.

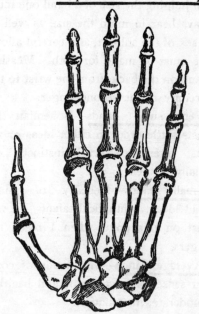

From that base emerge five long and straight bones, scientifically called Meta-carpal Bones or Metacarpus, and which constitute the Hand minus the Fingers, or what I designate in this book as the Hand proper and the Palm.

Above the Metacarpus rise the four-teen Phalanges; two for the Thumb, three for each of the four fingers. I am bound to state that medical works consider the Phalanges attached to the Metacarpus as the First and the Nailed Phalanges as the Third. Desbarrolles, and all those who with him believe in the attraction and penetration of the vital (or electric) fluid through the Tips of the fingers have reversed the nomenclature, and call the Nailed Phalanges the First Ones and so on, downwards to the Hand Proper.

II. The Hand as a Whole.

1. Size.

In judging the size of a hand one must always bear in mind the size as well as the sex of the subject, and careful allowance must be made for both. Measure a hand on the back, from the wrist to the extremity of the second finger.

Very small hands—Bohemian instincts; little order in either ideas or actions; oftentimes cruel instincts, especially in men.

Small hands—Delicacy of mind; broad ideas; synthetical talents. I will insist on this point when I reach the Fingers.

Average hands—The hands of common sense, practical gifts, and healthy, if moderate, imagination.

Large hands—A love and aptitude for minutiæ and details; analytical talents. I will pay my respects to this characteristic when I reach the Fingers.

Very large hands—A mania for useless details; the hand of the martinet and meddlesome, never satisfied employer.

2. Hair.

In a woman—A hairy hand denotes cruelty, or, at the best, mannish instincts.

In a man—Slightly hairy—Prudence, energy, self-possession.

Very hairy—Violent nature; inconstancy.

No hair at all—Effeminacy, cowardice; presumption.

Hair on thumb only—Inventive genius (tradition).

Hair on the two lower phalanges of the fingers—Stiffness of demeanor; lack of simplicity.

Hair on all phalanges—Ardent, easily aroused disposition.

Light colored hair on the hands—People easily influenced and often lacking in passion.

Dark colored hair—Quick, passionate disposition.

Reddish colored hair—Most excitable natures.

III. The Hand Proper.

To compare Length of Hand Proper with Length of Fingers, take your measurements on the back of the hand; the Hand proper extends from the wrist to the lower knuckle of the second finger; the size of the Fingers is taken from the above knuckle to the tip of the second finger.

1. Hand Proper Longer than Fingers.

A. With pointed tips (very seldom met, as the two characteristics contradict each other)—If thick at the base—self-indulgence; laziness, useless dreaming.

B. With conical tips—Aptitude for the mechanical parts of the fine arts. Opera singers have frequently such hands; rather sensuous disposition.

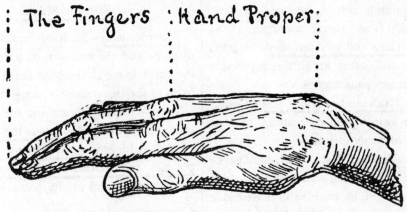

THE DIVISIONS OF THE BACK OF THE HAND.
[Design taken from life; the subject was 100 years old.]

C. With Square tips—A useful hand; will execute well other people's orders or ideas; an excellent military hand.

D. With Spatulate tips—A very active hand, love of sports; poor intellect, little understanding of details.

E. With characterless tips—The elementary hand (which see further): the hand of the unskilled workman, the navvy, etc.

2. The Hand Proper.

The Same Length as the Fingers.

This constitutes the most harmonious combination. (See special chapter on The Finger Tips, as the indications therein given all apply to Hand proper and fingers thus evenly balanced.)

3. The Hand Proper Shorter than the Fingers.

A. With pointed tips—Idealism; imagination at its best; generally accompanied by a well-developed Mount of the Moon.

B. With conical tips—Imagination mingled with a practical view of things. A clear, rapid insight into other people's true nature. A quick comprehension of details; in artists, inspiration and execution happily blended; the hand of high-class musicians; generally composers or actors who take infinite pains in creating their parts.

C. With square tips—The best hands for everyday life, especially in business. Not easily deceived, and always hard workers and attentive to minute details.

D. With spatulate tips—Activity at its best, except that sometimes it loses itself in minutiæ; indefatigable in outdoor exercises; great travelers and discoverers; versatility; wit.

IV. The Hand Proper and the Palm.

The Thickness of the Hand and its Consistency Combined are to be judged by pressing the center of the hand with the Index on the Back and the Thumb inside. The roughness or softness of the skin must not enter into consideration.

A. Thick and very hard—Instincts verging on brute animality.

B. Thick and hard—A primitive,

rather rough nature, but with strong, good points and native honesty.

C. Thick and medium hard—A good worker who cares for little else; kindly but not amorous nature.

D. Thick and medium soft—Capacity for enjoying all pleasures without falling into any excesses.

E. Thick and soft—Self-indulgence and laziness; danger ahead; is a sign also of a very bright imagination; desirable in artists, poets, musicians, etc.; dangerous in the commonplace hands.

F. Thick and very soft, "flabby"— Sensual instincts, hatred of any kind of labor; selfishness without restraint.

G. Thin and very hard—Cold, heartless, calculating disposition, even to crime.

H. Thin and hard—Selfishness, avarice, narrow-mindedness.

I. Thin, narrow and meager—Feeble temperament; indecision of character; cold imagination, if any.

J. Thin and soft—Weak constitution yielding to physical temptation.

K. Thin and very soft—Vicious disposition; often morbid tendencies; in an otherwise very good hand: gift of intuition.

L. Transparent—The palm of seers and saints; and, in a bad hand, the palm that goes with an utterly diseased imagination.

V. The Palm.

The Palm, distinct from the Fingers, extends from the root of the fingers to the first bracelet of the Rascette, and from the root of the Thumb (base of second phalanx) to the Percussion.

1. Size and Shape.

Narrow palm—Lack of imagination, of pluck and cheerfulness, on account of the small space allowed for the development of the three mounts along the Percussion—Mercury, Mars and the Moon. (See chapter on the Mounts of the Hand.)

Wide palm, if in good proportion with the size and character of the fingers— Strong health and evenly balanced temper.

Too wide; in that case it is generally thick—The exaggeration of the Mounts of the Moon, Mars and Mercury will result in a vicious imagination, a violent temper and deceiving instincts. (See chapter on the Mounts of the Hand.)

A square palm; met generally with spatulate fingers—Great love of activity, mostly of a physical nature.

2. Color and Character of the Skin.

Very pale—Selfish disposition; anæmia.

Yellow—Morbid disposition; biliousness.

Pink and mottled—Hopeful, cheerful disposition; well balanced constitution.

Red—Quick temper; superabundance of blood.

Very red—Violent temper; danger of apoplexy.

These colors are not easily discerned in the hands of people actually working with their hands; the above indications apply therefore more usually to persons without occupations, or whose occupations are mental rather than manual.

Extra smooth skin, of the kind

called "satin skin"—Tendency to rheumatism and gout.

Dry skin—Tendency to fever; perspiration being insufficient may also cause skin diseases.

Damp skin, especially if the sweat is cold and clammy—Very serious liver trouble; often ill-balanced moral nature.

VI. The Palm Proper.

The Palm Proper extends only from the base of the Mounts to the third angle of the Triangle, and from the Line of Life to a normally placed Line of Liver, not including any Mounts. It is also called the Plain of Mars, and includes both the Quadrangle and the Triangle.

A. Flat but high (i. e., on a level with the Mounts under the fingers)—Great, sometimes indomitable, pride; egotism; often violent nature.

B. Flat but low—Timidity; insignificance of life and aims; sometimes cowardice.

C. Hollow—Moderately so, it has no special meaning and does not interfere with the other indications.

D. Very hollow:

(1). More so toward the Line of Life—Domestic troubles.

(2). More so toward the Line of Head—Brain trouble or apoplexy.

(3). More so toward the Line of Heart—Disappointment in love; heart weakness.

(4). More so toward the Mount of the Moon—Nervous or internal troubles.

(5). In General—Failure in life. Loss of money.

Be careful to distinguish between a really hollow palm and a normally shaped palm appearing hollow solely on account of the neighboring high Mounts; in this case the hollow has no importance, and the reading must bear upon the development of the Mounts.

VII. The Nails.

It has often been said by scientists of recognized capacity, that the nails are nothing but the electric fluid within us solidified by exposure to the air, thus becoming a kind of intermediary substance between the said fluid and the human skin and flesh. Balzac wrote in Louis Lambert:

"When one thinks that the line separating our flesh from the growing nail contains the unexplained and invisible mystery of the incessant transformation of our fluid into horn, one must admit that nothing is impossible in the marvelous transformation of the human constituting elements."

Short nails—Inquisitiveness, intuition, energy. In a weak hand: frivolous disposition.

Short, hard, and partially covered with skin, and even flesh—Quarrelsome disposition, especially if they are broader than long. Seen at its worst on what I call a clubbed thumb. (See chapter on Thumb. A German scientist observed that after a violent access of rage the nails of the subject under examination would become softer for a while.)

Short nails with a soft palm—The born critic's attribute; irony and even scorn.

A short nail on the second finger, the nails of the other fingers being almond-shaped—Irritability, but only at times; always extreme sensitiveness to criticism.

Short and pale—Deceitful disposition; physical and moral weakness.

Short and red—Violent temper.

Short, square-shaped and bluish—Heart trouble.

Short, quite broad and square at the bottom—Passionate anger. If wider than long—Unsufferable stubbornness.

Short and triangular shaped; The point of the triangle nearest to the phalanx—Threatened paralysis.

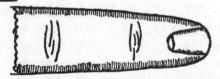

Short, narrow and curved—Danger of spinal troubles.

Large (both broad and long) and rounded at the base—Clear, sound judgment.

Long nails, especially if thin and brittle—Weak physical nature, often lack of intelligence.

Long, thin and curved—Sore throat and weak respiratory organs. If ridged or fluted—A sure sign of consumption.

Long, thick and curved, somewhat like a claw—Violent disposition in love and other intercourse with one's fellow-beings.

Long, thin, narrow—Timidity and cowardice; often found in convalescing persons.

Moderately thin and narrow—Excellent general disposition.

Perfect nails, white, almond-shaped and naturally polished, moderately long and thick—Happy nature, satisfactory state of health; strange to say, it has been observed that perfect almond-shaped nails are frequently found on the fingers of conceited and selfish subjects, especially women.

If pink on the outer edge—Short fits of anger, never malicious.

Ridges on the nail of a certain finger— Held by Desbarrolles to indicate a stronger devotion and aptitude of the subject to the particular art or profession which that finger represents more specially.

Cross ridges—Dr. Bain, a famous physician, states that in his experience the presence of a deep cross ridge on a nail announces a coming disease which will manifest itself by other symptoms before the nail has grown so that the ridge gets to the edge of the nail. The nature of the disease can be judged by the finger upon which this nail is found. The thumb nail is particularly interesting in this connection. As it takes six months for a nail to be entirely renewed it is easy to estimate in how long a time the illness will be due.

Not only the modern physician, but the most ancient in the art, believed that the shape, color, etc., of the nails denoted certain diseases. Hippocrates (460-357 B. C.) wrote that the

Nail of the first finger much bent inward indicates scrofula and consump-

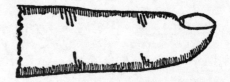

tion; and to this day this diagnosis is accepted as correct.

I decline introducing into this work— which is essentially a practical, and, as far as possible, reliable Guide to Handreading, the unsubstantiated indications furnished by the white or dark spots on the nails and by the examination of the moons at the lower part of the nails. A branch of Chiromancy known by the name of Onychomancy (divination by the nails) obtained some success in the XVII. Century, but it never reached that point when it could be admitted on a par with the more ancient and more satisfactorily verified Palmistry, and I prefer leaving it out of my present treatise. I may state, however, that Medical men have often admitted in my presence, that

Numerous white spots on the nails indicate poverty of the blood and defective circulation, while

Black or bluish spots on the nails frequently accompany poisoning of the blood, especially in cases of cholera or yellow fever, and even typhoid fever, diphtheria and small-pox.

THE FINGERS.

As stated several times already, in the appellation of Fingers, Palmistry does not include the Thumb, which is honored with a separate and distinct treatment as playing a considerable part in the economy of the hand.

There are, therefore, only Four Fingers to Palmistic Hands; they are designated as follows, the first name being the one I use exclusively through this work:

The First Finger, or Index, or Finger of Jupiter.

The Second Finger, or Middle Finger (Medius), or Finger of Saturn.

The Third Finger, or Ring Finger (Annularius), or Finger of Apollo.

The Fourth Finger, or Little Finger (Auricularius), or Finger of Mercury.

In examining Fingers we are naturally called upon to observe,

I. Their Position.
II. Their Length.
III. Their Shape.

And this Chapter will therefore be divided into these three heads, with proper subdivisions, separating such indications as refer to All the Fingers and those that pertain to Each Finger by Itself.

I. POSITION.

1. Alignment of the Bases of all Fingers.

Fingers set evenly on a line above the mounts are said to indicate success. An absolutely even line is very seldom met with, and would not be either natural or pretty.

Any finger set below the others loses some of its power.

The First finger "low-set" reduces the size of the Mount of Jupiter and gives awkwardness in social matters, often caused by an unfortunate combination of conceit and ignorance. (See chapter on Mounts.)

The Second finger is seldom displaced; to some extent, owing to its position in the middle (counting the Thumb as a fifth finger), it acts as a sort of balancing pole.

If the Third finger is set below the second finger, the qualities revealed by the former will be prevented by circumstances from full cultivation.

The Fourth finger "low-set"—Circumstances are against the subject, and his life will be a struggle. The subject will lack much of the influential cleverness that characterizes the fourth finger when high-placed and long.

2. Leaning of the Fingers toward each other.

First Finger.

Toward Thumb—Great desire for independence.

Toward the Second Finger—Morbid pride.

Second Finger.

Toward the First Finger—Superstitious sadness.

Toward the Third Finger—Less morbidity.

Third Finger.

Toward the Second Finger—Morbid vanity.

Toward the Fourth Finger—Art practiced solely for the money there is in it.

Fourth Finger.

Toward the Third Finger—Science and art happily blended; or business ability happily blended with artistic aptitudes.

3. Closeness of the Fingers.

Showing no light between—Meanness of disposition; avarice.

Showing light between—Inquisitiveness; the greater the amount of light the more intemperate the curiosity.

This seems in contradiction with the theory of the Knots. On that account I pay but little attention to this ancient tradition.

4. Spaces between the Bases of the Fingers.

When pronounced they indicate:

Between First Finger and Thumb—Generosity.

Between First and Second Fingers—Independence of thought.

Between Second and Third Fingers—Thoughtlessness of the future. "Happy-go-lucky" disposition.

Between Third and Fourth Fingers—

Independence of action; Bohemianism.

All the Fingers falling apart easily—Unconventionality.

If they keep close together most of the time—Stiffness in intercourse with others.

One Finger coming forward prominently—The quality or defect represented by that finger will be uppermost in the subject's nature.

5. Bent and Flexibility of the Fingers.

Bent is the natural position when the subject does not know he is observed. Flexibility is only judged by touch.

Bent forward—Avarice; meanness; excess of prudence; cowardice.

Bent backward—Unconventional instincts; jovial disposition; talkativeness.

Stiff—Practical nature; rather conventional; sometimes hard and unyielding disposition.

Flexible—Still more Bohemian disposition; inquisitiveness; no idea of the value of money.

II. LENGTH.

1. Length of All the Fingers.

Very long fingers—Meddling disposition; ever finding fault; sometimes cruel out of mere tormenting instincts; the poisoner's fingers

Long fingers—Love of detail; aptitude for doing small things well. Analytical capacities; sensitiveness over trifles.

Long, thin fingers—Diplomats; deceivers; card sharpers; pickpockets.

Average fingers—Well balanced organism; sometimes very commonplace nature.

Short fingers—Quick understanding of things taken as a whole; synthetical aptitudes. Intuitive faculty (with smooth joints).

Very short fingers—Bohemian, unconventional instincts; often laziness; selfishness through indifference; incapacity to understand and practice the common duties of life. Cruelty again, this time to obey rude, primitive instincts; the ruffian's fingers.

Equal to the third finger—Great desire for fame and riches.

Much shorter than the third finger—Lack of ambition; love for a humdrum existence.

Second Finger.

Much longer than the first finger—Morbidity even to folly.

Equal to the first finger—Life ruled by ambition.

Shorter than the first finger—Insanity,

2. Length of Each Finger.

First Finger.

IN FAIR PROPORTION.	TOO LONG.	TOO SHORT.	CROOKED.
Moderate love of rule; an active, intuitive disposition.	Tyranny.	Dislike to responsibility.	Lack of honor.

Second Finger.

Prudence.	Morbidity (especially if flat).	Frivolity.	Hysteria. Murderous instincts.

Third Finger.

Artistic sense. (Love of the beautiful.)	Love of speculation (gambling).	No love of beauty. Mercenary in art productions.	False idea of art; using art for wrong purposes.

Fourth Finger.

Versatility; desire for general improvement.	Crafty instincts.	Dangerous rapidity in coming to conclusions.	Want of honesty.

3. Length of the Fingers Compared With Each Other.

First Finger.

Longer than the second finger—Almost insane, domineering spirit.

Equal to the second finger—Love of power (Napoleon's index).

Much shorter than the second finger—Timidity; reticent in everything.

First Finger.

Much longer than the third finger—Abnormal, unhealthy ambition.

taking the form of mania for greatness.

Second Finger.

Much longer than the third finger—Morbidity interfering with the success of the subject in art, literature or money making.

Equal to the third finger—Gambling disposition.

Shorter than the third finger—A disposition to take desperate risks; foolhardy enterprises, amounting almost to insanity.

Third Finger.

Much longer than the first finger— Love of art, but no ambition to sustain it and bring about results.

Equal to the first finger—Great desire for fame and riches.

Shorter than the first finger—Ambition blinds the subject as to his real (small) merit.

Third Finger.

Much longer than the second finger— Taking deperate risks.

Equal to the second finger—Gambling instincts fully developed.

Much shorter than the second finger— Morbid instincts will ruin all prospects.

Third Finger.

Unusually longer than the fourth finger—Ambition will be altogether in the direction of the fine arts, and will meet with great success.

Almost equal to the fourth finger— Versatility; convincing power used for god or bad (the rest of the indications will tell).

Fourth Finger.

Almost equal to the first finger— Talent for diplomacy and statesmanship. Also seen in the unscrupulous politician.

Almost equal to the second finger— Scientific powers of an extraordinary type.

Almost equal to the third finger—Versatility. Power of influencing others. In a bad hand—A cheat.

4. The Phalanges Taken Separately.

First Finger.

Normal First Phalanx.	Normal Second Phalanx.	Normal Third Phalanx.
Love of and respect for Religion. Gift of intuition. Excess—Superstition.	Ambition, pride. Excess—Vanity.	Desire to rule. Excess—Love of power carried too far.

Second Finger.

Gravity. Excess—Melancholy. Religious insanity even to suicidal mania.	Love of agriculture. Excess—Extreme, unnecessary caution in choice of occupation or in business.	Economy. Excess—Avarice.

Third Finger.

Artistic inspiration. Excess— Unbalanced artistic tendencies.	Common sense blended with talent. Excess—Mercantile instincts stifling inspiration.	Love of brilliant show. Excess— Foolish display.

Fourth Finger.

Eloquence; love of science for its own sake. Excess—Lying.	Aptitude for science and inventions. Excess—Science used for guilty purposes.	Business talent. Excess—Thieving disposition.

I give herein an illustration of a finger, with a carefully prepared scale that will allow the student to judge by actual measurement whether a phalanx is normal or in excess. He may measure the length of any finger from the lower (outward) knuckle—where the Hand Proper ceases and the Finger begins—and divide this length into ten equal parts.

A normal Third Phalanx will be 4½ Tenths in length.

A Normal Second Phalanx will be 3½ Tenths in length.

A Normal First Phalanx will be 2 Tenths in length, not counting, of course, the portion of the nail that is allowed to grow over and above the tip of the finger.

Any marked (not insignificant) deviation from these proportions of 4½, 3½ and 2 ought to be considered as an Excess or Deficiency.

As a Deficiency in the length of a phalanx almost invariably determines an Excess in another phalanx of the same finger, it is quite sufficient for the student to know how to read the Excess as it becomes the ruling element in that particular finger.

III. SHAPE.

1. Outside of Tips and Knots.

Inside puffiness of the third phalanges —Selfishness; laziness; love of good living, often carried to excess.

Third phalanges wasped or waist-shaped—Daintiness in food and raiment; delicacy of mind.

2. The Finger Types.

In Palmistry, in the department called Chirognomy, to which this Part Second of my present book is devoted, para-

mount importance is given to two distinct features in each finger:

First—The shape of the Tip of the first (or nailed) phalanx.

Second—The Existence or Absence of more or less visible Knots at the joints of the phalanges.

These two features have to be examined simultaneously to avoid useless repetitions. In other words, I shall give you, at one and the same time, my readings of the

Four kinds of tips—Pointed, Conical, Square, Spatulate, in connection with—Smooth joints, first joint knotted, second joint knotted, both joints knotted.

Let me give you fuller definitions of the names applied to the various kinds of finger tips.

Pointed—The finger tapers from the root to the tip, where it ends in a decided point.

Conical—The finger tapers from the lower joint to the tip, where it ends in a rounded, thimble-like cone.

Square—The finger preserves very nearly the same width from root to tip, where it ends sometimes in a decided square, but more generally in a semi-rounded square.

Spatulate—The finger continues the same width from the root to after the upper joint, where it widens and ends in the form of a druggist's spatula, more or less pronounced.

3. The Finger Tips by Themselves.

The tips of the first phalanges show the type of the hand, and consequently the class to which it belongs. If they are:

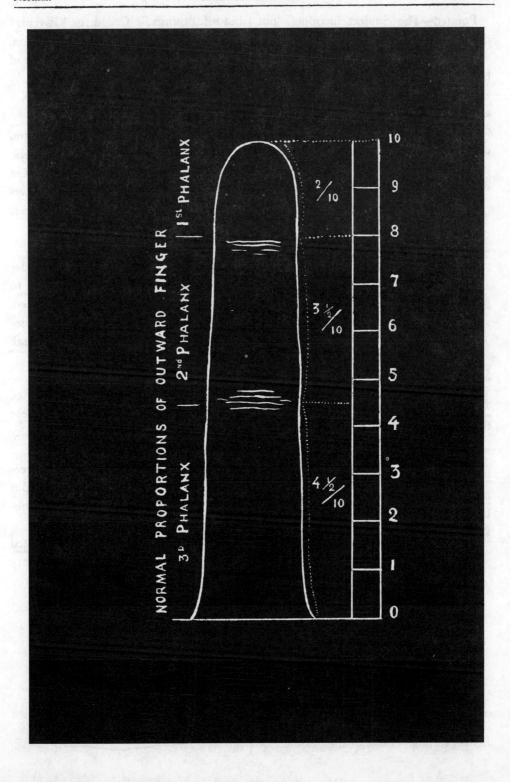

Pointed—The Subject imagines, but does not execute.

Conical—Reason and imagination blended.

Square—Reason is uppermost, rules alone.

Spatulate—Execution without the gift of conception and little reasoning power.

4.　The Knots by Themselves and What They Stand For.

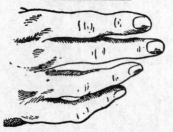

The Upper Knot, called also "The Philosophical Knot"—Order in ideas.

The Lower Knot, called also "The Material Knot"—Order in material things.

5.　Comparative Study of Types.

Let me now study and interpret each of these Types of Finger Tips and combine them with smooth and knotted fingers.

A.　The Pointed Fingers.

Smooth.

Poetry of soul and heart. Ecstatic religious feeling. Love of the "essence of beautiful things." Called the "Psychic" fingers. No order in ideas or action. Often incurable laziness. But the gift of intuition.

With First (Upper) Knot.

Struggle between inspiration and reasoning. The believer begins to doubt. The poet loses part of his genius. On the other side, inspiration is put to better advantage in the execution of works.

With Second (Lower) Knot.

Here the artistic gifts of a higher order are interfered with by a tendency to practicality which will not be silenced. The artist or poet will be more successful financially, but far from his pure ideal.

With Both Knots.

The natural qualities of the pointed tips are lost to a great extent by these two knots, which drag down the lofty ideals of the smooth pointed fingers.

Inspiration will often be in the direction of inventions or discoveries. But as a rule, this discord will render the subject moody and dissatisfied.

Pointed fingers are very rare. Pointed Fingers with Knots are extraordinary exceptions.

B.　The Conical Fingers.

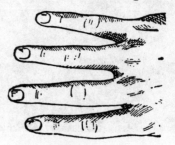

Smooth.

The poetic gift is more sensual, less ethereal. The beautiful will be cultivated in the solid and visible form, with still a hatred for rigorous logic and a great independence in thought and manners.

With First (Upper) Knot.

The artist is more dominated by practical reasoning. He calculates his efforts and aims at success with a set purpose, but still with a grand idea of art. Found in the hands of all gifted musicians, dramatic actors of high caliber, etc., etc.

With Second (Lower) Knot.

Combination and moral force are added to the artistic talent. But the subject will be quite practical in the handling of his interests and insist on the proper (moneyed) recognition of his talent.

With Both Knots.

Here we have the most desirable type for the artist, the inventor, the literary man, the musician, the actor who has to face the world and make his way through it. His genius will always be of just the kind that is wanted by his time, and he will know how to husband it to full profit. In conical hands the knots will be found seldom, and always be very slight.

C. The Square Fingers.

Smooth.

Love of philosophy, social science, reality in art; well-ordained literary works; a talent for conceiving business plans. Little enthusiasm: much inspiration, though, but strictly ruled over by reason. This is a strong and precious type.

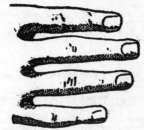

All the subjects with square tipped fingers, whether smooth or knotted, are independent to a degree, and generally truthful.

With First (Upper) Knot.

The tendencies of the square type are bettered by this knot. They are born to love reasoning, and this knot will cause them to excel in it; they'll discuss everything, religious beliefs included; they'll be hard to convince; they are regular Thomases. They have a good capacity for intelligent, useful work.

With Second (Lower) Knot.

This will increase the practical bent of the subject, but reduce his capacity for properly judging the cause before the effect. This type is that of the model employe, the disciplinarian, the pedagogue. Duty before everything; no discretion used. Obey, and, above all, be orderly.

With Both Knots.

Love of the natural sciences, of history, archæology, law. An excellent financier, fanatic of symmetry; prefers common sense to genius. Has no love for art, poetry, fiction. Apt to prefer the useful to everything else, and to drag down ideals when he has occasion to. But he is exact, honest and indispensable in all well-ordained commonwealths.

In Square Fingers, knots—especially second knots—are very frequent, almost the rule.

D. The Spatulate Fingers.

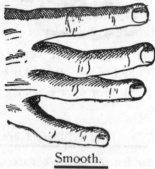

Smooth.

Instinctive understanding of real life; an imperious need of activity, generally physical. Fondness for open air sports and occupations, for politics and the management of men, for travel.

With First (Upper) Knot.

Here we have the type of the aggressive infidel, of the scoffer at every ideal, of the "born kicker." He hates sentiment, and has little use for ideal art. He wants art applied to industry. He loves realism, and is a positivist to an extreme degree. Fond of exact sciences and of researches in the domain of useful inventions.

With Second (Lower) Knot.

The second knot will give still more intensity to the instincts developed by the smooth spatulate tips. The love for the beautiful is here at its lowest, but the fondness for well-ordered enterprise is at its best. Great generals.

With Both Knots.

Stronger than ever is the taste for activity in and out of doors. He will call science to his help in his vast enterprises; his mind is never satisfied if it does not tire his body.

In Spatulate Fingers knots are very frequent, especially the Second knot. Distinguish carefully between the spatulate shape and the lower broadening due to the presence of the first knot.

6. Each Finger Tip Taken Separately.
First Finger.

Pointed—Intuition, high ideal of religion.

Conical—Perception, love of reading.

Square—Love of truth.

Spatulate—Exaggerated love of action.

Second Finger.

Pointed—Morbid fear of the supernatural.

Conical—Healthy belief in religion.

Square—Prudence.

Spatulate—Activity.

Third Finger.

Pointed—Ideality in art, poetry.

Conical—Artistic thought.

Square—Truth in art.

Spatulate—Love of movement in art (drama).

Fourth Finger.

Pointed—Science loved for its own sake.

Conical—Tact.

Square—Able to teach.

Spatulate—Good at active business.

THE THUMB.

All modern Palmists attach such importance to the symptoms revealed by the Position and Shape of the Thumb, that it seems to me essential to inform the student why, physiologically speaking, the Thumb ranks so high among the constituting elements of Palmistry. For that purpose I shall ask permission, in this chapter and the following, to quote freely from Captain d'Arpentigny's standard work, La Science de la Main (3d Edition, 1865), using in most cases the excellent translation of Mr. Heron-Allen, modified according to my understanding of the French text (and French is my native tongue), without the exhaustive comments of the translator. To avoid cumbersome quotation marks, the paragraphs in smaller type may be considered, once for all, as belonging to the great book above mentioned.

The superior animal is signalized by his possession of a hand, the man is signalized by his possessing a thumb.

The thumb of the monkey, which is barely flexible, and for this reason scarcely able to be opposed, i. e., be made to act in conjunction with any of the other fingers, is looked upon by many naturalists as nothing more than a movable nail. Whereas, on the contrary, the human thumb is so situated and organized as to be able always to act in an opposite direction to the other fingers, and it is by this power that it symbolizes the inner or moral sense which we oppose to our will, and through it to the temptations of our instincts and our senses.

Proofs of this assertion abound; thus, for instance, idiots, who are idiotic from birth, come into the world either without thumbs or with thumbs which are powerless and atrophied; and this is perfectly logical, for where the essence is absent, its symbol also must be wanting. (See the typical Idiot's Hand in our next chapter.)

Professor Sir Richard Owen, in his monograph On the Nature of the Limbs, calls attention to the fact that the "Thumb, which is the least important and constant digit of the anterior extremity in the rest of the mammals, becomes in man the most important element of the terminal segment, and that which makes it a hand properly so called."

Infants, up to the time when their intelligence begins to be developed, keep their hands continually closed, folding their fingers over the thumb; but in proportion as, with the body, the mind becomes developed, the thumb in turn folds itself over the fingers.

Epileptic patients in their fits fold their thumbs before the rest of their hands, which shows that this evil, which is instinctively apprehended before it is actually felt, affects the organization by which one perceives and knows, before it affects the organization by which one merely feels.

These principles laid down, I shall proceed as I did with the Fingers by interpreting the indications furnished by

I. The Position of the Thumb, meaning by this the fact of its being more or less detached from the Hand Proper, a wider or narrower angle being thus opened between the base of its second phalanx and the Side of the Hand, when the thumb is stretched downward to its full extent.

II. The Size of the Thumb, from the base of the second Phalanx to the tip of the first or nailed Phalanx.

III. The Shape of the Thumb. This will complete the indications concerning the Thumb as a whole.

Taking each Phalanx separately, as I have done, for the Fingers, I will examine,

IV. The First (or nailed) Phalanx.
V. The Knot between the Phalanges.
VI. The Second Phalanx.
VII. The Combinations of Phalanges.

I. POSITION.

Too high—Idiotcy (also short and ill-shaped).

High—Lack of adaptability. Meanness in money matters.

Low—Generosity; intelligence.

Normal—Meaning to be found in form and size.

Close to the fingers—Avarice.

Away from the fingers—Spendthrift disposition.

II. SIZE.

(Without distinguishing between phalanges.)

Very long—The head governs rather than the feelings; obstinacy, not always wise.

Long—Fine capacity for thought and action; the subject is his own master.

People with large thumbs are governed by their heads (source of all feelings of exclusiveness), and are more at ease in an atmosphere of ideas, than in one of sentiments. They judge things better by reflection than on the spur of the moment.

A large thumb with smooth fingers, conical at the top—Success in art or literature is reached by method, logical deduction, not intuition. With square or spatulate fingers—Love of action but lack of proper reasoning. With knotty fingers and square or spatulate tips—Reason has the upper hand in all the subject's undertakings; in fact, he lacks all impulsiveness, all intuition and oftentimes loses himself in complicated combinations that never come to anything.

Short—Irresolute mind; weak reasoning.

Very short—The subject will be carried constantly from one extreme to another.

People with small thumbs are governed by their hearts (source of all tolerant feelings), and are more at home in an atmosphere of sentiments than in one of ideas; they appreciate things more at a rapid survey of them than on reflection.

It is more easy for large-thumbed subjects to overcome the tendencies of their natures than for people with small thumbs. Generally speaking, a thumb which is small, mean and poorly formed announces an irresolute mind and a wavering disposition in those things which are usually the result of reasoning power, and not of sentiment or of instinctive knowledge.

A small thumb with smooth fingers—Talent or at least aptitude for one of the fine arts or literature. If the fingers are conical—The talent in question aims to a high ideal; if the fingers are square or spatulate—The talent will lie in a clever rendering of real life. With knotty fingers—If the fingers are conical—Method and logic modify the natural intuition. If the fingers are square or spatulate—The gift will be entirely in the line of science and business.

You must not, however, conclude that because you have a large thumb and knotted, spatulate fingers, you are necessarily gifted with the capacity of excelling in all practical sciences and occupations; nor that because you have a small thumb, smooth and conical fingers you are necessarily gifted with pre-eminent talent in every branch of the fine arts; on the contrary, the pursuit of a single science or art, or of a small number of sciences or arts (to an extent limited by the scope of the faculties of each individual). absorbs as a rule, the whole of the stock of genius with which God has endowed the generality of men.

III. SHAPE.
(Without distinguishing between phalanges.)

Thick—Primitive tastes; often uncouth ways; also blunt honesty.

Flat—Nervous disposition; meanness.

Broad—Violent outbursts. If short besides—Fits of stubbornness that do not last.

Slender—Poetic and artistic genius, or at least refined tastes.

Stiff—Plenty of common sense; often stubbornness, exaggerate caution, secretiveness.

Thrown back naturally—Generosity, artistic gifts.

Flexible—Spendthrift disposition; unconventional tendencies.

IV. THE FIRST PHALANX.

A. Size.

Very long—Despotism. Ungovernable temper.

Long—Strong, healthy will power.

Short—Want of self-control.

Very short—Weakness of will power, also often silly obstinacy; carelessness. Chronic discouragement.

It is well to keep in mind that will power is at its best only when we govern ourselves as well as we influence others.

B. Shape.

Conical—If long—Artistic gifts. If short—Lazy imaginings; inconstancy.

Square—If long—Will power tempered by love of fair-play. If short—Impartiality that lacks resolution to decide.

Spatulate—If long—The will here is that of a commander in the field. If short—It will leave the chief of an expedition in the lurch for lack of quick determination at the right time.

Broad—Obstinacy. If short—Fretfulness.

Flat—Insignificant, nervous personality.

"Clubbed" (i. e., broad, thick and rounded)—The murderer's characteristic phalanx. (See, in next chapter, the Murderer's Hand.)

Thick—Violent, often lascivious disposition.

Slender—Refined in action. If long —It will have recourse to most courteous means to succeed in what he resolves to do, "the iron hand in the velvet glove."

V. THE KNOT BETWEEN THE PHALANGES.

The existence of a more or less pronounced knot on the joint between the first and second phalanx modifies the above readings in accordance with the principles laid down in the preceding lessons. It must be remembered that this single knot corresponds to the first (or upper) knot on the fingers; it increases, therefore, the reasoning power of the sec-

ond phalanx and reduces the intuitive quality of the first phalanx.

VI. THE SECOND PHALANX.

A. Size.

Very long—Discusses everything to death; trusts nobody and nothing. Paradoxical to a degree.

Long—A good, strong reasoner; a correct logician.

Short—The reasoning power is weak, or is used by fits and starts.

Very short—Lacks the simplest common sense; hates to think before acting.

B. Shape.

Broad—if long—A good understanding of material things. If short—A primitive type of intellect.

Flat—In this case, logic lacks healthy development; often false logic.

Thick and clumsy—A lower grade of brains; the primitive type again.

Slender—Refinement in thought; sometimes nervousness affecting the reasoning power.

Wasped or waist-shaped—Quick, sharp, brilliant intellect; love of things intellectual.

NO THIRD PHALANX.

I refer the reader to the Skeleton of the Hand, found in a preceding chapter, for the proof that the Thumb has only two phalanges, and not three, as is commonly believed. The falsely so-called Third Phalanx is in reality the Mount of Venus, and will be studied later under that name.

VII. THE COMBINATION OF PHALANGES.

In a normally shaped hand the propor-

tion between the First and Second Phalanges is 2 to 3; in other words, if you measure a Thumb from its base (or lower knuckle) to the Tip, the First (or nailed) Phalanx must extend over two-fifths of the total length, and the Second Phalanx over three-fifths. Above or below this proportion the Phalanges must be considered as abnormal. Pay attention to this measurement when applying the following readings:

A long First and a short Second—Recklessness in thought and action. Will power is not influenced and controlled by reason.

'A short First and a long Second—"Talkers that are not doers;" they reason things fairly well, and lack the gift of execution.

THE LEADING TYPES OF HANDS.

Now that we have reviewed together —and interpreted—the diverse elements that enter into the exterior physiognomy of a hand and examined successively,

The Hand as a Whole,
The Hand Proper,
The Palm,
The Palm Proper,
The Fingers,
Each Finger Separately,
The Finger Tips,
The Finger Knots,
The Phalanges,
The Thumb,

I have two more chapters to bestow upon the Study of Chirognomy. The present one will be devoted to a combination of these various indications as are found in Fourteen Pure and Mixed Types, some of them beautifully delineated by d'Arpentigny, the others prepared by me from the most frequent examples that have come under my notice.

In the chapter closing this Part Second, I will give you an adaptation of Desbarrolles' semi-humorous, semi-serious method of judging people's dispositions from a cursory examination of their hands and without letting them suspect that they are under examination.

So far I have called your careful attention to four categories of Finger Tips:

the Pointed, the Conical, the Square, the Spatulate. These—in their purity and without admixture of contrary elements—characterize respectively:

I.   The Psychic Hand (pointed),
II. The Artistic Hand (conical),
III. The Useful Hand (square),
IV. The Necessary Hand (spatulate),

giving them here the names adopted by d'Arpentigny himself.

To those have to be added:

V. The Philosophical Hand (knotted), which, as we know, presents itself with Tips of the conical or square, or spatulate shape;

VI. The Elementary Hand, and

VIII. The Brutal Murderer's Hand, already much more mixed in their characteristics, and, in many respects, returning to the lower animal features. Of the Elementary Hand, at its worst, I find two very close counterfeits in

VIII. The Brutal Murder's Hand, and

IX. The Congenital Idiot's Hand.

These lead me to those commonplace types of Hands, which combine in their Finger Tips two, three and even four of the original four shapes:

X., XI., XII. and XIII. are descriptions of the hands most frequently met with among these Mixed Types. Finally:

XIV. The Woman's Hand

will give us an insight into the tendencies and most frequent characteristics of the weaker sex.

The reader may think perhaps that when I indulge in long, somewhat flowery descriptions of certain distinct Types of Hands, abandoning for a moment the sober teachings embodied in this work, I am playing false to my pledge to place practicality ever to the front, leaving severely aside all dithyrambic outbursts or fanciful picturings of impossible cases. Such imaginative sketches, I admit, will be found in this chapter and also at the end of Part Third in the minute descriptions therein inserted of the Seven Signatures of the Mounts; but the fact of my introducing them in this book, borrowing their main elements and much of their wording from d'Arpentigny and Desbarrolles, is not in any manner of means an act of desertion from the standard I have adopted as my own.

No, here again, even here, I have aimed to be directly useful to the future Hand-reader, whose tuition I have undertaken and whose mind has to be trained through more than one kind of drill before it acquires the suppleness that is one of the essentials of a successful Palmist. The gift of generalizing the ideas, principles and rules once laid down, understood and memorized, is one that cannot be too soon cultivated; for when the time comes for you to take hands within your grasp, their owners will not ask you for a lesson in Palmistry, but for information of a clear, broad, definite character, about their physical, mental and moral natures, from which can alone be deduced such facts in their past and future lives as the lines may or may not reveal. And how are you going to avoid "giving a stone when you are asked for bread," if you do not learn, from the Masters, how to grasp, to combine, to harmonize the separate elements that constitute now Chirognomy, now the study of the Mounts, now Chiromancy in its infinite minutiae?

Such a learning is obtained from just such descriptions as I have inserted in this chapter, and in another one further on; and although the perusing of these particular pages could be left out of the curriculum of your present studies without depriving you of any absolutely indispensable element of knowledge, yet in the training of a Palmistic mind the reading of those sketches of leading types occupies, in my opinion, a place that it would be decidedly unwise to leave empty.

I. THE PSYCHIC HAND.

"The Psychic Hand," says d'Arpentigny, "is of all hands the most beautiful, and consequently the most scarce, for rarity is one of the conditions of beauty. It is small and slender, compared with the rest of the body. It has a medium Palm, smooth Fingers (or fingers with the Knots barely perceptible), the nailed Phalanges long, and tapering to a point, a small and elegant Thumb. Whenever the Psychic Hand is large and more distinctly knotted, it possesses force and combination, but loses much of its spontaneity."

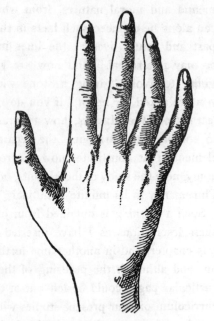

"Let common sense," writes the master, "be the guide of the Useful Hands,—hands of which order, arrangement, and unity are the sole ambitions; let reason be the solitary beacon of the Necessary Hands, ever carried, as they are, towards liberty and truth. The Psychic Hands bear to those two types the same relation the Conical bears to the Spatulate type; they add to the thinker's works the same elements the artist adds to the artisan's works: beauty and ideality; they gild them with a sun-ray, they raise them upon a pedestal, and open men's hearts to them; the soul, left behind by Philosophical Hands, is their guide; truth in matters of love is their end, and openheartedness their means.

"The Psychic Hand is not, as novelists persistently claim, the exclusive privilege of old families. Always scarce in our countries, it really exists nevertheless everywhere, even among the lowest classes, where it vegetates ignorant of itself, misunderstood and disdained, on account of its comparative inaptitude for manual labor.

"Conical Hands look for imagination and art everywhere; Square Hands, for rule and arrangement; Knotted Hands, for human reason. It is Divine reason Psychic Hands look for everywhere. They pay no attention to form, save in the domain of art, convinced, as they are, that civilization is not the absolute consequence of any particular form of religion; that liberty is not the absolute consequence of a democratic form of government; and that slavery is not the absolute consequence of an autocratic form of rule. In their eyes, religious faith is a fact as real as a rational certitude; so they excuse, even when they do not accept, the peculiarities of all religions.

"Psychic Hands are in an immense majority in Southern Asia, whence comes the essentially religious, contemplative, and poetic spirit of the nations which inhabit it; whence come also their respect for maxims (synthesis), and their disdain for methods (analysis); whence comes the preference they feel for holiness (source of repose) over science (source of activity); whence comes the languishing condition of arts, trades, and agriculture among them, and their theocratic and despotic governments, which are of absolute necessity for nations to whom reason and action are a torment. Thus, among us, are Spatulate and hard Square Hands in majority, whereas in India it is the Pointed and Soft Hands which numerically are in the ascendant.

"All nations—however different (physically and morally) they may be from one another, whatever may be the form of their government, the spirit of their culture or the nature of their ideas upon beauty, worth, truth, and usefulness—agree unanimously in giving Pointed Fingers to pictorial or sculptured representations of angels or good genii, with which each race, according to its education, considers the heavens to be peopled."

The entire human race sees nothing but beauty and elegance in a Pointed-fingered Hand.

"The Racial Psychic Hand, liberally endowed as they are, have only an imperfect comprehension of the things pertaining to real life: they look at them from too high a pinnacle to see them well. Spiritualists are endowed with lyricism, mysticism, prophetic ecstasies, a luminous, snythetic understanding of all human knowledge; but the talent of applied sciences, including that of the government of men, is wanting among them, unless, as in India, they only have to deal with people belonging to their own type. Again, it would be a great mistake to suppose that the Psychic Hands are better protected against the errors incidental to the imperfections of our natures, than the others; the world of ideas is not less perilous and deceitful than that of things real. For, if in their enthusiasm, Spiritualists are always ready to sacrifice themselves, they exact from others the same unlimited devotion to their ideals. With their synthetic method of thought, no isolated senti-

ment, no idea of detail can either touch their hearts, or alter their convictions, or turn them from their objects; it is in their eyes that the end justifies the means; if occasion should arise they will shed blood unhesitatingly—their own blood, or other people's—their own without regret, that of others without remorse. The Inquisitors of old Spain were men with thin Hands and Pointed Fingers."

II. THE ARTISTIC HAND.

The Artistic Hand is characterized by smooth Fingers whose nailed Phalanges assume the form of Cones or of elongated Thimbles. Plastic arts, painting, sculpture, monumental architecture, poetry of the imagination and of the

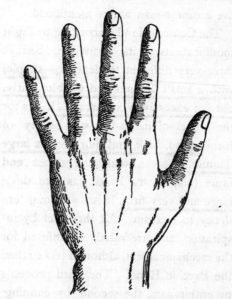

senses, cultivation of the beautiful in the solid and visible form, romantic charms, antipathy to rigorous deduction, desire of social independence, propensity to enthusiasm, subjection to phantasy—all these qualities and defects are distinctively represented by the Artistic, the Conical Hand.

The Palm is here larger and thicker than in the Psychic type; it is much more "of the Earth, earthy;" it is soft—sometimes too soft—as such genius as the Artistic Hand possesses is frequently accompanied by what the active business man, with his elastic or even hard Palm and his Square or Spatulate Fingers, rather contemptuously calls "constitutional laziness." Dreaminess, self-concentration is needed and practiced by the owners of Conical Hands during the period of conception, of incubation of the thought, in art, music, literature, that will call forth, perhaps, some day, the plaudits of the whole world—including the business-man above mentioned.

The Conical Hand, according to slight modifications in its formation, betrays three very different tendencies;—supple, with a small Thumb and a Palm fairly, but not excessively, developed, it has for the object of its endeavors, beauty of form; broad, thick, and short, with a large Thumb, it seeks wealth, greatness and fame (Napoleon's hand was like this); large and very firm, it has a strong tendency to fatalism. All three act by inspiration, and are relatively unfitted for the mechanical arts, although less so than the Psychic Hand. The third proceeds by enthusiasm, the second, by cunning, and the first obeys the suggestions of pleasure.

"Whoever has a hand thus formed," writes d'Arpentigny, "will attach himself, instinctively and without reflection, to the picturesque aspect of ideas and things: he will prefer that which pleases to that which pays. So long as a thing is beautiful it does not matter if it be true or not; greedy of leisure, of novelty, of liberty, at the same time ardent and timid, humble and vain, he will have more energy and enthusiasm than force and power. He will pass suddenly from the loftiest exaltation of mind to the profoundest despair. Incapable of command, and still more incapable of obedience, attraction will be his guide through life, rather than duty. Inclined to enthusiasm, he will live in constant need of excitement, and the activity of his mind will render regular domestic life heavy and uninteresting to him. In a word, he will be a man of sentiments rather than of ideas, appreciating the colors of a thing rather than its features; he will be light in character, he will have ingenuousness and eagerness, an imagination of fire, and, too often, a heart of ice."

Let us now push this type to extremes, and what do we find?

A fairly large Palm, smooth fingers, a weak Thumb, still more Conical Fingertips, i. e., large appetites for sensual pleasures, without sufficient moral control, and a mind lacking the strength to subject the senses to its dominion, the whole built upon a foundation of only slightly spiritual ideas. And this pictures—says d'Arpentigny—the character of artists, for in truth, beauty is the only thing they prefer to pleasure.

"Subjects of the Artistic types," writes the master, "do not share the ideas of the other types upon right or wrong, upon what is good or what is useful; they often possess instinctive religious faith, because it saves them the trouble of reasoning, without robbing their esthetical sense of any pleasurable feelings; but they will not stand political despotism, because its essential principles are the levelling of ranks, uniformity and monotonous quietude—conditions strongly contrary to their natures; their's therefore is generally relative liberty, such as is found under aristocratic governments, for such rulers have always used as their most effective instruments of power, luxury, pleasures, magnificent displays, and art in its highest manifestations. They are therefore the natural friends and patrons of the Artistic Hands.

"Generals with the Conical, Artistic Hand proceed by inspiration, and move by sallies; they are gifted with prowess, promptitude, passionate instincts, boastfulness, and the talent of acting impromptu; they attach more importance to passing glory than to solid, durable success."

The typical Woman's Hand, which we shall study at the end of this chapter, belongs, to a great extent, to the family of Artistic-Conical Hands.

III. THE USEFUL HAND.

"The Useful Hand," says d'Arpentigny, "is of medium size, but large rather than small, often with Knotty Fingers, the nailed Phalanges of which are square, that is to say, their four sides extend parallel up to and including the Tips (you must not take any notice of the curve, which nearly always finishes of the points of the fingers); a large Thumb, with the base thereof (the Mount of Venus) well developed, the Palm of medium dimension, and rather firm."

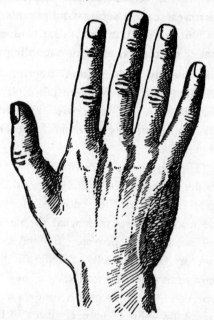

Perseverance, foresight and the spirit of order and conventionality, with a love of truth and fair play, characterize the individualities revealed to us by Useful Hands.

"The possessors of such hands have a deep preference for similitude and homogeneity. They know wherein things which differ are similar, and the points in which things that seem similar in reality differ; which faculty constitutes the spirit in which the various degrees of hierarchy range themselves in clearly defined lines, and in which, according to them, lie the principles of political power and wisdom. They intentionally confound discipline with civilization, i. e., they are narrow-minded respectors of the letter of the law, for they range all rules as duties, subjecting thoughts to thought, men to man, and only tolerating such impulses of the mind, the soul, and the heart as reason (considered from its narrowest aspect) accepts and permits.

"One law of all others is dear to them, that of continuity, and it is according to that rule, by tradition and transmitted law, that their development takes place. Such intelligences, otherwise vigorous, have no wings; they can expand but they cannot rise.

"The earth is preëminently their abode; they can see nothing beyond the social life of man; they know no more of the world of ideas than what the naked eye can know of heaven. Beyond this, they are always ready to deny all that they cannot feel or understand, and to look upon the limits of their understanding as the limits of nature. Even in literature, what of ideality these Useful Hands can comprehend stops short at a very narrow limit. They keep away from idealism just as they do from boldness of thought or novelty of form.

"Their tastes are in the direction of moral, political, social, and philosophical sciences; didactic, analytic and dramatic poetry; grammar, form, language, logic, mathematics, love of literary exactitude, meter, rhythm, symmetry and arrangement, strictly defined and conventional art. Their views of things are just rather than wide; they have great commercial talent; they have positive but moderate ideas, with the instinct of duty and of the respect due to authority, of the cultivation of practical truth and of good behavior, with a strong paternal instinct;

in fact, generally speaking, having more brains than heart, they prefer what they discover to what they imagine.

"In social relations, they require security and exactitude; in life, moderation. Circumspect and far-seeing, they like what is clearly known, and suspect the unknown. Born for the cultivation of commonplace ideas, they pay less attention to the actually real than to the apparently real; they recommend themselves by their good sense, rather than by their genius; by their cultivated talents, rather than by the faculties of imagination. Such subjects will accept none but the man who is well taught, disciplined, molded and trimmed upon a certain pattern. Where the man of learning shows himself in all his glory, they go to seek their models and their examples.

"Townsmen rather than citizens, men of the Square-Handed type prefer certain privileges to absolute liberty. Authority is the base of all their instincts, the authority of rank, of birth, of law and of custom; they like to feel and to impose the yoke."

Useful Hands love order for itself, admitting freely to their lives everything resulting therefrom.

The above, very brilliant description, mostly adapted from d'Arpentigny himself, culling here and there his best paragraphs, explains sufficiently why the Useful Hands are very generally provided with knots, or, at least, with distinct Second Knots, which complete and "round up," so to speak, their more decided idiosyncrasies.

IV. THE NECESSARY HAND.

By a Necessary Hand is meant one, the nailed phalanges of whose fingers present the appearance of a more or less flattened out spatula. I want to deal here

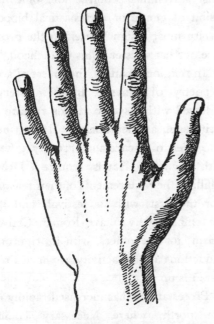

with those Spatulate Hands whose Thumbs are large, with those in which the instinct peculiar to these hands, supported by the promptings of the brain, makes itself the most clearly manifest. (As to consistency, the Palm is always elastic and often quite hard.)

"The Necessary Hand," writes d'Arpentigny, "has undoubtedly its origin in the latitudes where the inclemency of the climate, and the comparatively sterile nature of the soil render locomotion, action, movement, and the practice of the arts whereby the physical weakness of man is protected, more obligatory than they are under more southern skies. Larger Spatulate Hands are therefore

much more numerous in Scotland than they are in England, in England than they are in France, and in France than they are in Spain, and in mountainous than in flat countries.

"For the following reasons the most stable colonies are formed by Spatulate-Handed people rather than by others. Almost insensible to art or to poetry, they are endowed with a very small share of the instincts which lead to moral instability. They attach themselves to a country for the material benefits which accrue to them therefrom. Manual labor is agreeable to them, and it is the same with all kinds of active exercise. They suffer from the absence of the necessaries of life, but not from the absence of the superfluous, for they are only slightly sensual.

"Their love of locomotion renders them comparatively insensible to the annoyances of expatriation. Accustomed, as they are, by the multiplicity of the wants which assail man in our northern latitudes, to rely principally on their own exertions, they have no innate objection to solitude. Finally, they are apt at sciences which are merely those of physical necessity, and which in ordinary life affect only things which are constant and immovable."

Whence comes the severely practical common sense of the North Americans, if it is not from these "working hands," scattered over a space which they can cover and conquer, whilst resting their faith upon institutions that harmonize with their instincts?

Wherever they are in majority, as is

the case in England and the United States, liberty, in its broadest meaning, is the base of all political institutions; a fact which does not prevent, but rather proves, that of all nations in the world the English and the Americans are the most prone to exclusiveness and individuality.

The self-confidence of Spatulate subjects is extreme; they possess in the highest degree the instincts of real life, and by their natural intelligence they rule matters mundane and material interests.

"With smooth Fingers, the Necessary Hands like comfort as well as elegance, but their elegance is of a fashionable rather than artistic kind. It is from the restless crowd of Spatulate subjects that we get these everlasting measurers, whose admiration for works of architecture is in exact proportion with the greater or less bulk of these monuments; their instinct of grandeur is not in the form, it is in the mass; they are governed by mathematics.

"In the north, where Spatulate and Square hands are in a majority, the artist is swallowed up by the artisan; in Italy, in Spain, in France, the artisan is effaced by the artist. In the North there is more opulence than luxury, in the South there is more luxury than wealth.

"Spatulate hands are valiant, industrious, and active; they have the power and the genius of Cyclops; in old days they forged impregnable armor, and covered the earth with battlemented castles which they reared themselves upon the crests of rock promontories, protected by deep waters and impenetrable forests. Every gentleman, descended from the old fighting nobility, has necessarily a Spatulate hand. If his fingers be Pointed, he must search his pedigree for some infusion of gentle or ecclesiastical blood, or else must resign himself to the presence of a bar sinister in his escutcheon.

"In religious matters, the lovers of art, of poetry, of romance, and of mystery, endowed with Psychic Hands require a Deity such as they imagine Him to be. The lovers of science and of reality, gifted with Necessary Hands, require a Deity fulfilling the requirements of their reason. For the first, with its festivals and its contemplation, we have Roman Catholicism; for the others, with its rigorous deductions and its activity, we have Protestantism.

"Protestantism has increased rapidly in the north, where Necessary Hands abound, and has hardly penetrated at all in the south, save in mountainous districts, where the same hands, for the same reasons, are equally abundant.

"Tactics, manœuvres, encampments, sieges, military and naval architecture, strategy of temporization and delay, are the especial qualities of the Military or Naval Commander whose Hands are Spatulate. He has theory, method, and science, and cares more for success than for glory. His subordinates are well fed and housed, for he attends to those details upon which success is so often based."

Platonic affections, fiiial, paternal and

parental, are distinctly the attribute of the Necessary (and often of the Useful) Hands.

Devoted to manual labor and to action, and consequently endowed with feelings which are more energetic than delicate, constancy in love is more easy to them than it is to minds which are poetic, and which are more attracted by the charms of youth and beauty than restrained by a sense of duty.

Finally, the large, fat, soft, Spatulate Hands, (forming a sort of abnormal type) do not do much themselves, but like to see others working hard; they do not travel themselves, but delight in reading tales of voyages, traversing the habitable globe, riding, as one might say, on the shoulders of the energetic and actual traveler. These are not any longer, in spite of the shape of the Finger-tips, the Necessary Hands so highly praised by d'Arpentigny.

V. THE PHILOSOPHICAL HAND.

The Palm rather large and well developed, but bony; both Knots well marked in the Fingers; the nailed Phalanx half Square, half Conical, a combination producing with the upper Knot a kind of egg-shaped spatula; the Thumb large and indicating the presence of as much logic as will-power, i. e., composed of two phalanges of equal or practically equal lengths—this constitutes, for d'Arpentigny, the Philosophical (or Knotted) Hand.

We have seen that the Spatulate Finger-tips are drawn irresistibly toward that which is materially useful; that the

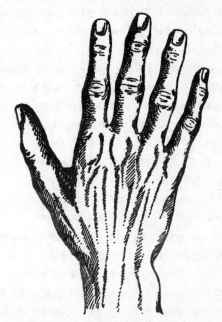

tendency of the Conical Fingers is toward beauty of form, i. e., art; and that the inclination of the Square Finger-tips tends toward social utility, average and practical ideas, and realizable combinations.

"By their Knots," writes d'Arpentigny, "Philosophical Hands are gifted with calculation, with a more or less rigorous power of deduction and with method in thought and action; by their quasi-Conical Tips they have the intuition of a relative form of poetry; and by the whole combinations of formations, including, of course, the Thumb, they have the instinct of metaphysics. They plunge into the outer as well as into the inner world, but they seek less after the form than after the essence of things, less after beauty than truth.

"More than any of the other types, they show themselves athirst for the severe enthusiasm which is diffused by the inexhaustible reservoir of higher moral, experimental, philosophical an æsthetic sciences."

Contrary to the Useful Hands, which appeal to subordination, to authority, to usage, to custom, to conventionality, to faith and to predestination, the Philosophical Hands appeal to reason, to examination, to proof, to liberty and to free thought.

Alone, the Philosophical type, doubtless because, to a certain point, both worlds are known to it, can understand and appreciate the other types.

As is the case with nations, individuals do not attain, excepting in ages of greater or less advancement, the perfect intelligence of their philosophical faculties, which, to come into being and develop themselves properly, require at least the light of experience. Philosophical hands, like those belonging to the other types, exist in all classes of society; only the genius which they represent becomes abortive, or manifests itself but very imperfectly among persons who are chained by their ill-fortune to gross labors.

The philosophers with Necessary or Useful hands study the problems of facts, of practical ideas, of realities, of politics, and so on.

The philosophers with Conical or Pointed Hands tend toward strange beliefs, speculative ideas and obtruse researches, and so on.

Hands of the quasi-Square and quasi-Conical formation generally reveal eclecticism, and it is for this reason that d'Arpentigny has given them, above all others, the name of Philosophical Hands.

When they are large, they incline to analysis; when they are small, they incline to synthesis; with a small Thumb they are guided by their heart, with a big Thumb they are led by their head.

VI. THE ELEMENTARY HAND.

Here we abandon what I call the pure types, already considerably modified by the occasional addition of the Knots, and we reach inferior grades of Hands, all deviating, more or less clearly, from what d'Arpentigny has called, very aptly, the Elementary Hand.

It is characterized by stiff, heavy Fingers, by a short, clumsy Thumb with the nailed Phalanx turned back, often of the "clubbed" type; by an extremely thick

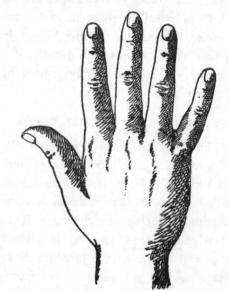

and hard Palm, and by Finger-Tips rounded and shapeless, somewhat of the Square type.

"Among the European races," writes d'Arpentigny, "these Hands undertake unskilled manual labor, the care of stables and the endless routine of coarse work, which may be carried out by the dim flickerings of the light of instinct.

"To these Hands belong war, when no personal prowess and no intelligent leadership are needed; to them belongs colonization, when it is merely a matter of mechanically watering the soil of a foreign land with the sweat of the laboring brow. Shut in, on all sides, by material instincts, their opinions are formed in a groove, which is inaccessible to reason, and their virtues are generally those of a negative nature. Governed as they are by dull routine, they proceed more by custom than in answer to their passions.

"Strangers to anything like enthusiasm, Elementary hands indicate feelings which are heavy and sluggish in rousing themselves, an imagination either asleep or wanting, an inert soul, and a profound indifference about everything but the rough needs and pleasures of the immediate present.

"In the Elementary Hand one finds a perfect demonstration of these axioms that 'organs which are practically insensible can only convey imperfect ideas to the brain;' that 'the outer man, is merely the reflection of the inner man;' and that 'as is the body, so is the mind,' and vice versa.

"Except in polar latitudes, real Elementary Hands are no longer to be found, save among nations of Tartar or Slavonic origin. Among the latter races, however, they exist in large numbers and in some localities they are to be found without any admixture of the more nobly endowed types."

And yet Elementary Hands are, almost invariably, more accessible to the charms of poetry or simple music than to those of science. It was to the lyric measures of Orpheus, and to the harmonies of the flute of Apollo, that in the old Greek world the first communities of men were formed, and the first towns were built.

"In the depth of the forest, or on the deserted sea shore," d'Arpentigny tells us, "by night, when the boundless ocean moans with the murmur of the tempest, Hands which are Elementary are, more than any other type, troubled by phantoms, specters and pallid apparitions, in proportion as their Finger-Tips are more or less Conical. But whatever be the form of the nailed phalanx, their possessors are always much influenced by superstition.

"Elementary-Handed subjects, whom neither inertia nor insensibility has been able to protect from pain and sorrow, succumb the more readily to their attacks, from the fact that they are generally entirely wanting in resources and in moral strength."

VII. THE ARTISTIC-ELEMENTARY HAND.

Here we have a not infrequent improvement on the Elementary Hand, an improvement one meets especially among those men of talent, or even genius, who emerge from the very lowest ranks of society, urged on by an invincible force, which pushes them to the highest places in the banquet halls of humanity. Great poets, famous musicians, illustrious painters, sculptors, orators, generals, are thus coming, every day, to the front, as if a magic wand had touched them on the brow. And yet the main characteristics of their humble origin are still visible, not only in their manners, their habits, their tastes—all these may have been more or less modified by association with the upper classes—but above all, and without possible dissembling, in the shape of their hands—the hands of their father, the clown, the peasant, the low-grade laborer. Their hands will remain to the last day—in spite of the laurel wreath voted them by popular acclaim—Elementary Hands; but they may show such modifications as will reveal to us much of the strange mystery of their surprising career. And this is especially true of heaven-inspired artists. Many of them possess broad, heavy, almost Square Palms, rather firm, though not exactly hard, Fingers heavy at the base, but ending in Conical tips; no Knots; a Thumb better than the Fingers, with a first Phalanx broad and thrown back, and a second Phalanx short.

These are the characteristics of the Elementary Hands refined by the introduction of the Conical Tips (inspiration, intuition, artistic gifts), and of a powerful First Phalanx of the Thumb, proclaiming the determined will-power that has led the street Arab or the country churl from the gutter or the pig sty to the highest honors in the gift of the great.

I am, in all fairness, bound to add that this interpretation of the Artistic-Elementary Type is not the d'Arpentigny

reading of it; in fact, it is diametrically opposed to it. The master sees in that seventh type—created, or rather classified, by himself—a lowering of the Artistic Hand, not a raising up of the Elementary Hand.

With the reader's permission I will stand by my guns—i. e., my theory in the case—for I hold it to be logical and I have proved it true in a large number of most interesting instances.

VIII. THE MURDERER'S HAND.

After having considered with you an Improved Elementary Hand, I shall examine, quite independently from the d'Arpentigny doctrine—the main features of which we have gone over together—the great deterioration of the Elementary Hand, as manifested in the Brutal Murderer's Hand. Its characteristics may be enumerated as follows:

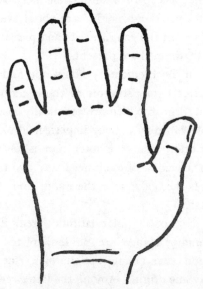

A thick, heavy Palm, reddish in tint, and broader than the average; short, awkward and stiff Fingers, generally crooked; often Spatulate; no Knots to speak of, although sometimes the second joint may be clumsy and thick; a Thumb with a "clubbed" First Phalanx and a Second Phalanx very much undersized.

These observations were made years ago in the hands of Tropmann, who, single-handed, killed a family of seven people, all in half an hour, at Pantin, near Paris; of Dumolard, the Lyons assassin, who murdered, nobody knows how many poor servant girls; of Avinain, the Parisian butcher, who killed and cut to pieces several confiding victims, and of several other infamously prominent criminals.

It is the typical hand of the drunken brute of the lower classes; rarely found among educated people, no better at heart, perhaps, but craftier in the satisfying of their murderous instincts.

Desbarrolles, whose wide experience and ever-honest investigating spirit I have trusted for so many years, insists especially upon the existence, in this particular kind of murderer, of the "clubbed" Thumb, the influence of which, the Master says, causes the possessor, when his wretched, diseased nature is moved to crime to "see red" and to strike and strike his victim with blind ferocity and with sensations akin to a horrible delight. He adds that he has often conversed with visitors to his studio in whose hands he saw the very same indications met with in the brutal murderers whom he sought in the Prisons or Penitentiaries—the indications of an uncontrollably violent temper. Whenever inclined to be confidential, these

subjects confessed to him that, at certain hours in their lives, the thirst for blood had come upon them with such imperiousness as almost to swamp their reason and power of resistance; before their eyes a bloody film came to pass between sight and object, and they had felt in their very bones that they were but a hair-breadth away from becoming actual murderers.

Strange to say, this very same characteristic has been observed by the writer on the battlefields of 1870-71, in the many hand-to-hand fights he witnessed or took part in, during the Franco-Prussian war. The Soldier, when his blood has reached a certain high temperature, i. e., after the first period of nervous emotion akin to physical cowardice has been conquered, becomes almost entirely oblivious of his nature as a civilized being, and returns with extraordinary rapidity to a state of savagery. The brutal murderer's instinct seems to fill him like rank alcohol—and the better fighter he proves to be, the nearer to the Murderer's Hand will his hand type be found.

IX. THE IDIOT'S HAND.

In my paragraphs on the Brutal Murderer's Hand, I did not hesitate to qualify his horrible propensity to take human life as a disease, and I believe that this affirmation is in accord with the dicta of the most prominent scientists of our times, who are now transferring from the Moral to the Physical domain these abnormal manifestations of an ill-balanced nature.

And this brings me still lower down

in the scale of Hands, which we have begun reading downward since we diagnosed, with d'Arpentigny, the Elementary Hand. Below the Criminal, almost in a level with him, we meet the Congenital Idiot, the half-developed brain, the Child for Life.

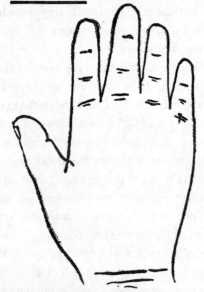

[This example, taken from life, is wider and better than the average.]

His hand will be so ill-shaped as often to be justly called crippled. The Palm will be thick, soft, longer than the Fingers and generally narrow; this narrowness increased by the position of the Thumb, set very high and only half detached from the side of the hand; very short, besides, clumsy and ill-shaped. The Fingers are hardly more than one-half the normal size; their Phalanges are twisted and their Tips rounded and shapeless; I have often found them inclining to the Spatulate type, a sign of the violent disposition, so often found in those poor, half-witted creatures.

I do not pursue farther my downgrade study of hands. Soon we should reach the lower Human Races, then the Ape. As for the Insane—not born insane—the shapes of their hands vary as much as did their own original tendencies before the dark shadow settled upon their brain.

X., XI., XII., XIII. MIXED HANDS.

Here I have not to antagonize but to complete the remarks and definitions of d'Arpentigny concerning those Hands, the most commonly met with—I might almost say the only ones we meet—to which he has applied the name of Mixed.

They include, in my opinion, those Hands in which the Finger-tips do not all four belong to one and the same type, but which present, generally, two Finger-tips of a type and two of another. Rather disdainfully, d'Arpentigny says of such hands (which are, after all, the hands that make the world go):

"The intelligence which is revealed by a mixed hand is one which partakes of the nature of the intelligences attached to each of the forms represented. Without these hands, that is to say, without the mixed intelligence peculiar to them, society—deprived of its lights and shades, and without moral alkalis to effect the combination of its acids, and to amalgamate and modify them, would advance only by struggles and leaps." And he adds:

"Well, it is to mixed hands that the intelligence of mixed works of intermediary ideas belong; of sciences which are not really sciences, such as administration and commerce; of arts, which are not the outcome of poetry; and of the beauties and the relative realities of industry.

"Men whose hands present the forms of a particular type have minds which are more powerful in one direction than versatile; men whose hands are of mixed types have minds which are more versatile than powerful. The conversation of the former is instructive, that of the latter is amusing; it is for these latter above all, that a powerful education, judiciously adapted to the development of the most prominent faculty of their minds, is an immense benefit.

"Apt for many pursuits, mixed hands nevertheless often excel in none in particular; a great moral indifference is their endowment. The hand which belongs to a particular type, on the contrary, is the sacred shrine in which God has placed the imperishable germ which is destined to renew or to reveal every art, every science hitherto ignored, or for a long time lost sight of. Its promptings, too imperious to be disobeyed, too significant to be mistaken, give it the clear knowledge of itself; it knows what it wants, and, like the animals which are guided by an infallible instinct, it desires nothing that it cannot possibly attain."

Now that we have been told, rather too plainly, what are the weak, contemptible points of these Indispensable Hands, let me give you the principle which I have found rules most of the Combination of Finger tips:

The First and Fourth Fingers—in the great majority of hands—are of a more Pointed or Conical type than the Second and Third Fingers of the same hand.

And I explain this by referring you to the Introduction to this work and to my Chapter on Lines in General in Part Third. In both places, I mention the fact of the Vital or Electric Fluid penetrating

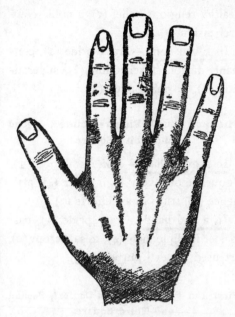

through the First Finger—always, comparatively pointed or conical, so as to better attract the same fluid; this is the Aspir. The Expir takes places through the fourth finger, the Projector, as the first finger is the Attractor—hence the pointed or conical tendency of the fourth finger.

Of course it would be impossible to present a complete list of all the possible Combinations of Finger-Tips, but the following will be found the most frequently met with, and for the others I refer you to my separate readings for every finger, which can be easily combined by any intelligent student. Remember that all that is supplied you is a hint, pointing out the right direction in which to seek for wider, logical interpretations.

First and Fourth Fingers Pointed, Second and Third Conical.

In a good hand—Lofty ambition (1), love of science for its own sake (4), a healthy religious belief (2), a noble comprehension of art (3).

In a bad hand—Crazy pride (1), constant dishonest scheming (4), superstition (2), art misapplied (3).

First and Fourth Fingers Pointed, Second and Third Square.

In a good hand—Lofty ambition (1), eloquence of a very high order (4), prudence (2), truth in art efforts (3).

In a bad hand—Crazy pride (1), past master in diplomacy (4), misanthropy (2), art used for evil purposes (3).

First and Fourth Fingers Conical, Second and Third Square.

In a good hand—Love of reading worthy fiction (1), aptitude for science and inventions (4), prudence and love of agriculture (2), mind much inclined toward art, music, literature (3).

In a bad hand—Vanity (1), commercial dishonesty (4), false idea of religion (2), art practiced for lucre (3).

First and Fourth Fingers Conical, Second and Third Spatulate.

In a good hand—Love of reading books of travel (1), speculations in far-off lands (4), constant activity (2), painters, writers, etc., of historical subjects (3)

In a bad hand—Loud bragging (1), Napoleons of finance (4), irreligion (2), realism in art (3).

XIV. THE WOMAN'S HAND.

"The tendencies of each type among women are," says d'Arpentigny, "the same as they are among men, only, those which are peculiar to the Spatulate and Square types are much less intense among women, by reason of the suppleness of their muscles, than they are among us." (I add, by reason of their delicate nerves.)

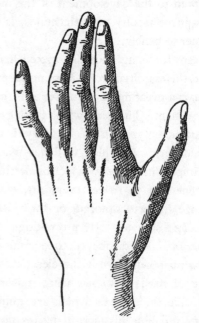

"Out of a hundred women in France," the Master claims, "forty belong to the Conical type, thirty to the Square, and thirty to the Spatulate type. These two latter types, of which the all ruling power is Mind, outweigh the former, of which the all-absorbing influence is Imagination.

"Few women have Knotty fingers, for few women are gifted with the talent of combination. Among intellectual labors, they generally choose those requiring more tact than science, more quickness of conception than strength, more intuition than reasoning. It would be otherwise if they had strongly Knotted fingers; then they would yield less easily to the inspirations of fantasy, and, just as the intoxicating qualities of wine are neutralized by the addition of water, so would theirs be by reason.

"Before combining Finger Tips and the other indications of Chirognomy, I will now divide women into two categories: those with large Thumbs, and those with small Thumbs. The former, more intelligent than sensitive, are attracted by serious, solid works, by books of history, travel, biography; the latter, more sensitive than intelligent, are captivated by the brilliant side of life.

"The cares of maternity being extremely difficult and complicated, their practice requires an instinct of a higher grade than that which is revealed in the Elementary Hands; these hands, therefore, are extremely rare among women."

"Women with Spatulate Hands and small Thumbs possess a great fund of affectionate freedom, an imperious desire of action and movement, a thorough understanding of real life.

"Order, arrangement, symmetry, and punctuality reign, without tyranny, in the homes which are governed by these calm managers with Square Fingers and a small Thumb.

"Do you lay siege to the heart of a beautiful woman whose Fingers are Square? Speak the language of common sense and do not confound singularity with distinction; remember that she has

less imagination than brains, and that her mind is more just than original. Do not forget that she has the social instinct strongly developed, and that she combines with respect for what is regulated by good taste a great love of domination.

"Religious institutions governed by rigidly-severe and narrow rules, where nothing is left to discretion, recruit nearly all their adherents from among the female subjects of the Square type.

"See these little soft, supple hands, almost fleshless, but rosy, and with faintly marked Knots: they love brilliant phrases, which, like lightning, cast a sudden bright flash of wit around them; they live with their minds alone.

"With women whose hands are hard, whose Fingers are Conical, whose Thumbs are small, do not hesitate to skillfully and flatteringly excuse, justify, applaud peccadilloes of the tender description. They love all that is brilliant, and rhetoric has more empire over their minds than logic. They are governed by three things: indolence, fancy and sensuality."

"Fingers which are delicate, Smooth, and Pointed in a woman's hand, when their meaning is completed by a Palm both narrow and elastic, without softness, indicate tastes ruled far more by the heart and soul than by the mind or senses, a charming mixture of exaltation and indolence, a secret disgust for the realities of life, and for recognized duties; more perfunctory piety than faith. These Hands, whose possessors are at the same time calm and radiant, expend their sovereign influence in a constant flow of inspiration and grace. Common sense, which of all human qualities is the most fruitful, but not the most exalted, pleases them far less than true genius."

All this is d'Arpentigny's semi-ironical plea in favor of the various types of Woman's Hands. He evidently had the Latin race in his mind's eye when penning these sprightly descriptions; and although America contains all the types in their purity as well as their most curious and unexpected combinations, my experience has taught me that the most thoroughly American Hand, in woman, can be correctly defined in these short paragraphs, which I had occasion to use in former books and lectures.

First of all, let it be clearly understood that by the typical Woman's Hand, I do not mean the hand of the woman of genius, or even the hand of the woman of unusual beauty, in shape and features. I mean the hand of the average woman, of the woman "womanly," the mother, the sweetheart, the daughter; the woman of the home, with her love, her patience, her divine devotion, but also with her imagination ever awake, her lack of logic, her sudden intuition, replacing sedate, sober reasoning, her whims and unexplained likes and dislikes. Of this Woman's Hand the picture is found in this section and it tells the following tale:

Remark, first of all, that the Tips of these Fingers are neither Spatulate nor Square; they belong evidently to the Conical type, but not often so pronounced. Now, the possessors of such fingers are ruled by impulse, rather than

calculation; they are predisposed to love beautiful things; they pass quickly from the acme of felicity to the lowest depth of despair; they need excitement in their lives and are not—alas!—they are not always constant.

The second observation is that in this hand there are no Knots. Especially the First joint is decidedly smooth, meaning, as you know, the absence of logical, philosophical bent of the mind. Generally the Second joint is slightly Knotted, a sign of order in material things. This is more clearly seen in the typical housewife, than whom there is no creature on earth that distributes more real, solid happiness around her.

The third remark refers to the Thumb: It is generally somewhat large, in the American woman, who is allowed so much liberty in her intercourse with men; that means that she is born naturally sensible and cautious in affairs of the heart; in other words, that she holds her sensations under the control of a well-balanced will.

A small Thumb would prove disastrous for a woman whose lines would not belie this disposition to excessive coquetry, unreasonable jealousy and unreliable nerves. Society belles, I am sorry to say, are very frequently afflicted with a puny Thumb. They are very seductive, as a rule, but very fickle and somewhat fond of coming mighty near the fire "that sometimes scorches."

Short-Thumbed women do not keep secrets, nor do they keep their word, nor are they over-scrupulous when talking scandal. Fingers of diversified types and shapes—stragglers, I call them—are often found in connection with these short Thumbs; when close together they have wide spaces for the light to pass between, an indication of a never-satiated inquisitiveness.

Large-Thumbed women are somewhat slower in understanding, but withal shrewd and calculating. They consider marriage as a matter of business, not passion; they are common sense all over; sometimes they will be found worrying needlessly, domineering in spirit, even loud-voices and "mannish;" still, they are the ones to be trusted.

VARIOUS TYPES OF WOMAN'S HANDS.

[From G. W. Gessmann's "Die Frauenhand."]

THE DREAMER.   THE EMOTIONAL.   THE GLOBE-TROTTER.

THE HOMEBODY.   THE DRUDGE.   THE QUICK-TEMPERED.

CHIROGNOMY IN EVERY DAY LIFE.

[Adapted from Desbarrolles.]

We have constantly occasion to meet people in a social or business way whose leading characteristics it would be of the very highest importance for us to know. They may be persons in a position to influence our whole lives, persons who may become our employers, if properly approached, or whose recommendation would be all-powerful in case we should apply for a city, state or government office. In a word, they are people whose good-will would be very useful if not essential to our future welfare. To please them, to meet with their approval, may be, at the time, of the utmost importance to us; and it is evident that if we knew a little of their nature we might treat them in such a way as to secure their support. It is not a question of flattering them, but simply to avoid antagonizing their hidden weakness. And to obtain such a precious result it is pleasant to know that we may call Palmistry to our help, with infallibly good results.

Of course, I do not mean the delicate, minute Chiromancy that unravels so slowly the tangled lines of the hands. No, I have in mind simply that branch of Palmistry called "Chirognomy," which bases its observations and conclusions on the shape of the palm, the fingers, the thumb. All these stand in full view whenever you are granted an inter-

view by high or low dignitary; you need not his permission to feast your eyes upon the peculiarities of his prehensile extremities. And a single glance will tell you the tale.

To be fully practical I will run over the various types you are bound to meet, and to each observation I will append a memorandum of the attitude that it will be proper, prudent and success-producing for you to adopt.

Let us first busy ourselves with the thumb of the interviewed party and see what it reveals to us when examined with a sharp, quick and accurate eye.

If the first phalanx of the thumb, the nailed one, be very long, you have before you the thumb of a despot, of the man with an uncontrollable, domineering spirit.

"Praise him to the skies. Any flattery will be accepted as the truth. Be humble, and you will please."

If the same phalanx be only of a middling size you have to do with a man endowed with the force of inertia.

"You must look for his weak points in the other fingers before you know how to handle him."

If the same phalanx be a very short one, its owner will be weak in his will-power, apt to run down from the acme of enthusiasm to the lowest degree of dis-

couragement; he will be of an unde-
cided nature and it will be very difficult
to bring him to a point.

"In that case act with energy, force
yourself upon him. Be even angry if it
suits the purpose. You will conquer the
fort by main fighting."

If the same phalanx be broad, as well
as short, you have a firm will to tackle
with. If it be very broad, that firm will is
nothing but stubbornness, often foolish
obstinacy.

"This is evidently one of the hardest
cases you will ever meet. Your only
possibility of success is to persuade your
man that your ideas are his own; you
may thus please him to such an extent
that the desired result be reached."

If this same phalanx be broad and
rounded like a playing marble, it is a
sign of violence and of unconquerable
stubbornness.

"Be patient. Let the fit of anger pass.
It may be just as well, perhaps, to come
back later; but all hopes are not lost, for
the short thumbs always yield in the
end."

If the thumb be bent back when the
hand is open, count on the generous instincts of your man.

"All you have to do then is to tell a
sad story, and even to give your voice
the tremulous tones of genuine grief; you
will reach his will through his heart."

But if the thumb be bent far back you
will have to deal with a prodigal, a spendthrift, who gives his influence as freely as
he would his money, and with just as little reason.

"That is the case, if ever, to ask all you
want and a little more."

Now we come to the second phalanx
of the thumb. If it be long and thick,
you are in the presence of logic and common sense.

"Be clear in your statements and avoid
any reasoning that might be contro-
verted easily."

If the second phalanx be short and
thin, whilst the first one (the nailed one)
is very long, will-power will have its own
way blindly, and without listening to the
appeals of reasoning.

"That is the case when you must ask
for anything that is absurd and unreasonable."

We are done with the thumb. Now
for the fingers. When they are very
long and very thin, without knots at the
joints, and when their tips are pointed,
the subject under inspection is possessed
of exaggerate mystical ideas; he is sure
to be fond of the supernatural and an
adept in the occult sciences.

"All you have to do is to show your
sympathy with this line of study, and, for
a little while, to humor his hobby in that
direction."

When the fingers are very pointed,
the subject has a disposition to lie, a continuous affectation of manners and a deceptive appearance of effusive kindliness.

"Follow suit and be yourself exaggerate in your demonstrations and polite
even to flattery."

If the fingers be short, and especially
if the nails be gnawed, the person is nervous, easily angered, fond of criticizing

and of discussing endlessly the smallest matters. For him nothing is done well that is not done by himself.

"This is a difficult case. Do not try to fight too hard. Give way. Seem convinced. Perhaps you may appease this restless fancy that feeds on other people's hopes."

If the fingers be square-tipped, you will be in the presence of a truthful and intelligent nature.

"Fall in line yourself and be sincere, clear in your statements and concise."

These same fingers give to the subject a spirit of fair play.

"Therefore it is essential that you should have a claim based on reality, or appearing to be, and that your request should not interfere with that of a better man."

These same fingers are indications of a spirit of order and correct reasoning.

"You had better speak quietly, distinctly, to the point, and with all your arguments well-marshaled forward."

If the fingers are spatulate, that is, if they grow wider at the tip, you are in the presence of a mind in love with independence in its widest meaning.

"You will surely please him if you attack abuses and speak of reforms like a true radical."

These same spatulate fingers are the characteristics of a love of outdoor sports, of extended traveling and of untiring activity.

"Do not fear to speak of athletics, football, even the race track and boxing ring. Show yourself a man who knows not what the word weariness means, both in business and recreation."

If the fingers be very spatulate, you have to deal with an Atheist, and probably a Socialist or Anarchist.

"You will find the way to his favor by being still more of an Atheist, a Socialist or an Anarchist."

If the second finger be particularly spatulate, the subject will be of a morbid disposition.

"You had better then show yourself also saddened by life's hard struggle and speak in a subdued tone about the melancholy experiences of your existence."

If the first joint (the upper joint) of each finger is visibly knotted, your man will be endowed with a philosophic mind.

"You may fearlessly wrap up your request in all kinds of abtruse reasonings."

If the second joint, the one between the middle phalanx and the lower phalanx of each finger, be markedly knotted, you will have to deal with a man who is orderly to a degree and who has all business details at his fingers' ends.

"Now is the time to show yourself a model business man, with almost a mania for classification and minute arrangements."

People with the above knot will be very careful in their dress and extremely regular in all their habits.

"It will be prudent to show yourself also dressed with the utmost care, and with the outward appearance of a model employe."

If the fingers be very long, the owner will have a mania for details in every thing. He is sure to have invented some extra minute classification of some sort or other. He will examine you from head to foot and note every little defect in your face or garb.

"Let us hope that you come to him prepared for such inspection, as he only admits to his favor such people as possess the same outward characteristics as are his own."

If he possesses short fingers he will only grasp general features and will have a natural hatred for full details and all red-tape business.

"When you approach him you may be dressed without any particular care, but you had better be quick about your requests, and not enter into details that would surely tire him out and dispose him ill toward you."

If his fingers are smooth, i. e., showing no knots at the joints, he will be easily impressed and be quick to understand half-expressed wishes.

"Speak rapidly, allow him to interrupt you; you may feel certain that he has grasped your meaning when the words have hardly been uttered."

Fingers fat at the inside base, where they are attached to the palm, denote love of good living, selfishness and material instincts.

"You had better talk of all the good times you have had and propose to have. Offer him the best cigars that can be bought for money, and, if you can, invite him to a recherché dinner. Show yourself a man of the world and a merry companion."

Should you notice that the third finger is smooth and at the same time spatulate at the tip, you will have to deal with a man who is fond of all beautiful things in nature and art.

"Do not hesitate to talk Painting, Sculpture, Music or Literature, according to the bent which you will find, after a few words, to be his."

Should the third finger be the same length as the second finger it is an invariable indication of a gambling propensity; your man will be fond of taking risks in business and of leading adventuresome expeditions into dangerous countries.

"You may talk to him about remarkable poker games and mention incidentally that you know of some big mine that only needs some care and investment to prove a millionaire-maker. Anything in that line that you may say will be welcomed with delight, and you must listen with sympathy to similar tales that he is sure to pour into your ears."

Now, at some times, the hand will open, and you will be able to inspect the root of the thumb, which is called, in Palmistry, the "Mount of Venus." If it be well-developed and bulges somewhat, but not too much, you have before you a man habitually kind in his disposition and inclined to help his fellow-beings.

"Answer back in the same tone by displaying a most benevolent disposition toward your fellow-creatures."

When he shakes hands with you, if the hand is hard you have to deal with a man of action, and if it is hot, besides, with a man of feverish activity.

"Then mention your overwhelming

occupations and your love for unceasing work."

If the hand is very hot and yielding, the indication will be that of constitutional laziness, and you had better pay attention to the following interpretation of this special characteristic:

"Never place any confidence in a lazy body, even if he speaks kindly to you. He is selfish at heart, and after you are gone, with the echo of his last pleasant words in your ear, he will never give you a second thought and certainly not move one step to assist you."

Finally, should you meet with a man whose fingers are ill-shaped, twisted, with very short nails and a thumb club-shaped, you may know that this man is a dangerous acquaintance, and the sooner you are out of his office the better for you.

These various items of information are not given here in a haphazard, arbitrary fashion. They are really based on the experience of hundreds of men who have both knowledge and belief in this branch of Palmistry, which has been rendered famous by Captain D'Arpentigny, the valorous officer of Napoleon the First, who gathered together the marvelous threads with which he weaved the science of Chirognomy.

DESBARROLLES AT THE TUILERIES.

One evening during the heyday of the Second Empire, when its structure seemed built on the rock and the Dynasty of the Napoleons assured of a century of power and prosperity, Desbarolles was summoned to the Imperial Chateau of the Tuileries—since burned to the ground by the Commune rioters—and invited to examine and read the hands of Napoleon III., and his beautiful wife, Eugenie.

The first indication that met the eyes of the great Chiromant when bending over the hand of Queen Hortense's son was the total absence of any line or sign of future greatness. The Chirognomy of the hand showed the sovereign under his true colors: a confirmed libertine, a dreamer and a deceiver, a reckless man without principles or scruples, extraordinarily lucky in his past adventures, but with the saddest doom in prospect. In health matters, the exact date of his death (1873) and the nature of his fatal ailment (stone in the bladder) were both clearly marked on the Line of Life and the lower Mount of the Moon. And a Line of Mars, following the Line of Life with the precision of a second rail on a railroad track, was read by Desbarrolles in his favorite manner as "a brilliant existence terminating in exile."

And, in the Empess' hands, the ill-luck in store was also strangely in evidence, at the very hour of her greatest triumph. First, Desbarrolles announced the death of a near relative: the Duchess of Albe, Eugenie's sister, in perfect health at the time of the reading, died within a year. Then he spoke, hesitatingly, of a great fatality which was to assail the Empress in her 47th year. The courageous woman listened calmy to the revelation; simply asking:

"I shall die on the scaffold, shall I not? A Gypsy, who foretold my accession to a throne, when she read my hand in my girlhood days, also predicted that I should be beheaded at the very date you mention."

"There is no signs of such a tragedy in the hand of Your Majesty," Desbarrolles replied; "and yet this star on the Mount of Mars, connected with a line of influence from the Mount of Venus that cuts the Line of Life at 47, is a sure token of a coming catastrophe."

"Can nothing prevent it?"

"Nothing, I fear."

"Let it come, then," exclaimed the brave lady, and withdrawing her hand, she went on chatting most cordially with her guest concerning the topics of the day.

On September 4th, 1870, Empress Eugenie, then in her 47th year, fled from the Tuileries palace, just as the mob was entering it from the other side, and, deserted by her courtiers, owed her safe escape to the devotion and coolness of her American dentist, Dr. Evans.

Desbarrolles' prediction was accomplished.

PART THIRD

The Mounts of the Hand

"Our body was most probably constructed, even in its less noble parts, so as to attract as large a quantity as possible of this *electric fluid* which it is bound to further elaborate; and, in our higher faculties, the active agent of our moral and physical perfections is doubtless some fluid more refined than electricity, although it preserves many of its characteristics. In a word, *thought* is but a ray of this heavenly fire that penetrates every living thing on earth and unites in the closest bond all the various elements of the created world. In the human organism, it sometimes reaches the highest attainable degree of perfection."—*Herder's Ideas on the Philosophy of Human History.*

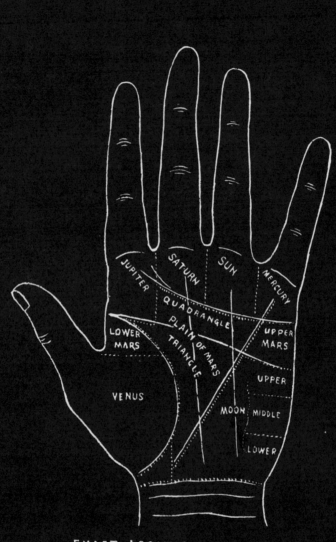

EXACT LOCATION OF THE MOUNTS
PLAIN OF MARS   } = QUADRANGLE AND
" OR PALM PROPER "   TRIANGLE .

THE MOUNTS OF THE HAND.

These slight elevations—bundles of muscles they are—found around the palm, like a wreath of peculiarly interesting indications, have been properly called Mounts. They are seven in number, if simply their appellations are considered; they are eight in reality, since one of them is duplicated.

That their importance is not due to the more or less development of the muscles that cover them, I had occasion to call your attention to in the Introduction by Desbarrolles, which gives sufficient stress to the existence of these hundreds of nerve-terminals, if the expression may be used for the purpose, distributed all over the human palm, but more especially and in greater numbers over what I call the Palm proper (Plain of Mars) and within the Mounts, especially those under the fingers. These Pacinic or Pacinian Corpuscles are thus defined in the famous Medical Dictionary of Dunglinson.

"Small bodies connected with the cutaneous nerves of the palms and soles. . . . . . . In each corpuscle there is the termination of a nervous filament." I have already described the Mounts that contain them as reservoirs of the mysterious fluid that seems to be the very essence of life or the nearest manifestation of it discovered so far by our limited senses. That they be called Mounts needs no explanation; their form is sufficient motive for the appellation. And as to the names of stars or of ancient dethroned divinities by which they have been known for centuries past, there is no interest for the practical student, intent upon the acquirement of profitable knowledge, in wasting paper or time expatiating at length upon them.

It is more to the point to give out here my scheme of study of those most important features in the human palm, so important, indeed, that I have decided to give them a separate department all to itself in this work, instead of starting my Chiromantic Observations with such indications as pertain to the Mounts.

The first notion that it is important to impress upon the student's mind is undoubtedly

I. The Positions of the Mounts; this, of course, applies to their normal positions, comparatively seldom met with in the examination of hands. Displacements form a separate section in this chapter. Next come

II. The Meanings of the Mounts; not only in their normal shape, but also when exaggerately developed, or when totally absent. Each of these meanings, for each Mount, is combined with this essential feature of the Finger tips, giving thus three different readings in connection with each of the four different types of finger tips. As a sort of corollary to this section come

III. The Meanings of the Mounts when displaced from what constitutes their normal positions; this applies more specially to the Mounts at the base of the fingers, although I give readings for the eight Mounts.

I found interesting to group in two short sections all information about

IV. The Mounts as they reveal Tendencies to Illnesses.

V. The Mounts as they indicate Suicidal Tendencies.

Finally a most important chapter presents to the readers the Physical, Moral and Mental types revealed by the marked predominance of one or the other Mount over all the others.

Here I will add only one short piece of advice and a warning:

You can never study the Mounts too long and too closely. A thorough investigation of the Mounts, added to a conscientious study of all Chirognomical observations, ought to suffice to enlighten you fully as to the physical, mental and moral nature of the subject under examination. You really have already within your grasp the key to those mysteries of the human body and soul you are bent upon probing to the quick.

But by neglecting to give the study of the Mounts the closest attention, you are doomed to failure—and you shall deserve to fail.

I. THE POSITIONS OF THE MOUNTS.

1. Mount of Jupiter: at the root of the first finger; limited by the Line of Head, by the Side of the Hand and by an imaginary line running straight down between the first and second fingers until it reaches the Line of Head.

2. Mount of Saturn: at the root of the second finger; limited by the imaginary line above mentioned, by the Line of Heart and by another imaginary line running straight down from between the second and third fingers until it reaches the Line of Heart.

3. Mount of the Sun: at the root of the third finger; limited by the second imaginary line mentioned in the preceding paragraph, by the Line of Heart and by an imaginary line running straight down from between the third and fourth fingers until it reaches the Line of Heart.

4. Mount of Mercury: at the root of the fourth finger; limited by the second imaginary line mentioned in the preceding paragraph, by the Line of Heart and by the Percussion of the Hand.

5. Upper Mount of Mars: immediately under the Mount of Mercury, following along the Percussion. In a normally built and lined hand, the Upper Mount of Mars occupies the space between the Line of Heart and the Line of Head. Inside the Hand it extends to where a normal Line of Liver cuts the Quadrangle.

6. Mount of the Moon: immediately under the Upper Mount of Mars, along the Percussion; its limits in a normally built and lined hand would be: at its upper part, the Line of Head; at its lower part, the first Bracelet of the Rascette, and inside the hand, first the Line of

Liver until it reaches the Third Angle of the Triangle, and secondly, the Mount of Venus from that point down to the first Bracelet of the Rascette.

7. Mount of Venus: In a normally built and lined hand it is inclosed between the root of the thumb (base of the second phalanx) and the Line of Life, and between the first Bracelet of the Rascette and an imaginary horizontal line crossing the hand from the bottom of the angle formed by the thumb and the first finger.

8. Lower Mount of Mars: A Mount rather difficult to locate by sight, as it is not very frequently met with in very prominent shape. It stretches between the above imaginary horizontal line and the foot of the Mount of Jupiter, at the starting point of a normally placed Line of Life. Inside the hand it extends to the Line of Life, forming thus a kind of triangle.

I call the attention of the reader to this double Mount of Mars. I call the first one the Upper Mount of Mars, because it is situated altogether above the Line of Head; I call the other the Lower Mount of Mars, because the whole of it is found below the Line of Head; both, in a well-built and lined hand, touch the said Line of Head. All the works on Palmistry published to this day, although recognizing, sometimes, the distinct existence of the Lower Mount of Mars, have paid it but little attention. It is not, of course, as important as the other Mounts, by any means; but it is there and deserves regular, logical treatment.

II. THE MEANINGS OF THE MOUNTS.

(In this section they are supposed to be in their regular normal position.)

The principles ruling the existence, absence or undue prominence of the Mounts are the following:

Normal and in position—The quality at its best.

Absent—The quality absent also.

Abnormally prominent—The quality in excess, hence the defect or vice corresponding logically to that quality.

These readings, and those referring to the Displacement of the Mounts, only concern Smooth Mounts without any independent Lines or Signs. A long chapter is devoted to the meaning of each Mount, when marked by this or that line or sign. For the present, let it suffice to lay down this rule:

"A Mount is considered present and active, athough it be not marked by any rising, if it is marked by lines and signs."

The readings below are supposed to be made from a "good" or, at least "fairly good" hand. In a hand otherwise "bad" the reader will have to radically modify the readings, in accordance with logic and common sense.

The Mount of Jupiter.

WITH	NORMAL.	IN EXCESS.	LACKING.
Pointed fingers.	High religious ideal.	Superstition.	Absence of veneration.
Conical "	Lofty pride.	Artistic conceit.	No respect for others.
Square "	Pride in everyday life.	Vanity.	Absence of self-respect
Spatulate "	Pride in great enterprises.	Boasting.	Vulgarity.

The Mount of Saturn.

	WITH	NORMAL.	IN EXCESS.	LACKING.
Pointed fingers.		Poetic melancholy.	Intense morbidness.	Cares nothing for the supernatural.
Conical	"	Morbidness.	Saddest view of art, etc.	Realist in art matters.
Square	"	Love of solitude, not misanthropy, though.	Hatred of mankind.	Chronic indifference.
Spatulate	"	Love of agriculture and other safe, but active, occupations.	Aggressive hatred of others.	Works hard but cares little for others' society.

The Mount of the Sun.

		NORMAL.	IN EXCESS.	LACKING.
Pointed fingers.		The exquisite dreamers.	Genius confining to insanity.	Art has no place in their dreams.
Conical	"	Idealistic artists, writers, etc.	Talent overrating itself.	Clever, but not truly gifted.
Square	"	Artists of high stamp, but practical.	Cupidity stifles real talent.	No love for or intellectual enjoyment.
Spatulate		"Artists fond of excitement and noise who picture them on canvas or in books.	Braggards, without any talent; always on the go, doing wretched work with a great noise.	Hatred for art and all mind-culture.

The Mount of Mercury.

		NORMAL.	IN EXCESS.	LACKING.
Pointed fingers.		The master's intuitive science.	Dreamers of new religions.	Fine thoughts ill combined.
Conical	"	Divine eloquence.	Inventors of practicable things.	Eloquence handicapped by some physical or moral defect.
Square	"	The great inventors.	Dangerous schemers.	No scientific gifts nor business ability.
Spatulate	"	The great discoverers.	Adventurers who stop at no crime.	Active to no useful purpose.

The Upper Mount of Mars.

		NORMAL.	IN EXCESS.	LACKING.
Pointed fingers.		The courage of the martyr.	The violence of the religious persecutor.	A coward in his creed.
Conical	"	The courage of the patriot.	The violence of wounded vanity.	A coward in facing the public.
Square	"	The courage of the soldier.	The violence of the disappointed schemer.	A coward in everyday life.
Spatulate	"	The courage of the explorer.	The violence of the ruffian.	A coward in the field of battle.

The Mount of the Moon.

		NORMAL.	IN EXCESS.	LACKING.
Pointed fingers.		Imagination at its best.	Sheer insanity.	(Never seen.)
Conical	"	The gifted artist.	Extravagant vanity.	Imitation in art matters; actors.
Square	"	Healthy love of poetry, etc.	Absence of common sense.	Humdrum existence.
Spatulate	"	Love of nature.	Often violent insanity	Action never brightened by one thought of "what could be."

The Mount of Venus.

WITH	NORMAL.	IN EXCESS.	LACKING.
Pointed fingers.	Ideal love.	Vicious imaginings.	Above even the idea of love.
Conical "	Material love of a poetical character.	Inconstancy.	Artist wedded to his art.
Square "	Honest family love.	Sensuality.	Indifferent to the charms of the other sex.
Spatulate "	A lover or husband who wants in his mate a comrade in his incessant agitation.	A Mormon or a Turk; will have a wife or sweetheart in every State in the Union.	Finds the other sex an incumbrance in his active existence.

The Lower Mount of Mars.

	NORMAL.	IN EXCESS.	LACKING.
Pointed fingers.	Heavenly resignation.	Unhealthy chastising of the flesh.	Sensitive soul.
Conical "	Stoicism.	Hard-heartedness.	Easily offended.
Square "	Patience.		Much afraid of physical or moral pain.
		Passive cruelty.	
Spatulate "	Ignores what pain or fear means.	Active cruelty.	A coward.

III. DISPLACEMENTS OF THE MOUNTS.

When I speak of Displacements of the Mounts I must also mention my system of locating them, so as to know, for instance, if an elevation found between the roots of the first and second fingers is the Mount of Jupiter inclines toward the Mount of Saturn or the latter inclines toward the Mount of Jupiter. This method, by the way, applies only to the Mounts under the fingers, as the others can be located by simple, cursory inspection.

To succeed in this rather minute search necessitates the use of a magnifying glass, if the examiner be not endowed with especially sharp eyesight. In either case the reader must look for these tiny lines, which form the very outward texture of the skin. At the point constituting the apex or summit of each Mount these lines will be found grouped in designs marked very much like this. I have also attempted to show apexes in the print of a hand. Four such apexes

and no more are found across the hand directly under the fingers; each of them

represents, as I said, what ought to be the summit of a Mount, when they are all four located properly; any displacement can thus be easily given its proper signification.

A Mount to be at its best must be placed directly under the finger it may be said to belong to; for is not the Mount the continuation of the third phalanx? The Mount must not be abnormally developed and must be relatively firm under a gentle touch. If the consistency is soft it means that the quality it represents has not been made use of by the subject; the nervous fluid hardens the substances it acts upon; at least for a time. Look at the same fingers, front

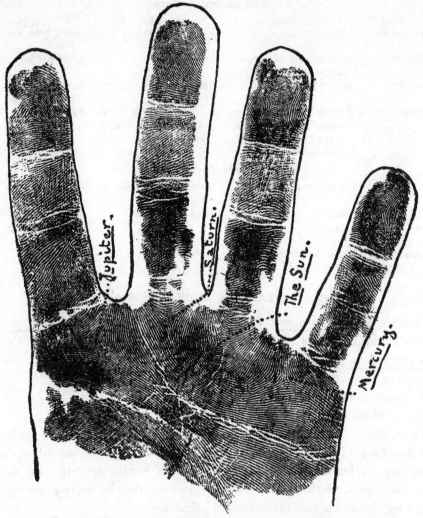

THE APEXES OF THE MOUNTS—FOR LOCATING ANY DISPLACEMENT.

and back, and you will grasp my meaning and agree with me.

Mount of Jupiter.

Toward the first finger—Egotism, vanity.

Toward the Mount of Saturn—Self-consciousness.

Toward the Line of Heart—Pride in affection.

Toward the Line of Head—Pride in intellect.

Toward the Line of Life—Pride in family.

Mount of Saturn.

Toward the second finger—Intense love of solitude.

Toward the Mount of Jupiter—Morbid pride.

Toward the Mount of the Sun—Less morbidity.

Toward the Line of Heart—Apprehension in love.

Mount of the Sun.

Toward the third finger—Affectation in attitude toward the public.

Toward the Mount of Saturn—Selfish love of animals.

Toward the Mount of Mercury—Shrewd management of one's artistic talent.

Toward the Line of Heart—The Gift of Mercy.

Mount of Mercury.

Toward the fourth finger—Sense of humor; eloquent after-dinner speaker.

Toward the Mount of the Sun—Eloquence of a flowery character; business blended with love of art.

Toward the Percussion—Business success.

Toward the Upper Mount of Mars—Making a trade of fighting; the mercenary soldier.

Upper Mount of Mars.

Toward the Percussion—Pluck.

Toward the Palm proper—Aggression.

Toward the Mount of the Moon—The power of hypnotism.

Mount of the Moon.

Toward the Upper Mount of Mars—Imagination well within control; a love of harmony (in music).

Toward the Rascette—Wild imaginings.

Toward the Mount of Venus—Imagination intensifies the emotions.

Toward the Palm proper—Imagination increases the aggressive force.

Mount of Venus.

Toward the Thumb—Emotions rule the will.

Toward the Rascette—Sensuousness.

Toward the Mount of the Moon—Sensuality.

With the angle of the Thumb (space between Thumb and First finger) well developed—A love of melody.

Lower Mount of Mars.

Toward the Mount of Venus—Power of endurance through affection.

Toward the Mount of Jupiter—Power of endurance through pride.

Toward the Thumb—Power of endurance through sheer will.

IV. THE MOUNTS AS THEY REVEAL ILLNESSES.

These tendencies are indicated either by the abnormal prominence of the Mounts or by their being covered with confused lines.

Mount of Jupiter—Apoplexy; rush of blood to the head; lung troubles.

Mount of Saturn—Nervous irritations; hemorrhoids; fluxes of blood downward; troubles with the legs, teeth and ears; paralysis; hemiplegy; rheumatism; vice and its consequences.

Mount of the Sun—Heart-beatings; aneurism; troubles with the eyes, up to loss of eyesight.

Mount of Mercury—Bilious troubles; liver diseases; jaundices; extra nervous irritations.

Upper Mount of Mars—Sore throat; bronchitis; troubles with the blood, whatever their forms.

Mount of the Moon—Diseases of the bladder and kidneys; dropsy; stone; weakness of eyesight and sometimes blindness, but always as a consequence of the lymphatic dispositions which belong to the Mount of the Moon; anæmia, gout. Also female troubles.

Mount of Venus—Diseases of the generative organs.

Lower Mount of Mars—Same reading as the Mount of Venus (which see).

V. THE MOUNTS AS THEY INDICATE SUICIDAL TENDENCIES.

I. The possessor of a predominating Mount of Jupiter seldom commits suicide, except when deeply humiliated in his overwhelming pride; or else he, a man of pleasure, feels that his sensual satisfactions are about to vanish. In that case he tries to bring down everything else within a general conflagration or some other great disaster of which he is proud to be the instigator.

2. The possessor of a predominant Mount of Saturn will throw himself from a high place or choose asphyxiation by gas, coal damp, etc.

3. A predominant Upper Mount of Mars will induce the possessor to use the revolver, the dagger or the razor to cut short the thread of life.

4. A predominant Mount of Mercury inspires the idea of suicide by poison. This, by the way, is not unusual with an exaggerate Mount of Saturn.

5. An exaggerate Mount of the Moon will induce its possessor to have recourse to drowning to free himself from the burden of existence.

6 and 7. Neither the Mount of the Sun nor the Mount of Venus inspires any desire to commit felo da se. The possessor of a large Mount of the Sun is too fond of life and of too sunny a disposition, and a predominant Mount of Venus supplies the owner with an unlimited supply of consolation in the dark moments of life.

The reader will kindly bear in mind that the exaggerate prominence of any of these Mounts is not "per se" evidence of a tendency to suicide; this tendency must be confirmed elsewhere in the hand, or rather in both hands, before any such surmise be allowable. But when the evidence is all in and its weight is sufficient, then the Mount will tell us the probable mode of suicide toward which the subject has an inborn inclination.

THE SIGNS IN GENERAL.

Before I examine the various independent lines and signs that are frequently met with on the Mounts or at the places where certain absent Mounts ought to be located, I must give you a list of the Sixteen Signs most frequently discovered on the inside of the hand. They are

spots, black spots and white spots. The shape, usually round, is often elongated and irregular.

II. The cross; it is either of the Latin form or the Greek (St. Andrew's) shape.

III. The star; any addition of a single branch or ray to a cross transforms it into a star, although stars of six

DOTS or Spots	CIRCLES.	ISLANDS	SQUARES
ANGLES	TRIANGLES	CROSSES	GRILLES
STARS	SIGN OF JUPITER	SIGN OF SATURN	SIGN OF The SUN
SIGN OF MERCURY	SIGN OF MARS	SIGN OF The MOON	SIGN OF VENUS

I. The spot or dot; most generally a small, deep indentation in the skin, the color of which it retains.

There are besides; red spots, bluish

rays are more frequent.

IV. The circle (quite rare).

V. The square.

VI. The Triangle.

VII.   The angle.

VIII.   The island. This is seldom found elsewhere than on, or rather in, a line. It is considered as an island only when the line that contains it runs before and continues running after it splits to reveal the island. In other words, an island open at one end must be considered only as a branch of a line. Neither must a slight split in a line be considered an island.

IX.   The grille or gridiron, although generally represented on the Mounts under the fingers by a design similar to the one in the engraving, may assume much larger proportions, as it often does on the Mount of Venus, when it sometimes covers the whole Mount by the combination of lines concentric to the Line of Life with horizontal Influence Lines. On the Mount of the Moon also, rays and cross-rays frequently form a grille of large proportions.

The other seven signs are the Planetary Signs, referring to each of the names given to the Mounts. Although but seldom met with, they are considered interesting enough—even if only on account of traditional antiquity—to deserve detailed mention in these lessons. They are,

X.   The Sign of Jupiter.

XI.   The Sign of Saturn.

XII.   The Sign of the Sun.

XIII.   The Sign of Mercury.

XIV.   The Sign of Mars.

XV.   The Sign of the Moon.

XVI.   The Sign of Venus.

I have met in several hands the Sign of the Moon (the crescent), and the Sign of the Sun (a circle with a dot in the center, sometimes with a smaller concentric circle). Once I discerned clearly the "h" which constitutes the Sign of Saturn. The other signs I have never located. Of course one does not expect them to occur in a perfect form; if they are only roughly but indisputably marked, the readings belonging to them ought to be accepted and made use of.

LINES AND SIGNS ON THE MOUNTS.

I. ON THE MOUNT OF JUPITER.

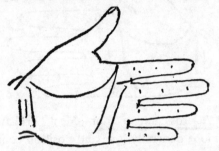

A strong, red line on the Mount separating the first and second fingers—Weakness of the intestines.

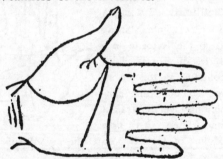

A single line—Success.
You will find the single line feature to be favorable on every Mount, if uncut and not written crosswise.

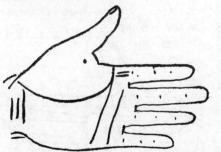

Two lines—Ambition divided in its purpose and hence unsuccessful.

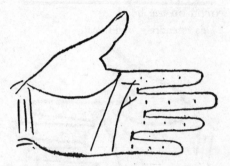

A line crossing a branch of the Line of Heart—Misfortune through, or in, love. Often read as—A love union ending wretchedly.

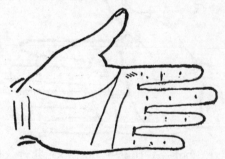

A succession of short lines arranged ladder-like—A poor life suffering from repeated losses.

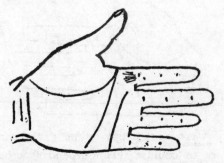

Many confused lines—Persistent but

unlucky efforts toward success. If they cross each other—Loose morals, generally of a Falstaffian character.

In that case they really form a grille (which see below).

Capillary cross lines (hair lines)—A wound on the head.

This is entirely traditional.

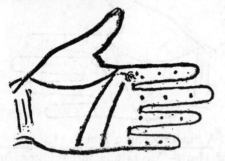

A sprig on the Mount—Apoplexy.

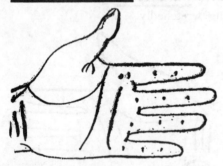

A spot—A ruined position; loss of fortune and reputation.

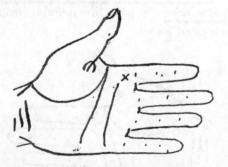

A cross—A happy union. (Take care not to confuse this independent cross with a line from the Line of Life barred

on the Mount; the latter would mean—Social ambition thwarted.

For approximate date of this union, see my special chapter on dates.

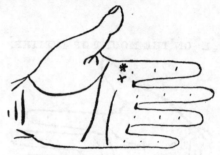

A cross and a star—Most brilliant union; generally love and position combined.

Very Difficult Beginnings. Finally Fortune Coming to the Subject Through a Brilliant Union.—A Line of Fate starting from the Rascette in a series of crosses which continue up to, and after, 20, after that continuing very straight and fine. On the  Mount of Jupiter a star, one ray of which helps forming a cross of union.

"A young actress who had had a great deal of hard times to go through, managed to attract the attention of the old King of Holland at Baden Baden. He interested himself in her success, and she soon became well known and wealthy."

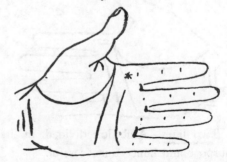

A star—Ambition fully satisfied; sudden rise in life.

Born of a Mother Who Died When the Child Came in the World.—A star, clearly marked quite at the beginning of the Line of Life, or on the edge of the hand near the Line of Life. It generally corresponds with a star (of death) on the Mount of Venus.

"Desbarrolles states that he has seen such a star in the hands of illegitimate children. It is really found near where stars prognosticating fires are found. Only those are generally higher up along the side of the hand."

Ambition Interfered with by a Revengeful Enemy.—One branch of a deeply marked star on the Mount of Jupiter is continued by a line which cuts the Line of the Sun on the Mount of the Sun.

"A woman pretended to have been compromised by D., a famous French dramatist. She created such a scandal that, although her statements were false, he failed to receive, that year, a much coveted distinction."

A square—Sober sense guiding one's ambition. Preservation from social failure. Capacity to command.

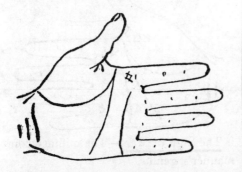

Self-possession is the sine-qua-non of "the chief;" the square protects him against the intoxication of success. This applies just as well to business men, speculators and society leaders of both sexes.

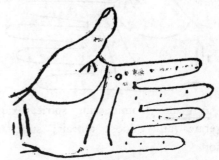

A circle—Success. (Very rare).

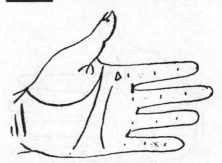

A triangle—Diplomatic cleverness; a subtle politician.

And now, for the first time, we meet the grille, also frequently called gridiron, whenever the lines and cross-lines forming it are wide apart. As a matter of fact, a grille as a small, separate sign is of very uncommon occurrence. On the Mount of Venus and the Moon it occupies the major portion of, if not all, the Mount. On the Mounts below the fingers it is often represented by many confused lines, and is generally read just as these confused lines would be. Grilles destroy the efficiency of the Mounts and are the equivalents of exaggerate Mounts; in other words, they turn qualities into defects and even vices. Derbarrolles says, very correctly, that they "chain down" the virtues of the Mounts and allow the evil instincts to take and keep, the upper hand.

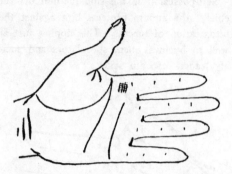

A grille—Domineering spirit; exaggerate vanity; loose morals; superstition.

The wrong kind of religious tendency comes into play.

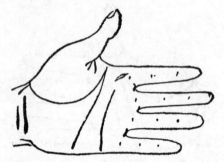

An island—Ambitious career ruined by the mad actions of a relative or close friend. (Will be generally connected with a line of influence. See further on).

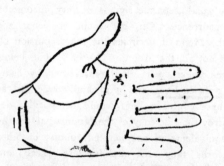

The Sign of Jupiter—An intensity in the good qualities of the Mount.

The Sign of Saturn—Caution, love of occult sciences.

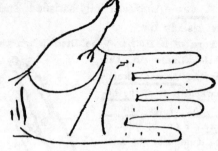

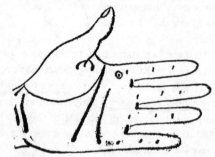

The Sign of the Sun—Eloquence and love of the fine arts.

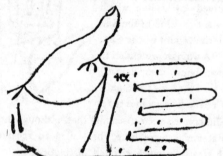

The Sign of Mercury—Administrative ability; statesmanship.

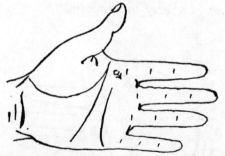

The Sign of Mars—The military commander's genius.

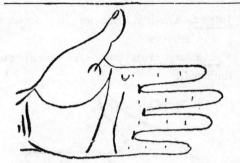

The Sign of the Moon—Ambition led astray by imagination.

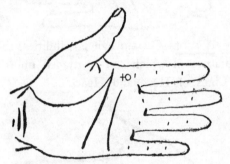

The Sign of Venus—Dignified, deep and constant love.

Should the Mounts be exaggerated, these astral signs ought to be interpreted as indicating the counterparts, or defects corresponding with the qualities that may have been ascribed to them above.

II. ON THE MOUNT OF SATURN.

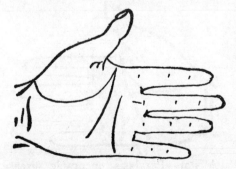

One single line—Very great luck.

One deep line forming the end of a broken Line of Fate—Peaceful but

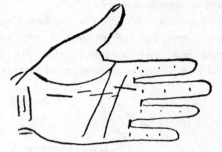

monotonous ending of life.

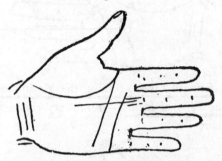

Two parallel lines—(often taken for sister lines to the Line of Fate)—Success, late and laborious.

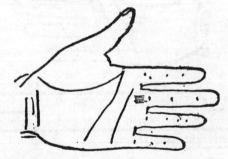

A number of lines—The more numerous the lines, the greater the ill-luck.

Deafness. Wound in the Legs.—A line of Head broken under the Mount of Saturn. On that line a number of very deep dots close together. An exaggerate Mount of the Moon. A number of vertical lines on the Mount of Saturn and the third pha-

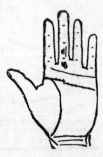

lanx of the second finger.

"The subject, a mixture of the Saturn and Venus type, had suffered from a grave nervous illness, culminating in deafness. He had had an accident that maimed one of his legs."

Several Lines crossing the Mount and the Line of Heart—Hereditary rheumatism.

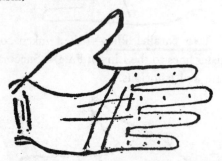

A Line across the top of the Line of Fate—Unavoidable misfortune, if the line of the Sun does not end especially straight and strong.

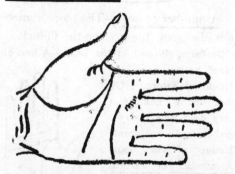

Many lines scaling the Mount ladderwise in the direction of the Mount of

Jupiter—Gradual rise in life toward public honors.

Capillary cross lines—A wound on the breast.

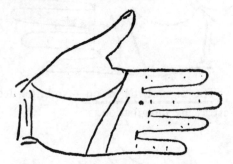

A spot—Certain evil possibilities, the nature of which can be traced on the Lines of Head and Heart.

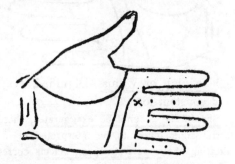

A cross—Childlessness; tendency to make an evil use of occult sciences. Extreme liability to accidents.

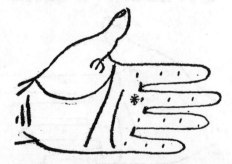

A star—Paralysis; incurable disease. If very strongly marked in both hands and with other signs (which see)—Death on the scaffold.

If the star is faint and poorly formed —Ill health and trouble at the close of life.

Paralysis.—A star on Saturn. A star on the middle part of the Mount of the Moon; a very much rayed and crossed Mount of the Moon; and often a sloping Line of Head, while the Line of Heart starts from the Lines of Life and Head in fatal cases.

"The subject died at 36 from the consequences of sexual excesses."

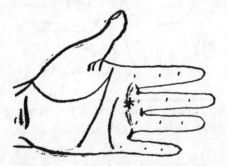

A star almost in the middle of a double or triple Girdle of Venus—Terrible venereal disease, to be soon followed by death.

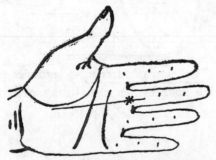

A star, with the line of fate entering deeply into the second finger—Danger of assassination. Should the hand be generally bad—Murderous tendency.

A circle—A favorable omen, specified

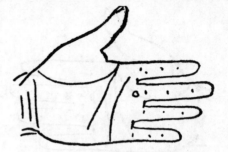

by other indications. (Very rare).

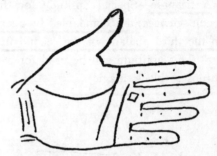

A square—Preservation from some great fatality read elsewhere in the hand.

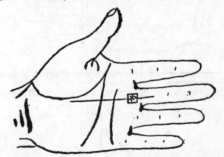

A star within a square—Escape from assassination.

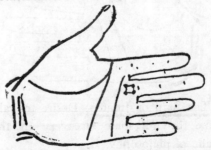

A square with red dots at the corners —Preservation of life in a fire.

A triangle—Special aptitude for the occult sciences; if accompanied by a star on the third phalanx of the second finger—This aptitude will be used for evil purposes (black magic).

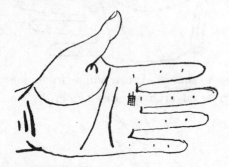

A grille—Lack of luck through life, especially in old age. Often imprisonment.

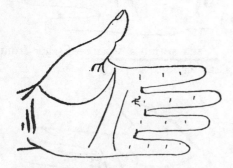

The Sign of Jupiter—Desire to gain fame through some discovery in the realm of philosophy.

The Sign of Saturn—Intense devotion to the study of all things mysterious—

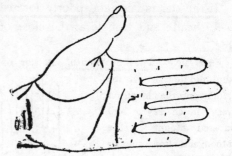

religion, philosophy, occult sciences, etc.

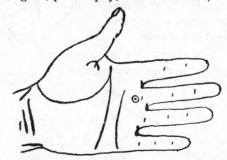

The Sign of the Sun—A love for artistic beauty in nature, and fine language in expressing one's thoughts.

The Sign of Mercury—Aptitudes for high mathematics and astronomy.

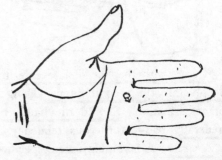

The Sign of Mars—A combative spirit in the discussion of religious or philosophical problems. Found in the hands of old-time inquisitors and fanatics.

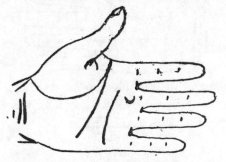

The Sign of the Moon—Morbid imagination. Often insanity.

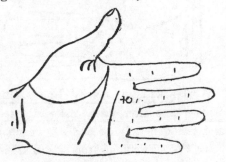

The Sign of Venus—A mixture of passion and despondency in the love of the opposite sex.

With an exaggerate Mount, apply the principle laid down at the end of the signs on the Mount of Jupiter.

III. ON THE MOUNT OF THE SUN.

One deep and straight line—Wealth

or fame, or both. One career only.

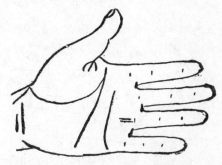

Two lines—Real talent but poor success; two conflicting talents. Except when one of the lines is clearly a sister line of the Line of the Sun (which see).

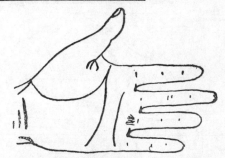

Many confused lines—Artistic tendencies, unfortunately interfered with by scientific instincts; inspiration stopped midway to realization. In money matters—Many schemes coming to nothing profitable.

Capillary cross lines—A wound on either arm.

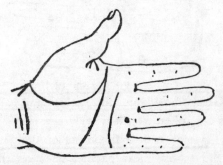

A spot—danger of losing reputation

and social standing.

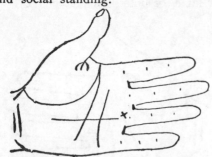

A cross with a good Line of the Sun— Success. Often lofty religious ideal. If the Line of the Sun be poor—Tendency to religious insanity (with other indications). Often near—not touching the Line.

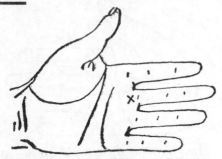

A cross without a good Line of the Sun—Artistic blunders marring success. Wild speculating. Ill balanced intellect.

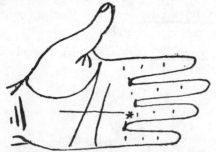

A star with a good Line of the Sun— Great fame due to genius and hard work; often wealth.

A star with a fine Line of the Sun and several clear parallel lines on the Mount—Great wealth and generally

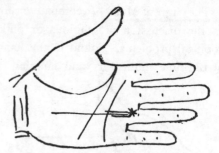

fame or at least high social standing.

These lines have been called by ancient authors Lines of Reputation.

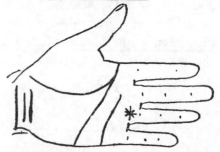

A star without a good Line of the Sun—Fame after many risks incurred; and not generally of a desirable character. Wealth coming too late to secure happiness.

Life Saved in a Fire.—On the Upper Mount of Mars under the Mounts of the Sun and Mercury and close to the Line of the Sun, a St. Andrew's Cross surrounded by a square with a deep dot at each corner. (Mars and the Sun both indicate fire.)

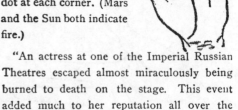

"An actress at one of the Imperial Russian Theatres escaped almost miraculously being burned to death on the stage. This event added much to her reputation all over the world."

A square—Business ability protecting the artist from being exploited. Protection against the intoxication due to

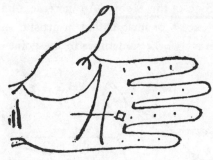

great financial success.

A triangle—Science assisting art to success.

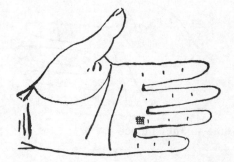

A grille—An almost insane vanity, sometimes culminating in real lunacy. Very little talent magnified tenfold by the subject.

A circle—Much fame. (Very rare).

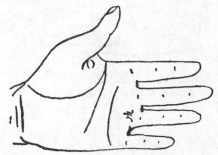

The Sign of Jupiter—Eloquence in statesmanlike discourses.

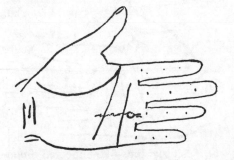

An ill-formed circle at the base of the Mount with a poor Line of the Sun—Eyesight endangered.

The Sign of Saturn—A tendency to wierdness in the manifestations of artistic genius. In a bad hand—Misuse of an aptitude for occult sciences.

The Sign of the Sun—Artistic genius intensified and bringing fame and for-

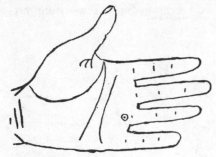

tune to the subject.

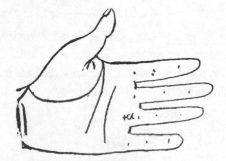

The Sign of Mercury—A very remarkable money-making talent.

The Sign of Mars—Found frequently in the hand of a painter or writer of military subjects.

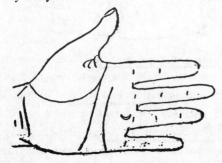

Sign of the Moon—An increase, often an excess of imagination in artistic and literary work; sometimes to the point of incoherence.

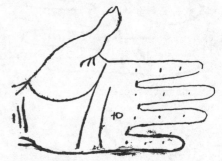

The Sign of Venus—Idealization in the love of poetry and art.

If the Mount be exaggerate, apply the principle laid down at the end of the observations on the Mount of Jupiter.

IV. ON THE MOUNT OF MERCURY.

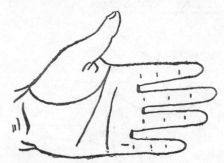

One single line—Unexpected financial good fortune. If very deep—Great scientific aptitudes.

From three to six strongly marked

parallel lines—An aptitude for medical studies—The same lines in a woman's hand—The subject will be attached to and often marry a medical man; she will prove an excellent nurse.

The above lines with a prominent Mount of the Moon—Found in the hands of people who are always doctoring themselves for real or imaginary ailments.

A Physician With Strong Atheistic Tendencies.—A Saturnian type, with a short Line of Head, ending just after cutting the Line of Fate. Spatulate second finger. A cross between the third and fourth fingers; strong medical stigmata on the Mount of Mercury.

"A doctor whose disposition was at the same time that of an agnostic and that of a very superstitious and saddened man. His brain power was not strong enough to guide him in his search after truth; he had vague religious instincts, fought against by the skepticism of his second finger."

(For vertical and cross lines on the Mount when on, or near, the Percussion, read in connection with the Lines of Union—See Chapter on Lines of Union.)

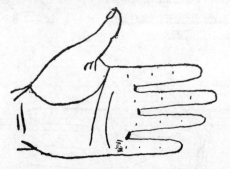

Many mixed lines—Shrewdness not of the best; scientific aptitudes, danger-

ously directed.

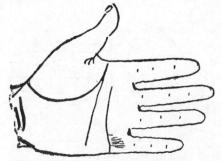

Many mixed lines reaching as low as the Line of Heart—Unwise generosity in the spending of money.

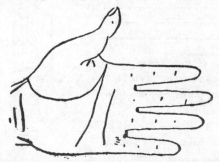

Many very short vertical lines in a woman's hand—Chattering habits.

They are generally mixed with children lines causing confusion (See Chapter on Lines of Union.)

Capillary cross lines—Wounds on the legs.

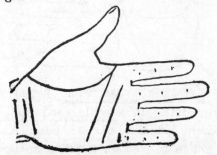

A short cross line—A heavy loss through theft.

A spot—Failure in business.

A large black spot like a lentil—The

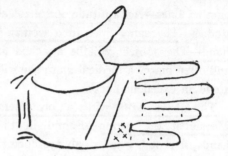

A star in a bad hand—Persistent dis-

movements of the subject's body are interfered with through accident or illness.

Dislocation of the Thigh Bone.—A deep and black dot as big as a small lentil low down on the Percussion of Mercury. (In the center of the Mount it is the indication of the highwayman or burglar's propensities).

"This was found in the hand of a young man whose thigh bone had been dislocated in infancy. A good Mount of Mercury means agility."

honesty. In a really good hand—A remarkable talent for assimilating other people's ideas and projects not necessarily to make use of them.

Husband, an Embezzler, Ran Away With Trust Funds and His Wife's Money.—A star on the Line of Fate connecting with a Line of Influence cutting the Line of Life at 30. Touching the extremities of a Line of Union a big star on the Mount of Mercury.

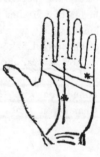

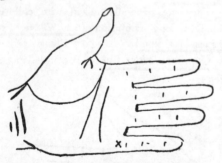

A cross in a bad hand—Deceiving disposition. In a really good hand—Positive indication of mimic talent. Also a gift to be pleasant to all, even those we dislike. Diplomacy in business and social circles.

Several small crosses—Unnatural vices.

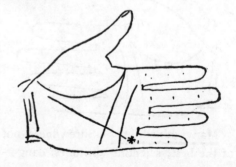

A cross or star at the upper part of a good Mount with a very fine and long Line of Liver not touching the Line of Life at the start—Very constant and even brilliant business success.

This is a new reading, by a distinguished British palmist, which I have frequently found correct.

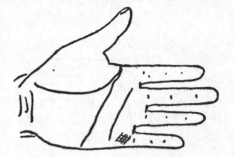

A circle—Violent death by poison.

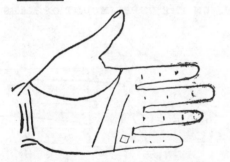

A square—Preservation from heavy financial losses.

A triangle—Shrewdness in politics, generally of the lower grade.

A grille—Prognostic of violent death to take place during or on account of some swindling enterprise on the part of the subject.

I had occasion to see this marking in the hand of a bank cashier who committed suicide on being discovered to be an embezzler for a large amount.

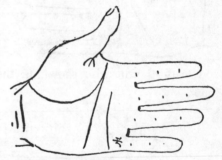

The Sign of Jupiter—Fame and power reached by science or eloquence.

The Sign of Saturn—Talent tinged with sadness.

The Sign of the Sun—Talent for astronomy and natural philosophy; intense admiration of God's creation.

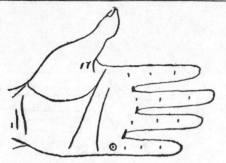

The Sign of Mercury—Intensifies the

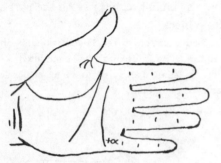

good features otherwise shown in the Mount.

The Sign of Mars—Violence and theft combined; the highwayman's characteristic.

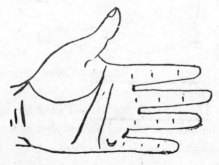

The Sign of the Moon—Wild scheming disposition that will deceive the subject himself and his friends and associates.

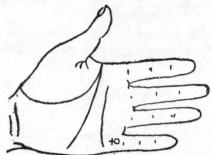

The Sign of Venus—Sensible love, that thinks of the future of both parties.

With an exaggerate Mount, the principle laid down before, must be applied and the reading modified in consequence.

V. ON THE UPPER MOUNT OF MARS.

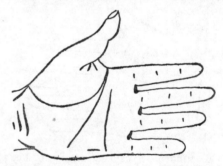

One line—Courage, sang-froid.

Several lines, rather confused—Violent temper, lasciviousness, brutality in love; a very bad omen for the general success of the subject. Also bronchitis and disease of the larynx.

Horizontal lines from the Percussion —Enemies; for each line an enemy; their length and depth indicate their power.

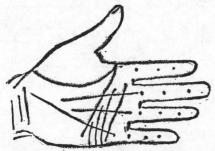

If they cross the Line of Liver—The health is affected by these enmities; if they cross the Line of the Sun, money matters are affected; if they cross the Line of Fate, the career is endangered; if they cut the Line of Life, relatives or supposed close friends are the guilty ones.

In that last case see Chapter on the Lines of Influence.

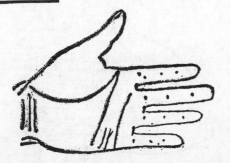

Crossed Lines from the Percussion or simply on the Mount, particularly if deep and forked—Severe throat and bronchial troubles.

Laryngitis.—Two mixed horizontal lines from the Percussion on the Upper Mount of Mars ending in a fork.

"A lady complaining of bronchial troubles was told that the above marking revealed a trouble in the larynx, not the lungs."

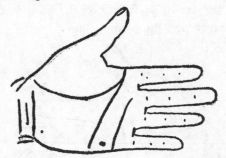

A spot—A wound in a fight. With an exaggerate Mount—The wound was inflicted by the subject.

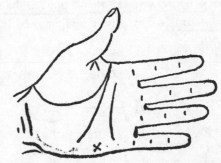

A cross, with an exaggerate Mount —Danger from the quarrelsome or stubborn disposition of the subject. With a fairly developed Mount—Danger of bodily harm to be suffered by the subject.

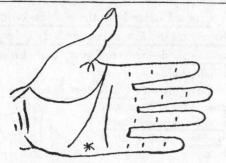

A star, with an exaggerate Mount—Homicide committed by the subject through furious anger or jealousy. With a normal Mount—Danger of assassination. (See confirmation elsewhere and particularly on the Mount of Saturn and the second finger).

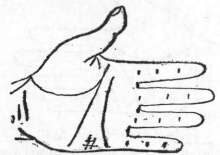

A square—A violent temper held in check by reason. If the Mount is below normal—Protection against bodily harm.

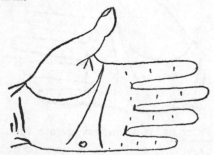

A circle—A very bad omen; often a wound in the eye. (Rare).

A triangle—Excellence in military tactics.

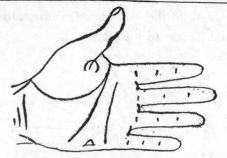

A grille—Hemorrhage. Great danger of violent death. With an exagger-

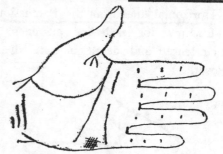

ate Mount—Decided murderous instincts.

A grille over the lower part of the Mount extending to the upper part of the Mount of the Moon—Serious intestinal trouble. Often catarrh of the stomach.

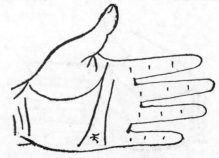

The Sign of Jupiter—The characteristic of the insatiable conqueror; met also in the hands of the "lady-killer."

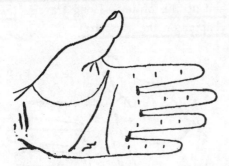

The Sign of Saturn—Disposition both morbid and murderous, found in the poisoner's hand when his fell deed has been incited by a desire of revenge, not by a thirst for lucre.

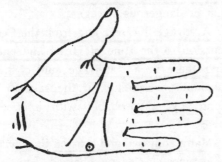

The Sign of the Sun—Love of show, of vivid colors; childish vanity satisfied with a bright uniform or a gem.

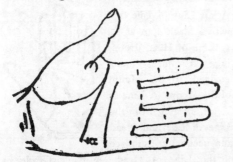

The Sign of Mercury—The love of conquest and triumph on the field of business; found in the hands of plungers on the exchange or on the turf; in the hands of born gamblers.

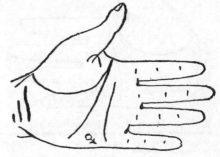

The Sign of Mars—Intensifies the merits or demerits of the Mount.

The Sign of the Moon—Violent insanity is threatened.

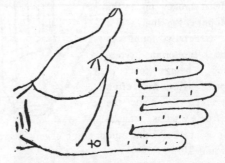

The Sign of Venus—Violence in love matters.

With an exaggerate Mount apply the principles laid down at the end of my readings of Jupiter.

VI. ON THE MOUNT OF THE MOON.

A single long line—A presentiment of evil.

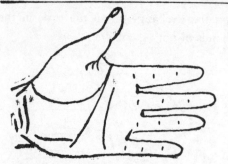

A line down the Mount with a short one crossing it—Tendency to chronic

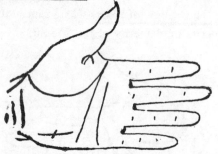

rheumatism or gout. Especially in the middle portion of the Mount.

Fatal Aneurism Caused by Gout.—A cross on the Mount of the Moon and a Line of Heart broken under the Mount of the Sun.

"Generally found in the Jupiterian types, who, being fond of good living are often attacked hy gout; the extreme pains caused

by gout often bring about some severe heart troubles."

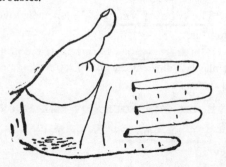

Many confused lines—Visions, insomnia, nightmares.

Clear vertical lines from the Rascette and up the Mount—Long travels. (See chapter on the Rascette).

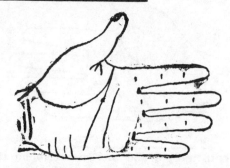

Horizontal lines starting from the percussion—Voyages. If they are crossed, broken or islanded—Unpleasant or dangerous voyages.

A voyage line reaching from the Percussion to the Line of Heart and ending there in a star—The subject will abandon everything for the sake of a long voyage, probably with a sweetheart.

Many confused and crossed lines with a sloping, starred or chained Line of Head—Tendency to insanity.

Young Man Who Believed Himself Haunted by Ghosts.—A fair Line of Life, but with a black spot at 19. A Line of Head drooping at once, quite chained, to the Mount of the Moon. A Line of Heart, starting from the Line of Life and Head and occupying the place

of the Line of Head. A triple Girdle of Venus virtually occupying the place of the Line of Heart and starting with a big star on the Mount of Jupiter. The Lower Mount of the Moon rayed and cross-rayed; just above this a large St. Andrew's star.

"A young man was affected, from his 19th year on, with a peculiar monomania. He believed himself the chief of a band of spirits who surrounded him. He had been addicted to vicious practices, and his nervous system was shattered. This star on the Mount of Jupiter with one ray penetrating quite deeply into the first finger is often found in the hands of insane people who believe themselves occupying high positions."

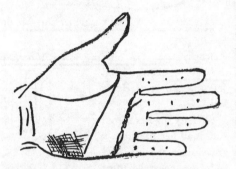

Many confused and crossed lines with a chained or islanded Line of Heart—Inconstancy in love affairs; often downright immorality.

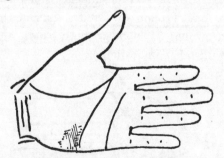

A series of crossed or confused lines at the upper part of the Mount—Chronic diarrhea; if very heavy and forming a kind of grille—Intestinal troubles of the gravest nature.

Many confused and cross lines at the bottom of the Mount—Bladder troubles; often Diabetes or Bright's Disease

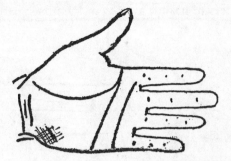

of the Kidneys. In women—Infallible sign of female troubles especially if there is a star at the connection of the Lines of Head and Liver.

Capillary cross lines—Wounds on the body.

A spot—Some disease of the nervous system from hysteria to raving madness; the Line of Head will complete the diagnosis. Is often read as a cross (which see below).

Intestinal Abscess.—A blue spot on the Line of Life at 20; another blue spot, quite important on the Upper Mount of the Moon.

"A friend of Desbarrolles almost died from a dangerous abscess in the intestines.

A cross—Superstitious, dreamy disposition. If large, a deceiving nature, or, at least, one prone to bragging. In matters of health: a cross in the upper part

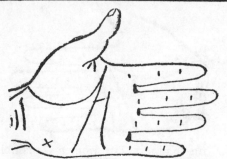

—Intestinal troubles; in the middle— Gout or rheumatism; at the bottom— Bladder, Kidney or Womb troubles.

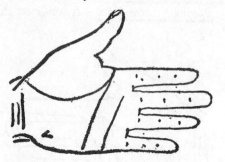

An angle—Great danger of drowning.

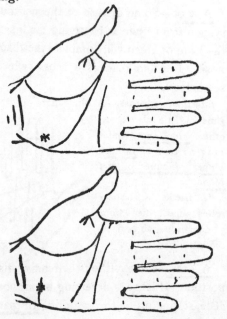

A star—Danger of death by drowning. On a line of voyage—Danger of shipwreck.

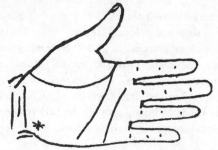

A star on the lower part of the Mount —Dropsy.

Dropsy.—A star on the lower Mount of the Moon, chained and yellowish Lines of Heart and Life.

"A lady had suffered almost all her life from a grave liver trouble and had been operated three times for dropsy."

A star with a far drooping Line of Head on a very prominent Mount and a bad Mount of Saturn—Suicide by drowning (if found in both hands, and with other indications).

A star connected by a Line of Influence with the Mount of Venus or the Line of Life—Hysteria or insanity often of an erotic character. (See chapter on Lines of Influence).

Diabetes.—A long voyage line from the lower Percussion of the Mount of the Moon cutting the Line of Life, with a star on the Mount.

"A young man afflicted with a terrible thirst (for water) was soon to be troubled with severe diabetes; water caused his illness."

Disease of the Bladder: The Stone.—A much chained and poor Line of Heart. A Line of Head broken under the Mount of Saturn and sloping down into the lower part of the Mount of the Moon and ending in a star; that part of the Mount being much rayed and

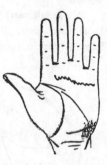

cross-rayed, a ray of the star extending to the lower palm (the bottom of the triangle).

"Seen in the hand of an old soldier, who pretended never to have been ill, but acknowledged being troubled with calculi (or stones) in the bladder."

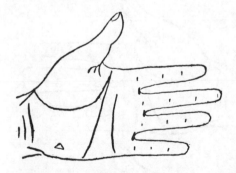

A triangle—Wisdom in the use of high imaginative faculties.

A grille—Melancholia; nervous troubles; troubles of the womb and bladder.

Read what I have to say about confused lines and cross lines on the Mount. Grilles, on the Mounts of the Moon and Venus are

practically the equivalents of these confused and crossed lines.

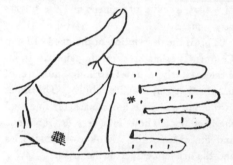

A grille with a star on the Mount of Saturn—Danger of partial apoplexy or paralysis. Often the star alone is enough.

A poor line of Heart, indicating defective circulation of the blood foretells (with the above grille) coming apoplexy. A poor line of Head, telling of an impaired brain, paralysis.

A grille with a fine Line of the Sun—Poetical imagination; often found in literary women's hands.

This is the equivalent of an exaggerate Mount of the Moon, which I consider as acceptable in the hands of people of genius.

The Gifts of Invention and Method United in the Same Hand.— The Line of Head cross- ing the whole hand and forked before cross- ing the Line of the Sun, the lower prong go- ing low down into the Mount of the Moon, where the Mount is much rayed. The Mount

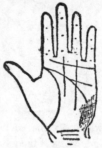

of Venus is quite prominent and the fingers very square.

"This is the description of the hand of Leon Coignet, the famous French painter. It in- dicates clearly a most striking mixture of imagination and practical ability. The Lines of the Sun and Fate are remarkably fine, and the hand, as a whole, is a very desirable one and fits exactly the well-known tendencies and the brilliant career of the artist."

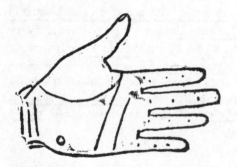

A circle—Danger of death by drown- ing.

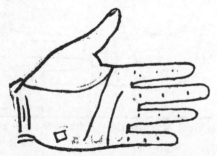

A square—Protection against the bad

markings or exaggerate development of the Mount.

Three Times Saved From Drowning.— On three Lines of Voy- age on the Percussion of the Moon, three stars, each surrounded by three squares. Besides that, the Line of Head, Heart, Fate and Sun formed a beautiful square.

"A gentleman had been almost miraculously saved from drown- ing on three different occasions."

The Sign of Jupiter—Dreams of ex- travagant power and position.

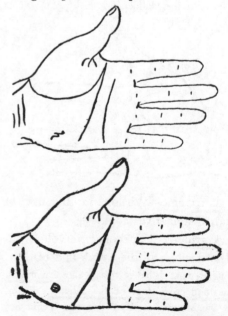

The Sign of Saturn—Religious insanity.

The Sign of the Sun—Extravagance in poetical and artistic manifestations. The folly of wealth.

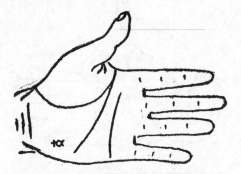

The Sign of Mercury—The taste for speculation pushed to extremes and to financial ruin.

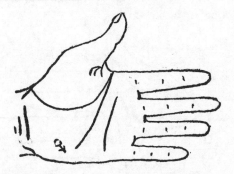

The Sign of Mars—A strong tendency to brain fever; raving mania.

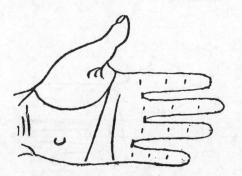

The Sign of the Moon—Diseased imagination; nightmares, insanity. In a

hand otherwise good—Evil influences of a person of the other sex on the subject's life.

The Sign of Venus—A constant search after strange, new sensations.

Again I call your attention to the principle laid down at the end of my readings of the Mount of Jupiter.

VII. ON THE MOUNT OF VENUS.

Two or three vertical lines—Ingratitude. More frequently (and logically), Inconstancy.

I have never verified these readings to my full satisfaction.

Lines concentric to the Line of Life —(aside from the Line of Mars, which see)—They represent the subject's love affairs which will not be under his or her control.

For this and the next observations see also the Chapter on Lines of Influence on, or from, the Mount of Venus, etc.

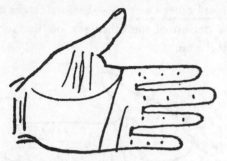

Strong, deep, horizontal lines from the root of the second phalanx of the thumb to the Line of Life—Overpowering influence of the opposite sex upon a portion of the subject's life. If any of these lines are islanded—The love affair in question will have been of a guilty nature.

A quantity of lines much crossed—A

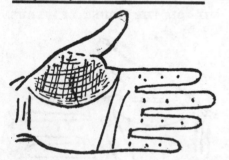

passionate disposition. If the Mount is flat and hard—The sign of the heartless debauchee already worn out.

This is really what is called a grille on the Mount of Venus, a small grille being rarely met with there.

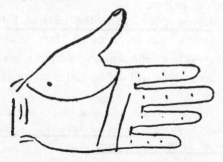

A spot—Some serious disease connected with a love affair. A black spot —A venereal disease.

Capillary cross lines—Wounds on the body.

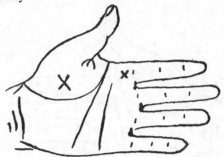

A St. Andrew's cross, quite large— An only love. With a similar small cross on the Mount of Jupiter—A happy love affair, with the "one" woman or the "one" man on earth.

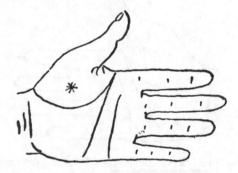

A star—Death of a relative or close friend.

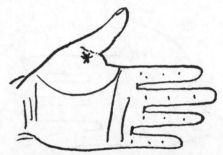

A star very near the second phalanx of the thumb—A marriage or liaison that will be the subject's whole life.

I have never verified this very ancient reading.

Girl Mother Abandoned with Her Child.
—Two lines clearly traced on the Mount of Venus, close to the second phalanx of the thumb and cut by two distinct crosses.

"Seen in the hands of several poor girls who had been seduced and then abandoned with their offspring."

Three stars close to the line and together—The subject will be much loved by a person of the other sex, but it will all end in disaster. (Traditional).

I never saw this sign and I should hesi-

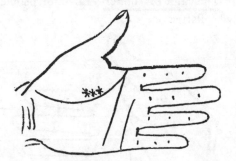

tate very much before giving it this meaning. It is more likely to mean three deaths in the subject's family.

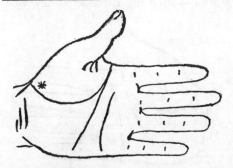

A star at the base—Misfortune due to a person of the opposite sex.

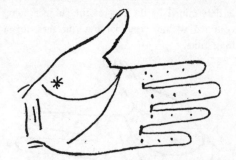

A star at the base with a sloping Line of Head—Diseased imagination.

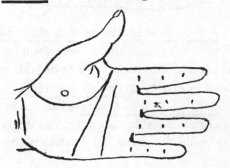

A circle (very rare)—Chronic ill health.

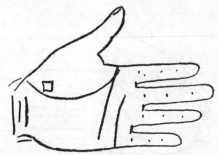

A square at the lower part of the Mount quite close to the Line of Life but not touching it—Imprisonment or cloistered life.

I must state here, emphatically, that I never saw this sign in the hands of people about to be imprisoned or about entering convent life. But, on the contrary, I have noticed it very frequently in the hands of people who had led a recluse's life, either by inclination or by order of court. For me it (this square) is determined by the fact of the subject being confined within very narrow quarters for a long time.

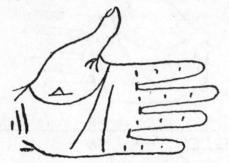

A triangle—Calculation (in a bad hand —venality) in love affairs; often found in the hands of husband or wife or both in what is known as French marriages.

A grille in a bad hand—Lasciviousness and unhealthy curiosity. The larger the grille the worse the lascivious tendency.

As stated above the Grille on the Mount of Venus generally covers the whole Mount.

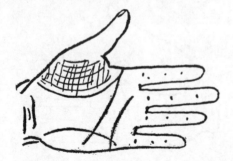

The Mount grilled all over, with a well marked Line of Intuition—Disposition to dream prophetic dreams or to conceive correct presentments.

This reading is historical, not personal to the author. A much rayed Mount of the Moon would certainly have this meaning.

An island crosswise—An advantageous opportunity of marriage has been missed.

Never verified by me.

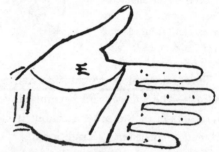

The Sign of Jupiter—Love for people who flatter one's vanity.

The Sign of Saturn—A melancholy, morbid—often unnatural kind of love.

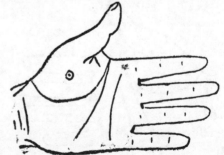

The Sign of the Sun—Idealistic, platonic love.

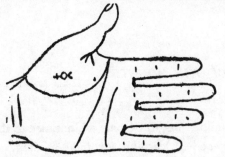

The Sign of Mercury—Mercenary love.

The Sign of Mars—Brutal disposition in all love affairs; the animal instincts overpowering the higher feelings.

The Sign of the Moon—An erotic imagination. A thoroughly bad sign.

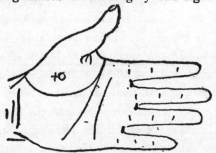

The Sign of Venus—Increased qualities otherwise shown by the Mount.

Once more I call your attention to the principle laid down at the end of my readings of the Mount of Jupiter.

VIII. ON THE LOWER MOUNT OF MARS.

I found most of the indications relating to Lines and Signs upon the Upper Mount of Mars, to apply here also very correctly, leaving out, of course, most of the aggressive features. The two following readings I think interesting to add to the list:

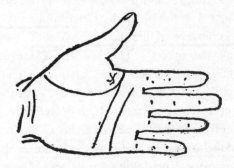

An ill-formed cross.—Tendency to suicide. (Very rare.)

It seems that in that case, the resignation, typical of this Mount, has given place to despair.

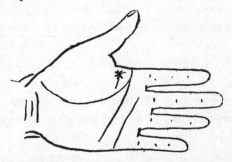

A star on a horizontal line—Misfortune or death for the person for whom this Line of Influence stands, not the subject, but a relation or close friend.

THE SIGNATURES OF THE MOUNTS.

As a natural consequence of the importance given in Palmistry to the Presence, the Exaggeration and the Absence of the Mounts, the ancient teachers of the science directed their patient study toward those types, physical, mental and moral, which are represented in the hands by the absolute predominance of one particular Mount over all the others. The Modern Palmists have added their quota of minute and well classified observations to the treasures inherited from their forefathers, and have finally reached very similar conclusions; so that now they claim such occasional predominance of one Mount over all the others, to be accompanied almost invariably by certain physical, mental and moral features, the knowledge of which is considered by Desbarrolles to be one of the essential acquirements of every well-equipped chiromant.

I need not insist in this chapter upon the fact that the astrological aspect of the question, alluring though it may seem to be, is to find no place in my book. Not that I deny the probability of the greater orbs, be they stars or planets, exerting over this little earth and its denizens certain influences of no mean importance; but simply because I consider the study of this most curious and captivating theory too complex and too minute not to become a hindrance to the practical learning of hand-reading. I have decided, from the start, to turn away from such impedimenta, to pass them by, so to speak, almost unheeded, for the goal I keep in constant view proves fully sufficient to absorb my best and most strenuous efforts.

Therefore the reader will understand that the words Jupiterian, Saturnian, Solar, Mercurian, etc., used through this chapter, are not to be understood in the astrological meanings of "born under Jupiter, or Saturn, or the Sun," etc., but simply indicate that, in the hands of the subject under examination, the Mount of Jupiter, or Saturn, or the Sun, etc., has been found distinctly predominating—"ruling," if you prefer—over all the others.

The pictures inserted through this chapter will be found to represent, rather roughly, the Mount that overshadows all the others, and the type of palm and fingers more generally found associated with such a predominance. The apex of the Mount is not indicated in the same manner as in the section I devoted to the Displacements of the Mounts; but the purpose of these engravings being different, I allowed the artist to express the idea in his own way, and the result is certainly clear, if not pleasing. Still the skin-markings of the apex are the only ones the student must pay attention to whenever placing the Mounts below the fingers where they belong.

I shall now divide the examination of what I call the Signature of each Mount into three paragraphs:

I. The Physical peculiarities of the type.

II. The Health peculiarities of the type.

III. The Mental and Moral peculiarities of the type.

I. THE MOUNT OF JUPITER.

Those people in whose hands the Mount of Jupiter is found predominating over all the other Mounts are called in Palmistry Jupiterians.

I. Physical Peculiarities.

The Jupiterians are strongly built and of middle height. Their complexion is

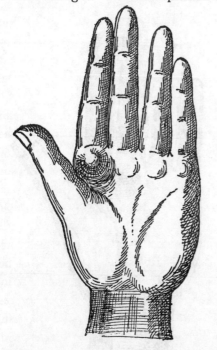

light and clear-colored; they are rather fleshy. Their voice is sonorous, their eyes are large, smiling and melting; the pupils are large, round and limpid; the eyelids are thick and with long eyelashes; their hair is chestnut in color, long, thick and curly, but they lose it early in life; their beard is also wavy; the eyebrows are bow-shaped and well marked; the nose is straight, but not specially long; the mouth is large and thick-lipped, with the upper lip slightly overlapping the lower one; they have long teeth, especially two long upper middle ones; their cheeks are fleshy and firm, with the bones not very prominent; the chin is long, with a dimple at the base; the ears are of medium size and rather close to the head; the neck is shapely; the shoulders and the back, quite fleshy; they grow stout rather early in life. They have much hair over the body and their feet are hard and plump. They perspire abundantly, especially on the summit of the head. They walk in a quiet, stately manner.

When the Jupiterian type is spoiled by other indications in the hands we are apt to find a lack of healthy glow in the whiteness of the skin; also straight hair, a short, ill-shaped nose and long, black teeth.

A good Jupiterian will have long, smooth, square-tipped fingers, with a first finger conically shaped, and above the average in size; a thick, half-soft palm, a long first phalanx of the thumb and the inside third phalanges quite plump.

II. Health Peculiarities.

The Jupiterian is both bilious and sanguine in temperament. He is subject to gout. Being a great drinker and eater, he is bound to suffer from his indulgence in that respect. His tendencies are sensual without being vicious, except when the type is shown to be spoiled by other undesirable indications in the hands.

III. Mental and Moral Peculiarities.

The Jupiterians are gifted for public life, statesmanship, high offices, even the army and important positions in the church. They are full of confidence in themselves, essentially good-natured and often warm-hearted and charitable. They are apt to spend money too freely and show a somewhat exaggerate contempt for everything mean and miserly. They are religiously inclined, but are fond of splendid ceremonies and of outward show of every kind. They are born aristocrats and conservative to a degree. They believe in law, order, hierarchy. They love peace, but hate all cheating and deceit and will fight without hesitation anyone who tramples upon their beloved tenets. They are easily pleased and keep their friends.

They grow to manhood easily. The proverb says that the Jupiterian "is early out of puberty and poverty;" the pure type is born lucky and is helped to success by its being a general favorite. A Jupiterian in music was Rossini; in painting, Rubens; their works are most correct illustrations of the type.

When other unfavorable indications show the Jupiterian type to be spoiled, he is insufferably overbearing, despotic, spendthrift, selfish to excess, a debauchee, who sacrifices wife and children to his vile habits and very soon becomes a weak and degraded object for general contempt. His luck is not with him any longer, and his detestable instincts culminate in scoundrelism, for his passions are devouring and he must satisfy them at any risk.

II. THE MOUNT OF SATURN.

Those people in whose hands the Mount of Saturn is found predominating over all the other Mounts are called in Palmistry Saturnians.

I. Physical Peculiarities.

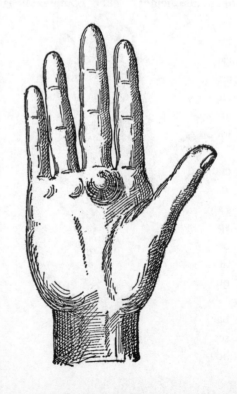

The Saturnians are tall, thin and pale; their skin is sallow, rough and dry, easily wrinkled; their hair is lanky, thick and dark; they lose it early; the face is long, the cheeks hollow, the cheek bones quite high; the eyebrows are black, upturned at the start and joined in the middle; the eyes are deep-set, dark and generally sad; they glisten only under the influence of anger or suspicion. The white of the eye is yellowish; the ears are large; the nose thin and pointed; the nostrils but slightly opened. The mouth is large, with thin lips, and the lower jaw prominent. The Saturnians have fine teeth, that deteriorate early; the gums are pale. Their beard is dark and abundant, except along the cheeks; the chin is large and heavy in its lower part; the neck is long, with strong, cord-like muscles, veins in clear sight and a marked Adam's apple. Their bones are massive in spite of the thinness of the type. They have a narrow, hairy chest and very high shoulders, giving them a stooping appearance. Arms and hands are muscular, but awkward and homely-looking.

Their fingers are long and knotty, especially the second finger, which has always a strong first knot. The tips are exaggerately square and quite often spatulate, especially the tip of the second finger. The first phalanx of the thumb is abnormally large and frequently flat.

The worst type of Saturnian is hunch-back or cripple and cross-eyed, with scant hair and a frightful thinness of body. Their fingers have, in an exag-gerate degree, all the characteristics enumerated above.

II. Health Peculiarities.

The Saturnian is the truly bilious type, in contradistinction to the Mercurian, who is nervoso-bilious. He is also subject to diseases of, and accidents to, the feet and legs; many cripples are Saturnian; they often suffer from varicose veins and lose the use of their legs comparatively early in life. They worry a great deal and suffer from chronic melancholia that frequently grows into sheer insanity. The worst Saturnian type dislikes water and is filthy, out of personal taste.

III. Mental and Moral Peculiarities

The Saturnian's main characteristics are sadness, on one side, and extreme prudence on the other. He lacks veneration and is a born doubter. He delights—in his own peculiar way—discussing forever the religious and economical problems of the time; his tastes are in the direction of occult sciences; he is also fond of chemistry, physics, medicine and even higher mathematics, and is often very successful in these branches of learning. He likes country life and agriculture, and, being essentially conservative and suspicious by nature, he prefers investing his money in farm lands as offering the least risk of loss. He has a strange, mysterious gift for discovering veins of precious metal or locating oil fields. He dislikes to obey, and incites others to riots, in which he takes but little active part, as his inborn prudence won't let him run personal risks. He prefers dark colors in his clothes and home furniture and is not fond of the everyday pleasures of life. He cares but little for other people's society and is not of an amorous temperament. Very strict, severe and abstemious priests are generally Saturnians; there are many Saturnians in the soberly-clad, silent and scheming Order of Jesuit Fathers. The Saturnian spends little, saves all he can, and when his type is very pronounced is a downright miser, often a filthy one. Among the ancient philosophers many were Saturnians; but among artists only those whose inspirations have some invariably sad strains, in color or tonality, can be called Saturnians; they prefer old-fashioned classical principles to romantic inovations, and have a sort of grayish monotony enveloping their well-shaped and orderly efforts. The Saturnian is slow, patient, tireless. He gambles passionately, but always plays a system, thus excusing his weakness by calling it scientific experimenting. As a rule he is very unlucky. Independence, even to license, is the Saturnian's main idiosyncrasy; he can bear no restraint; hence his love of solitude and often his dislike of mankind.

In its worst form this type transforms this passive misanthropy into malignant hatred and becomes dangerous to a degree. Prisons are full of Saturnians; poisoners are Saturnians; so are the cold-blooded tormentors of wife and children; so were the Inquisitors of old burning at the stake the victims of their intolerance. Finally, Saturnians have been considered the world over as possessing the evil eye and using their detestable power in blighting men's hopes and the fruits of the earth.

Let me add right here that the Saturnian type, even in its mildest form, is but very seldom met with; in the examination of hands even a moderately developed Mount of Saturn is exceptional. At times one discovers in hands a flat but somewhat rayed and cross-rayed Mount of Saturn; this is sufficient indication of Saturnian tendencies that will need watching.

III. THE MOUNT OF THE SUN.

Those people in whose hands the Mount of the Sun is found predominating over all the other Mounts are called in Palmistry Solar Subjects.

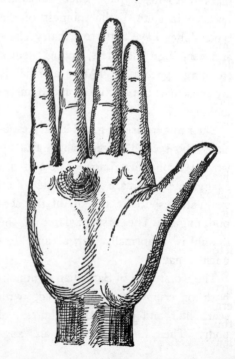

I. Physical Peculiarities.

The Solar Subject is of a height just above the average and is shapely and handsome; his complexion has a kind of a golden hue suffused with a healthy glow; his beard and hair are abundant, soft and wavy, of a beautiful, sunny shade of blond; his forehead is broad, but not too high; his eyes are large, almond-shaped, brilliantly lit and with the whites pure and limpid; their expression is both frank and sweet; the pupils are of a brown color, and the eyelashes long. The cheeks are firm and rounded, the nose straight and delicately chiseled, and the eyebrows beautifully curved. The mouth is not large and both jaws meet gracefully; the teeth are white and well-arranged in coral, colored gums. The voice is not very strong, but of a charming tone; the chin is round and not prominent; the ears are pink-colored, rather small and close to the head. The neck is long and fleshy but most gracefully curved; the body is not hairy at all. The chest comes forward in a healthy fashion, and, although small-boned, the limbs are shapely and agile.

The Solar Subjects are seldom stout; they are muscular, without superabundance of fat. They walk with firm elasticity and their movements show the absence of any effort; they are born athletes.

The Solar Subjects have smooth fingers, conical sometimes, but more generally with moderately square tips; the thumb is of average size, the second phalanx somewhat large. Palm and fingers are of equal size. They have occasionally a trace of the second knot.

When the Solar type is exaggerate and accompanied by undesirable indications in the hand, we find the subject rather undersized, with blond, crispy hair and a dark yellow complexion. He is often cross-eyed and possesses twisted, ill-shaped, sometimes spatulate fingers, with a flabby palm, the first phalanx of the thumb being extravagantly developed.

II. Health Peculiarities.

As a rule the Solar Subject enjoys a well-balanced health, the fact of his being essentially hopeful and looking only at the bright side of things contributing greatly to his physical welware. His weak point is his eyesight; the accidents that threaten him most are caused by fire. He is fond of the good things of life, but is too intellectually endowed to indulge in any excess, and his health is again the gainer by this disposition to moderation in everything.

Of course in the bad Solar Subject these advantages are reduced to a minimum; he often becomes totally blind, and is apt to die in a country far away from his birthplace.

Both in good and bad Solar Subjects, the organ found often in a poor condition is the Heart. They are frequently troubled with palpitations, irregular beats and even aneurism. When a feverish disposition is marked elsewhere in the hand, the Solar Subjects are generally affected by fevers common in the tropical countries, such as Yellow Fever, vomito negro, etc. Finally Solar Subjects seem to be chosen victims of sunstrokes.

III. Mental and Moral Peculiarities.

Intellectually the Solar Subjects are as richly endowed as they are physically. They learn everything almost by intuition and without the need of hard study, especially in the domain of fine arts or literature. They invent sometimes and imitate often, doing both with admirable skill and facility. Their versatility is surprising, and so is their love for everything that is beautiful in nature and art. They are consequently very fond of fine clothes, rich furniture and splendid jewels. They become quickly centers of attraction, and make ardent (if not constant) friends and bitter enemies—the latter, envious rivals. They have a clear, logical understanding of most problems, be it religious, intellectual, or even of a business nature, whenever business, by its character and scope, deserves the attention of a man of brains. The Solar Subject lights up every topic he touches. He is eloquent with ease—not always very deep, but ever pleasing and easily understood. He often reaches high positions and makes money without difficulty. As the proverb says, "he turns everything into gold." His weak point is his habit of speaking out his mind too quickly and too frankly; in fact, he likes to hear himself talk.

In religion he is not a fanatic, but an easily convinced believer, without a superstitious trait in him. By intuition he often penetrates quite deeply the mysteries of occult sciences; they attract him, and his brain power loves to tackle those high, difficult problems. His disposition is cheerful and kindly; he is not especially amorous, except of beauty for its own sake; women often abuse his good-humored laxity; as a husband he is not a success. He gets angry quickly, and cools off at once; he never bears a grudge and generally ends by making friends of his worst enemies, but his brilliancy inspires so much envy that he has but few real friends. He is not dissipated in his habits, and is fond of healthy open-air exercise; he is a great traveler over the face of the earth. His most ardent wish is to render his name both famous and esteemed. In the Solar Subject, at its best, there is no trace of egotism or vulgar ambition, but an intense thirst for the noblest kind of celebrity.

Modified by unfavorable indications in the hand, the weak points of the Solar Subject become terribly harmful to himself and others. He shows himself vain to a degree, with a love of nonsensical and ruinous display, and is so intent upon making the world speak of him that he would just as lief commit a crime if it put him at the head of the criminals of his time. He generally exaggerates greatly whatever little artistic or literary merit he may possess, and claims arrogantly "a place at the top" that does not in the least belong to him. If repulsed, he becomes intensely bitter and malignantly discontented, accusing everybody of being privy to a conspiracy against his legitimate dues. Then he begins, and continues, to show himself the relentless enemy of all those his petty talents cannot equal.

He is as unsuccessful as his brother—

the Solar Subject at his best—is triumphantly conquering.

IV. THE MOUNT OF MERCURY.

The people in whose hands the Mount of Mercury is found predominating over all the other Mounts are called in Palmistry Mercurians.

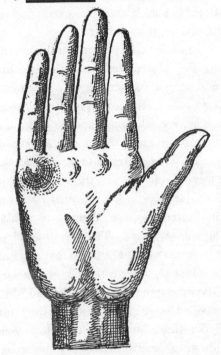

I.　Physical Peculiarities.

The Mercurians are small of stature, but well-built, with an elongated, pleasing face, which remains young-looking quite late in life. Their complexion is light, of the color of new honey, and the least emotion sends a blush to their cheeks; their hair is of a chestnut color and slightly curling at the end; their skin is soft, and the expression of their face very changeable; the forehead is rather bulging. Their beard is short, darker than the hair; the eyebrows thin,

curved and joined. Their eyes are deep-set, very quick and penetrating; sometimes restless, with yellowish whites and thin eyelids. Their nose is long and straight, with a rounded, dimpled tip. Their lips are thin, the upper somewhat fuller, and the mouth generally half open; the teeth are small, and the chin long and pointed, sometimes turned up like Napoleon's. The neck is strong, the shoulders sturdy, the chest broad and well-muscled; so are the limbs, although the bones are small. The voice of the Mercurian is decidedly weak, lacking sonority.

The hands of the Mercurian are large and the palm elastic, with fingers of mixed types, the fourth finger always conical. With the exception of a slight first knot, the fingers are generally smooth; they are very supple and skillful. The thumb is long, the second phalanx especially.

When the Mercurian type is spoiled by unfavorable indications, the subject is dark complexioned, and a sombre glow burns in the deeply sunk, shifting eyes. The hair is of an ugly, lifeless, blonde hue. The bad Saturnians have distorted features, with the grimacing characteristics of the ape, and are often hunchbacks of the malignant, hateful kind.

In the bad Mercurian type the hands are soft to flabbiness, the fingers are exaggerately long, twisted and bent backward.

II.　Health Peculiarities.

The Mercurian is endowed with a nervous-bilious temperament. His weak points are his liver and digestive organs. He is also apt to suffer from troubles of, and accidents to, the arms and hands, especially such troubles as interfere with the rapidity of his movements. On that account even troubles of, or accidents to, the legs have been indicated by evil signs, etc., on the Mount of Mercury.

III. Mental and Moral Peculiarities.

The Mercurian is quick in thought and action, and is fond of every manifestation in which his mental and physical alertness plays a part. He is skillful at all games, in and out of doors, and delights in oratorical contests in which his gift of repartee assures him success. He is a great judge of human nature and a clever manager. He schemes with tireless activity and possesses a real influence over his fellow-beings. No one masters better than he does the science of life. He is a deep student also; mathematics is generally his first choice; next to it medicine, and even the occult sciences. He cares for art and literature only in so far as they are close to human nature and appeal to his reason and his love of clearness. He is above all an excellent business man, frequently very ingenious in discovering new ways of making money. He is often an inventor, an excellent lawyer and a convincing teacher. His eloquence is built on facts, not fancies, and its triumph is that of quick, limpid logic. He is a born actor, and his mimic is genuinely true to life. He has the best points of the Saturnian, as far as inborn scientific talent is concerned, but is his superior in his handling of

men. He is not viciously inclined, or even amorous, but affectionate and equally tempered; a safe, not a gushing, friend. He loves his family and dotes on children. He has, at times, the gift of divination; but generally his mood is more of the merry, mildly-mocking kind. He is fond of traveling and likes nature and its beauties more than their artificial representations.

When afflicted with undesirable markings the Mercurian's natural gifts, become dangerous to a degree. His planning talent concentrates itself upon treacherous scheming, and he turns out to be a liar and a cheat of the deepest dye; he often pretends to be pastmaster in occult sciences for the sole purpose of making dupes. On the other hand the bad Mercurians are themselves childishly superstitious. They are found frequently among the professional tramps; the Gypsies are nearly all of the bad Mercurian type. Not only the bad Mercurians deceive others systematically and all the time, but they are often fool enough to deceive themselves and to believe in the "sure" success of their worst combinations.

V. THE MOUNTS OF MARS.

Those in whose hands the Mounts of Mars are predominating over all the other Mounts are known in Palmistry as Martians.

Desbarrolles, who recognized as Mount of Mars only what I call in this book the Upper Mount, confined his indications as to the signature of this Mount to a predominating Mount of

Mars along the Percussion, between the Lines of Head and Heart. My drawing, although entirely original to my work, follows this reading of the master. Of course a strong Lower Mount of Mars would simply strengthen these indications.

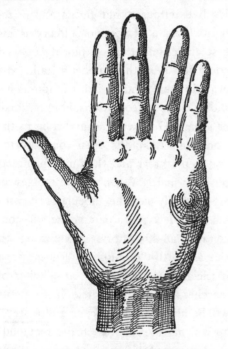

I. Physical Peculiarities.

The stature of the Martian is above the average; he is strong, without being heavy, with a small, thick head, an open brow and a very widely developed cerebellum (lower part of the back of the head). The face is round and the skin of a reddish hue (especially near the ears), often spotted and never thin. The hair is short, crisp, curly and of an auburn color. He has large, bright, daring eyes, the pupils either a brown or a rusty gray, looking at one fixedly and commandingly, the whites more or less bloodshot.

The mouth is large, with thin lips, the inferior one the thicker of the two; the teeth, of a yellowish enamel, are healthy but small and ranged like those of a dog. The eyebrows are thick, straight and low and the Martian often frowns.

His nose is sharp and long, often curved and beak-like; his chin turns up; his beard is short and hard to shave; his ears are small, but grow away from the head; his cheeks are thin and the cheek bones prominent. The neck is short, strong and of a bluish red, the veins much in evidence; the chest is splendidly developed, the shoulders broad and fleshy and the back covered with bulging muscles; the articulations are thick and the bones above the average in size; the thighs are relatively short, but the legs are well-shaped, and the Martian walks with a brisk, proud and determined step. His voice is powerful and of a commanding tone. His movements are so quick and unexpected that he often breaks things around him.

The hand of the Martian is hard, with thick, strong, short fingers; the first phalanx of the thumb is much larger than the second.

Whenever the hand of the Martian contains other unfavorable indications you will find him to be short of stature, with an inflamed face, a twisted mouth, a threatening, ever suspecting, look in his blood-injected, deep-set eyes, and a continual frown on his brow. The voice is rough, the skin is spotted with red, the hair droop, flat and colorless; the ears are long and the beard is stiff and ill-kept. The hands are thick and short, like that of the born bully, with a rough, red skin; the first phalanx of the thumb is club-shaped, and the inside third phalanges of all the fingers are bulging.

II. Health Peculiarities.

The Martian represents the sanguine temperament. He has really too much blood, or his blood is too rich. His habits—of which more in the next paragraph—are apt to over-excite this characteristic and bring to him loss of blood, apoplexy, skin diseases, inflammation of the inner organs. He runs a great risk of wounds in quarrels, and, being a born fighter, he rather courts such dangers, either in brawls, duels or battles.

At its worst the Martian will commit such violent crimes as will lead him to the scaffold.

III. Mental and Moral Peculiarities.

At its best the Martian is generous, magnanimous and a devoted friend. He throws his money away for other people's sake, as well as for his own, and he knows no fear. He has plenty of energy and perseverance and will go through any amount of peril and fatigue to bring an enterprise to success. But he has very little delicacy in his intercourse with his fellow-beings; he goes straight to his goal without minding the pain he may cause; and in his love matters he always acts audaciously, and often succeeds by his daring ways. He is very amorous by nature, not vicious, but simply physically excited to numberless love conquests. He is domineering and

refuses to listen to reasoning, which he probably would fail to understand. He is fond of good eating, of plenty of it especially; he prefers meats cooked rare and heavy, heady wines, to any culinary delicacies, and is especially fond of convival reunions and boisterous merriment. He likes circuses, bull-fights and prize-fights. As a profession soldiery is his first choice, next the exploring of wild countries, next the butcher's stall. His pride is great, and so is his fondness for showy clothes, decorations, honors, small or great. He always wants to be to the front, and manifests open contempt for the deep scholar and the quiet, planning business man. Whenever he tackles an art or profession he inoculates it with his own views; as a painter, he will concentrate all his efforts into putting on canvas battles or hunting scenes; as a musician, the composing or playing of marches, dances, and brass instruments will be his favorite work; as a litterateur, he will narrate endless stories of bloodshed, mingled with a good deal of braggadocio. With all his defects the true Martian is admired by the crowd and is a born chief, even in our time of effete civilization.

The worst Martian type—revealed by other disastrous indications in the hands —will be highwayman, burglar, ruffian, murderer. He is as dangerous to society as a railroad engine let loose in a crowded thoroughfare. He has to be suppressed as early as the law permits, either behind steel prison bars or on the scaffold.

VI. THE MOUNT OF THE MOON.

Those in whose hands the <u>Mount of the Moon</u> is found <u>predominating</u> over all the other Mounts are called in Palmistry <u>Lunar Subjects</u>.

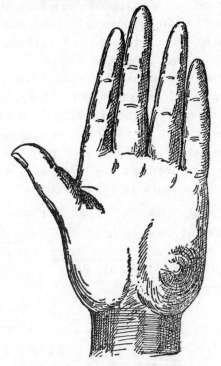

I. Physical Peculiarities.

The Lunar Subject is of a tall stature and has a round head, broad above the temples, with an insignificant brow and that part of the cranium that surrounds the eyes quite bulging His complexion is of a dead white, with occasionally the addition of a pinkish hue; his flesh is soft, for although the muscles are large they are sponge-like in consistency. He has very fine, supple, blonde hair, not thick, however, and no hair on the body. In his face, quite broad and full, the nose is small and round-tipped. The mouth is small and thick-lipped, as if al-ways pouting; the teeth are large, yellowish, badly-arranged, and they deteriorate early; the gums are quite in evidence and are usually pale. In the eyes, round large and bulging, the pupils shine with a dull, liquid, gray-bluish tint; the eyelids are large and thick; the blonde eyebrows are joined and poorly marked; the chin is fat, heavy and retreating; the ears are stuck close to the head.

The neck of the Lunar Subject is long, white, fleshy and streaked with many wrinkles; the chest is fleshy, but the tissues are flabby and unhealthy looking. The stomach is quite bulging, while the legs are heavy, thick at the ankles, with large homely feet. The inferior extremities often look swollen, as if waterlogged.

Of course, in such a type, the hands are bound to be fat and quite soft; the fingers are short, smooth and inclined to be pointed. The first phalanx of the thumb is much below average.

At its worst the Lunar type—when it is accompanied by other undesirable indications—if often affected with ill-smelling sweats and disturbed eyesight; the skin is of a livid white and covered with spots. The hands assume, in an extreme form, the above characteristics.

II. Health Peculiarities.

The Lunar Subject, being essentially of a lymphatic temperament, has a poor blood and cannot stand hard work or prolonged exertion. He suffers from hallucinations, going sometimes as far as actual insanity, and is constantly anxious about his health. The illnesses he is frequently troubled with are paralysis, convulsions, epilepsy; also different forms of insanity. He is in danger of drowning and of suffering from kidney, bladder and womb troubles, as well as rheumatism and gout; grave intestinal diseases are peculiar to his type.

III. Mental and Moral Peculiarities.

The Lunar Subjects are fickle, unreliable and selfish; they are fond of travel, because they tire quickly of any permanent home; they are cold, lazy, melancholy, poor lovers and worse husbands. They are more superstitiously than religiously inclined, and their minds, as well as their bodies, are slow and phlegmatic. Yet their imagination is ever at work feeding upon wide-awake dreams; they often have strange forebodings and are certainly more sensitive to nervous impressions than any other type. In art, in literature, they are romantic to a degree; also fond of poetry and music, but of harmony rather than melody. The male Lunar Subjects are generally effeminate in their shape and tastes; the female Lunar Subjects, without being virtuous, are tenderly devoted to those they love, their imagination endowing them with all kinds of fanciful qualities. Sailors belong to the Lunar type, and so do those who love water and all the occupations and recreations connected with it. Like water itself, they are hard to keep to one purpose; they promise but don't keep their word; they are more generous in talk than in action. They eat voraciously; they drink little, but like strong liquor. Their favorite tints are white and yellow-white.

A worse type of Lunar Subject—revealed by other bad indications in the hand—has all the bad traits above mentioned, increased tenfold. He is thoughtless, foolishly talkative, a liar and a slanderer; often perfidious and profligate, without real physical passion, but just in quest of some novel sensation. He is shamelessly selfish, insolent, a braggard and a coward. Such Lunar Subjects are very much to be avoided and are happily very easily discernible, their gray, watery eyes leaving a most unpleasant impression at the very first meeting.

VII. THE MOUNT OF VENUS.

Those in whose hands the Mount of Venus is found predominating over all the other Mounts are called in Palmistry Venusians.

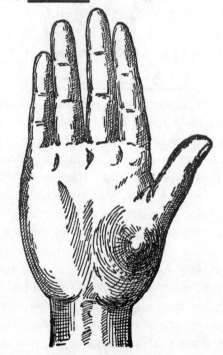

I.   Physical Peculiarities.

The Venusian has many traits in common with the Jupiterian, but there is in his nature something more feminine—in the good sense of the word—more tender and more deeply unselfish. He has the same white complexion, tinted with pink, but softer and more delicate. In stature he is above the medium height, with a round face wherein no bone is apparent; the cheeks are smooth, often dimpled, and the brow is beautifully curved, although of comparatively narrow dimensions; whenever he smiles or feels sad two or three perpendicular wrinklets are visible between the eyebrows, which are finely curved, abundant and silky, but not joined. His hair is long, dark colored, plentiful and supple; he keeps it until late in life. The nose is long and broad at the root, but shapely and rounded at the tip; the eyes are large, clear and beautiful; they are moist with sweet, voluptuous tenderness, slightly bulging and of a brown color; the pupils are wide and the eyelids so silky and fine that the bluish veins are visible. The mouth is small, with rather thick, red lips, especially the lower lip; well-orderd white teeth issue from coral-colored gums. The chin is round, plump, dimpled and rather long; the jaws are not massive. The ears are small and delicately shaped The neck is white, majestic and fleshy. The shoulders are narrow and gracefully drooping. The chest is not broad but full and healthy looking. The arms are plump. The hips are quite developed and rather high, in both sexes; yet the thighs, although long, as in the Greek statues, are graceful and lithe; the ankles are small and so are the high-instepped feet. The hands of a Venusian are plump and dimpled, soft but not flabby, with short, smooth fingers and a mottled skin; the thumb is short.

The bad Venusian type—revealed by other unfavorable indications in the hands—has a sickly, white complexion, and an unhealthy embonpoint. His flesh is flabby, his sunken eyes are bold and libidinous. His hair is often reddish, and his heavy, fat nose turns up at the end in an unshapely mass; his lips are very thick, especially the lower one; he walks with difficulty, is encumbered early with a large stomach, and his extremities are of a vulgar type; his voice is hoarse; even women of that species are thus afflicted. The hands are flabby and the shapeless, fat fingers are short and smooth.

II.   Health Peculiarities.

The Venusian, at his best, is strong and healthy, and his temperament is known as the nervous-sanguine—a most desirable combination. His cheerful disposition carries him over many minor troubles. He suffers, however, from such illnesses as come from disappointments in love, and also from various derangements of the generative organs, although the female Venusian has the difficulties in child-bearing and their consequences more usually marked on the lower part of the Mount of the Moon.

The Venusian at his worst suffers from

the consequences of his excesses and has to pay for them dearly, having often to face one of the most horrible forms of slow blood poisoning, known as syphilis.

III. Mental and Moral Peculiarities.

With the Solar Subject the Venusian divides the honor of belonging to the elite of mankind. He loves life in spite of all its miseries, and believes in its possibilities; the pleasing expression of his face reveals how truly he is in peace with himself and with all the world; and in fact he knows no selfishness and enjoys nothing better than to exert his spirit of benevolence all around him. He is fond of sociable intercourse, and is, above all, desirous to please and to be universally liked. He is not a great eater or drinker, although he is endowed, as a rule, with a remarkably good digestion. He loves delicate perfumes, the beauties of nature and simple melodious music; such music as goes straight to the heart. He is certainly sensually inclined, but his aversion to causing pain or damage to any living being keeps him away from such immoral deeds as might ruin others or bring sorrow to those he respects. Still the opposite sex plays the most important part in his life and influences his every act. Being truthful and constant himself, he is often deceived, but, like all those who truly love, he pardons easily and unrestrictedly. He hates all forms of quarreling, strife, warfare. He is only mildly ambitious, and then simply for the sake of the one he loves best of all and to attract her attention and her affection. In a word, he is the soul of kindness. If art appeals to him, he will display in it, to a rare extent, the gift of harmonious form and a thorough understanding of the beautiful in his choice of subject drawing and coloring. As a writer of fiction his work will be touching and elevating. No real great painter or musician or novelist may hope to reach the heart of the people if he be not to a high degree a Venusian.

The Venusian type at its worst—i. e., with other unfavorable indications in the hands—is that of the unscrupulous debauchee, the detestable profligate, often the erotic madman. All the thoughts and actions of the bad Venusian are directed toward obscenity and corruption. As he grows older he becomes more and more abject and revolting in his conduct, and it is quite a common occurrence to see his depravation land him into state's prison.

THE COMBINATION OF THE MOUNTS.

After devoting much space to the Signatures of the Mounts and minutely describing—with Desbarrolles—the complete type represented by each predominating Mount—supposing that particular mount to be indisputably above all the other Mounts—it is quite essential that I should say a few words of those types in which two Mounts seem to be about equal in importance and power. This, of course, will be much more frequent than the absolute supremacy of but one Mount, and therefore a clear table of these 28 possible combinations is sure to be very much in demand, and in constant, profitable use.

Here, however, I have left out the physical characteristics upon which I insisted in my Signatures of the Mounts; the Master has taken the trouble of presenting in his earlier book a list of those compound types, and it has never been translated, to my knowledge at least. But although this work of mine be large and comprehensive, it cannot include everything, and so I have had to limit myself to a brief interpretation of good and bad hands possessiong two Mounts equally prominent and overshadowing the others in importance. Of course, by this time, the reader knows what I mean by a good hand and a bad hand. By these words I refer to the other characteristics, either favorable or unfavorable, revealed in the hands under examination.

1. Jupiter and Saturn—Excellent luck ahead. Bad—Tendency to suicide.

2. Jupiter and the Sun—Fame and fortune. Bad—Insufferable conceit.

3. Jupiter and Mercury—Love and success in science and business. Bad—A deceiver and thief through love of show.

4. Jupiter and Upper Mars—Bravery; success as a commander. Bad—A cruel despot.

5. Jupiter and the Moon—Imagina-tion governed by sober pride. Bad—The monomania of titles, honors, etc.

6. Jupiter and Venus—Pure, respectable and respected love. Bad—Virtue succumbing to the temptations of vanity.

7. Jupiter and Lower Mars—Resignation at its best. Bad—Cowardice when threatened with loss of position.

8. Saturn and the Sun—High art tinted with sadness. Bad—Brain power affected by morbidness.

9. Saturn and Mercury—Love of science and occultism. Bad—Cheating instincts.

10. Saturn and Upper Mars—Choleric, combative temper. Worse—Cynicism, slow cruelty.

11. Saturn and the Moon—Remarkable gift for the study of occult sciences. Bad—Tendency to suicide through morbidness.

12. Saturn and Venus—Self-possession, quiet kindness. Bad—Intense jealousy.

13. Saturn and Lower Mars—Resignation due more to discouragement than any other feeling.

14. The Sun and Mercury—Perspicacity; brilliant eloquence; original business plans. Bad—Dangerously attractive scheming.

15. The Sun and Upper Mars—A love for shining in war; the great society leader's characteristic. Bad—Desire to shine at all risks.

16. The Sun and the Moon—Imagination at its best. Bad—Imagination leading healthy art astray.

17. The Sun and Venus—Love for, or by, a great artist, writer, etc. Bad—Fawning famous people.

18. The Sun and Lower Mars—Cheerful resignation. Bad—Affected resignation for show only.

19. Mercury and Upper Mars—Scientific warrior. Bad—Selling one's sword for profit.

20. Mercury and the Moon—An inventor's genius. Bad—Constantly conceiving rascally ways of making money.

21. Mercury and Venus—Sensible combination of love and prudence. Bad—The bartering of one's person, in marriage or otherwise.

22. Mercury and Lower Mars—Perseverance in one's plans in spite of hardships. Bad—Obstinacy in wrongdoing.

23. Upper Mars and the Moon—Crusaders, explorers in dangerous countries. Bad—Reckless military adventurers, cruel and revengeful.

24. Upper Mars and Venus—The typical soldier. Bad—The brutal conqueror in war or love.

25. Upper Mars and Lower Mars—A perfect combination of pluck and passive courage. Bad—Most violent temper.

26. The Moon and Venus—Ideal love. Bad—Lewd imaginings.

27. The Moon and Lower Mars—Suffering patiently for one's ideal. Bad—Sticking through thick and thin to one's foolish conceits.

28. Venus and Lower Mars—The patience of the unrequited lover. Bad—The persecutor of one's sweetheart or spouse.

PART FOURTH

Chiromantic Observations

Based upon the system of the ancient Chiromants, as explained, developed and vastly improved upon by ADRIEN ADOLPHE DESBARROLLES, a famous French painter and scientist, born in Paris, August 22, 1801, died there February 11, 1886. After obtaining marked recognition in the Paris Salons, he traveled extensively in Germany, Italy and Spain, and finally chose as his life work the rehabilitation of Chiromancy, at the time a most degenerate science. After fifteen years' close study, he published, in 1859, the first edition of *Les Mystères de la Main* (22d edition, 1895); in 1865, his *Almanac de la Main;* in 1869, his *Journal de Chiromancie*, and, in 1879, his *Révélations Complètes*, the largest book on the subject ever attempted. He added to these monuments of his indefatigable labor *Les Mystères de l'Ecriture*, the standard work on *Graphology*. For forty-four years, his whole time, attention and labor were devoted to *Palmistry* under its most varied aspects.

THE LINES IN GENERAL.

I. GROUPING.

The Map of the Hand, and the description that accompanies it, have already furnished the reader with a preliminary knowledge of the position of each of the fourteen Main Lines, which I shall group now in their logical sequence, as follows, giving each of them but one name, the appellation which it will keep all through this work.

   I. The Line of Life.
      The Line of Mars.
      The 3 Bracelets of the Rascette.
  II. The Line of Liver.
      The Via Lasciva.
      The Line of Intuition.
 III. The Line of Head.
 IV. The Line of Heart.
      The Girdle of Venus.
      The Lines of Union.
  V. The Line of Fate.
 VI. The Line of the Sun.

I put forward only Six Chief Lines, out of the Fourteen Main Lines; I do not even give way to a desire to have the number seven play a part in this series of lessons. We must keep out of, and above, all these ancient superstitions, respectable and highly interesting to the antiquarian though they may be. I want to obtain for you and for me the very limpidity of truth, and no such trifles must stand in our way.

Now the above classification explains itself. Division one, headed Line of Life, includes the Minor Main Lines upon which we read many details concerning the longevity and general health of the subject. They are, in fact, so closely related to each other that a perfect Line of Mars, or an excellent Rascette of 3 bracelets have, many a time, been known to entirely make up the worst deficiencies of a short, broken or chained Line of Life.

Division Two is, in truth, a subdivision of Division One, as it includes the Line of Liver, the presence of which, in a perfect shape, and not touching the Line of Life, also gives assurance of a green old age and of a life of fine health. The Via Lasciva and the Line of Intuition, I consider, as you will see later on, as simple modifications of the Line of Liver, often sister lines to it, and endowed with very similar meanings.

Division Three, headed Line of Heart, includes the Girdle of Venus, generally interpreted as a sign of vicious tendencies, and the Lines of Union, considered as the markings of serious love affairs, often legalized love affairs, i. e., Marriages. Here again we have a very simple and natural combination.

B. MEANING.

And now I am about touching upon a subject I have never seen treated by any author, ancient or modern, although, indirectly, the Sixteenth Century Palmists and the immortal Desbarrolles have indicated, if not expressed in so many words, opinions very much in accord with my own theory. I want to present herein a plea tending to explain why and wherefore this or that line has received the name it bears and been endowed by the Chiromants with its special qualities. This is certainly a delicate point to ventilate and yet, if it could be elucidated to the general satisfaction of the students, I truly believe they would feel relieved of one of their most persistent causes of embarrassment, whenever defending, against sneers or direct attacks, the science they love so well.

Let me open the debate, without further preliminary, by asking this plain question:

"Why, for example, are the Lines of Life, Head and Heart called by these names and supposed to relate to Longevity, Brain troubles and Heart disease?"

The starting point of my answer will take its source from the well-authenticated theory of an ambient atmosphere surrounding us, the nature of which is a mystery, the nearest to which we ever came being found in the vague appellation of electricity. It certainly exists; for new phenomena come daily to light confirming its extraordinary powers for good and evil. That it is attracted by points—be they lightning rods, or fingers, or hairs—is also undoubted. That our whole nervous system acts, first as a reservoir for this attracted fluid, and later as its conductor, is just as fully admitted by scientist and layman; that finally, from the brain where it has accumulated, it returns by an unceasing process of circulation to the points that attracted it, to be projected either into the common source it came from originally, or into other animated creatures— our fellow-beings, or the animals about us—is hardly more contestable nowadays.

With but slight differences as to the limitation of beliefs, all thinking men and women of our time, have reached, or are fast reaching, these conclusions. And those once admitted, the theory of the Chief Lines in the human palm is both logical in the extreme and most easy of comprehension.

The finger of Jupiter is by excellence the attractor, if I may coin the word; it is in constant communication with the outside world—if by that expression may be designated the reserve fluid, the nature of which remains the great X for all living scientists, be they named Kelvin, Edison or Tesla. At the base of that finger stands its Mount, its group of Pacinic Corpuscles, absorbing the fluid just acquired; and, from that Mount of Jupiter—my Map of the Hand will tell you so, if your own hand does not—start the three great streams of nervous fluid, named respectively: the Lines of Heart, Head and Life. Highest into the Mount rises the Line of Heart —and the circulation of the blood sets the arteries pulsating. Just under it, the Line of Head sends to the brain the effluvium received from the Mount; but what would it amount to if the first awakening had not resulted from the supreme battery, starting agoing the flow of life-bearing blood? And, third, but not least, comes the Line of Life, the combination of the sanguine and nervous elements of vitality, adding to both the digestive power which is to make the whole mechanism temporarily self-sustaining.

Thus have the three great lines—those which are known to precede and survive all others and which I have found, hundreds of times, to be sole-existent in hands of strong men, doing their task in this world with plenty of energy and sturdy vitality—thus have the three lines triumphantly explained their right to their ancient names, that came to us through Chaldean Astrology, Egyptian Magic, Aristotelian Philosophy and the deep cogitations of the great Palmists of the XVI., XVII., XVIII. and XIX. centuries, Desbarrolles first, foremost and the Master.

And now to complete my demonstration, shall I call your attention to the strange fact—so logical though—that only from the Mount of Jupiter start Chief Lines, the other Mounts, with the fingers at the base of which they stand, not being attractors but reflectors, and throwing out the fluid received through the first finger; thus the Lines connected with them start somewhere in the middle or at the bottom of the hand and terminate on these Mounts, after having—all of them—crossed one or more of the three original Jupiterian Lines: Heart, Head or Life.

Finally the Line of Liver—which ought to have been called all along the Line of Mercury—after crossing part of the Mount of the Moon (devoted to the lower secretions of the body) and the Upper Mount of Mars (where is to be read everything concerning the upper secretions from throat, bronchies and lungs), finally ends on the Mount of Mercury; and the bile, whose irregular flow is the cause of most of the ills human nature is heir to, finds thereon its outlet, as no finger in the hand possesses, in as strong a degree as the fourth finger does, the gift of projecting, now a moral or deleterious influence, now all undesirable physical impedimenta. The circle is complete; every finger, every line has done its logical work; the eternal going and coming of the mysterious fluid proceeds in its own tireless work; and it will do so as long as through the Index and the Line of Heart our pulse is set a-beating and the cells of our cerebral matter are kept nervously thrilling in their narrow quarters.

II. CHARACTER.

If the reader has given sufficient attention to the principles laid down in the preceding pages he will have no trouble grasping and storing in his memory the few following statements concerning the Character of the Lines:

First, as to Color; if normal and healthy, it must not be too vividly different or distinct from the general color of the hand; just a trifle higher in tint perhaps, of a faint, pink hue. We follow here the directions of the physician and accept his dictum that "A very white hand indicates a poor quality of blood and a superabundance of lymph; that a yellowish tint is evidence of liver trouble of a more or less serious nature; that a red hand indicates a superabundance of blood, and a very red hand a tendency to apoplexy." What applies to the inside of the hand is still more positive when the color of the lines is under examination.

In a moral point of view:

Pale lines are the token of weak, deceitful natures;

Yellow lines, of a sad, Saturnian temperament;

Red lines, of a violent disposition.

The general shape of the hand, the character of the nails, the prominence of certain Mounts, must, of course, verify, or modify the impression produced upon the examiner by the peculiar color of the subject's lines.

After Color, comes Length; but concerning this characteristic the only general rule that applies is that the Line of Life can never be too long, while there are certain limitations as to the length of the other Main Lines, which will be expatiated upon, in detail, in the chapters devoted to each of them respectively.

Width may be treated right here, as two short paragraphs will do it justice.

A line must not spread too much in its course, or it loses its qualities as a channel for the transmission of the nervous fluid—whatever name we please to give it. Like a river that runs over its banks, it ceases to be useful as a carrier and its shallowness destroys its efficiency.

There are two exceptions to this ruling, however, and these two exceptions confirm the rule. The first ten or twelve years on the Line of Life (see Chapter on Dates), and the final portion of the Line of Heart are found, in ninety-five cases out of a hundred, quite wide and often even malformed. This is due to the well-known fact that during the first period of every animated being's existence, his tenure of life is very shaky and uncertain—and this is made manifest by the poorly shaped Line of Life during those years. When the inevitable end grows near, another Line—this time the Line of Heart—shows signs of fatigue, even failure.

But, in health, all the lines are to be medium thin, straight and not too deep; and this brings me to the fourth characteristic—Depth.

No measurement and no sounding, of course, could be applied in this case. But a few months' experience will teach the student to recognize with sufficient accuracy those lines that have cut too deep a furrow into the hand, either all along their course, or only during certain periods. He will learn, also, without much questioning, that these deep stretches always indicate a strain, an effort on the part of the subject, and, if he follow the case long enough, he cannot fail to discover that this strain, this effort has played havoc with the subject's constitution and ambition, and, within a comparatively short time, often wrecked both. Too much fluid has been called upon by sheer will-power on the part of the subject, to run along these fragile channels cut out for its passage; the tension soon exceeds the power to sustain it, hence the crash, hence the catastrophe, generally ending in paralysis—if the Line of Head shows the abnormal depth—or in the bursting of a blood vessel—if the Line of Heart be at fault.

III. MALFORMATION.

There are four usual cases of Malformation of the Main Lines.

CHAINED LINES.	SPLIT LINE "MAGNIFIED"	FORKED LINES	UPWARD BRANCHES
DOWNWARD BRANCHES	TASSELS	BREAKS WITH FRAGMENTS OVER EACH OTHER	CLEAR BREAKS

They are often Broken, and this defect, interfering gravely with the circulation of the fluid, denotes a serious perturbation in the physical and moral condition of the subject.

But the Breaks are of two kinds. Either clear, leaving an unoccupied space—lengthwise—between the fragments, or the fragments overlay each other, thus allowing, so to speak, a new line above the broken one to continue the latter's work comparatively unimpaired. I need not say that the second kind of break is less alarming than the first, and must be read very differently. After the Break, the Split; a malforma-

tion frequently met with in the second portion of the Line of Heart, and indicating, as I stated before, the gradual weakening of this important organ, as years advance. Elsewhere, this split ought to be considered with great concern, as it is equivalent to the cutting of the Line, showing it to lose its value as a fluid carrier and become rapidly worthless. I must warn the student against considering those splits on the Line of Heart as elongated islands. In no case must a split be read as an island, as it certainly has nothing to do with a love affair, except in so far as it might affect the subject's physical health.

The Chained or Linked formation is also very frequently met with. In the chapter devoted to each line I shall give full readings as to its meaning. I simply want to remind the reader of what I said above concerning Lines of Life chained at the start (delicate childhood), and the Line of Heart chained at the end (poor circulation of the blood after the change of life in woman and the great climacteric in man).

An Islanded line is seldom met with; but distinct, separate islands on the line are of daily occurrence; they are the objects of my close attention all through this book.

IV. DUPLICATION.

After the malformation, come, in logical sequence, the supplementary formations, or the Duplication of certain lines. These are called by the generic name of Sister Lines, although they are but very seldom found accompanying a line along its whole course. They are more usually marked upon the Mounts which are the normal, terminal locations of these lines; and there they run along these main lines for a little while. Full clear readings concerning them are given in the places where they belong.

But the student must be warned at once against the mistake of accepting as sister lines the two split halves of one line. While the sister line is always considered as an assistance to the line it duplicates, splitting, on the contrary is one of the most unwholesomely dangerous indications the hand reveals. A magnifying glass will never fail righting the attentive student in that respect before he commits himself to the consequences of such a startling reading.

By Forks, Branches and Tassels are designated formations which partake of the nature of Splits, since they seem detached from the very substance of the Line and of the nature of Duplications as they often add to the strength of the Line which they actually enrich. Full details concerning these modifications in a Main Line are found in the chapter devoted to it. Let me simply state here that I have systematically called Forks such branchings of a Line found at its start or termination only; everywhere else they are named Branches.

V. ABSENCE.

Some of the Main Lines are very frequently altogether absent from the hand; seldom, however, are the same Main Lines absent from both hands. In order of frequency—or infrequency

rather—I would say that of the Six Chief Lines,

The Line of Life is never absent.

The Line of Head very rarely, even if it be only present in embryo.

The Line of Heart, seldom. Whenever it happens: a very grave omen.

The Line of Fate and the Line of the Sun, more frequently, although one of the two is fairly certain to take the place of the other. As the reader will be told later, these two lines are often considered sister lines and replace each other quite satisfactorily.

The Line of Liver is often absent; and many prominent Palmists consider its absence as a boon. I'll discuss the question at length in its proper place.

The first bracelet of the Rascette is always there. The second bracelet, often; the third, seldom, at least in a clear, satisfactory shape.

The Line of Intuition and the Via Lasciva, being simply modifications, or at most, sister lines, of the Line of Liver, their absence is of no particular consequence.

The Line of Mars is rare—at least in its entirety.

The absence of the Girdle of Venus—happily very frequent—is quite desirable.

As to the Lines of Union, it is my experience that, at least one is found in every hand. I do not remember more than three exceptions to this statement.

And now that I have rapidly surveyed the principal characteristics of the Fourteen Main Lines—distinguishing emphatically betweeen the Six Chief Lines and the <u>Eight Minor Main Lines,</u> I shall undertake, with the kind reader at my elbow, and plenty of illustrations to lighten up my path, the minute description of, and the many readings concerning this queen among Chief Lines—the <u>Line of Life,</u> preceding it, however, by my <u>theory of Dates and how to discover them on the Lines of Life, Fate, etc.</u> As soon as I enter the study of the Lines I have frequent occasion to refer to this theory; it is necessary therefore to present it as a sort of general introduction to the Lines.

THE VANISHING OF THE LINES.

[Adapted from Desbarrolles.]

Many years ago a gentleman called upon me for the purpose of consultation. It was in the winter time and he wore a heavy Macfarlane. He asked—and was granted—permission to keep this garment on his shoulders during his visit. Then he stretched his left hand and I said to him at once:

"You are a military man, sir."

"That may be," he answered, rather curtly; "kindly proceed."

"I mentioned the fact because I notice here the sign of a wound; and yet it was not incurred in war."

"What do you mean?" he exclaimed; "this hand was never wounded!"

"I mean that this wound whose sign—not scar—is marked upon this hand, if inflicted on the battlefield would have brought you promotion and honors, while, on the contrary, it ruined your prospects and compelled you to abandon your profession."

"It did," acknowledged my visitor; "I escaped Solferino without a scratch, only to be crippled by the awkward handling of a shotgun while crossing my own preserves. I received the whole load in the shoulder; the nerves were doubtless grievously affected, for my hand has grown useless; it has lost all sensation; it is just like dead."

"Would you kindly show me that hand?"

"Willingly; but, in appearance, you'll not find it in any way different from the left hand which you have just examined;" and he pushed with difficulty his right hand from under the cloak and laid it on the table.

The back of this hand seemed just as healthy and natural as its sister hand. But inside, its palm was absolutely smooth, all vestige of lines or signs had disappeared.

Thus these lines had begun to vanish from the very hour the nerves connecting the hand with the brain had ceased to operate. Had there not been a constant, direct correspondence between the cerebral matter and the nervous centers in the palm, the hand, although rendered useless, would have preserved the lines that it possessed from birth. This constatation, repeated a hundred times and more, under various circumstances, especially in cases of paralysis, leaves no doubt in my mind as to the close connection between brain and palm; it confirms triumphantly the declaration of the world-famed historian and exquisite psychologue, Michelet:

"The convolutions of the brain are written in the Hands."

HOW TO RECKON TIME IN THE HAND.

I. HOW FAR PALMISTRY GOES IN THE MATTER OF DATES.

In my previous works on Palmistry, my Hand Book, published in 1883 (exhausted), and my recent Practical Palmistry (1897), I have presented my readers with the two more ancient systems for marking dates upon the Lines of Life and Fate—the only Lines upon which such marks are usual and necessary. I am going to insert in these lessons a method which I personally practice, which was adopted by Desbarrolles himself in his practice during the latter part of his life, and which prominent British palmists consider the most reliable. It has, at any rate, the merit of being simple to a degree, and the results attained by its cautious and attentive use are very generally satisfactory.

But I must say right here, what I am never tired repeating, that, according to both rule and tradition, absolutely exact dates are not to be found in the hand; I mean by this that the day, the month or even the year are not to be determined. Anything closer than two years, either way, if not to be expected, counted upon, is nevertheless often obtained by the very careful combination of the various elements found in both hands of the subject. To hope for more is to deceive one's self, or the subject, or both. Every honest palmist must not hesitate stating this fact when reading hands. At no time have respected chiromants claimed more exact results. Of course, if the exact age of the subject is told the reader, he or she may give his statements a more direct, positive form. (I need not state here that the age of the subject, at the time of the examination, is not revealed in the hand). But the amount of knowledge supplied will be practically the same. I will now proceed in my detailed explanation.

II. TIME MEASUREMENT ON THE LINE OF LIFE.

You measure with a white thread the Line of Life from its starting point to its meeting with the first bracelet of the Rascette. If the Line of Life stops before that, you will follow and measure the curve it would occupy if it did terminate at the first bracelet.

This first measuring done, you cut the thread at the terminating point. You then double it and mark with ink its new terminating point. Each of the two halves of the thread you divide into five equal sections.

The markings completed, you stretch the thread on the hand, following exactly the Line of Life, and beginning at the beginning, you memorize the following figures corresponding with each of the ink bars you have traced upon the thread.

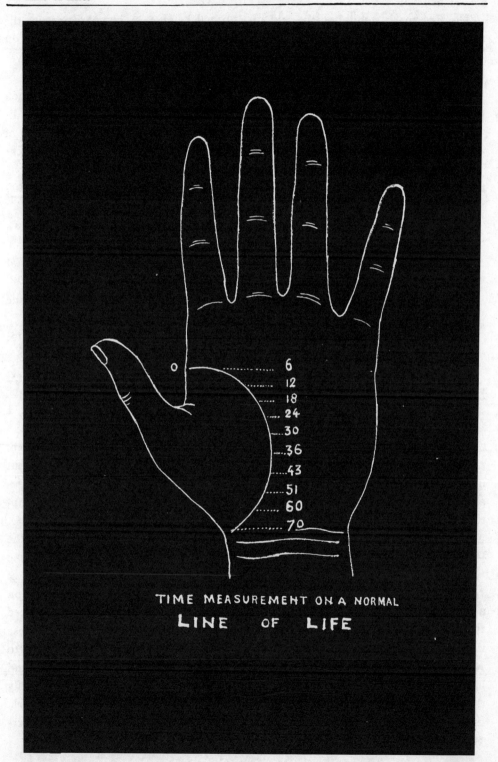

TIME MEASUREMENT ON A NORMAL
LINE OF LIFE

The first mark stands for the end of the 6th year.

The second mark stands for the end of the 12th year.

The third mark stands for the end of the 18th year.

The fourth mark stands for the end of the 24th year.

The fifth mark stands for the end of the 30th year.

(This is the middle of the thread).

The sixth mark stands for the end of the 36th year.

The seventh mark stands for the end of the 43d year.

The eighth mark stands for the end of the 51st year.

The ninth mark stands for the end of the 60th year.

The end of the thread marks the 70th year.

As you see, the spaces, as soon as the heyday of life in people of our race and clime is passed, contain a gradually increasing number of years. We are going down hill, and the decline is quicker and quicker. Who ever passed his fortieth year knows that but too well.

III. TIME MEASUREMENT ON THE LINE OF FATE.

Again I measure with a white thread a straight line from the first bracelet of the Rascette to the root of the second finger, i. e., the upper portion of the Mount of Saturn. But instead of folding the thread into two halves, I ignore that portion of it that goes further than the Line of Head—provided that Line of Head is normal; and if it is not normal I judge, by comparison with the normal type, the location where it ought to be cut by the Line of Fate. The lower portion of the thread (below the Line of Head) I fold into three equal parts; then stretching it again along the space indicated above (the fact of the real Line of Fate being shorter does not interfere with the operation).

At the upper end of the first (lowest) third I mark the fifth year.

At the end of the second third I mark the 20th year.

At the end of the third third (i. e., at the meeting with the Line of Head, whether real or imaginary), I mark the 35th year.

Above the Line of Head I do not measure by the thread any longer, but

At the meeting with the Line of Heart I mark the 50th year.

At the root of the second finger I mark the 70th year.

The Line of Fate goes no further; past that age, in ninety-five cases out of a hundred, a man's life is purely vegetative, and its incidents are of no importance.

I have to call your attention to the fact that the measurements on the Line of Fate are modified by the length of the hand, while the measurements on the Line of Life are mostly influenced by the breadth of the hand. These slight differences are left, however, to the sound judgment of the student, and the experience he or she will gradually acquire in this delicate part of the work. With the above system these differences will be of very little account.

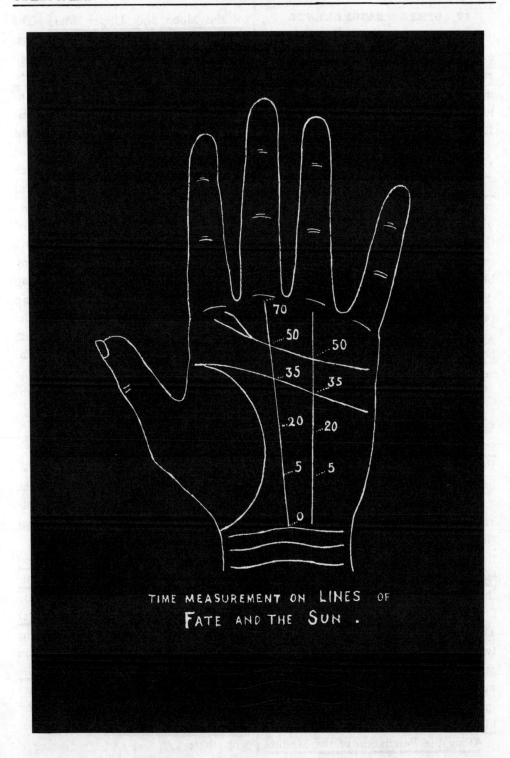

TIME MEASUREMENT ON LINES OF FATE AND THE SUN.

IV. OTHER MEASUREMENTS.

On the Line of the Sun—Follow the exact system and scale described in reference to the Line of Fate, keeping in mind that the Line of the Sun is often to be considered as a sister line to the Line of Fate.

On the Mount of Mercury, along the Percussion—This refers exclusively to Lines of Union and their position between the Line of Heart and the root of the fourth finger. After long hesitation—for here we are on very uncertain ground—I found that this space ought to be scaled from downward upward, and divided into two halves, the lower one representing the years from 15 to 30 for girls or women, and from 18 to 35 for boys and men. The upper portion contains the rest of the subject's life time.

Along the Line of Union—Here the children are marked by tiny upright lines. The earlier born will be found furthest from the Mount, that is on the Percussion entirely. No closer dates can be obtained upon such narrow ground.

On the Mount of Jupiter. This again refers exclusively to Unions, and the signs by which they are represented on the Mount are crossed with, or without, stars. The space on the Mount, between the Line of Life and the root of the first finger is again to be divided into halves. The lower portion includes the years between 15 and 30 for girls and women, and between 18 and 35 for boys and men. The upper portion contains the indications referring to the rest of the life of the subject.

Along the Percussion of the Mounts of the Moon and Upper Mars—The space has been divided by Desbarrolles, in his Revelations Completes (2nd Edition, page 258), into thirty equal parts, beginning from ten years old, at the connection of the first bracelet of the Rascette with the lower part of the Mount of the Moon, up to a normally placed Line of Heart where 70 is marked; each of these divisions including a period of two years. Dates of voyages are, according to the master, to be reckoned in obedience to this scale. Personally I have never found it to answer, with any degree of certitude. I prefer being guided by an imaginary line continuing each of these Lines of voyage up to its crossing the Line of the Sun or the Line of Fate, when a fairly correct date can be attained on either of these lines, the first to be used as a scale only in the absence of the second.

V. ONE MORE IMPORTANT REMARK.

Has for object to warn you against mixing up the date indications found on the Lines of Life and Fate. The principle to follow in the premises is the following:

Whenever you have read an indication and a date on the Line of Life, should the Line of Influence (See my Chapter on the Lines of Influence, etc.) that cuts the Line of Life cut also the Line of Fate or even terminate upon that Line in a sign, do not count the date again; the whole indication has been settled once for all as to time on crossing the Line of Life and you must stop there.

THE LINE OF LIFE.

I. POSITION AND DIRECTION.

Normal. Starting from under the Mount of Jupiter, encircling the Mount

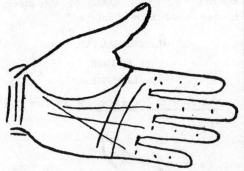

of Venus and the Lower Mount of Mars, provided both are normally placed and of average superficial dimensions.

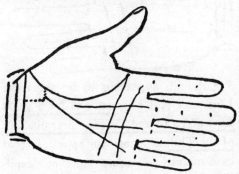

This portion of the Mount of Venus between the Mount of the Moon and the Line of Life (normal) indicated in the above illustration by a dotted line is not enclosed by the Line of Life; but for all ordinary readings it may be stated that the Mount of Venus is all within the Line of Life.

Lying closer to the second phalanx of the thumb, especially if there is a star at the intersection of the Lines of Head and

Liver—Childlessness; difficulty in child-bearing.

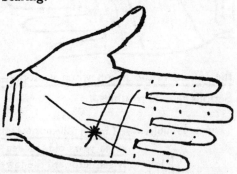

By reducing the space occupied by the Mount of Venus proper, the generative power of the subject is reduced that much; hence the above reading.

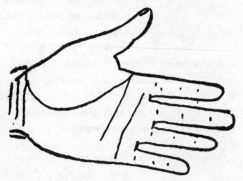

Coming out in a great circle into the palm of the hand, and reaching or ending close to the Mount of the Moon—Longevity of unusual duration.

This is in accordance with the principle given below: "The longer the Line, the longer the life." In this case the Line of Life will probable enclose the whole of the Mount of Venus.

Normal for awhile and then starting almost straight to the lower portion of

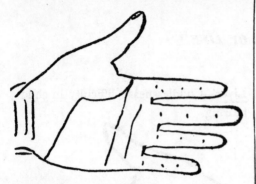

the Mount of the Moon when it stops—
Serious female troubles.

Womb Troubles.—A Line of Life, normal up to 30 years old, sudden-

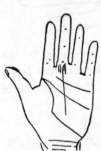

ly starts toward the lower part of the Mount of the Moon when it ends near the Rascette. The Mount of Venus low but much rayed and a Mount of Saturn with several vertical lines.

"Seen in the hand of a lady suffering from the consequences of unfortunate child bearing; this position of the Mount of the Moon either exaggerate or much rayed always indicates—in woman—troubles of the generative organs."

Congenital Idiotcy—Both hands ill shaped,

with dwarfed thumbs and crooked fingers. In the Left Hand a Line of Life forming, at 30, a right angle ending at the Percussion, with a small islanded Line of Heart. In the right hand a chained Line of Life and Head, several islands on the Line of Heart and a star on the Mount of the Sun (a most curious sign

doubtless inherited from some brainy parent).

"Seen in the hands of a young girl 14 years old whose face was comparatively intelligent, although she was really afflicted with idiotcy from birth. This Line of Life in the Left hand crossing over to the Mount of the Moon is often an indication of epilepsy."

II. CHARACTER.
(a) By Itself.
1. LENGTH.

The shorter the Line, the shorter the Life.

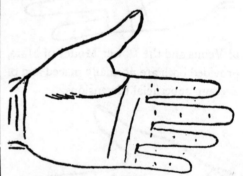

Although appearing to be short the Line may still be sustained by a good Line of Head and a strong first phalanx of the Thumb; soon will appear in that case minute downward lines, or "capillaries."

A strong will-power has been known to keep up life in an otherwise debilitated body; the nervous fluid absorbed by a strong thumb and circulated by a good Line of Head will allow the subject to fight against a physical weakness which might cause his death if not energetically resisted. We will find similar indications, with appropriate cases, as we proceed farther in the study of the Line of Life.

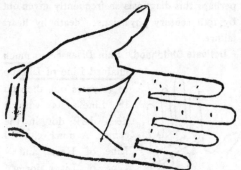

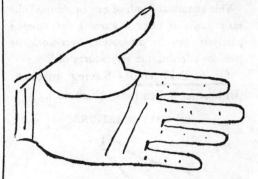

A short or poor Line, if the Line of Liver does not connect with the Line of Life and goes up, straight and even to the Mount of Mercury—To a great extent this is admitted to make up for the defective Line of Life.

A fine Line of Liver denotes a perfect digestion, and with a good stomach there is a strong probability that life may be prolonged.

Short in both hands—Death at the date indicated on the hand. (See also the Line of Mars, the Rascette and the Line of Liver.)

I take this occasion for repeating that a long and even **perfect** Line of Life in both hands, while it promises a long life to the subject, does not necessarily guarantee it. This excellent marking simply announces that an important capital of life is granted the subject by his Maker; but it is only by properly husbanding it that it will last the full allotted time.   Other signs in the hands will most probably appear as warnings of a possible curtailing of this inestimable privilege of longevity. Physical or moral defects that may terminate the subject's life prematurely and perhaps abruptly are there to be read and heeded. Hence the extraordinary usefulness of Palmistry as a mentor and a guide.

2. COLOR, WIDTH, DEPTH.

Of various thicknesses throughout its course—Capricious and fickle temper; uneven state of health.

It is well known that people with frequent periods of ill-health are generally moody and very easily put-out.

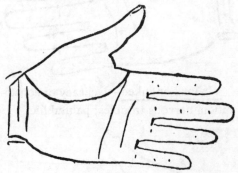

Thin and meager in the center—Ill health during that portion of life. A spot terminating this thinness—Sudden death (with other indications).

Pale and wide—Ill health, bad instincts, feeble and envious character.

The Paleness of the Lines always indicates poverty of the blood or defective circulation. A line too broad loses much of its value as a carrier of electricity; it is like an overflowing, shallow river that ceases to render its accustomed services.

Deep and red—Violence and brutality of temper; feverish disposition.

This observation applies to all the main Lines.

Very deep all through—Brusque manners; often violent ways; rapid wearing out of the system.

This abnormal depth of one or more of the main Lines is often a warning of coming paralysis due to dissipation, over-work, or troubles affecting the very source of life.

Of a livid color—Raving madness (with other indications, which see).

3. MALFORMATIONS.

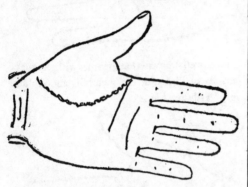

Chained or linked—Delicacy of constitution, nervous troubles; painful life.

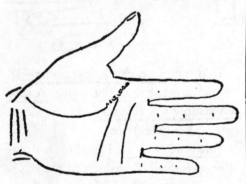

Chained or linked under the Mount of Jupiter—Bad health in early life.

The Line is very generally chained at that place which comprises the first six or eight years of one's life. During that period, human beings are especially frail—as is shown by the Tables of Mortality—and even when they escape what is known as "Childhood's diseases," their hold on life is weak to a degree. Hence the chained or linked formation. It is interesting to notice that the same formation is very generally **found** toward the termination of the Line of Heart, explaining

perhaps this diagnosis so frequently given out by 19th century physicians: "death by heart failure."

Delicate Childhood. Skin Disease.—A much chained Line of Life up  to 12 years old, then on the Line a star with a deep, dark dot in the center. A much chained Line of Heart, and a Line of Liver formed ladderwise by small fragments. Very short nails. The Line of Head separated from the Line of Life at the start and widely forked at the termination. A long, broad-tipped Thumb.

Poor, Diseased Eyesight Until Past Twenty.—A Line of Life chained up to 20. A Line  of Head separated from the Line of Life and beginning under the **Mount of Saturn, had** been gradually attached to the Line of Life by capillary lines. A star on the 3rd phalanx of the third finger toward the second finger.

"A young professor of law, afflicted with very poor general health and eyesight up to 20; had short nails (critical mind). Recovered somewhat from the trouble with his eyes; but the organ remained very weak."

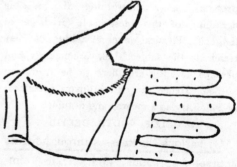

Formed of small lines arranged ladderwise—Poor general health during the period of life represented by the space occupied by this ladder-like formation.

(b) In Combination with other Indications.

A long fine Line, without any Lines of Fate or Sun in the hand—A healthy but uneventful existence, with but little chance of making money.

A short Line in both hands with all the other main lines above the average in clearness and directness and with a good first phalanx of the thumb—The duration of the Line will be most probably prolonged by the moral energy and well sustained efforts of the subject.

III STARTING POINTS AND FORKS AT THE START.

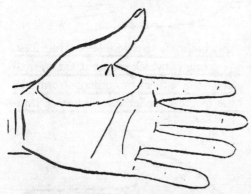

Starting on the Mount of Jupiter—Great ambition fully rewarded.

Slightly separated, at the start, from a good Line of Head—Energy and go-ahead spirit; enough pluck to face an au-

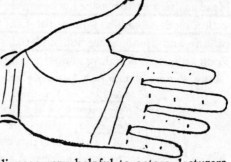

dience; very helpful to actors, lecturers, preachers, teachers, lawyers.

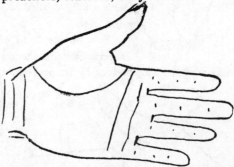

Separated, at the start, from a good Line of Head—The above characteristics are somewhat accentuated, with the addition of some recklessness and haste in the taking of decisions or in the judgment of situations.

A strong second phalanx of the thumb and knotted fingers will counterbalance this tendency to take risks without properly weighing them. On the other hand, a very long first phalanx of the thumb, and short, smooth fingers would increase the danger.

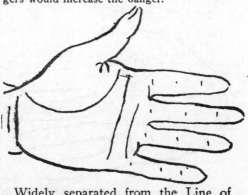

Widely separated from the Line of

Head at the start, the space between filled with a mesh of capillary lines, the Lines of Life and Head being full and red—Foolhardiness amounting almost to folly.

Ultra Nervous Nature in a Literary Man.—

A Line of Life widely separated from the Line of Head. A fragment of a Girdle of Venus cut by a small Line of the Sun. Pointed fingers with a fully-marked second knot.

"Seen in the hand of a very excitable literary man who met with ill-luck in his profession.

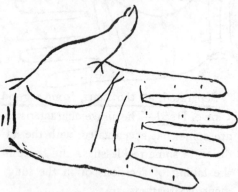

A short outside fork at the start, in a good hand—Justice of soul; fidelity. With an exaggerate Mount of Jupiter—Indecision, fantasy.

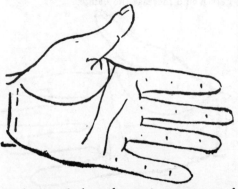

A short fork at the start, one prong of

which starts from the side of the hand—Inconstancy.

The starting points of the Line and the prongs of its forks must not be looked for back of the hand, but must only be followed up to the edge of the hand.

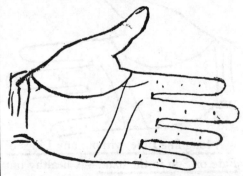

A long fork deep into the Mount of Jupiter, if uncrossed—Ambition crowned with success.

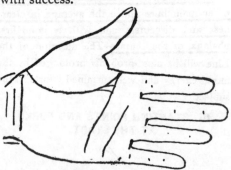

Beginning with a double or triple fork, one prong of which starts at the normal place, the other or others from the Line of Head under the Mount of Jupi-

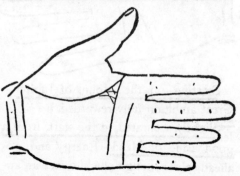

ter but no farther inside the hand—Fortune and honors to the parents of the subject which ultimately benefit the latter.

If the prongs above mentioned are crossed before reaching the Line of Head —As many lawsuits lost; these law suits affect the fortune or the honor of the parents of the subject and thus indirectly the latter.

IV. TERMINATION AND FORKS AT THE TERMINATION.

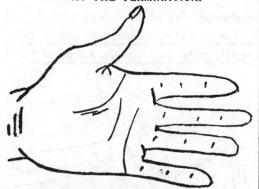

Terminating abruptly, with a few short parallel lines—Sudden death. If the short parallel lines are not there death may not be sudden but it will take place at the date indicated on the Line, if the marking is repeated in both hands.

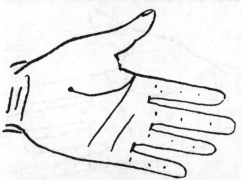

Terminating abruptly, with a black dot at the end—Death by accident or violence. (If repeated in both hands and with other indications.)

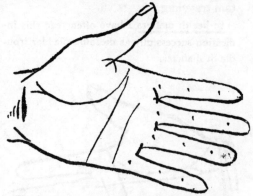

Forked at the termination—General weakening of the system; more rarely: overwork and old age accompanied with poverty.

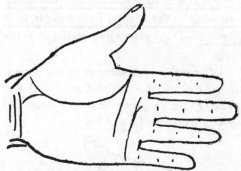

Forked at the termination, the prongs more widely separated—Rheumatism; more rarely: the life will end in poverty away from the country of one's birth.

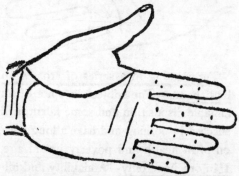

Forked at the termination with a long prong crossing the Mount of the Moon to the Percussion—Long voyages or distant traveling.

In health matters I have often read this indication successfully as meaning bladder trouble or diabetes.

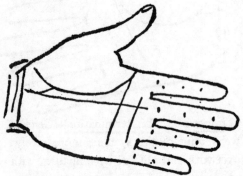

Forked at the termination, one prong running to the Line of Fate and merging into it—Dull, vegetative ending of the life.

Of course in this case, as in all similar ones, the date must be read on the Line of Life—where the prong leaves the main Line —and not on the Line of Fate.

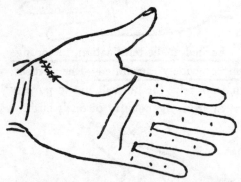

Terminating in a series of crosses, in both hands—The subject in spite of an amiable disposition and some talent, will succeed in nothing and have a long period of ill health and poverty in old age. If in one hand only—Amiability and talent.

Tasseled at its extremity—Poverty through loss of money late in life. Gen-

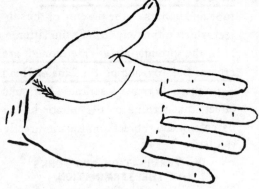

eral weakening of the system.

Tasseled at its termination, one of the tassels going deep into the Mount of the

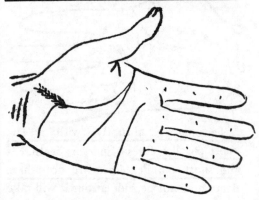

Moon—Prospective insanity; probably of a senile character.

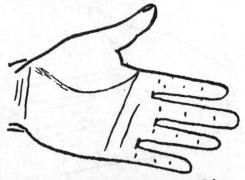

At the termination of a short Line a number of Capillary lines gradually appearing and gaining in strength—The bad omen indicated by the short line has

been annulled by much care and precaution.

V. BRANCHES.

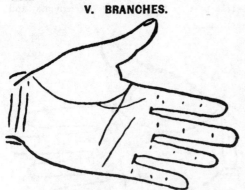

A branch starting early and reaching into the Mount of Jupiter—Successful ambition; egotism.

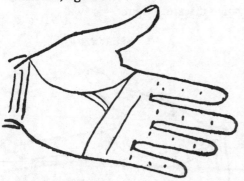

Branches reaching but not cutting the Line of Head, about its center—Honors and riches.

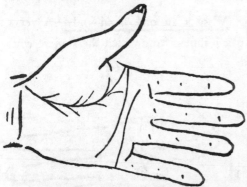

Upward branches on either side—Fine health, ambition satisfied and generally riches.

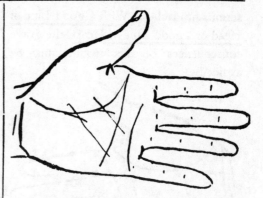

Upward branches cut crosswise by lines of influence—For each cut, a lawsuit or legal separation.

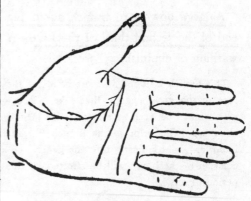

Downward branches on either side—Loss of health and wealth.

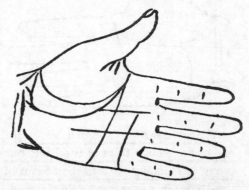

A very large branch descending in a wide curve almost from the starting point of the Line down to the Rascette—Very serious headaches. With a good Line of Head or a good Line of Heart, the grave consequences of this trouble may be avoided.

A large downward branch about the end of the second third of the Line—A warning of diminishing forces.

This branch is found in most hands at the date of the great change that takes place—with women between 40 and 46; with men at about 49. The color of the branch is quite important, as it indicates how the general circulation of the blood will be affected by this period of crisis.

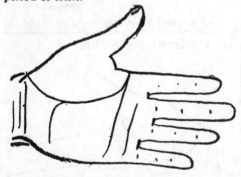

A large downward branch about the end of the second third of the Line, one prong terminating far into the Mount of the Moon; in a firm hand—Restlessness, love of travel. In a flabby hand, with sloping Line of Head—Restlessness only satisfied in vice.

Of course in both cases, imagination (represented by the Mount of the Moon) plays a great part in the subject's movements and actions.

A downward branch from a black spot on the Line—Nervous complaint left by some disease. Gout.

VI. BREAKS.

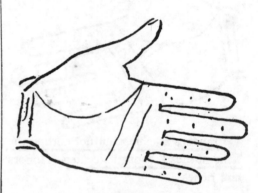

A break in one hand only—A very grave illness from which the subject will

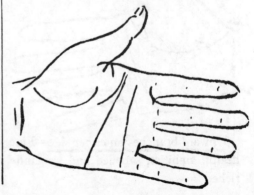

surely recover; especially if the two fragments overlay each other.

A break in both hands—Great danger of death, especially if the lower fragment turns inward toward the Mount of Venus.

A Very Serious Venereal Disease—A triple, much broken Girdle of Venus, starred under the Mount of Saturn, the star connecting with a cross line from the Mount of Jupiter. A broken Line of Life in both hands, and the nails long, brittle, convex and ridged.

"A young man hopelessly ill from the consequences of reckless dissipation. The poison in his blood was finally affecting his lungs and consumption had set in. Died a few years later."

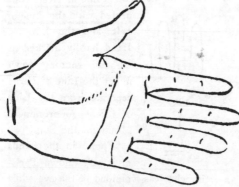

Broken up and laddered—Period of continuous ill health.

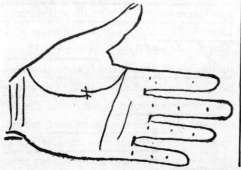

Broken but both fragments overlaying each other and joined by a short, distinct cross bar—Recovery from severe illness.

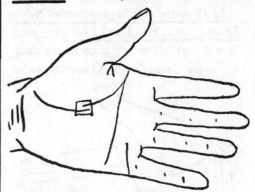

Broken within a square—Signal preservation from great bodily danger.

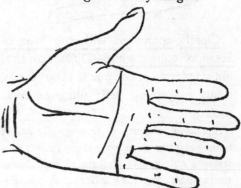

A broken end of the Line merging into the Line of Fate—Great danger to life averted by sheer good luck.

VII. CONNECTED WITH THE MAIN LINES.

(a) Directly.

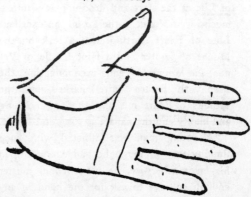

Connected in a sharp angle with the Line of Head—Prudence and average common sense.

In all matters of Angles formed by the Lines of Life, Head and Liver, the reader will find full information in my chapter on the Triangle and Quadrangle.

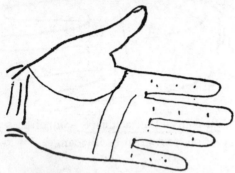

Closely connected with the Line of Head for quite a while—Diffidence; timidity; extreme sensitiveness about everything concerning self; ultra-conservatism.

This disposition may be succcessfully fought against and triumphed over if the subject possesses a strong first phalanx of the Thumb and a good, long Line of Head, as the will-power persistently exerted can do wonders.

An Only Love, with Extreme Timidity in Expressing It—A normal Line of Life with a big cross on the Mount of Venus and a Line of Head attached abnormally to the Line of Life at the start and drooping low into a much rayed Mount of the Moon; an excellent Line of Heart starting with a fork on the Mount of Jupiter and a faint Girdle of Venus; the Mount of Venus predominating; the Mount of Saturn quite marked, but the Mounts of Mars missing; the fingers long and knotty and the nails also long and brittle.

"A young man was afflicted with such timidity that, although he had everything in his favor otherwise, he never could muster enough courage to ask for the hand of any young lady. He was deeply in love with one most suitable girl whose parents would have accepted him as a son-in-law for the asking, but no consideration in the world could make him let anyone discover his love, and he remained a bachelor for the rest of his life."

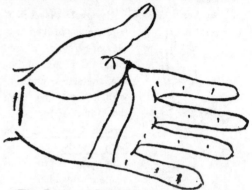

The Lines of Life, Head and Heart all joined together at the start—An omen of sudden but not necessarily imminent death.

A Wound in the Eye—A line of Heart connected with the Line of Life; and the Line of Head hardly marked at all and running down under the Line of Heart separate from the Line of Life. A prominent Mount of the Sun.

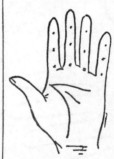

"Found in the hands of a well known Parisian artist who was wounded in the eye while fencing."

The connection of the Lines of Life and Heart with a very small or ill-formed Line of Head always indicates some accident or sudden illness. When the Mount of Jupiter is prominent it indicates rush of blood to the head. If the Mount of Saturn is prominent, a wound in the leg or legs; if the Sun is prominent, wound in the eye; if the Mount of Mercury is prominent, grave and acute bilious trouble; if the Mount of Mars is prominent, quick and fatal lung illness; if the Mount of the Moon is prominent, paralysis; if it is the mount of Venus, the trouble will be due to venereal diseases.

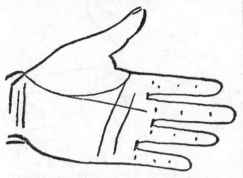

Connected with the Line of Fate, at the starting point of the latter—The subject's family has ruled his or her exist-

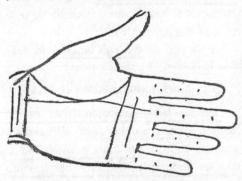

ence; if connected farther up the Line of Fate—The influence of the family will be

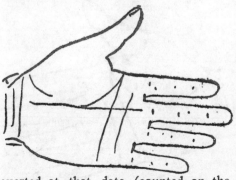

exerted at that date (counted on the

Line of Fate).

If a broken end of the Line joins the Line of Fate—Great danger to life which has been averted, or will be averted by good luck.

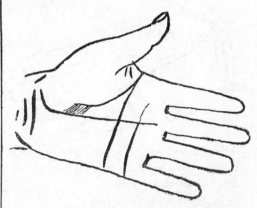

Capillaries from the termination of a short Line of Life to a Line of Fate that starts from where the Line usually terminates—Preservation from the evil consequences of a short Line of Life.

Interesting Case of Great Longevity.—A  Line of Life broken in both hands at 60 is connected at its abrupt termination, by many capillary lines, with a very fine Line of Fate which starts from the Rascette and turns around the thumb just where the Line of Life ought to have been; an excellent Line of Liver.

"An old man of 85 years of age had those markings in his hands; he had been very ill between 60 and 65, but had fully reccovered and was still feeling hale and hearty."

Connected with the Line of the Sun—at the starting point of the latter, and in both hands—Success in art, music or literature. Brilliant fortune.

The type of the subject and his or her aptitudes, judged at an earlier period of the ex-

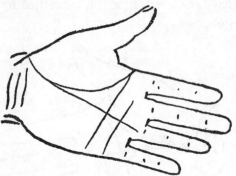

amination, will settle whether talent or money is to be read on that particular Line of the Sun. Sometimes, both.

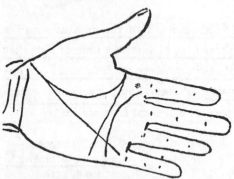

Connected with the Line of Liver— Weak general health, and with a narrow Quadrangle due to the Line of Heart curving toward the Line of Head— Fainting fits.

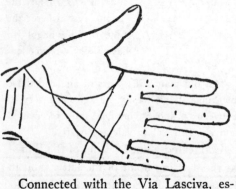

Connected with the Via Lasciva, es-

pecially if the latter starts inside the Mount of Venus and is wavy and long— Lasciviousness; often life shortened by sensual excesses.

(b) By Means of Minor Lines.

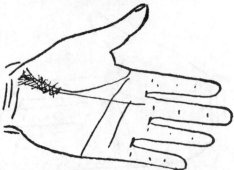

The Line, at its termination, covered up, so to speak, by a number of confused lines that connect it with a Line of Fate much cut up at the start—Poor health in old age due to privations in the early portion of the subject's life.

See Chapter on **Lines of Influence** for further indication of a similar nature.

VIII. BARS, CAPILLARIES AND SIGNS.

Capillary lines dropping from or attached closely to the Line—Weakness, loss of vitality; especially when found at the termination of the Line not in sufficient number to indicate gradual recuperation.

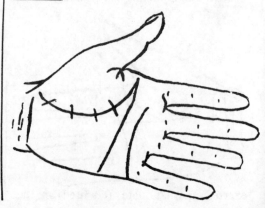

<u>Cut by thin, short lines or bars</u>—For every cut an illness of not a very grave nature.

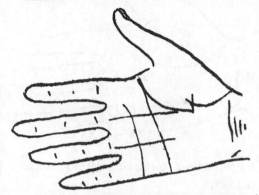

<u>A bar across the broken fragments of the Line overlaying each other</u>—Recovery from a grave illness.

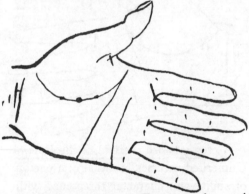

<u>Dots on the Line</u>—For every dot a minor casualty. <u>A number of dots</u>—Unsatisfactory state of health.

Tape-Worm.—<u>A blue spot on the Line of Life</u> marked the date of the trouble, and there were many confused lines at the upper part of the Mount of the Moon, much developed at that point. A poorly formed star was found amid those confused lines.

"These markings were found in the hand of a

man troubled with the tape-worm. Persistent constipation would also be indicated by either an exaggerate swelling of the upper Mount of the Moon and even the Upper Mount of Mars, or by lines and cross lines on that same place. Should a light blue spot, sometimes growing to the shape of a star or a crescent, be found there, it would indicate constipation of a persistently dangerous character."

<u>A bluish spot</u>—Typhoid, malarial or cerebral fever.

<u>Red dots, if many</u>—Feverish disposition.

<u>Black dots</u>—Always indicate grave diseases or other serious troubles. <u>A deep black dot</u>—A dangerous wound.

<u>A very deep black dot at the termination of a broken line</u>—Sudden death, often by assassination (if repeated in both hands). <u>With a dry skin and a prominent, or much rayed Mount of the Moon</u>—Grave nervous trouble.

Gout.—<u>A deep cross line on the middle Mount of the Moon. A black spot on the Line of Life at the date of the first attack. Short nails.</u>

"Both gout and rheumatism are indicated by the above line and also by a cross well marked, or by confused lines on the middle Mount of the Moon."

<u>White dots, when confirmed by ominous signs on the Line of Head</u>—Injury to the head or eyes.

<u>A triangle near the termination of the Line</u>—Loquacity and falsehood. But <u>with good Lines of Head and Heart</u>—Tact and eloquence.

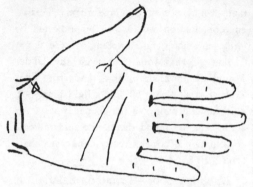

A cross at the starting of the Line, es-

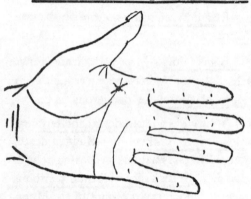

pecially if a dot be found upon it—Accident in early life.

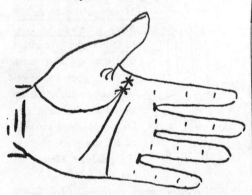

Two crosses at the beginning of the Line—In a woman, sensuousness and immodesty.

A series of crosses at the termination; in one hand only—Amiability and talent. If in both hands—Versatility never of

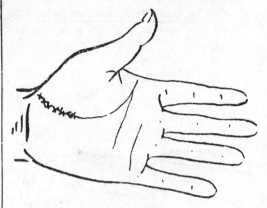

much real use to the subject; poverty in old age.

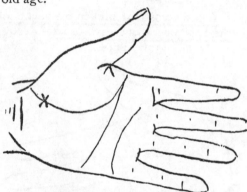

A cross toward the end of the Line—Unmerited reverses in old age; a person of ability and character threatened with ill health at that period of life.

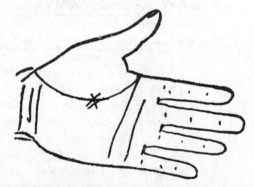

A cross cut by a downward branch—Infirmity from which the subject will not recover.

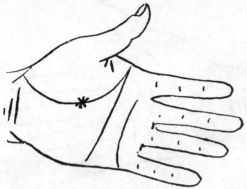

A star—An accident, a fatality in the subject's existence.

Asthma. Disease of the Spleen—A star at 70 on the Line of Life. A star on a much chained Line of Heart under the Mount of Saturn. A very narrow Quadrangle.

"A man died at 70 from what was supposed to be a liver ailment. It was proved that his very lymphatic disposition had affected his heart, through poverty of the blood, and that, besides, his breathing was difficult. Finally a swelling of the spleen was discovered as the main cause of death; it resulted from this poor quality of the blood."

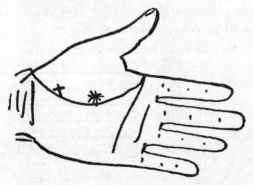

A star or cross on the Mount of Venus touching the Line—Troubles from some

member of the subject's family or some intimate friend.

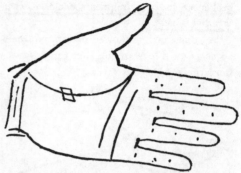

A square on or near the Line (with one exception which see below)—Always a sign of preservation from grave illness or trouble, or of rapid recuperation.

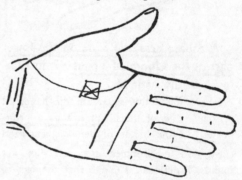

A St. Andrew's cross within a square on the Line—A great danger will be incurred, but its consequences will not be harmful.

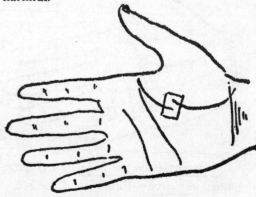

Broken inside a square—Recovery

from a serious illness.

Saved from Poisoning—A Line of Life broken at 30, both fragments enclosed within a big square.

"A young girl swallowed poison as a consequence of a love trouble, but the dose was too large and she was saved."

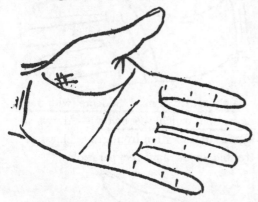

A square near the Line on the lower part of the Mount of Venus—Imprisonment, or monastic life.

I have found this square in the hands of prisoners and of nuns, but not as a prognostic. In the hands of persons sentenced (justly) to imprisonment no such sign was found. From that, I judge that the fact of being enclosed for a length of time within a small space determines the sign.

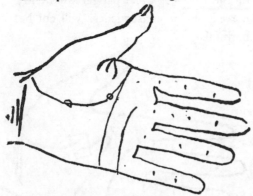

Two circles on the Line—Total blindness; one circle—Blindness of one eye.

An island at the beginning of the Line

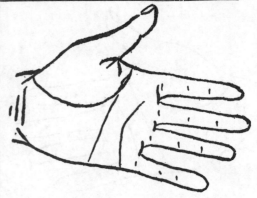

—inherited illness; sometimes mystery of birth.

Deaf and Dumb from Birth—An island at the start of a Line of Life cut by many bars and worry lines. An island at the termination of a very long Line of Head. A very high Mount of Mercury. No Line of Fate.

"A remarkably intelligent young man deaf and dumb from birth."

An island on the Line—A grave illness or serious trouble, the cause of which will be shown elsewhere on the hand; often due to some form of excess.

If there is no other indication, the island refers to some trouble of the digestive organs, as such illnesses attack more directly the very principle of animal life.

A Lethargy or Catalepsy of One Month.—The Line of Life broken at 28; the upper fragment turned up and formed an outward island extending quite a distance back. The Line of Head started under the Mount of Saturn and descended in clean broken fragments. A similar Line of Heart. No other main Line.

"A small man, Saturnian type, with knotted fingers, remained a whole month in a state of apparent death, from which he woke up a well man."

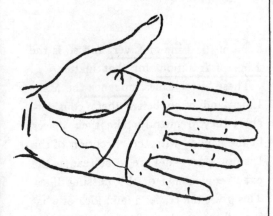

An island on the Line with the Line of Liver wavy—Biliousness and chronic indigestion.

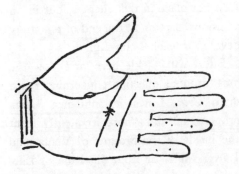

An island on the Line with a star on the Line of Head—A serious illness at the date of the island. If the star is under the Mount of Saturn—The lower limbs affected. Otherwise the general reading will be—Brain trouble or consumption according to the chirognomical indications (which see). Often small pox.

Illness Having Deprived the Subject of the Use of His Legs—An  island on the Line of Life between 30 and 42. A star on the Line of Head under the Mount of Saturn. A Girdle of Venus; a very poor Line of Head forked at an otherwise normal termination; a very poor Line of Heart.

"Several years of paralysis of the lower limbs caused by some hereditary brain trouble."

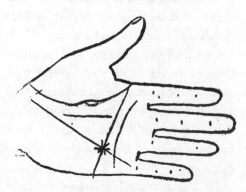

An island on the Line with a star at the connection of the Lines of Head and Liver—Sterility; difficulties in childbearing and their consequences.

Displacement of the Womb.—An island on  the Line of Life between 35 and 45; the lower portion of the Mount of the Moon much rayed and crossrayed. A poor Line of Heart.

"Found in the hands of a lady who had suffered for many years from a displacement of the womb. The trouble had affected her general health, especially the functions of the heart."

LINES OF INFLUENCE IN GENERAL.

Besides the Fourteen Main Lines enumerated in the chapter on the Map of the Hand and each of which is the object of a separate study, there are, in the majority of hands, a certain number of minor lines, almost infinite in their variety and seeming to defy all orderly classification and logical reading. I do not pretend to catalogue and interpret them all in this work; but several hundreds of those most frequently met with I shall group, describe and read to the best of my ability, basing myself upon the experience of the masters and upon my own.

To begin with, I will give to these minor lines the generic and general name of Lines of Influence; subdividing them at once into Sister Lines, meaning those that accompany a main line for a stretch without even touching it, and Cross Lines or Lines of Influence proper.

In the first category belong some of the Main Lines themselves; and later I shall expatiate at leisure upon this fact which I consider as one of the essential principles of intelligent, easily legible Palmistry. For the present, let it suffice for me to state that the Line of Mars is the Sister Line of the Line of Life; the Line of the Sun is the Sister Line of the Line of Fate; the Via Lasciva is the Sister Line of the Line of Liver, and so is the Line of Intuition, for that matter.

These Sister Lines influence the Main Lines and often better them considerably; they frequently take their places in the hands—with the exception of the Line of Mars—and are to be read as the exact equivalents of the missing lines. This gives the reader a faint idea of what is really meant by Influence Lines.

Now there are—especially on the Mounts—a number of shorter, less important Sister Lines influencing, completing, sustaining, seldom hurting the Main Lines; the exact reading of these I do not place in this chapter, but in an additional section at the end of the study devoted to each Main Line.

But I will tackle here and now the most arduous question concerning those many Cross Lines or Influence Lines proper, that start more frequently from the inside of the Mounts of Venus and Lower Mars, or from the Line of Life, and reach various points in the hand. They have been called, by recent authors, Worry Lines, and Desbarrolles has occasionally mentioned them as Lines of Sorrow ("Lignes de chagrin"), without attempting, however, to group them under any special head. Other Lines of Influence start from the other side of the hand, from the Mounts of the Moon and

Upper Mars. There are comparatively few of them, and, as they generally terminate at, or across, the Lines of Fate or the Sun, they will be properly read in the additional sections following the study of these lines.

One word more, before plunging in medias res and it is a word of encouragement as well as warning to the beginner.

"Some hands will present to your inspection an extraordinary number of those lines, almost taking your breath away, as if puzzling your brain before an illegible scroll. In such cases, all that can—and must—be done is to cut the Gordian Knot, and to make a selection of a limited number of lines, longer, clearer and more significant than the others; those you will read with prudent care. The rest will be noticed in bulk by simply jotting down in your notebook: ultra-nervous temperament."

I have something more to say yet before I raise the curtain that is to reveal to us so many interesting things—for in the Influence lines lie most of the exact details as to facts, events, past and future, with their approximate dates, that Orthodox Palmistry can furnish us with. Some of these lines, although long and sufficiently deep to deserve a reading, may be broken on their course, and the first impulse of the novice will probably be to discard them at once, on that account. This would be a great mistake, however, for the influence thus revealed has existed or will exist just as truly as if the Line was perfect all through; only you will have to add to its reading that the influence has not existed—or is not to exist—continuously, but by fits and starts, so to speak, and will let go its hold at times. Kindly bear this in mind when studying, with close attention, this first—and main—department devoted to the Lines of Influence.

LINES OF INFLUENCE FROM THE MOUNT OF VENUS,

THE LOWER MOUNT OF MARS, OR THE LINE OF LIFE.

To make reference easier and quicker, I have divided these Influence Lines, so very important to locate and read properly, into Two Divisions, each one of them subdivided, as follows:

I. Lines of Influence inside of the Mounts of Venus or Lower Mars.

a. Concentric to the Line of Life.

b. Cross Lines.

II. Lines of Influence from the Mounts of Venus or Lower Mars, or the Line of Life.

a. Ending within the Triangle and cutting no main line.

b. Ending on one of the other Mounts.

c. Merging into or just cutting one or more of the other Main Lines.

d. Starting from a sign.

e. Ending in a sign.

f. Starting from a sign and ending in a sign.

I. Lines of Influence inside of the Mounts of Venus and Lower Mars.

a. CONCENTRIC TO THE LINE OF LIFE.

For Main Line Concentric to the Line of Life, see the chapter on the Line of Mars, and the Map of the Hand.

Other concentric lines, further inside the Mounts of Venus and Lower Mars. Influences of persons of the other sex upon the subject. The stronger and

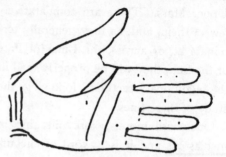

A line starting with several branches

longer the Lines and the nearer to the Line of Life, the more powerful these influences.

A line pretty far down the Mount of Venus, running parallel to the Line and rising to the Lower Mount of Mars— the person in whom the subject is interested will drift away more and more.

b. CROSS LINES.

A line from the Line to the Lower Mount of Mars. (In a woman's hand), unfavorable attachment in early life having caused great sorrow to the subject.

from the Line and terminating on the Lower Mount of Mars—Repeated persecutions worrying the subject (a woman) through the passionate nature of the man in the case.

I am bound to state that the two observations above have never been verified by me personally, and that Desbarrolles and the trustworthy ones among modern Palmists have not given them any value. The many wrinkles at that particular place in the hand, determined by the constant activity of the thumb, although they doubtless have a signification of their own, are yet unexplained satisfactorily. The lower Mount of Mars, at its best, means resignation, persistency; and at its worst, stubborn obstinacy. Logically, all lines from it ought to be interpreted with those general meanings ever in mind

II. Lines of Influence from the Mounts of Venus or Lower Mars, or the Line of Life.

a. ENDING WITHIN THE TRIANGLE AND CUTTING NO MAIN LINE.

In general, Lines cutting the Line of

Life from the Mounts of Venus or

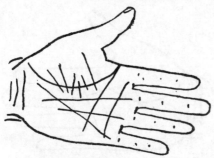

Lower Mars, when they do not cross any other line than the Line of Life—Interference of relatives.

A number of those lines—Nervous nature—worried about trifles.

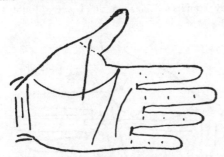

A deep line from the second phalanx of the thumb across the Mount of Venus and just cutting the Line—Great sorrow from the death or faithlessness of some one much loved.

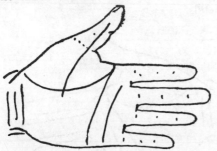

If this Line comes from the first phalanx of the thumb—Death from a metallic weapon (sword or dagger).

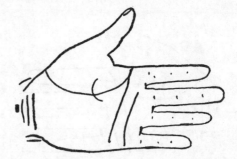

A semi-circular Line just crossing the Line of Life—Sudden grave illness or even death.

b. CONNECTING WITH ANY OF THE OTHER MOUNTS.

General Indication of Importance.—Besides the various readings that will be found under this head there is a much wider one, very difficult and delicate in its application, which may be defined as follows:

Lines of Influence from the Mounts of Venus or Lower Mars to any of the other Mounts, are quite frequently to be interpreted as pointing out the type—the astral type—of the person whose influence has been, is or will be exerted upon the subject. Now, these astral types have all been described in a special chapter entitled Signatures of the Mounts. This most interesting element of knowledge has to be used with extreme prudence, as it is closer to the occult than anything else, perhaps, in Palmistry. Here again, I must ask the examining student not to speak rashly and not to depend upon the inspection of the Lines. His chirognomic work, if conscientious and thorough, will be his only guide when attempting to find the physical type of the influence acting upon the subject.

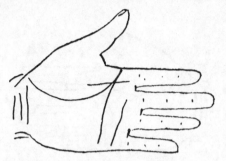

A Line to the Mount of Jupiter—Ambition, egotism, success; higher progress in one's position.

Strengthened if it ends with a star on the Mount of Jupiter; weakened or an-

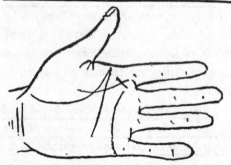

nulled if crossed by a bar, or some other minor line or, worse still, a cross.

Although this line may (and probably will) cut the Line of Life at a very early stage, its meaning will apply not to the childhood of the subject, but to his, or her, general career.

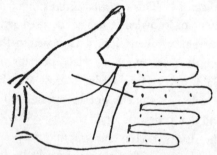

A Line to the Mount of Saturn.—Accident from a quadruped or vehicle; will prove fatal if the Line ends with a fork.

Modern Palmistry includes in this indica-

tion all kinds of vehicles, even to cable-cars, trolley-cars, and railroads.

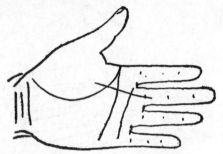

A Line cutting the root of the second finger.—Danger in child-bearing; womb troubles in general.

Generally confirmed by a star at the connection of the Lines of Head and Liver and by confused Lines on the Lower Mount of the Moon.

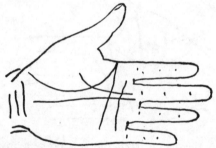

A Line to the Mount of Saturn, acting as a sister line to the Line of Fate.—Increase of wealth, due to the subject's efforts, assisted by relatives or intimate friends.

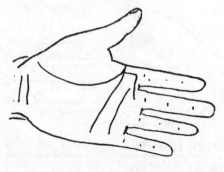

A Line from the Line of Life going

straight up the Mount of Jupiter then curving toward the Mount of Saturn, where it ends—Deep religious feeling in early life; also found in the hands of ambitious and somewhat worldly ecclesiastics.

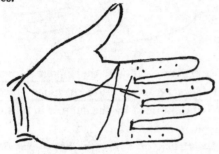

A Line to the Mount of Saturn, ending in a fork—Unhappy marriage.

This is to be taken in connection with other signs (which see); otherwise the above reading obtains.

A Line from the Mount of Venus cutting a small upward branch of the Line of Life and ending on the Mount of Saturn—Divorce.

It is more usual for this line to end under or even upon the Mount of Mercury, when it also means legal separation or divorce, more especially if it cuts a Line of Union.

A clear, straight Line from the Mount of Venus to the Mount of the Sun—Celebrity or wealth, or both, coming to the subject in accordance with his special capacities, aided by his family or

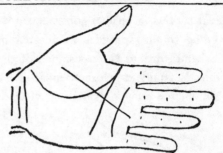

close friends.

Be sure that it is not a regular Line of the Sun.

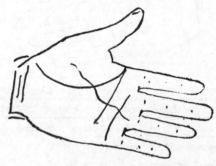

An indistinct or wavy or broken line from the Mount of Venus to the Mount of the Sun—Obstruction to the possible celebrity or wealth of the subject according to his special aptitudes, through some defect to be found elsewhere in the hand.

In this case the subject has received the assistance of his family and friends, but has not made the best use of it, or the assistance was not very real and effective.

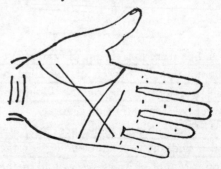

A clear, direct Line from the Mount of Venus to the Mount of Mercury—

Great success in business or science (according to the aptitudes manifested in the hand), due to the assistance of the subject's family or close friends.

Be sure this is not a regular Line of Liver.

An indistinct, or wavy or broken Line from the Mount of Venus to the Mount of Mercury—Obstruction to success in business or science (according to the special aptitudes of the subject).

Here again he did not make the most of the opportunities offered him by his family or close friends, or their assistance was not worth much.

A line from the Mount of Venus cutting an upward branch of the Line of Life and terminating on the Mount of Mercury—Separation or divorce.

A Line cutting the Lines of Fate, Head and the Sun and ending on the Upper Mount of Mars—A wound at the date marked on the Line of Life; probably a wound inflicted by a relative or

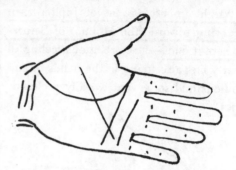

dear friend. Should the Upper Mount of Mars be exaggerate or much lined, Wound inflicted by the subject in a fit of anger.

Description of a Person Who Is the Object of a Fatal Love. —A very deep Line of Influence from the Mount of Venus, cutting an upward branch of the Line of Life and ending on the Mount of Mercury after cutting all the principal lines.

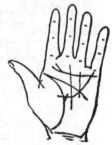

"A fatal love ruining the subject's life, especially after a separation from the loved one. The subject—a man—was infatuated with a woman of the Mercurian type."

Minor Children Financially Ruined by the Death of Their Father on Account of the Law Suit of One of His Lady Loves Against His Estate. — A fairly good Line of Life; a good Line of Head connected with the Line of Life; a Line of Influence starting from the

Mount of Venus, cutting at 25 years old an upward branch of the Line of Life; then islanded, then starred as it crossed the Line of Fate and finally ended on the Mount of Mercury.

"A young musician, friend of Desbarrolles, was despoiled of his father's fortune by a law suit won by one of his late father's mistresses. The fact of the Line of Influence ending on the Mount of Mercury pointed out the type of woman, who was a decided Mercurian."

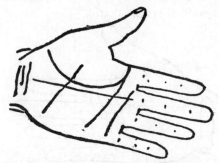

A Line cutting the Line of Fate and ending on the Mount of the Moon—Misfortune through interference of persons of the opposite sex.

c. MERGING INTO OR JUST CUTTING OTHER MAIN LINES

Projected Guilty Intrigue Threatened to End in a Catastrophe. —A very straight and deep Line of Influence starting from an island on the Mount of Venus cuts a star on the Line of Life at 30 and ends at the Percussion of Mars after cutting a star at the connection

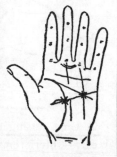

of the Lines of the Head and the Sun. A double Girdle of Venus. A Line of Fate stopped short by the above Lines of Influence and resumed only after 40.

"A handsome woman consulted Desbarrolles, who told her that she was about giving way to a hysterical and guilty love which, he knew, would end in a terrible catastrophe in which her good name, her future, and even her reason, would become involved. She acknowledged that she could not resist the temptation to abandon an excellent husband for the sake of a very young man who, up to

that time, was not even cognizant of her passion for him."

A Line cutting the Line of Life and merging into the Line of Fate—Relatives or close friends will seriously inter-

fere with the subject's career. Is sometimes read to indicate the exact date of a serious union of the subject.

A Line cutting the Line of Life and just cutting the Line of Fate—Relatives will oppose the subject in business and worldly affairs, and often force him, or her, to give up the career they are best fit for.

Seduction by a Married Man.—An elongated island beginning on the Mount of Venus cut the Line of Life at 18 and after touching the Line of Heart merged into the Line of Fate on the Mount of Saturn. A similar island on an otherwise good Line of Fate.

"A young girl had been led astray, at 18, by a wealthy married man, who remained a long time her protector. The fact was repeated twice in the hand."

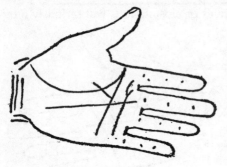

A Line terminating at the Line of Head.—Relatives will interfere with the freedom of the thoughts and opinions of the subject.

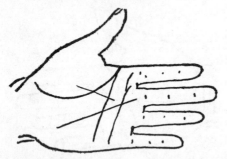

A Line cutting the Line of Life and Head.—Head or brain troubles; generally due to sorrow or vexations from relatives, who may sometimes be right in their actions toward us.

Omen of an Unfortunate Marriage.—Two lines of influence from the Mount of Venus, cut upward branches of the Line of Life at five years' distance and ended within the Quadrangle after cutting the Line of Heart. The Line of the Sun was broken and inter-

rupted between these two lines of influence.

"A young girl had a suitor to her hand. Desbarrolles foretold her that if she married him she would be separated legally within 5 years and that, at the time, her husband would undergo a dishonorable trial; the facts happened as prognosticated."

A Line cutting the Line of Life and terminating at the Line of Heart—Heart disease due to persecution or unfaithfulness of relatives or very close friends.

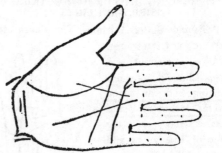

A Line cutting the Lines of Life and Heart—Interference of relatives in the subject's affections.

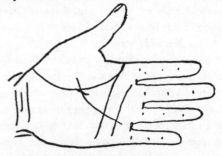

A Line cutting an upward branch of the Line of Life and also the Lines of

Head and Heart—Troubles in married life, culminating in legal separation or even divorce. If it cuts also a Line of Union—The divorce is sure to take place.

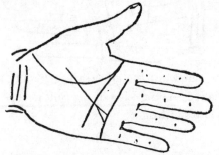

A Line to the Line of Heart terminating in a fork—Separation or divorce.

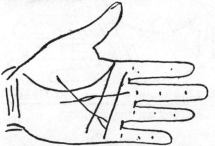

A Line to the Line of Heart terminating in a fork with an island on the Line of Fate—Guilty intrigue resulting in scandal and divorce.

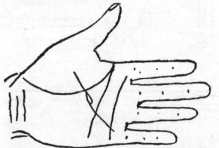

An island on a Line from the Line of Life to the Line of Heart—A guilty love affair fraught with the most serious consequences.

A Line merging into the Line of the Sun—Assistance of one's relatives in the

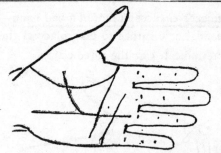

struggle for life; generally success and good reputation.

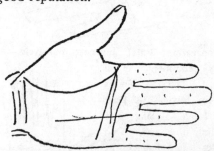

A Line from near the starting point of the Line of Life cutting the Line of the Sun—Troubles or loss of money, in early life, due to the financial ruin or disgrace of the subject's parents.

Loss of Fortune of the Parents in the Early Life of the Subject.—A star on the Line of Fate at 5 years old; about the same date a Line of Influence cut the Line of Life and ended after cutting the Line of the Sun. But the Lines of Fate went up straight and  fine from the star on, ending in a triple fork on the Mount.

"Dr. Toisac, a famous Paris physician, had great difficulty in obtaining an education, his parents having lost all their money when he was a child. However, by his own unaided efforts he became famous and wealthy."

A Line cutting the Line of the Sun—Interference of relatives spoiling the

subject's chances in life; in a bad hand—
Scandal or disgrace to take place at the
date indicated at the intersection.

Separation; Fatal Journey; Paralysis.—A
very prominent, much
rayed Lower Mount
of the Moon. A Line
of Head sloping and
ending in a star. <u>Two
Lines of Influence</u> at
5 years' distance cut-
ting upward branches of
the Line of Life and
both ending after cutting
the Line of Head.

"A lady chiromant, met in Egypt. The
marks on the lower Mount of the Moon indicated a kind of paralysis special to women.
The two Lines of Influence referred to an unfortunate marriage and to a separation from
that husband. She had thus been doubly
warned."

<u>A Line from the Mount of Venus cut-
ting an upward branch of the Line of</u>

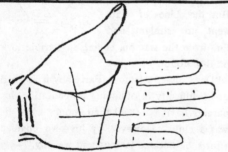

<u>Life and ending at a line of the Sun</u>—A

law suit won; the adversary generally a
relative. If the Line of the Sun is cut—
A law suit lost.

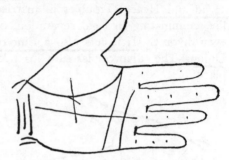

<u>A Line cutting a Line of Union</u>—
Divorce against the subject.

An island on a line cutting a line of
Union—A divorce pronounced against
the subject who has had some guilty love
affair.

<u>A Line from the Mount of Venus, cut-
ting an upward branch of the Line of
Life and merging into a prong of a
forked Line of Union</u>—A sure divorce
decided in favor of the subject.

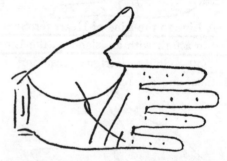

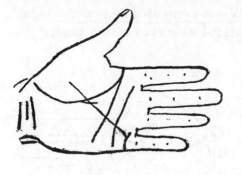

d. STARTING FROM A SIGN.

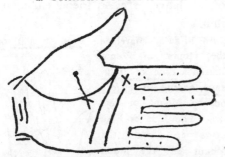

A Line starting from a dot on the Mount of Venus and cutting a small upward branch of the Line; on the Mount of Jupiter, a clear well formed cross—A love marriage sure to end in separation

Unfortunate Marriage; Illicit Attachment; Death of the Object of This Love; Two Law Suits. — An enormous Mount of Jupiter with a very hollow palm. A line of influence starting from the Mount of Venus and ending in a star on the lower Mount of Mercury confin-

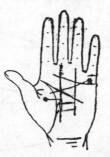

ing to the upper Mount of Mars. An island on the Line of Fate cut at the top by an influence line starting from a star on the Mount of Venus at 28. A deep dot on the marriage line, two lines of influence starting from the Line of Life and each cutting a small upward

branch at 30 and 40 respectively. A beautiful Line of Fate after the island is cut by a number of bars on the Mount of Saturn. The Line of the Sun remarkably fine.

"A lady of very high station married at eighteen to a worthless spendthrift. He was a Martian and an officer. (See first Line of Influence for the type.) She loved another man, who died. She was legally separated from her husband and later had to fight a long law suit to save a portion of a large inheritance."

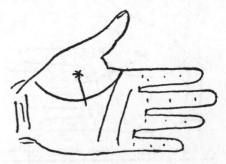

A Line from a star on the Mount of Venus just cutting the Line of Life— The death of a relative or close friend at the date indicated on the Line of Life.

Widowhood. —A hand with good lines, all there, but with a deep black dot on a Line of Union, and with a Line of Influence starting from a star on the Mount of Venus and cutting the Line of Life at 30.

"Desbarrolles met one day on the boulevard in Paris a friend he had not met for some time. The latter confided to him that he had married a woman who rendered his life unbearable and that he had decided to break the tie. As there was no divorce allowed in France at that time and as, on the other hand, he was very fond of his little girl—the only issue of this marriage—he had almost decided to gather all the money he could and to leave the country with his child. Desbarrolles asked permission to look into his hands, and saw in both the above signs of widowerhood to occur within two years. He begged his friend to postpone all action for awhile so as to avoid the unpleasant scandal connected with it. He obeyed the suggestion, and two years later he was a widower."

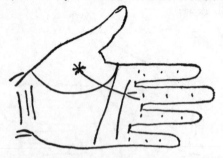

A Line starting from a star on the Mount of Venus and ending in a fork on the Mount of Saturn—Unfortunate marriage, the subject's spouse either dies or becomes insane.

Death of Husband in a State of Insanity After an Unfortunate Marriage.—From a star on the Mount of Venus started a Line of Influence cutting the Line of Life at 25 and ending in a fork on the Mount of Saturn. Another line across from the Line of Life to  the Mount of Jupiter, forming a big cross with a line from the side of the hand to the Mount of Saturn.

"A young lady had married an old man, who had died insane through the morbid excess of his love for his bride. Ambition alone had induced her to marry him."

A Line from a star on the Mount of

Venus to the Mount of the Sun—Quarrel following as a consequence, the death

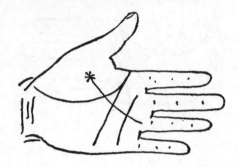

of a relative or close friend ending in ruin.

An Ill-Fated Marriage.—From a star on the Mount of Venus started a Line of Influence, ending in a fork on the Mount of Saturn. The Line of Fate came up from the Mount of the Moon first starred, then broken.

"A young woman had married a comparatively old man, who had died insane; later she had herself an affair of the heart which for a time ruined her prospects. Finally her life resumed a smooth course."

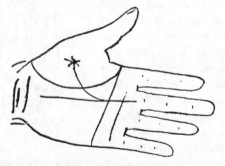

A Line from a star on the Mount of Venus joining and merging into the Line of Fate—The above quarrel will end in good fortune.

Double Inheritance Through Deaths at Short Intervals.—A Line of Fate and a Line of the Sun both starting at 30 years old. The first is met at the start by a Line of Influence from the Mount of Venus, starred twice inside the Mount.

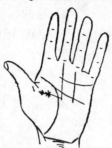

"Two successive deaths, at six days' distance, bring two large fortunes to a young man whose life until then had been far from prosperous."

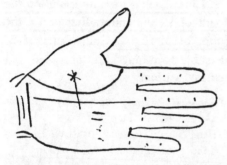

A Line from a star on the Mount of Venus cuts the Line of Fate—The death of a relative or close friend seriously affects the subject's career.

Widowhood. Many Troubles. Brilliant Future.—A very poor Line of Fate up to 17. A line of influence starting from a star on the Mount of Venus cut the Line of Life at 28; and also cut a Line of Fate which ended as it met the Line of Head. A fine Line of

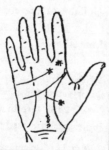

the Sun starting from the Lower Mount of the Moon came up unbroken to 40, broken again at 44; was finally resumed and rose, quite brilliant, into the Mount of the Sun. A star on the Mount of Jupiter; a star also at the start of the Line of Heart.

"A lady whose youth, up to 17 had been very poor had married well at that age. Her husband had died when she was 28 leaving her penniless, although he had been supposed, for years, to be one of the richest men in Paris. Fortunately almost at once she had become acquainted with a rich foreigner, but, as she was about marrying him, there had been opposition on the part of his family. Finally, after many worries, they had been married, and since then she had known none but prosperous days, as her second husband was both very wealthy and very devoted.

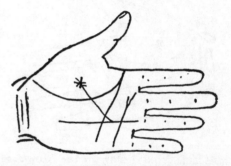

A Line from a Star on the Mount of Venus merging into a good Line of the Sun—Increase of fortune through the death of a relative or close friend.

Fatality Having Ended in Financial Success.—A line of influence starting from an island on the Mount of Venus cut an upward branch of the Line of Life and merged into an extremely fine Line of the Sun, which was starred at its connection with the Line of Heart.

"The death of her lover who had left a lady a large fortune was the cause of a law-suit which she won, thus becoming wealthy. The star on the Line of Heart then indicated sorrow but not financial disaster."

Inheritance. —A line of influence from a star on the Mount of Venus blending into a fine Line of the Sun at the beginning of the latter in the Triangle.

"A young man had lost his mother when he was 3 years old— the date of the cutting of the Line of Life—and had inherited from her a large fortune."

A Line from a star on the Mount of Venus cutting the Line of the Sun— Loss of money as a consequence of the death of a relative or close friend.

A Line starting from a star on the Mount of Venus and cutting a short upward branch of the Line of Life—Law suit as the consequence of the death of a relative or close friend. When cutting the Line of the Sun—Loss of a law suit. When merging into the Line of the Sun —The law suit won. Also a prognostic

of inheritance. The law suits above mentioned generally result from quarrels about the estate left by the deceased.

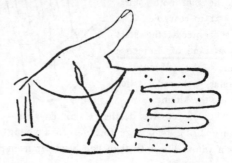

A Line starting from an island on the Mount of Venus and ending under the Mount of Mercury—Guilty intrigue of the subject ruining his prospects, at least for a time.

Temporary Insanity Caused by a Great Love.— A normal Line of Head widely forked at the termination. A line of influence from an island on the Mount of Venus shows a deep black dot as it crosses the Line of Heart on its way to joining a sloping Line of Union. A line connects this black dot with a star at the end of the upper prong of the Line of Head.

"Some time before 30 a young man suffered deeply in his love for a married woman. His grief acted for a while on his brain. The fork at the termination of the Line of Head indicates how easily he was deceived."

A Line starting from an island on the Mount of Venus, cutting an upward branch of the line of Life and merging into the Line of the Sun—Guilty intrigue with law suit and final success for the subject.

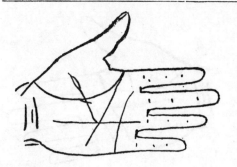

Fame and Success Due to Great Love-Sorrow. — From an island on the Mount of Venus a Line of Influence cut an upward branch of the Line of Life and ended at the starting point of a fine Line of the Sun, going up from the Line of Head. A Line of Union  curved abruptly down to the Line of Heart.

"A man of great talent had seen a guilty intrigue, upon which he had staked his whole life, broken by an unavoidable separation. His grief had induced him to greater efforts in his profession and he had become famous and wealthy."

e. TERMINATING IN A SIGN.

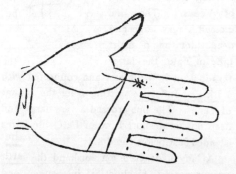

A Line from the Mount of Venus to the Mount of Jupiter ending in a star— Ambition crowned with brilliant success.

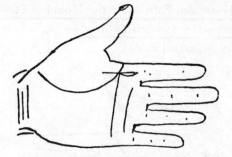

A Line to the Mount of Jupiter ending there in an island—Severe illness of the respiratory organs.

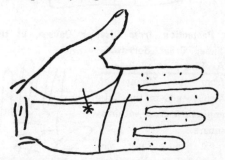

A Line across the Line of Fate terminating in a star within the Triangle—A serious loss of money.

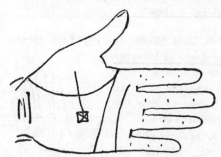

A Line from the Mount of Venus ending inside of the Triangle in a cross within the square—A Love trouble in reality saves the subject from much greater trouble; probably from an unfortunate marriage or dishonor.

A Line islanded from the Line of Life to the connection between the Lines of

Heart and Fate under the Mount of Saturn—(In a woman's hand).—Seduction by a married man.

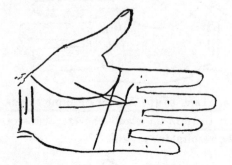

Protection from Disaster Causes, at the Time, Great Sorrow.— A Line of Influence from the Mount of Venus ends in the Triangle in a cross within a square.

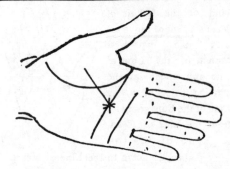

"A young lady was prevented by her family from marrying a man she cared much for He proved shortly afterwards to be a scoundrel and a cheat."

Two Love Affairs Injuring Each Other.— Two Lines of Influence, close to each other, end together at a star on a Line of Fate that stops shortly after.

"A lady was given up by an admirer who discovered that she was favoring another man at the same time; the gentleman she lost was by far the better catch."

Two lines meeting in a star on the Line of Fate—Two simultaneous love-affairs ruining each other. Has also often been found to mean: Repetition of the same trouble.

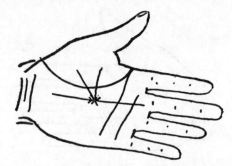

A Line terminating in a black spot or star on the Line of Head—Worries due

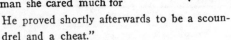

to relatives or close friends causing some sort of serious brain trouble.

A Guilty Intrigue, the Cause of a Terrible Catastrophy. —A Line of Head, normal, but terminating in a big star and connected with a Line of Influence starting from the Mount of Venus. The line crossed a very large and deep dot on a short Line of Fate, the latter

terminating in a big star and connected with a Line of Influence starting from the Mount of Venus. The line crossed a very large and deep dot on a short Line of Fate, the latter islanded just below the dot.

"A lady had given her husband the most serious reasons to show his just anger, and in the hour of discovery had been wounded by him in the head."

A Line terminating at a black spot or

disease of a grave nature.

star at the connection of the Lines of Head and the Sun—Troubles of the eyesight,

Trouble With The Eyes.—At the age of 30 a long black indentation on the Line of Life. One year later a Line of Influence from the Line of Life ended at a deep black spot at the connection of the Lines of Head and the Sun. The latter continued its way very brilliantly. For ten years after that the Line of Life was in poor shape, the indentation extending fully that time.

"Seen in the hands of the charming song writer, Nadaud. Following a long and painful period of neuralgia he had suffered in his eyesight, one of his eyes being almost lost. For fifteen years his general health had suffered from this trouble."

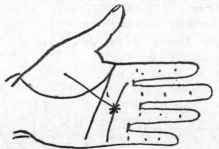

A Line terminating in a black spot or star on the Line of Heart—Worries due to relatives or close friends causing heart

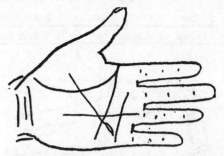

A Line cutting the Line of the Sun and terminating in an island—Disgrace and public scandal, the result of a guilty intrigue.

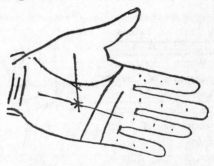

A Line cutting an upward branch of the Line of Life and terminating in a star on the Line of the Sun—Loss of a ruinous law suit; or great legal scandal.

Divorce. Law Suit. Loss.—A star with a deep dot in the center on the third phalanx of the third finger toward the fourth finger. A Line of Influence from the Mount of Venus cutting an upward branch of the Line of Life and ending in a star on the Line of the Sun, low down in the Quadrangle.

"A lady, divorced from her husband, had to fight a law suit which jeopardized her whole fortune. In fact, she never recovered from the loss."

f. STARTING FROM AND TERMINATING IN A SIGN.

A Line starting from a star on the Mount of Venus and ending in a star in-

side the Triangle—Great disaster following the death of a relative or dear friend.

Two Great Fatalities in a Woman's Hand —A Line of Influence starting from a star on the Mount of Venus cutting the Line of Life at 25 and ending in a star inside the Triangle. A second line of influence from the Mount of Venus cut the Line of Life at 30 and joined the star inside the Triangle.

"The subject—a maiden lady—lost her mother when she was 25, and her father remarried when she was 30; the stepmother rendered her life very unhappy. Hence the mark of disaster."

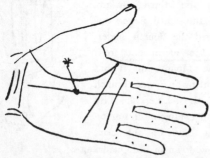

A Line starting from a star on the Mount of Venus and ending in a dot on the Line of Fate—The career of the sub-

ject is—for a time at least—wrecked through the death of some relative or close friend.

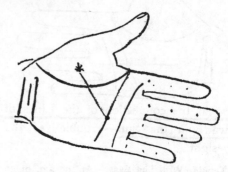

A Line starting from a star and ending in a dot on the Line of Head—Death of a relative or close friend from severe brain trouble. Sometimes the death determines brain trouble in the subject.

Grief, After Separation from, and Death of a Beloved One, Ending in Mild Insanity. — A sloping Line of Head; a Line of Influence starting from a star on the Mount of Venus, cutting an upward branch of the Line of Life and ending in a deep black dot on the Line

of Head after cutting the Line of the Sun.

"A lady over 30 years old had lost a very dear one and been financially ruined, afterwards, by a law suit concerning the will of the deceased; she became afflicted with monomania caused by an excess of grief."

An Abscess in the Head. The Consequence of the Death of a Relative Having Caused a Law Suit. —A Line of Influence starting from a star on the Mount of Venus and cutting an upward branch of the Line of Life ends at a deep spot on the Line of Head

after having cut the Line of the Sun. On the Line of Head a star within an island is also found.

"A lady suffered severely from a law suit following the death of a relative. Not only did she experience a heavy financial loss, but the trouble brought about an abscess in the head, from which, however, she recovered, as it pierced outwardly."

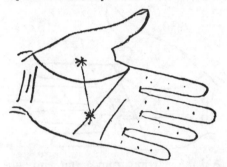

A Line starting from a star and terminating in another star on the Line of Head—Death of a relative or close friend in a state of insanity.

Brain Troubles of a very Serious Nature. Desired Career Hindered by the Subject's Family.—A thick, much rayed hand; an enormous Mount of Venus; a short thumb; square fingers; a Line of Head widely separated from the Line of Life and drooping

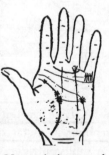

down the Mount of the Moon; it is starred just before the actual drooping begins; the medical stigmata are found on the Mount of Mercury, but crossed by one deep line; a deep Girdle of Venus cutting the Lines of Fate and the Sun, the latter ending in a triple fork. The Line of Life was starred at 8 years old and again at 23 and 25, this last star connected by a Line of Influence with the star on the Line of Head, both stars with a deep black spot at the center.

"A man had suffered from brain fever at 8 years old. At 23, he thought he had a vision that ordered him to become a priest. His family refused their consent; he finally yielded, became a physician and married. But two years later his vision came back to him, disturbing him constantly and finally causing his death in a state of furious insanity. His whole fate had been ruined by hysteria in his system (Girdle of Venus cutting too deep into both of the leading vertical lines)."

Serious and Persistent Loss of Blood from the Bowels.— A very much rayed and cross-rayed hand, a strongly marked Girdle of Venus and a badly chained Line of Heart; a Line of Influence from a star on the Line of Life, ending in a star at the termination of a sloping Line of Head.

"A very hysterically inclined woman; had suffered severely from a long bowel complaint of the gravest character. The second star placed thus on the Upper Mount of the Moon, where intestinal troubles are usually marked, had a dark, threatening color."

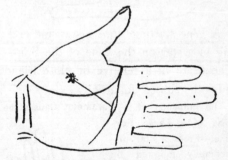

A Line starting from a star and ending in an island on the Line of Head—The death of a relative or close friend from either brain trouble or consumption; the chirognomic observations, (palms, fingers, nails), must settle which.

These three readings may often be read accurately by applying them to the subject; stating, in that case, that the death of the relative or close friend determined <u>in the subject</u> some brain trouble or even insanity.

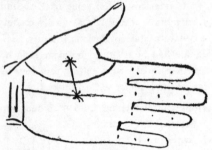

<u>A Line starting from a star and ending in a star on the Line of Fate</u>—The death of a relative or close friend ruins the subject's prospects at least for a time. The date to be read on the Line of Life.

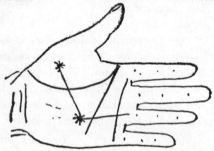

<u>A Line starting from a star and ending in a star on the Line of the Sun</u>—The death of a relative or close friend ruins the subject financially.

The Influence of a Paramour Causes the Loss of a Large Fortune.—From a <u>star</u> immediately followed by an island on the Mount of Venus <u>starts a Line of Influence</u> which cuts an upward branch of the Line of Life and ends in a star on the Line of the Sun in

the Quadrangle.

"Found in the hand of a lady who was despoiled of an inheritance that should have come to her from a near relative. The latter died leaving all his fortune to a mistress; a law suit ensued, based upon undue influence, but it was lost by the subject. In the hand of the subject's young son the identical markings were found."

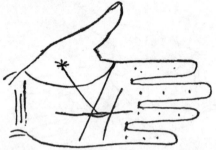

<u>A Line starting from a star and ending in an island on the Line of the Sun</u>— The death of a relative or close friend ruins the subject financially.

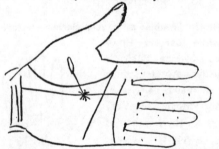

<u>A Line starting from an island and ending in a star on the Line of Fate</u>— A guilty intrigue ruins the career of the subject at least for a time.

A Line starting from an island and ending in a dot or star on the Line of Head—Guilty intrigue affecting the subject's brain.

Cruel Separation Bringing About a Happier Fate. — The Line of Heart starting from the Line of Head is crossed by a bar under the Mount of Jupiter; a square of preservation was formed around this cross by a line from the beginning of the Line of Life going up

the Mount of Jupiter, then crossing toward the Mount of Saturn, where it meets a fine Line of Fate. The fourth side of this square is formed by a good Line of Head. Inside the Mount of Venus a line of influence starting from an island cut an upward branch of the Line of Life and ended in a star on the Line of Fate. An influence line from the Mount of the Moon merged into the Line of the Sun.

"A lady was abandoned by her lover (a married man), and this was for her a great sorrow and disaster. But she was protected from the consequences of both by the coming forward of another admirer, both wealthy and constant."

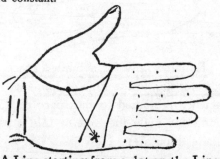

A Line starting from a dot on the Line

of Life and ending in a star on the Upper Mount of Mars—Hemorrhoids.

A Line starting from a star on the Mount of Venus and ending in a star on the Mount of the Moon—Insanity resulting from the loss of a relative or close friend.

Disastrous Death of a Near Relative.—A Line of Influence starting from a star on the Mount of Venus and cutting an upward branch of the Line of Life ended in a star on the Mount of the Moon, on a sloping Line of Head.

"A French officer lost his mother, who died insane. Besides his grief, he had to fight a law-suit about the will left by the old lady."

ADDITIONAL CASE

Grief; Lawsuit; Palpitations of the Heart. Result .—The Line of Heart chained from start to termination. A Line of Influence from the Mount of Venus, cutting an upward branch on the Line of Life, reached and just cut the Line of Heart under the Mount of Mercury.

"A friend of Desbarrolles. Tormented all his life by a wicked woman from whom he finally separated legally. Had his health ruined by his sorrow and troubles. His heart and liver had been particularly affected. The woman was of the Mercurian type."

THE LINE OF MARS—THE RASCETTE.

To complete Division One (see p. 141), I have to present here the few observations that have been gathered concerning the Sister Line of the Line of Life, called The Line of Mars—doubtless because it often starts inside the Lower Mount of Mars—and the three Bracelets of Life constituting the lower boundary of the Palm and called, together, The Rascette. These four lines have always been considered as concerning especially the Longevity of the subject or the state of his health. In fact, most of the other observations brought forward concerning these lines I have found purely traditional and difficult to explain logically; besides, I failed to find the meanings given them warranted in the few cases when they happened to come under my personal examination. Still, they are worthy of enumeration, and the student, in his diagnosis, may find them more reliable. I begin with

THE LINE OF MARS.
I. POSITION AND DIRECTION.

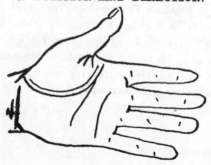

Normal.

Running close and parallel to the Line of Life, on the Lower Mount of Mars and the Mount of Venus—It corrects many of the breaks and defects of the Line of Life. It gives assurance, self-respect, and, with a good Mount of Jupiter, a desirable amount of pride. Also a promise of success and fortune when confirmed elsewhere.

Running quite parallel to the Line of Life, like the two rails of a track, especially along the latter portion of the Line of Life—Death away from one's own country. (See p. 80.)

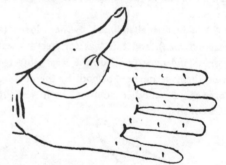

Running only for a limited space as a sister line to the Line of Life—Its influence is limited to the space of time indicated upon the Line of Life it partially duplicates.

II. CHARACTER.

Slightly more pink than the natural coloring of the skin and with a hand announcing decision and perseverance—

Of great assistance to an officer in command, or to a society leader with an important function to manage.

Too deep or broad, with red coloring—A sign of great heat and violence in sensual passions; of an easily aroused anger; of a masterful spirit. Especially so in a thick, hard hand with exaggerate Mounts of Mars and highly colored lines.

III. STARTING POINTS AND FORKS AT THE START.

At the date corresponding to its starting point—A love affair began, or is to begin.

Traditional—This is very much in the line of the observations I inserted on page 174, concerning the Lines of Influence concentric to the Line of Life (which see).

IV. TERMINATION AND FORKS AT THE TERMINATION.

Accompanying only the final portion of the Line of Life, in a hand containing indications of a very violent nature—Tendency to murder. Especially if the Line is deep and red.

Terminating in a fork, one prong of which enters the Mount of the Moon—

Intemperance of every kind, due to a

superabundance of the animal nature; often amounts almost to brutal insanity.

Terminating in a fork, one prong of which enters the Mount of the Moon and ends in a star—Alcoholic intemperance. Add to this a black spot on the Line of Head—Death from delirium tremens or alcoholic insanity.

V. BREAKS AND SIGNS.

These must be read as Breaks and Signs in the Line of Life, and always in connection with it.

SPECIAL OBSERVATONS.

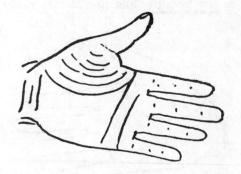

Other sister lines of the Line of Life, further inside the Mount of Venus—Influences of other people over the subject's life. The intensity and duration of this influence reckoned in accordance to the length, depth and nearness of these lines to the Line of Life..

This belongs more properly to the chapter on Lines of Influence within the Mounts of Venus and Lower Mars (pp. 173-4).

Other indications relating to the duration of life and to its happiness or ill-luck are found in these three lines on the wrist, called the Bracelets or Restreintes (because they restrict or limit the hand), and the combination of which constitutes

THE RASCETTE.

Desbarrolles says of the Rascette:

"It is traced in that portion of the hand which is devoted to material instincts, and therefore all lines inside the palm that droop down to it are debased thereby and lose much of their intellectual and moral meaning."

This will be found confirmed in my Chapter on the Line of Head. Remember that this does not apply to such lines as rise from the Rascette, as they really

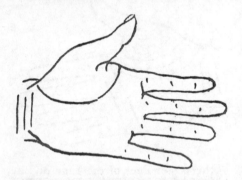

indicate an ennobling, not a debasing tendency.

There is a great deal here that is purely traditional and which has not been very clearly demonstrated—in my opinion. Certainly the first Bracelet is an interesting study that deserves attention; the other two, being practically out of the field over which Chiromancy concentrates its observations, may be looked upon simply as additional evidence, strengthening such indications gathered elsewhere, inside the palm.

I. POSITION AND DIRECTION.

One of these Bracelets clearly marked and unbroken—An omen of twenty-three (23) to twenty-eight (28) years of life.

Two such bracelets—Announce a life of from forty-six (46) to fifty-six (56) years.

Three such bracelets—Give promise of a life of betwen sixty-nine (69) and eighty-four (84) years.

Many works give to each of the bracelets a meaning of 30 years of life. I have never found them to exceed 26; in fact, in the hands of very old people, octogenarians, etc., I have found four bracelets; although they have not always been very visible, as, at that age, the skin is so exceedingly wrinkled all over the hand as to lend but very little reliable assistance to the inquiring palmist.

It was also believed by the old chiromants that three fine bracelets—with a poor Line of Life—meant fortune, or success, or both, but without health to enjoy them.

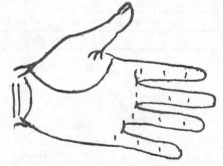

The first bracelet high on the wrist and convex in form—Troubles in the generative functions, especially in childbearing, etc.

It is of the utmost importance not to mistake the first bracelet for a deep Line of Voyage from the lower part of the Mount of the Moon to the Line of Life, or for a Line of Influence from the Mount of Venus to the Mount of the Moon. Both these indications will be found interpreted on p. 114 and p. 179 respectively.

II. CHARACTER.

The Three Bracelets very clear, well defined and colored—Health, wealth, good fortune; a smooth, easy existence.

Poorly formed—A life of extravagance, and (with other confirmatory signs) of dissipation.

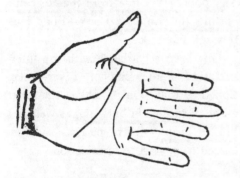

The first bracelet chained—A life of much hard work and care, but with final success crowning these efforts.

III. CONNECTED WITH THE MOUNTS.

A line from the Rascette to the Mount of Jupiter—A long and successful journey.

This line generally crosses the Mount of Venus. When it comes through the Mount of the Moon, it is most decidedly a sea voyage.

Two lines from the Rascette to the

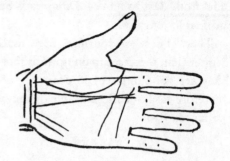

Mount of Saturn, crossing each other there—The subject will not return from one of these long journeys.

The element of ill-luck is here quite manifest.

A line from the Rascette to the Mount of the Sun—Reputation acquired through associating with people in high position met in one's travels. Also—more frequently—interpreted as "travels in tropical countries."

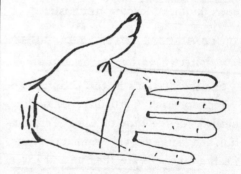

A line straight to the Mount of Mercury—Indication of sudden wealth.

It acts in that case as a sister line to the Line of Liver.

Lines from the Rascette to the Mount of the Moon—Journeys (by land, when these lines do not cross the Mount of the Moon); for every line a journey; the longer these travel lines, the longer the journeys; two such lines absolutely parallel from start to finish—Dangerous but profitable journeys.

These lines of journey are much fainter than the three main upward lines; they are quite different in character and therefore easily distinguishable by an experienced eye.

IV. BREAKS.

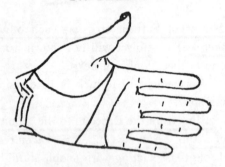

The three bracelets breaking in a point, one above the other, under the Mount of Saturn—Inordinate vanity and untruthfulness, leading to disaster.

V. CONNECTED WITH THE LINES.
Directly or by Minor Lines.

See the Sections in the Chapters devoted to each particular main line, headed, for the Line of Life, "Termination and Forks at the Termination," and, for the Lines of Fate, the Sun and Liver, "Starting Points and Forks at the Start."

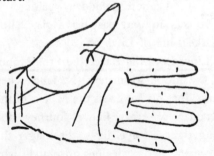

Travel lines from the Rascette, ending at the Line of Life—Death on a journey.

These lines are properly Lines of Influence, but tradition has given them this meaning, which is radically different from that logically attributed to Lines from the Mounts of Venus and Upper Mars and the Line of Life (which see).

A poor, wavy line from the Rascette, cutting the Line of Liver—Poor luck through life.

This is in accordance with my interpretation of the Line of Liver—mentioned further—which makes the latter a line of success in business, as well as a line of health—when perfect and unbarred from start to termination.

VI. SIGNS.

A cross in the center of the first bracelet, if the latter is finely shaped and unbroken—A life full of difficulties, but ending comfortably and peacefully.

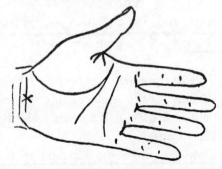

A line from the Line to the Mount of Jupiter, with a cross or angle on the first bracelet of the Rascette—Wealth coming, through a very successful journey.

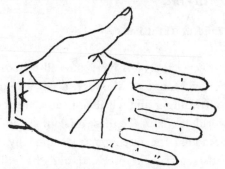

An angle at the center of the first bracelet of the Rascette—Money by inheritance and position of honor coming to the subject in his, or her, old age.

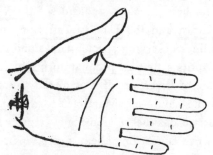

A triangle with a cross inside—Large fortune by inheritance.

A star in the middle of the first brace-

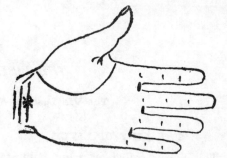

let in a good hand—Inheritance; in a bad hand—Immorality.

The five indications concerning Signs on the Rascette are so absolutely illogical, when thus giving highly satisfactory meanings to such untoward signs as crosses, angles and stars, that I must class them among purely traditional observations. They are, however fully indorsed by Desbarrolles.

As I stated above, I attach but little importance to the third bracelet, and have not absolute faith in the second. Often deep wrinkles are formed by the habitual wearing of gloves, which assume the shape (but not the meaning) of the third, and sometimes the second bracelet. But, on the other side, the first bracelet is of real value in palmistic readings.

THE LINE OF LIVER.

The Via Lasciva—The Line of Intuition.

THE LINE OF LIVER.

This line is called by many Palmists the Line of Health, and is considered by them simply as an accessory to the Line of Life. While willingly admitting that this line confirms in many instances the promise of longevity revealed in the Line of Life, and while it certainly completes the indications obtained from the third of the Chief Lines concerning the good or bad working of the digestive organs, the Line of Liver ought not to be neglected in the study of the subject's business career, for does it not terminate on the Mount of Mercury and contain all the elements already examined under the heading of this Mount and that of the fourth finger? Here and there we find in the leading chiromantic works observations that can be logically explained only by this reference to the business idiosyncrasies of the Mount of Mercury. I have simply completed these scattered indications and united them into one homogenous reading.

I have been struck by the fact that a perfect digestion and an active liver contribute greatly to clearness of thought and rapidity of action; two essential qualities for a successful business man. Hence the close connection between a perfect Line of Liver, a well-proportioned Mount of Mercury, a fairly long fourth finger and a brilliant career in the world of affairs. To these, of course, must be added the intelligence denoted by a satisfactory Line of Head, and the will-power revealed in a strong first phalanx of the thumb.

There is a second remark concerning the Line of Liver which has its natural place here. I always considered the Via Lasciva and the Line of Intuition, not as lines deserving special names and descriptions, but as peculiar forms of the Line of Liver, or—if it be already found in the hand—as sister lines to that important channel of vital fluid. However, I write concerning them under separate headings, somewhat against my better judgment and simply on account of the general use of these names, etc., by the later English palmists. Desbarrolles mentions the Via Lasciva, which he calls La Voie lactée (the Milky Way); but the Line of Intuition he treats simply as a curved form of the Line of Liver along the Percussion of the Mounts of the Moon and Upper Mars.

This will explain a few—to my mind, useless—repetitions the reader will meet with in this chapter.

I. POSITION AND DIRECTION.

Normal.

Starting from above the Rascette, not touching the Line of Life, and going

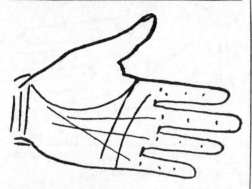

straight up to the Mount of Mercury— Longevity, good health (especially of the digestive organs); success in business.

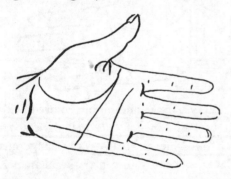

Taking its course quite near the Percussion—Sign of a changeable, ultra-nervous disposition; also of many voyages. It is often taken then for what is called the Line of Intuition, and, in fact, has very much the same meaning of "Gift of Clairvoyance," although perhaps less pronounced.

Turning a kind of semi-circle from the Mount of the Moon to the Upper Mount of Mars or Mercury—Clairvoyance. This is really the Line of Intuition (which see).

II. CHARACTER.

a. By Itself.

Entirely absent—Quick mind, alert disposition.

No biliousness, hence none of that heaviness caused by the poor working of the liver. Many palmists consider the total absence of a Line of Liver as a most favorable health indication, proceeding from the idea that "your liver is surely in perfect order when you do not notice its existence."

For years I followed this reading, but I finally accepted the Desbarrolles interpretation of "frequent headaches," as, in the majority of cases that came under my notice, I found the absence of the line to be accompanied with imperfect digestion, hence headaches.

Thick and short—Impaired digestion in old age.

This follows the above reading, as its shortness would cause it to be absent at that time of life.

Straight and very thin—Stiffness of manner.

Red throughout—Brutality and inordinate pride.

This applies to all lines.

Red at the start—Tendency to palpitations of the heart; especially if connected with the Line of Life. These palpitations will be due to poor digestion.

Thin and red about the middle—Tendency to bilious fevers.

About the middle would mean where it crosses the Line of Head; hence the feverish disposition.

Of varying colors and red where it crosses the Line of Heart—Apoplexy.

Fits of apoplexy are generally forthcoming—in subjects so predisposed by the poor quality of the blood or imperfect circulation—shortly after heavy meals; they are really determined by a faulty digestion.

Red at its termination—Chronic sick headaches.

Of a yellow color—Serious liver troubles.

It is seldom that one line only is yellow; they are generally all of that color or none at all.

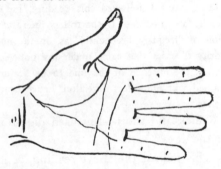

Wavy—Biliousness; in its worst form, with a damp, cold hand. Also poor success in business; and in a bad hand—Confirmatory indication of dishonesty.

b. In Combination with other Indications.

Absent, with hard hands and square-tipped fingers—Activity.

Absent, and with a developed Mount of Mercury—Vivacity in word and action. Quickness of repartee.

Straight, not joined with the Line of Life, and with a well-formed Rascette—Longevity.

Long, narrow, clear and straight, with a normal Line of Head extending clear across the hand—Good memory.

It is a well-known fact that the ab-

sence of all biliousness is a great help to persistent memory.

Long and fine with a short Line of Life—Often makes up for the insufficiency of the Line of Life.

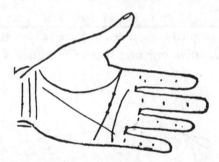

Very narrow and highly colored, with a broken Line of Life and dark spots on the Line of Head—Very dangerous fever; generally of a malarial character.

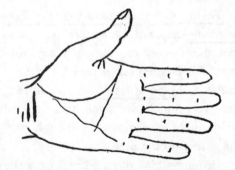

Irregular or wavy, with a poor, narrow Line of Head—Indigestion. Inferior business capacity.

Poor, with all the other lines in the

hand also feebly marked—Paralysis.

This is more positively indicated when the hand itself is paralyzed; then that line (with all others) will soon disappear altogether from the affected hand. (See p. 147.)

Poorly traced and with a narrow Quadrangle, due to the Line of Heart curving too much toward the Line of Head—Asthma and hay fever.

Wavy, with a poor Line of Head and a total absence of the Line of Heart— Weak heart. Tricky, unreliable business ways.

Long and wavy, with a similar Line of Fate and the second phalanx of all fingers rather longer than the others— Bad teeth.

Remember that the state of the teeth is marked upon the Mount of Saturn (and the Line of Fate that terminates

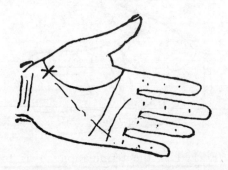

there). Bad digestion is sure to bring about the decay of the teeth, and vice versa.

A poor line, with a poor Line of Head and a cross near the termination of the Line of Life—Poor general health, especially in old age.

Deep and not extending beyond the Quadrangle, while touching both the Lines of Head and Heart on either side —Danger of brain fever.

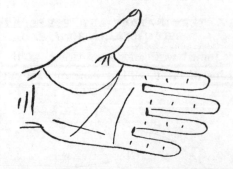

Forming a cross, with the Line of Head on the Mount of the Moon— Over-excited imagination.

This can only take place if the Line of Head droops considerably out of its normal direction, and if the Line of Liver runs comparatively close to the Percussion. Either of these displacements—taken by itself alone—would be read almost in the same manner.

III. STARTING POINTS.

Starting from the Rascette, straight and direct to the Mount of Mercury—Good digestive power. Excellent business success.

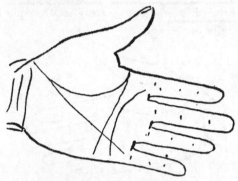

Starting from the Line of Life and with a narrow Quadrangle, due to the Line of Heart curving toward the Line of Head—Fainting fits, due to imperfect digestion.

IV. TERMINATION AND FORKS AT THE TERMINATION.

Joined with and terminating at the Line of Head, with a Line of Life cut

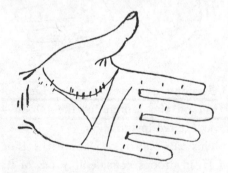

by many bars—Brain disease, brought about by a disturbed liver. It will be generally of a "melancholia" character.

Terminating on the Mount of the Sun, with a complete Rascette, well marked —Wealth.

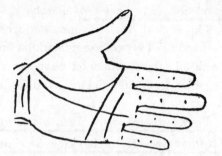

Take care not to mistake this for a Line of the Sun.

Wavy or broken, terminating on or near the Mount of the Sun, and with

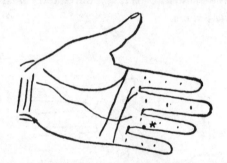

black dots or stars on the third phalanx of the third finger—Very serious fever in a tropical country.

Straight and so long that it crosses the whole of the Mount of Mercury—Longevity. Only true if the Third (lower) Angle of the Triangle is open, broad and clear.

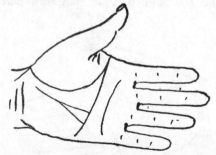

Forked at the termination so as to form a triangle with the Line of Head

—Intense love of honors and powers; great aptitude for occult sciences.

This is rather an abnormal disposition that might be dangerous for the health of the subject's brain.

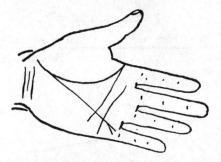

Forked on the Mount of Mercury—Languor; weakness; generally in old age.

V. BRANCHES.

Throwing branches toward the Mount

of the Sun—Changes (for the better) in one's business.

VI. BREAKS.

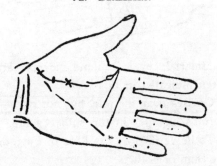

Breaks on the line, confirming breaks, bars, crosses, stars or islands on the Line of Life—As many breaks as many illnesses. Also a sign of chronic indigestion. Also indications of successive reverses in business, due to the subject's incompetence or poor health.

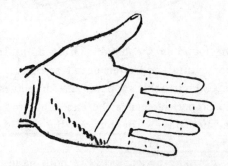

Broken in fragments arranged ladderwise—Very severe liver trouble. Succession of business losses.

Organic Trouble. Skin Disease.—A chained beginning of the Line of Life, this portion of it ending in a star with a deep, dark dot at the center. A badly chained Line of Heart. A wavy and forked Line of Head; short nails; domineering first phalanx of the thumb. The Line of Liver formed of a succession of fragments placed ladderwise.

"A young girl, after a delicate childhood, was attacked by an organic disease that left her a mark for life in the shape of an ugly skin trouble. She was irritable, despotic and not over-sincere."

VII. CONNECTED WITH THE MAIN LINES.

Forming a clear triangle, open at the base, with the Lines of Life and Head—

One of the most favorable indications to

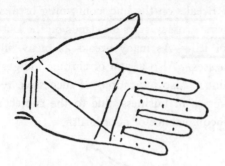

be found in the hand. Great aptitude for natural and often occult sciences.

Of course this supposes the three lines to be perfect; hence the excellent prognostic. (See Chapter on the Quadrangle and Triangle.)

Forming a clear cross in both hands, with the Line of Head on the Upper

Mount of Mars—Talent for the occult sciences.

This is still clearer when the line runs close to the Percussion. I explained this above.

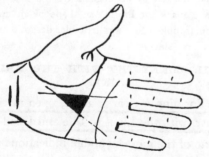

Forming a small (minor) Triangle with the Line of Head and the Line of Fate—Aptitude for the occult sciences, or the gift of intuition, and, if very straight and clear—Clairvoyance.

VIII. SIGNS.

Deep bars across the Line—As many illnesses. Weak digestion. Business re-

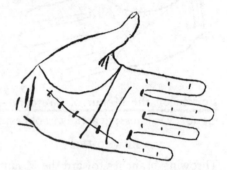

verses. The deeper the bars, the more unfavorable the omen.

Closely connected with the Line of Life, but irregular in its course, with red and bluish spots on the Line of Life —Heart disease, due to poor digestion or liver troubles.

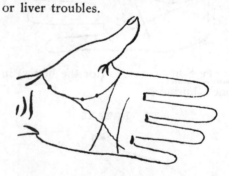

Malarial, even typhoid, fevers are often indicated in this wise.

Crosses near the line, but not on it— Serious changes in the subject's life.

To be verified on the Line of Fate, or the Sun, or both.

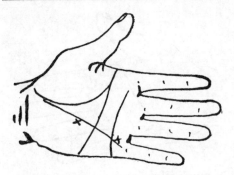

A cross toward the termination of the

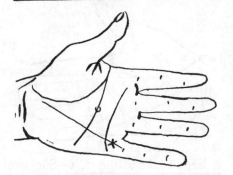

line, with a circle on the Line of Head—Blindness.

This is the sign I have met with most frequently when examining blind subjects' hands. More frequently yet, this cross is accompanied by a break of the Line of Head or the Line of Heart under the Mount of the Sun, the circle being absent.

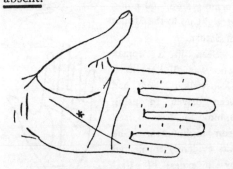

A star close to the line inside the triangle—Blindness.

A star on the line—Sterility; child-

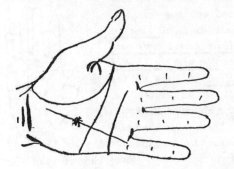

lessness; troubles connected with child-bearing. Especially so if it is found at the

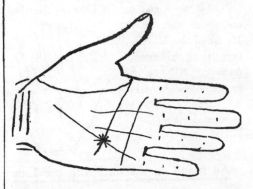

connection of the line with the Line of Head, with a Line of Life running close to the thumb. Also jaundice.

Sterility Through Torpidity of the Generative Organs.—Besides the regular star at the connection of the Lines of Liver and Head, which indicates disorder in or malformation of the generative organs, there was found a deep dot at the bottom of the Mount of the Moon.

"The owner of these markings, although well conformed, suffered from an inactivity of the organs that prevented pregnancy. This dot by itself will indicate womb troubles or, in both sexes, disease of the kidneys."

Sterility.—A Line of Life encircling a very narrow Mount of Venus and with one conspicuous island. A Line of Liver starred at its connection with the Line of Head. A cross on the Mount of Saturn. A fair Mount of the Sun.

"Seen in the hand of a woman had been brought forth successively three children who died in birth. Finally, by dint of almost incredible care, she became the mother of a strong and healthy babe."

Jaundice.—A star on the Line of Liver on the upper part of the Mount of the Moon—A jaundice of one month's duration. A black spot or dot instead of a star— A jaundice of six months' duration.

An island on the line, with the Line

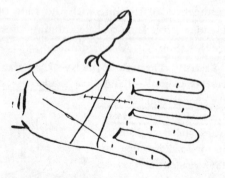

of Fate or the Line of the Sun broken or cut by a deep bar—Bankruptcy.

With many islands and narrow, fluted nails—Consumption.

This is more usually revealed by the poor shape of the Line of Head, gener-

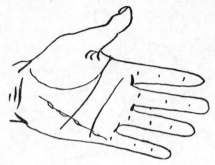

ally much islanded.

A large island at the start—Somnambulism.

Another Case of Born Somnambulism.— In the right hand, a very poor Heart Line and a Line of Liver islanded at the start, and going straight to the Mount of Mercury. In the left hand, a Line of Fate beginning with two islands forming an 8, and going straight up to the Mount of Saturn.

"Seen in a woman who was all her life a sleep-walker, and had been driven to using opium to free herself from nightmares. She was evidently tormented by an excess of astral fluid."

THE VIA LASCIVA.

I. POSITION AND CHARACTER.

Normal.

Running parallel to the Line of Liver, starting farther from the Plain of Mars

and ending on the Mount of Mercury; when traced clearly in both hands—Sensuality. Passionate thirst for money.

Wavy—Inconstancy. Ill success, often due to dissipation.

Considered as a sister line to the Line of Liver, it repairs many of its defects.

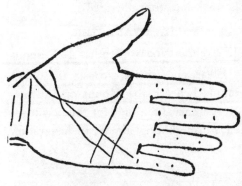

Wavy and long, starting from inside the Mount of Venus—Immorality. Life shortened by excesses.

II. TERMINATIONS AND FORKS AT THE TERMINATION.

Terminating on the Mount of Mercury—Good luck; eloquence; cleverness as a politician; generally accompanied by bad morals.

Forked at its termination—Impotence, languor; slow wasting away; generally due to excesses.

III. BREAKS AND BRANCHES.

Same meanings as those read on the Line of Liver.

IV. CONNECTED WITH THE MAIN LINES.

a. Directly.

Cutting the Line of Liver—Grave indication of liver troubles; also annihilation of the business qualities the Line of

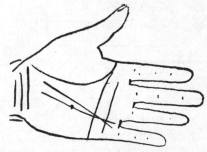

Liver may have shown up to the date of the cut. To be read in the hand of a voluptuary—Success in business destroyed by excessive love of the other sex.

b. Minor Lines.

Connected with the Line of the Sun by a line not cutting the latter—Wealth.

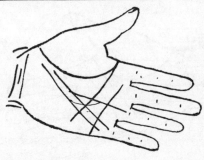

Connected with the Line of the Sun by a line cutting the latter—Heavy finan-

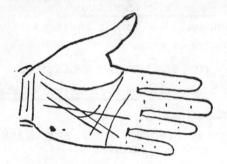

cial losses, or artistic success ruined by excessive love of the other sex.

Unexplained Pains in the Side.—A number of cross lines from the lower Mount of Venus to the Upper Mount of Mars, seemingly like a crowd of Lines of Liver and Via Lasciva.

"A lady suffered cruelly from constantly recurring abdominal pains, for which the most prominent physicians and surgeons failed to discover a cause, except that they attributed them to nervous over-excitement."

V. SIGNS.

A star—Riches, but much trouble to secure them, keep them and enjoy them; due to exaggerate influence of, or love for, the opposite sex.

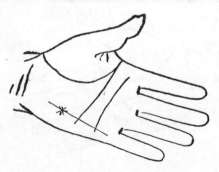

THE LINE OF INTUITION.

I. POSITION AND DIRECTION.

Normal.

Starting from the lower part of the Mount of the Moon near the Percussion,

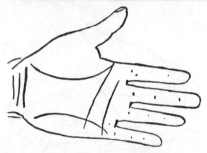

and coming up in a more or less accentuated curve to the Mount of Mercury, where it terminates also near the Percussion—A peculiar tendency to presentiments. A strong aptitude toward the occult sciences.

If found in the Left Hand only—The aptitude for occult sciences is there, inherited, but not cultivated.

II. CHARACTER.

In Combination with other Indications.

Clear, and with a cross in the Quadrangle beneath the Mount of Saturn—Very unusual aptitude for the occult sciences, amounting almost to inspiration.

This is the large, fine St. Andrew's cross called the Mystic Cross.

Clear, and with a high Mount of the Moon, more pronounced in its upper part—Mesmeric, hypnotizing power.

III. STARTING POINT.

The higher up on the Mount of the Moon is the starting point of the line, the more the subject will have his intuitive faculty under control.

IV. TERMINATION.

Terminating on the Upper Mount of Mars—Hypnotizing power of remarkable intensity.

The energy of the Upper Mount of Mars has here full sway and increases ten-fold the peculiar gift of the subject, as far as influencing others is concerned.

V. BRANCHES.

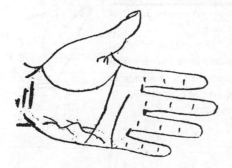

Short, wavy and branched, with the Mount of Mars exaggerated—A restless disposition, the result of ultra-nervousness. The subject will be extremely difficult to please.

VI. BREAKS.

Broken repeatedly—The intuitive tendency comes by fits and starts and cannot be relied upon.

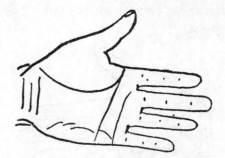

VII. CONNECTED WITH THE MAIN LINES.

a. Directly.

Forming a triangle with the Line of Fate and the Line of Head—Strong aptitude for occult sciences.

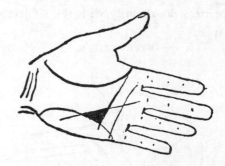

This is a form of the Minor Triangle (which find described farther).

b. By Minor Lines.

Found in both hands and crossed by Influence Lines from the Line of Life—The subject's relatives or close friends object strongly to his indulging in the

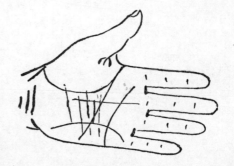

practice or even study of occult phenomena.

Found in both hands and crossed by
Lines of Influence from the Mount of
the Moon that also cross the Line of
Fate—These tendencies or aptitudes will
interfere disastrously with the subject's
career.

VIII. SIGNS.

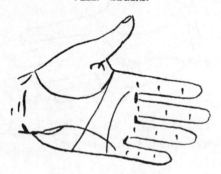

Starting in an island—Somnambulism; clairvoyance.

There are no stronger indications in
the hand concerning clairvoyant powers.
Seen more frequently, however, in the
hands of habitual sleep-walkers.

A Born Somnambulist.—A sloping Line of
Head. A large island at
the beginning of a very
clear and long Line of
Intuition.

"In the hand of a
young man who had
always been a sleep-
walker and was, besides,
prone to nightmares and
presentiments."

Extra Lucid Medium.—A line of Head
sloping far down into
the Mount of the Moon,
where it ends in a star.
A remarkably clear and
complete Line of Intui-
tion. A poor Line of
Heart.

"The excess of astral
fluid in a woman me-
dium had a tendency to
drive her gradually to
insanity."

THE LINE OF HEAD.

I. POSITION AND DIRECTION.

a. By Itself.

Normal.

Starting from the Line of Life at its beginning, rising ever so slightly toward the Line of Heart under the second

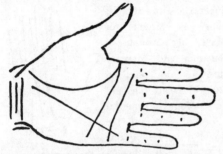

finger, and then increasing the space between them until it terminates on approaching the Percussion, which it must not reach—A will-power and an intellect fully up to, if not above, the average.

Straight and stiff like a bar from the Line of Life clear to the Percussion—Avarice; selfishness; cleverness in worldly matters; no idealism.

Running quite close to the Line of Life for a while—Brain fever.

It must keep absolutely distinct from the Line of Life to have this meaning.

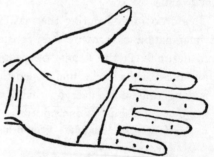

Running too close to the Line of Heart—Tendency to asthma or hay-fever.

This determines a Narrow Quadrangle, a sure indication of oppression—in matters of health, and of meanness—as a moral tendency.

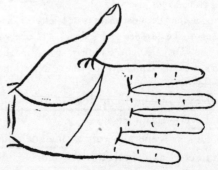

Slightly sloping down the Mount of the Moon—Intellectual faculties influenced by imagination.

Sloping deep into the Mount of the Moon—Exaggerate spiritualism; morbid superstition. More generally nervous troubles.

This drooping—denoting the mastery of imagination over matter—is considered desirable in the hands of people whose life-work is intellectual or artistic; it is dangerous in the everyday hand, as it will beget a disgust of one's duty.

A Specialist for Bladder Troubles.—Strong medical stigmata on the Mount of Mercury. A very sloping Line of Head ending deep into the Mount of the Moon.

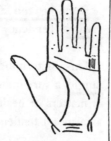

"A physician was introduced to Desbarrolles, who, after glancing at his hands, declared at once that he must make a specialty of diseases of the bladder and kidneys. It proved to be Dr. Leroy d'Estiolles, who, in the '60's was the authority on the subject, the world over."

Wavy and inclining toward the Line of Liver—Brain disease.

This is generally of a melancholia character, as it indicates the morbid influence of the Liver on the Brain.

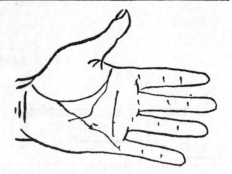

A Brilliant Girl Violinist.—Short, slightly spatulate, fat, smooth fingers; a short thumb; enormous Mounts of Mars; big Mounts of the Sun and Mercury thrown into one; a Line of Heart fine and very long; beautiful Lines of Fate and the Sun. A very long line of Head sloping down to the Rascette.

"The hand of Mademoiselle Tayaut, the young violinist prodigy, already revealing, at 14, the energy and passionate artistic temperament of the great virtuosa; she was a brunette with very bright complexion and a rather sensual face, but with the evidences of a warmhearted and cheerful disposition."

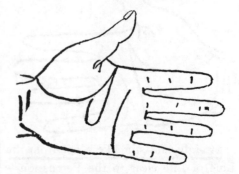

After partly crossing the hand, turning back and starting toward the Mount of Venus—Cowardice; lack of energy.

In this case it fails to reach the Upper

Mount of Mars (energy, courage), which is its normal terminating point.

b. In connection with other indications.

Rising toward the Line of Heart, with a Line of Liver starting from the Line

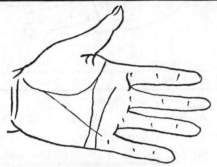

of Life—Tendency to fainting fits.

Generally due to a poor digestion. It is often a prognostic of coming apoplexy.

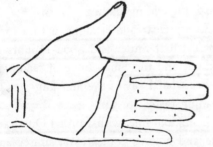

Rising toward the Line of Heart, under the Mount of Saturn, and then resuming its natural course—The subject will be rendered very miserable—up to insanity—by those he loves.

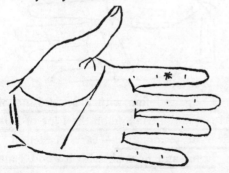

Sloping abruptly to the Mount of the Moon with a star on the second phalanx of the second finger—Insanity.

The Mount of Saturn, the second finger and the Mount of the Moon all represent by the nervous system, generally at its worst. [Star on wrong finger.]

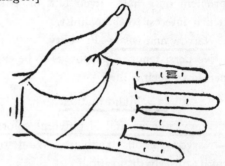

Sloping far down into the Mount of the Moon with the second phalanx of the first finger lined—Aptitude for occult sciences.

The first finger is essentially the Finger of Inspiration. It is considered the connecting link with the upper world. Its second phalanx has already absorbed the inspiration and causes it to pass through the crucible of human reason.

II. CHARACTER.

a. By Itself.

1. Length.

Absence—Constitutional brain trouble; dull intellect, often idiocy of a congenital nature.

Long, straight and clear—Common sense.

Short and clear, or long and faintly traced—Flightiness; lack of concentration.

In either case a poor line.

2. Color—Width—Depth.

Thin, toward the center—Nervous or brain trouble, to last as long as the thinness extends on the Line.

For the time measurement on the Line of Head, I refer the reader to the Appendix to this book, containing many a problem only half solved but of particular interest to the palmist.

Narrow and weak—Frivolity.

No persistency of purpose is to be expected of such a line.

3. Malformation.

Wavy, uneven and of different colors —Nervous bilious troubles. Want of spirit; miserly disposition.

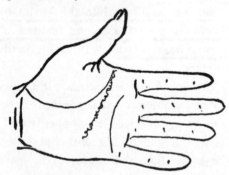

Chained or linked—Want of fixity in the ideas; chronic headaches.

b. In Combination with other indications.

1. Length.

Long and straight, with hands and fingers long—Love of details.

Long and straight with a very short fourth finger and very much marked knots—Tactlessness.

The fourth finger, in good shape and length, indicates aptitude for the clever management of people. The contrary rules obtain here.

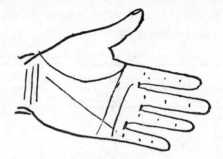

Extending clear across the palm, with a Line of Liver narrow, distinct and straight—Good memory.

A good memory needs a clear brain and an unclogged Liver.

Stretching like a straight bar across the whole palm, with a badly formed Triangle—Avarice.

The lack of the slight curve at the middle of the Line always indicates a hard, unyielding nature.

Long, clear and straight, with a long conical first finger and good Mounts of Jupiter and the Sun—Love of reading.

See what I say of the first finger as to reading tastes (p. 50).

Long and fine, with a broad Quadrangle and a long conical first finger and the others square—Fair mindedness.

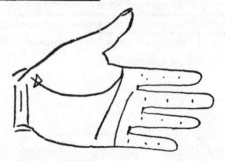

Long and fine with a good Line of Heart and a triangle on the Line of Life near its termination—Tact, discretion.

Long and normal, with a good Line

of Heart, and a first finger longer than the normal size—Great generosity toward one's friends, but more in giving them entertainments than by really helping them.

If too straight and stiff and with a poor Line of Heart—The generosity will be all spent upon oneself, especially for high living.

Long and sloping to the Mount of the Moon with a high Mount of Jupiter marked with a grille—Eloquence as a politician.

The presence of the grille simply exaggerates the Mount of Jupiter and is proof sufficient for me that this eloquence will not be exerted for worthy motives.

Long and fine with a moderate Mount of Venus—Constancy.

A good will-power and instincts moderately amorous are guarantees of constancy.

Long and fine, with high Mounts of Mars, Jupiter and Mercury—Unusual power of concentrating one's mind.

Long and sloping, in both hands, with a strong Mount of the Moon and the second and third fingers nearly the same length—Love of gambling; disposition to take great risks in business.

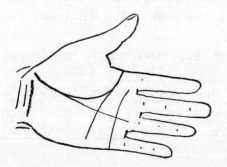

If this is added to a deep, long Line of the Sun—The risks will be taken in traveling in dangerous, probably tropical, countries.

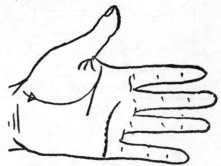

Short with a poor Line of Heart and a triangle on the Line of Life near its termination—Loquacity often harmful.

Lack of brains and a heartless nature are responsible for the most dreadful scandals.

Short with a low Mount of Jupiter and exaggerate Mounts of Venus and the Moon in a soft hand—Laziness.

No Mount of Jupiter—no ambition.

Short, with a narrow Quadrangle and a low Mount of Venus—Narrow mindedness; even uncharitableness.

The Low Mount of the Moon is evidence of little sympathy for other people's troubles.

2. Color—Width—Depth.

Pale and broad, with hard hands and a low Mount of the Sun—Dull intellect.

Paleness and abnormal width always indicate a wretched flow of vital fluid.

Long but faint, with an exaggerate Mount of Mercury—Perfidy.

Very Deep—A sure indication of a serious strain of the nervous system.

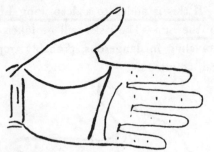

Thin (or short) and faint, with an ir-

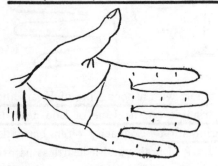

regular Line of Liver—Chronic indigestion, sick headaches.

3. Malformation.

Wavy and rising in an abnormal curve
to the Line of Heart under the Mount

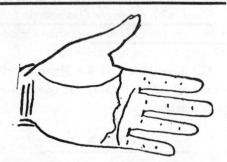

of the Sun or the Mount of Mercury—
Insanity.

To be confirmed in the other hand
and also by other signs, especially on the
Mount of the Moon.

Wavy, with a narrow Quadrangle and
a Mount of Mercury exaggerate—Dishonesty.

Meanness, cupidity and falsehood are
here combined to reveal the swindler
and the thief.

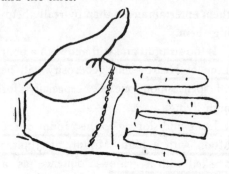

Formed in little islands with fluted
nails curved at the top—Consumption.

The curve is sufficient without the
fluting. If not seen in the Right Hand
—The inherited consumptive strain is
being gradually eliminated from the
subject's constitution.

Poor, with the Line of Heart absent
and the Line of Liver wavy—Weak
heart. Irresolute nature, generally led
to evil doings through the lack of these
two essentials: brains and affectionate
feelings.

Very poor with abnormally small
thumbs—Idiocy.

As will be stated further, the congenital idiot's hands also reveal a wretched
state of the circulation, by the poor
markings of the Line of Heart. Medical authorities confirm this reading.

III. STARTING POINTS AND FORKS AT THE START.

Not joined to the Line of Life at the
start, in a good hand—Self-reliance, energy. Better still with a firm hand and
square fingers.

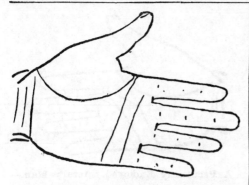

Not joined to the Line of Life, with exaggerate Mounts of Jupiter and Mars —Abnormal self-confidence.

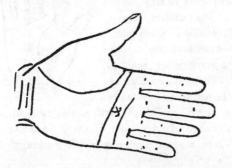

Not joined to the Line of Life at the start and with a badly formed cross in the Quadrangle—Exaggerate enthusiasm.

This is a counterfeit of the Mystic Cross, the presence of which imbues the blessed owner with almost heavenly enthusiasm and knowledge.

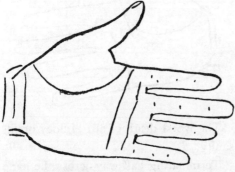

Far apart from the Line of Life at the

start with a flat Mount of Mercury and exaggerate Mounts of Mars and Jupiter

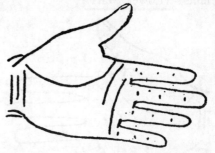

—Recklessness, extreme conceit. If the Line is short—Lack of intelligence.

With smooth fingers—Tactlessness.

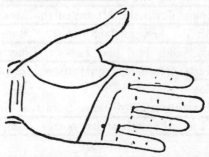

Not joined to the Line of Life but starting with a curve around the base of the Mount of Jupiter, then going clear across the palm—Extravagant conceit.

Starting inside the Mount of Venus or the Lower Mount of Mars—Extreme fretfulness and inconstancy; irritable disposition.

By partially crossing the Mounts, the

Line has destroyed to some extent their characteristics of amiability (Venus) and firmness (Lower Mars).

Not joined to the Line of Life, but starting on the Mount of Jupiter and sloping down the Mount of the Moon, with the first phalanx of the thumb broad and short and a poor Line of Heart—Obstinacy, quarrelsome disposition.

Starting some distance from the Line of Life, although at its normal height

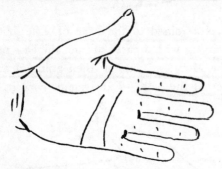

otherwise—Grave eye trouble in early youth.

It is as if a fragment of the line were missing. It is not to be read, as above, as a sign of recklessness or conceit.

Forked, as well as the Line of Heart, under the Mount of Saturn, one prong joined to the Line of Life, the other going toward the Line of Heart but not cutting it—Good fortune.

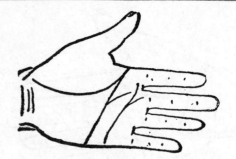

A Peculiarly Endowed Literary Man.— Lines of Head in both hands widely separated from the Lines of Life and quite short.

"The subject was a journalist of much talent but without the faculty of pursuing any topic to its natural conclusion. He had to be constantly prompted and finally fell to the rank of a wretched drudge for a cheap publisher. There was no continuity in the workings of his brains."

IV. TERMINATION. FORKS AT THE TERMINATION.

Terminating under the Mount of Saturn—Premature death or intelligence extinguished early.

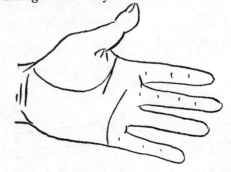

The worst death of all: Idiocy or insanity.

Terminating half way across the hand with badly developed Mounts of Jupiter

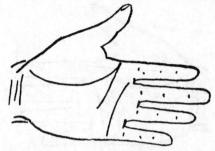

and the Sun—Lack of intelligence. With badly developed Mounts of Mars—Want of spirit, of courage, active or passive.

Terminating just before it crosses the

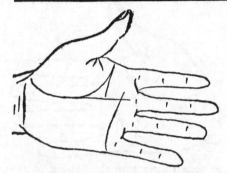

Line of Fate—Short, unhappy life.

Turning back toward the Line of Life

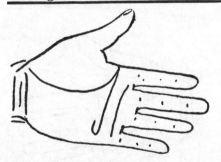

before its termination (after having entered the Upper Mount of Mars)—Self-confidence and exaggerate egotism bring about serious troubles.

Terminating on the Mount of Saturn —Death by a wound in the head. Also a sign of dangerous fanaticism.

If it terminates in that direction, but

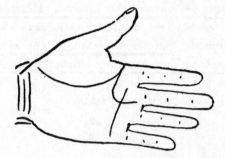

before crossing the Line of Heart—The wound in the head will not be fatal.

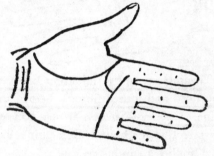

Fanaticism comparatively harmless.

Terminating on the Mount of the

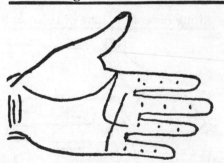

Sun—A passion for the fine arts or literature. If it terminates in that direction

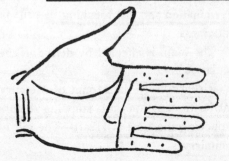

before it crosses the Line of Heart— Great chances of success in the same direction. Should the hands otherwise show no intellectual or artistic aptitudes —An all-absorbing desire to acquire riches without much labor.

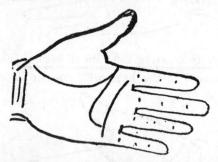

Turning up and terminating between the third and fourth fingers, below the Line of Heart—Success in art secured by scientific methods. Something like "art applied to industry."

In artistic hands—Fortune obtained by the same means.

Rising toward the Line of Heart at its

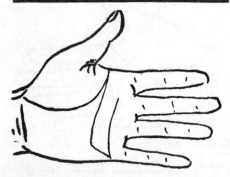

termination and just touching it—Fits of dizziness.

The brain is affected by defective circulation.

Rising toward the Mount of Mercury at its termination, but stopping before touching the Line of Heart—The gift of mimicry.

I have noticed this frequently in noted actors' han ; more generally, however, with the fork, which see further.

Rising in a curve at its termination

and penetrating into the Mount of Mercury—Tact and shrewdness in the management of affairs. In a bad hand— Duplicity.

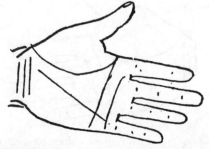

Terminating at the Percussion, but with a fine Line of Liver—Good Memory.

This is rather too long a Line of Head; but you know the saying, "he has a long head," meaning, "he remembers far back."

Running stiff and straight to the Percussion, with low Mounts of Jupiter and Venus, the thumb inward bent and the

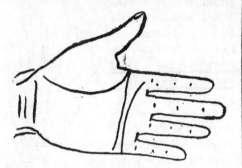

fingers close together—Selfish, miserly disposition.

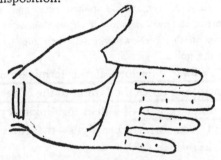

A very small fork at the termination—Imagination controlled by common sense.

This is really the normal termination of an average good Line of Head.

Forked at the termination, with a thick, soft palm, a short thumb and the third phalanx of every finger bulging in-

side the hand—Untrustworthiness.

This is the lazy nature of the voluptuary elsewhere described, and certainly one not to be relied upon.

Forked at the termination, with one

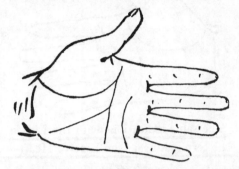

prong normal, the other low down into the Mount of the Moon—The subject will deceive himself first and others afterwards.

In the hand of genius, it reveals, however, a rich imagination and, on account of the straight prong, the gift of making money out of one's talents.

Sloping and forked at the termination, one prong to the Mount of the Moon and the other to the Mount of Mercury —The power to hypnotize; also crafty disposition in business; the thirst for money blinding the subject as to the means to secure riches.

Forked at the termination, one prong down the Mount of the Moon, the other rising and touching the Line of Heart— The subject will sacrifice everything to an affection.

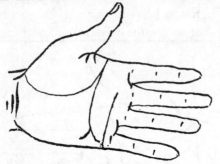

The same indications with the Line of Fate terminating at the Line of Heart—

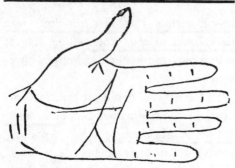

This passionate affection will ruin the subject's life.

The subject's brain power and all the possibilities of his life are here concentrated upon one being; hence the saddest probability of a total wreck.

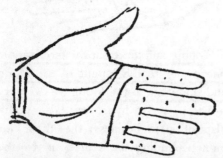

A fork at the termination, both prongs sloping low down into the Mount of the Moon—Diseased imagination; some-

thing of the Oscar Wilde form of aberration.

Perfidious Denunciator.—Exaggerate Mounts of Venus and the Moon, with absent Mounts of Mars. A rather fat hand. A drooping Line of Head forked at the termination.

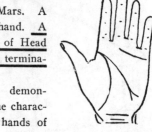

"Repeatedly demonstrated to be the characteristic of the hands of people who turn State's evidence, or betray their friends or country under the influence of fear; these two exaggerate Mounts reveal an inborn, remarkable poltroonery and a horror of physical pain. To save themselves from it, these fellows will sell their mothers to the police."

A long, fine fork at the termination, one prong down the Mount of the Moon, but not very low—Talent for diplomacy, and even—with other signs—the gift of clairvoyance.

Terminating in a three-pronged fork, one prong straight on, the second curving up to the Mount of Mercury, the third sloping a little way down the Mount of the Moon—Union of brain power, business talent and imagination; often seen in the hand of the successful artist or "litterateur," who sells his works to advantage.

I would expect to find just such a triple fork in the hand of an inventor who knows how to finance his patent to full advantage.

The Hands of the Famous German Painter, Cornelius.— A short, small, thin hand, with square-tipped, knotted fingers; a fairly long thumb, the second phalanx above average; short nails. A large Mount of Venus very much rayed, as was the whole palm. A fine

star on the Mount of Jupiter, and another, quite clear also, on the third phalanx of the first finger. The third phalanges were not plump; on the contrary, thin and dry. A very fine Line of Head with a long triple fork at the termination. A perfectly curved Line of Intuition. Lines of Fate and the Sun starting from an exceptionally long and clear Line of Life.

"Desbarrolles met Cornelius when the latter was 87 years old and had several long conversations with him. The Master of Palmistry, being himself no mean artist, was able to judge very accurately of the merits of the illustrious German, who, by the way, was French on his mother's side. A clever business man whose ambitions had been crowned to the limits of his desires; an excellent and bold draughtsman and a painstaking, classical painter, Cornelius always lacked warmth of coloring to give true life to his admirably grouped figures. All these qualities and defects were confirmed by the shape and markings of his hands, who showed that, with all his great talent, he lacked genius."

Forked at the termination, with one prong normal, the other only a little way down the Mount of the Moon—People clever to astuteness; business men of unusual shrewdness; successful lawyers; worldly clergymen; sometimes first-class actors sinking their personalities in the parts they act.

This is particularly the characteristic marking of the lawyer and the actor. This fork is the distinct proof of a capacity for seeing both sides of every question. It is not considered as an evidence of exceptional veracity.

Violent Temper Amounting Almost to Insanity.—A Martian type with a short thumb but a very long Line of Head widely separated from the Line of Life at the start and terminating in three prongs very close together. A star marked at 20 on the Line of

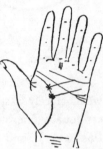

Life and another marked at 28 and both connected by Lines of Influence, the first with the Line of Heart, the second with the Line of Head.

"Seen in the hands of a lawyer whose temper was at times absolutely uncontrollable; the short thumb did not furnish him with will-power sufficient for conquering this tendency. Two serious incidents in his life had been the consequences of this easily aroused wrath: a duel when quite young; later a carriage accident as he was driving at a furious rate in the wake of a woman he was desperately jealous of; in both cases he had been severely wounded."

V. BRANCHES.

Bars cutting the Lines—Headaches.

A branch from the line deep into the Mount of Jupiter, terminating in a star—Success.

This is one of the few cases when a

star is considered as a favorable omen. The divergency of opinion upon the subject is quite remarkable. I feel more and more inclined, however, to follow the readings of a most brilliant English palmist, Mrs. Kathryn St. Hill, and to consider all stars as disastrous, except

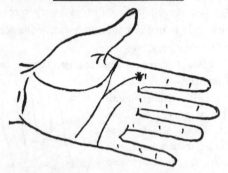

when closely associated with some exceptionally fine indications. And yet, in this case, I shall let the pleasant omen stand, as Desbarrolles is particularly emphatic in his favorable reading of Stars on Jupiter.

A branch from the Line ascending to the root of the first finger, but not cutting it—Ambition.

A branch from the Line deep into the Mount of Jupiter cut by a bar or terminating in a cross—Failure of one's main ambition.

With a cross on the first Bracelet of the Rascette—Wealth coming.

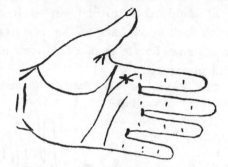

This is purely traditional. See what I say about it in my Chapter on the Rascette.

Three or more branches rising to the Mount of Jupiter—Riches; ambition

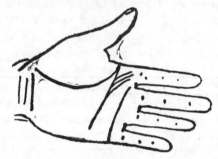

brilliantly successful.

A branch from the Line rising into

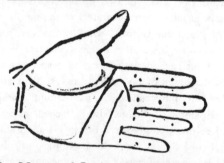

the Mount of Jupiter and then turning toward the Mount of Saturn—Religious fanaticism; extravagant vanity.

I have seen this indication in the hand of a woman whose insanity was of the religious character.

A branch to the Mount of the Sun

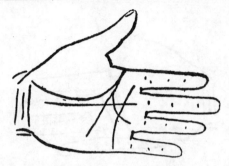

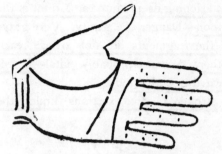

with a good Line of Fate—Riches. In an artistic hand—Brilliant success in the direction of the subject's talent.

ble of, the head. Many breaks—Headaches.

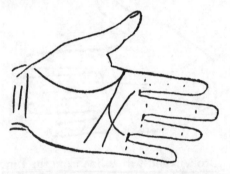

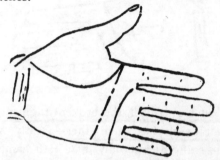

One clear branch to between the third and fourth fingers—Profitable success in artistic or scientific labors. Often read —Money made through discoveries or inventions.

Broken, but with an overlaying fragment continuing it at once—Recovery

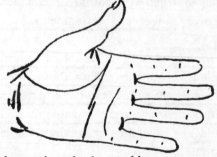

after serious brain troubles.

Broken under the Mount of Saturn

Throwing branches toward a well-formed Mount of Mercury—Business prosperity.

VI. BREAKS.

A break—A wound in, or severe trou-

and sloping deeply into the Mount of the Moon—Danger of insanity. Very grave if the fragments do not overly each other. Worse—probably fatal—if repeated in both hands.

Broken in two sections under the

Mount of Saturn, the broken fragments not overlaying each other—Death on the scaffold (true only if in both hands and with confirmatory signs). More generally a grave wound to either the head or legs; with partial or complete recovery whenever the fragments overlay each other.

Broken under the Mount of Saturn, with a Line of Life ending abruptly and generally cut by a bar at its termination, with a cross inside the Triangle (in both hands)—One of the signs of death on the scaffold.

This cross inside the Triangle is that famous fighting cross of the ancient palmists, indicating quarrelsome, often murderous, instincts. Remember that on that very spot the nerves of the hand are particularly numerous and sensitive. Hence, the ultra-excitement in certain natures.

Broken under the Mount of the Sun— Danger of hydrophobia. Danger of sun-

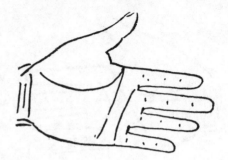

stroke. In general: Danger to the eyesight.

Broken, and with a line from the Line of Heart to the Line of Fate—Widowhood; or separation by death from a very dear one, not a relative.

Lack of Continuity in Thought and Action.—Very long fingers and an enormous thumb, with a long, drooping Line of Head broken in a number of small fragments.

"The young man who owned these characteristics was constantly starting to do great things

and displayed enthusiasm galore, only to collapse within a very short time, and to turn his changeable disposition toward some other project, just as ardently entered into, to be abandoned before half completed."

Broken in small sections—Serious, racking headaches; loss of memory; with

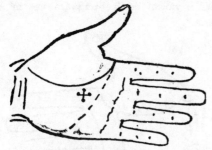

a cross in the Triangle, the rays some-times terminating in spots, and with short nails—Epilepsy in full operation.

Epilepsy.—Crooked fingers; short nails; double Girdle of Venus; a very long Line of Head broken in small fragments and drooping deep into the Mount of the Moon; in the center of the Triangle a big cross with a dot at the end of each arm.

"The man who displayed those markings had been subject to epileptic fits for many years and was gradually coming down to the level of a congenital idiot. This big cross—"the Cross of battle" —was imprinted upon the nervous center of the hand."

VII. CONNECTED WITH THE MAIN LINES.

a. Directly.

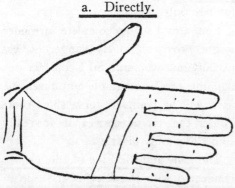

Joined in a very acute angle with the Line of Life—Prudence.

This is, after all, the normal shape of this angle; its quality depends greatly on the length, etc., of the Line; it means but little by itself. See Chapter on the Plain of Mars.

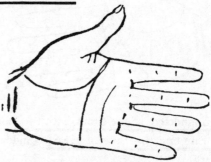

Closely connected for some distance with the Line of Life—Hesitating ways; diffidence.

A strong first phalanx of the thumb, a long straight Line of Head and a good Mount of Jupiter will triumph over this tendency. Hundreds of times I have found it in the Left Hand, and yet, in the Right Hand, the angle was formed so clear and open as to secure full freedom of thought and action.

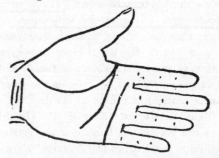

Joined with the Line of Life, rising toward the Line of Heart, then coming down and resuming its normal position —Blind or fatal passion; long engage-ment (or entanglement) never terminat-ing in marriage.

This will be due to a mixture of meanness (narrow Quadrangle) and physical passion.

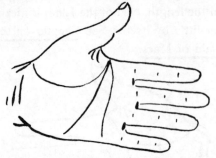

Connected, at the Start, with the Line of Life and the Line of Heart—Sudden death.

The Hand of Jules Gerard, the Famous Lion Killer.—A Saturnian type, but fortified by distinct Martian markings and brightened by a strong Mount of the Sun crossed by a deep vertical line. The Lines of Heart and Head joined at the start on the Line of Life, the latter

broken at 35 (in one hand), with the fragments overlaying each other. The Line of Head deeply forked at the termination. A high Plain of Mars. Square tipped and smooth fingers, the third finger the same length as the second. Medium thumb with good second phalanx. A cross in the Quadrangle touching the Line of the Sun.

"Jules Gerard, an officer in the French Army in Africa, was famous as the greatest lion-killer that lived in this century. He was fond of desert life and religiously inclined. He was bold to excess, generally hunting the lion single-handed, and yet he was shrewd in his methods and reasoned out to a fine point his most foolhardy expeditions. He almost succumbed to a terrible and prolonged attack of African fever; and finally

died a violent death, being drowned in Algeria."

Starting from the Line of Life under the Mount of Saturn—Neglected education and late development of the brain. With the same start, if the Lines of Life and Heart are short—Danger of sudden death.

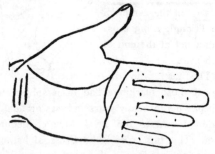

Losing itself into a Line of Heart that has come straight from the Mount of Jupiter—Unexpected happiness; love for one only.

I am afraid such a complete surrender might prove extremely dangerous, especially in a woman. So I consider this happiness to be as fragile and unreliable as it will be complete for a short time. Under the circumstances it is really something of a disaster.

The Line and the Line of Life closely connected with the Line of the Sun in both hands, with large hands and the

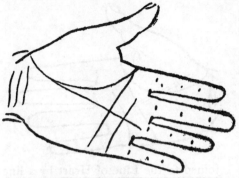

first angle very narrow—Extreme sensitiveness.

That means that the Line of Life and Head are connected too long. See explanation above. [The cut is poor.]

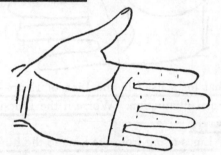

Joined with the Line of Heart under the Mount of Saturn—Fatal events, due to the surrender of reason to emotion.

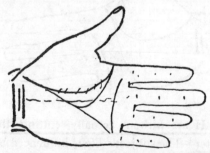

Joined with the Line of Liver, with a poor Line of Fate, many bars crossing the Line of Life and with an exaggerate Mount of Jupiter—Tendency to suicide.

The poor Line of Liver indicates gloomy thoughts; the bars on the Line of

Life, constant indispositions; the poor Line of Fate, a succession of misfortunes; the high Mount of Jupiter, a pride that can stand no reverses; all of these combined have led many a man to commit felo de se.

Joined with the Line of Liver, the Line of Life being forked at the start—Brain disease.

This will be of the melancholia character.

Forming a clear cross with the Line of Liver on the mount of the Moon—Diseased imagination.

This cross can only be formed by the Line of Head drooping greatly and the Line of Liver running comparatively close to the Percussion; each of these indications, taken by itself, is sufficient to explain the reading.

Not joined with the Line of Life at the start, but connected by minor lines or branches—Evil temper, uneven dis-

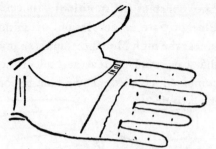

position. In a good hand—Brusquerie.

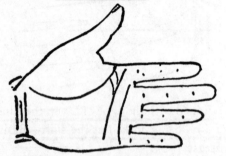

Not joined with the Line of Life at the start, but connected with it by a

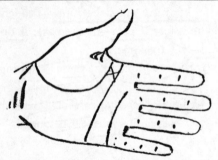

cross—Domestic troubles of a serious nature, in the family of the subject, who suffers the consequences of these quarrels without being an actor in them, on account of his age.

Often read correctly as a family law suit that ruined the subject's prospects in his infancy.

Lines from the base of the Mount of Venus cutting the Line of Life and the Line—Pecuniary difficulties due to one's family.

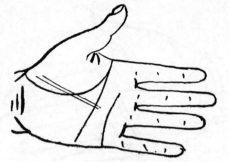

Joined to the Line of Heart by a line

that loses itself in the Line of Heart—Fatal infatuation. Worse if the Line is wavy.

Lines rising from the Line to the Line

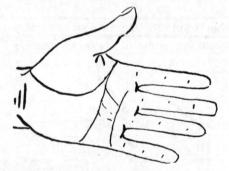

of Heart without actually cutting the latter—The subject's life is influenced by others, generally through friendships with people of the same sex.

A line toward the termination of the Line rising to the Line of Heart and being absorbed therein—Affection mastering reason.

The Line and the Lines of Life, Heart and Union cut by a line starting from

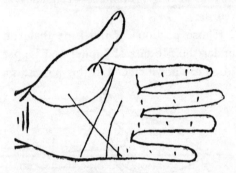

the Mount of Venus—Trouble connected with marriage or deep attachment for person of another sex.

See Chapter on Lines of Influence from the Mounts of Venus and Upper Mars and the Line of Life for a number of readings relating to the Line of Head (pp. 172-193).

VIII. SIGNS.

Many Bars—Headaches

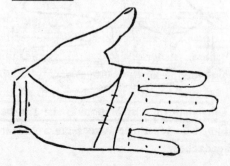

Wavy, straight or curved bars cutting

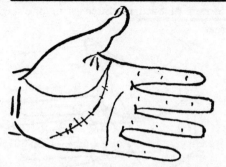

a sloping Line of Head—Headaches; danger of insanity.

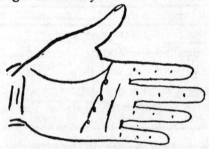

A knotting up of the Line—Tendency to murder; if pale—in the past; if deep red—yet to come.

I have seldom met these knottings. But the leading English palmists give it so much importance that I have inserted the reading where it belonged.

A deep, colorless indentation on the Line—Cruel neuralgia, to last one year or more.

White spots on the line—Discoveries or inventions.

White spots on the Line under the Mount of Saturn—Success in one's career.

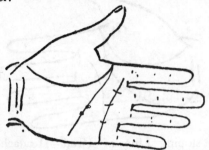

Bars crossing the Line of Heart, with white spots on the Line under the Mount of the Sun—Literary success.

Absolutely traditional, but curious. I met it twice. It seems that literary successes are generally associated with defective action of the heart, as the bars have certainly no other meanings. Or is it the rush of blood to the brain that is manifested in this wise?

White spots on the Line close to the Mount of Mercury—Success in scientific researches, generally practical in their character.

Dark spots on the Line with narrow and highly colored Lines of Life and Liver—Tendency to fever, often of a typhoidal, or at least malarial, character.

Pale and wide with black spots on it

and the Line of Life forked at the start—Very serious brain disease.

A bluish spot on the Line, where it forms a side of the Triangle, the Mounts

of Mars being prominent—Tendency to murder.

Those portions of the Line that run under the Mounts of Jupiter and Upper Mars are not included in this indication.

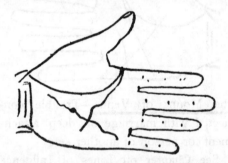

Irregular, either wavy or discolored, with a bluish spot on a wavy Line of Liver—Health troubles due to malarial influences.

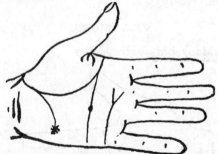

A black or bluish spot on the Line—Typhoid fever or excessive chronic headaches.

A dark spot on the Line with a Line rising from the lower part of the mount of Venus or the Line of Life and terminating on the Mount of the Moon in a star—Delirium tremens.

Here the symptoms of drunkenness are at their worst. Notice that this Line from the Mount of Venus to the Mount of the Moon is also read quite correctly as "dangerous kidney trouble." In confirmed alcoholism the kidneys are dangerously affected. Hence the similitude between the two readings founded on the same markings.

Black spots on the Line generally indicate, with the Mount of Saturn most prominent—Toothache; with the Mount of Venus most prominent—Deafness; with the Mount of the Sun most prominent—Disease of the eyes, especially with a star at the root of the third finger.

Deafness.—A Venusian—Saturnian subject. Fine Lines of Heart, Fate and the Sun. Several deep dots on the Line of Head. A line from the Upper Mount of Mars to the Mount of Jupiter, cutting deeply into the Main Lines. A cross in the Quadrangle under the Mount of Mercury.

"Seen in the hand of a distinguished painter, a lady, cruelly affected with deafness. She had had difficulties in childbearing, and, after that, her tendency to deafness had grown until she heard almost nothing; Desbarrolles considered the Line from the Upper Mount of Mars to the Mount of Jupiter as the marking of this infirmity in conjunction with the dots on the Line of Head."

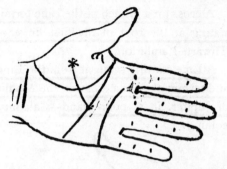

A black spot on the Line connecting by a Line of Influence with a star on the Mount of Venus—A cruel sorrow, (sometimes insanity), due to the death of a loved one. (See also Lines of Influence, p. 190.)

A cross or a deep bar when the Line forms a side of the Triangle—Grave accident; generally to the head.

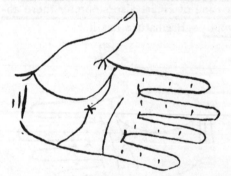

A cross on a wavy Line where it forms a side of the Triangle—Fatal accident; generally to the head.

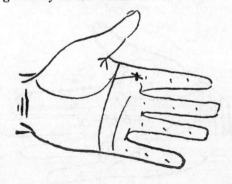

A cross on a branch of the Line terminating at the root of the first finger—Thwarted ambition.

A Line starting straight from the Line and terminating in a cross on the Mount of Jupiter, in a poor hand—Calamity coming.

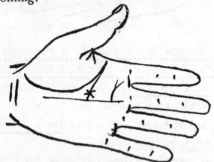

A cross on the Line, the latter stopping abruptly at the Line of Fate, with a Line of Heart also stopping there abruptly—Premature death.

A star on the Line—A wound in the head. If repeated in both hands—The wound will prove fatal.

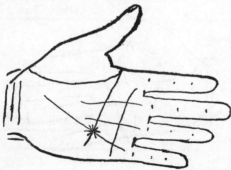

A star where the Line meets the Line of Liver—Danger in childbearing, or sterility.

Projected Guilty Intrigue Threatened to End in a Catastrophe.
—A very straight and deep Line of Influence starting from an island on the Mount of Venus cuts a star on the Line of Life at 30, and ends at the Percussion of Mars after cutting a star at the connection of the Lines of Head and the Sun. A double Girdle of Venus. A Line of Fate stopped short by the above Line of Influence, and regained only after 40.

"A handsome woman consulted Desbarrolles, who told her she was about giving way to a hysterical and guilty love which would end in a terrible caastrophe in which her good name, her future and even her reason would become involved. She acknowledged that she could not resist the temptation to abandon an excellent husband for the sake of a very young man who, up to that time, knew nothing of her passion for him."

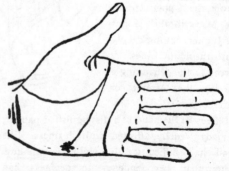

Sloping into the Mount of the Moon and ending in a star—Death by drowning. Often, suicide by drowning in a fit of insanity.

Sloping almost or quite to the Rascette and terminating in a cross or star

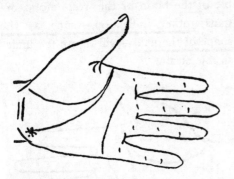

—Brilliant fortune.

This is so essentially traditional, that, in spite of Desbarrolles, I insert this reading regretfully.

Loss of Reason Through a Love Sorrow. —In the Left Hand a sloping Line of Head; on that line, under the Mount of the Sun, a star connected with the Mount of Venus by a Line of Influence cutting an upward branch of the Line of Life. From that star an elongated island stretched itself up to the Mount of Mercury. In the right hand, at the same date, a Line of Influence from the Mount of Venus, cutting an upward branch of the Line of Life, curved upward, cutting the sloping Line of Head under the Mount of Saturn, in the midst of a number of confused lines. From that confusion started the same elongated island reaching to the Mount of Mercury.

"The subject had grown insane from the sorrow due to the evil doings of his wife— a Mercurian, as seen by the terminating point of the islands; he had obtained a divorce; and was gradually regaining his reason, through deep studies, that led him to become a distinguished inventor."

Temporary Insanity Caused by a Great Love.—A normal Line of Head, widely forked at the termination. A Line of Influence from an island on the Mount of Venus shows a deep black dot as it reaches the Line of Heart on its way to joining a sloping Line of Union. A line connects this black dot with a star at the end of the upper prong of the Line of Head.

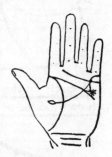

"Sometime before 30 a young man suffered deeply in his love for a married woman. His grief acted for a while on his brain. The fork at the termination of the Line of Head indicates how easily he was deceived."

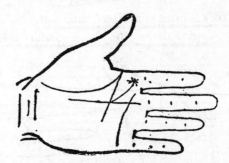

A short Line, with a prong of a fork at its start, ending in a star on the Mount of Jupiter—Fatal pride; especially if it connects with the Line of Fate.

By "fatal pride" is meant such a lofty idea of oneself as will cause one to risk almost anything rather than to "give in" and acknowledge one beaten.

A branch of the Line ascending to the root of the first finger and ending in a star—Successful ambition.

A circle on the Line and a cross high up on the Line of Liver—Blindness; the

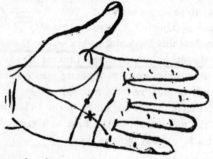

cross is often considered sufficient.

A triangle on the Line under the

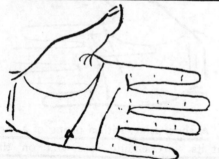

Mount of Mercury—Success in scientific researches.

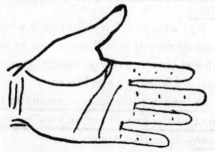

Islanded at the start—Inherited trouble of the brain or the respiratory organs; other indications—such as the shape of the nails—will locate the undesirable strain.

An island on the Line—Chronic neuralgia.

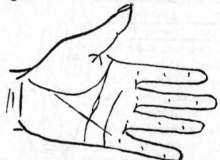

An island on the Line, with a Line of Liver turning red as it approaches the Line of Head—Brain fever of a bilious character.

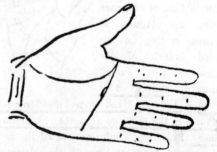

An island under the Mount of Saturn —Sure sign of serious deafness, often begins by a dot, then gradually enlarged to a fully formed island. It is generally accompanied by exaggerate Mount of the Moon—Lymphatic disposition.

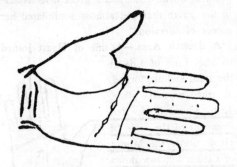

Islanded—Brain trouble resulting from intellectual overwork or dissipation.

Islanded, and with long, curved, brittle, often fluted nails—Consumption or at least great delicacy of the respiratory organs.

A very large island at the termination —Severe intestinal trouble.

The student must remember that intestinal troubles are usually marked on the lower part of the Upper Mount of Mars and the upper part of the Mount of the Moon; hence the above reading. (See Chapter on Signs on Mounts, page 113.)

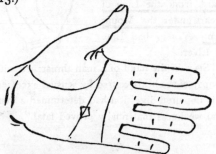

Running through a square—The intelligence of the subject saves him from the worst consequences of a grave accident or misfortune.

Threatened Softening of the Brain. Recovery.—In the Right Hand a Line of the Sun was starred on a Line of Head that crossed the whole hand; then it started again in fine shape up to the Mount of the Sun. In the Left Hand at the same spot a cross on the Line of Head was surrounded by a square; the Line of the Sun was superb.

"Seen in the hand of an American author of great reputation whom overwork and excess of smoking had brought to the verge of paresis. A total change of habits and a long European trip had saved him from the threatened disaster."

SPECIAL OBSERVATION.

Accompanied by a sister Line (very rare)—Inheritance.

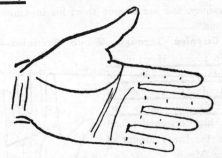

The two sister lines must be quite distinct and not consist simply of the line split in two, lengthwise, as this would be a most serious prognostic of insanity.

I wish to supplement this chapter by adding to it four very interesting observations of abnormal Lines of Head, gathered by Desbarrolles and never, to my knowledge, presented to the English-speaking public:

A Materialistic Philosopher, Almost Driven to Insanity.— Long, smooth, well-shaped fingers; a long and flat-tipped thumb. In the Left Hand only the three Chief lines visible. A very long but chained Line of Heart; a rather short Line of Head forked at the termination. In the Right Hand, a chained Line of Heart crosses the whole hand, but <u>the Line of Head was represented by a mere downward fragment under the Mount of Saturn.</u> No Lines of Fate or the Sun.

"Seen in the hands of a brilliant young scientist who had set his whole thinking power at work demonstrating the material nature of the vital principle and denying vigorously the existence of a soul. He had overworked himself to such a degree, pursuing his favorite studies, that he was on the brink of actual insanity, and had to stop short his investigations."

Crippled Through Womb Troubles.— <u>No Line of Heart whatsoever. A Line of Head crossing the whole hand like a bar.</u> A big horizontal island on the lower Mount of the Moon.

"Madame de C., a famous Parisian society woman, was condemned to spend her life stretched on a couch, on account of an incurable womb trouble. She was a very brilliant conversa-tionalist and her intellect brought in her drawing rooms the elite of the literary and political world. She had a great love trouble in her youth that had almost annihilated her power of affection."

A Broken Arm.— A line of Heart joined to the Line of Life at the start, ending, forked, at the normal place. <u>Just a much twisted fragment of the Line of Head, under the Mount of Saturn but low down in the hand.</u> A strong line, forming an angle from the starting point of the Line of Life to the Mount of Saturn. (This is Desbarrolles' description of the above sketch; I am inclined to think that the Line forming a right angle is really the Line of Head).

"Seen in the hand of a young man who suffered from a fracture of the arm just below the elbow."

Dropsy of the Heart.— In both hands a chained Line of Heart crossing like a bar at the normal place of the Line of Head. The Line of Head represented by a <u>small fragment downward from the Line of Heart under the Mount urn.</u> A very bad Line of Liver.

"Seen in the hand of a man threatened with dropsy of the heart caused by sensual excesses. His impaired digestion had determined a general weakness that finally proved fatal."

THE LINE OF HEART.

The Girdle of Venus—The Lines of Union.

This Division Three of the Main Lines, as I call it on page 141 of this book, includes the Third of the Chief Lines—the Line of Heart—and several minor Main lines that partake of its characteristics in a more or less important degree. Admitting that the Line of Heart indicates a smaller or larger amount of loving power, I find that the Girdle of Venus—the principal meaning of which is that of extreme sensuality—acts, in reality, as a sort of influence line over the said Line, increasing the revealed tendency toward physical passion.

Again, the Lines of Union, which I shall prove to be not Lines of Marriage —as usually believed—but mere Lines of Attachment, with or without the sanction of law or priest, do necessarily receive a great deal of influence from the Line of Heart which runs parallel to them, terminating—as they do—on the Mount of Mercury, which they enter from the Percussion.

These similarities in position and meanings are sufficient to explain why I have judged it proper and convenient to comprise these three manifestations of the same influential element, Love, under one and the same heading and in close vicinity to each other. I shall now begin with

THE LINE OF HEART.

which represents in the hand the circulation of the blood and the action of the heart—as far as health is concerned; and in the moral and mental world; the affections.

I. POSITION AND DIRECTION.

Normal: Running along the base of the Mounts below the fingers (except

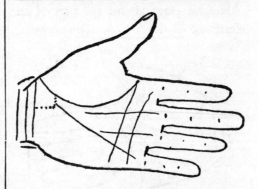

that it starts from inside the Mount of

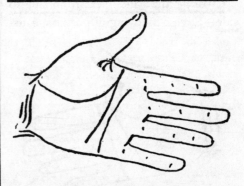

Jupiter) and ending at the Percussion.

Placed lower than its normal position —Coldness, selfishness. In a good hand—Indication of a steady flow of pure affection without physical attraction. In a bad hand—Avarice, duplicity, cruelty.

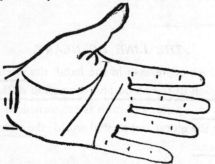

Placed very high in the hand, close to the bases of the fingers—Passionate, jealous disposition.

Here it plays almost the part of an elongated Girdle of Venus (which see).

Crossing the hand, clear from side to side—Excess of loving disposition, causing suffering to the subject; with a high Mount of the Moon—Exaggerate jealousy.

Crossing the hand like a stiff bar, from side to side, with a hard hand—Unfeeling disposition.

Lack of Synovia in the Knee-Joints.—The Line of Heart occupying the usual place of the Line of Head extending, quite chained, clear to the Percussion. A small fragment of a Line of Head dropping from the Line of Heart below the Mount of Saturn.

"An old man 75 years old had suffered for years, from a lack of oil in the knee joints; his stomach and heart were both in a very wretched condition."

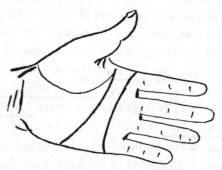

Sinking toward the Line of Head, with an exaggerate curve under the Mount of Saturn or the Sun, thus making a very narrow Quadrangle—Meanness of disposition; still more so with square-tipped and very smooth fingers.

The latter reading indicates a nature without an ideal and obeying its first, selfish impulses.

Sinking toward the Line of Head, as above, forming a very narrow Quad-

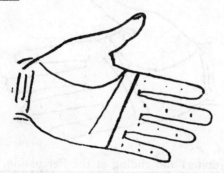

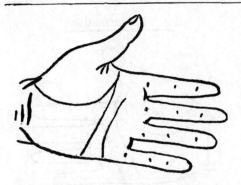

rangle, and with a prominent Mount of the Moon—Duplicity.

Imagination added to a mean, selfish disposition induces lying.

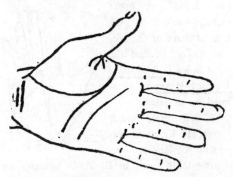

Sinking toward the Line of Head, as above, the latter connected too long at its start with the Line of Life—Stiffness and formality in manner and disposition.

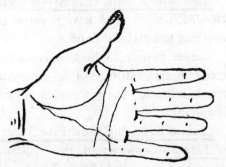

Sinking toward the Line of Head, as above, with a poor, wavy Line of Liver —Asthma, Hay fever.

II. CHARACTER.

a. By Itself.

1. Length.

Absent—Extreme coldness, physical and moral; selfishness; boundless avarice; with other signs, such as a prominent Upper Mount of Mars—Cruelty; also hemorrhage. If it has faded away —The heart has grown hard through disappointment in love.

This you can only judge, of course, if you have had a former occasion of examining the hand of the subject, or may depend on his declaration in that respect.

The longer it is and the farther into the Mount of Jupiter it starts from—The stronger and the more idealistic the love.

Long, clear and well traced—Lasting affection.

2. Color: Width: Depth.

Very red—Violence in affairs of the heart.

A dangerous person to be in love with.

Livid or yellow—Liver troubles.

This applies to all the Lines in the hand; in fact, when one is livid and yellow, they all show the same hue; it is not always the case with red lines.

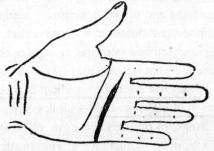

An unusually deep Line—Danger of apoplexy

The depth of a Line, when abnormal,

always indicates a strain that may soon reach the danger point.

Two Strokes of Apoplexy.　Great Sorrow.—A very deep Line of Heart in a hand otherwise poor in lines. Deep dots on that line.

"That unusual depth of the line I saw recently in a famous actress, who has suffered already from a stroke of paralysis. But with her the Line of Head was also extraordinarily deep."

Very pale and wide—Heart disease; poor circulation, dissipation having brought about a general weakening of the system.

The vital fluid has lost much of its beneficent value, and the traces of its passage through this particular channel are faint.

Very thin and long—Murderous instincts.

Thinness is not a quality in the Line of Heart as it is in the Line of Head. You will find a great difference in the general aspect of these two lines; I advise you to study their characteristics very closely so that, should one of them be absent and the remaining one occupy its place (an abnormal formation that is not uncommon), you may recognize the Line for what it really is.

Weak and poor, and ending branchless at the Percussion—Childlessness.

Branches on lines are signs of plenty of sap, of an exuberance of vitality, giving the power of reproducing the species.

3.　Malformation.

Chained—Flirtatious disposition. Imperfect action of the heart.

Change of Religion.—Knotty and spatulate fingers. A cross clearly marked on the first phalanx of the second finger, toward the third finger. A chained Line of Heart; a sloping Line of Head.

"A lady, very much tormented by many superstitious fancies, was absorbed for years in all kinds of religious investigations, hesitating constantly between the most strict Presbyterianism and entering a Catholic convent. She had been brought up a Romanist; but her knotted fingers finally drove her into rationalist protestantism."

Pale, broad and chained—A cold blooded roué who will have recourse to anything to satisfy his passions.

The evil passion, in this case, is not the result of the warmth of a generous blood; it is solely the outcome of vicious imaginings.

Chained and rising toward the Mount of Saturn—Contempt of the opposite sex. In a very bad hand—Unnatural vices. Otherwise misanthropy of the darkest dye, as Saturn hates company.

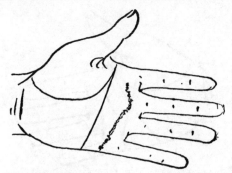

The **Tobacco Heart.**—In a very much rayed and cross-rayed hand, a Line of Head separated from the Line of Life and cut up in a number of short fragments. <u>A very poor Line of Heart. A double Girdle of Venus.</u>

"The abuse of tobacco smoking had rendered the subject wretchedly nervous and almost hysterical. His memory as well as his will power had vanished and the action of his heart was gravely injured by this excess of smoking."

b. In combination with other indications.

1. Length.

<u>Well traced and placed, with a strong first phalanx of the thumb—Constancy.</u>
Fidelity needs will power if it is to last.
<u>Well traced and placed, but with a</u>

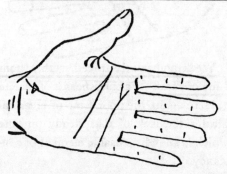

<u>weak first phalanx of the thumb—Inconstancy</u>; wayward loving disposition.

<u>A good line with a good Line of Head and a Triangle near the termination of a good Line of Life—Tact.</u>
Kindness of heart and brains are the necessary elements of tact.

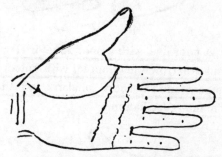

<u>A poor line, with a poor Line of Head and a triangle toward the termination of the Line of Life—Unkindness in speech;</u> foolish, harmful gossip. (See above.)

<u>A well developed Line, with somewhat exaggerate Mounts of Venus and the Moon—Romantic disposition.</u>
A man or woman who loves with the imagination, not the senses

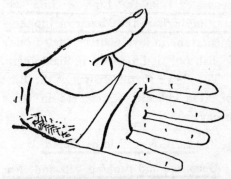

<u>Very long, with a prominent or much lined Mount of the Moon and a clearly marked Girdle of Venus—Almost insane</u> jealousy, generally of a physical nature and often without cause, since imagination, not common sense, rules over it.

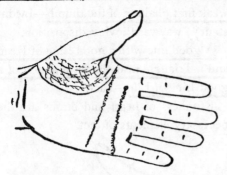

A poor line, with a poor Line of Head and a narrow Quadrangle, with smooth fingers and a short phalanx of the Thumb—Vacillation.

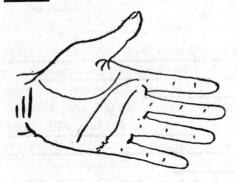

A poor Line with the Line of Head separated from the Line of Life and starting high on the Mount of Jupiter— Misfortune in love matters due to one's foolish ambition toward a brilliant union.

The above characteristics of the Line of Head indicate recklessness in one's behavior.

2. Color: Width: Depth.

Deep, red and running stiff and clear across the hand, from side to side, with a similar Line of Head and exaggerate Mounts of Mars—Tendency to murder.

Pale and wide, and with a Line of influence from the Mount of Venus to the Mount of Mercury or the Upper Mount

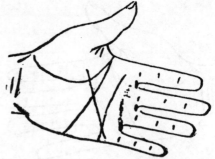

of Mars—Material love; extreme sensuality, resorting even to crime, especially with a broken or double Girdle of Venus.

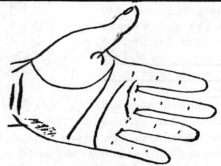

An unusually deep line with a strong Girdle of Venus and a prominent or much-lined Mount of the Moon—Unreasoning and unreasonable jealousy that will bring about disaster.

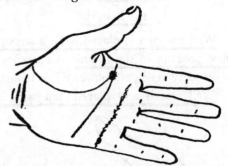

Weak and poorly traced, with a poor Line of Head—Faithlessness.

Here again, the poor Line of Head indicates the lack of that steady purpose which is an indispensable element of constancy.

Chained or poorly traced, with a similar Line of Head and a Mount of Venus, either exaggerate or covered with many cross-lines—Constant flirtations or even guilty intrigues.

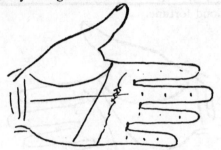

Chained at its intersection with the Line of Fate—Love trouble (or heart disease) having interfered with the subject's career.

III. STARTING POINTS AND FORKS AT THE START.

Starting from inside the third phalanx of the first finger—Lack of success in all directions.

The principle is that whenever a main line penetrates a finger, its best qualities turn into defects. We have seen that this is the case with all exaggerations, in the shape of fingers, mounts, etc.

Starting from far up into the Mount of Jupiter and forkless—Ideal love, with

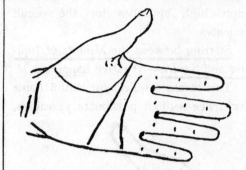

no trace of sensuality (if not contradicted by other indications).

This is again somewhat the exaggeration of a good thing.

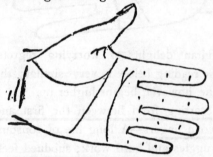

Starting from the center of the Mount of Jupiter, especially when forked—The highest type of love—pure, deep, steadfast.

Completely encircling the Mount of Jupiter, at the start—Jealousy, more ideal than sensual in its character, if the hand is otherwise good. Under the name of Solomon's Ring it is held to denote high aptitudes for the occult sciences.

Starting between the Mounts of Jupiter and Saturn—Negative happiness.

This means a quiet, uneventful home existence without passionate yearnings,

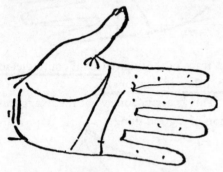

exultant delights or worrying regrets. The reading below is very similar; the Line, however, begins higher up.

Starting from between the first and second fingers—A long life of constant struggles and hard work; subdued feelings of love.

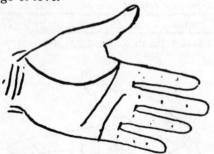

Starting under the Mount of Saturn

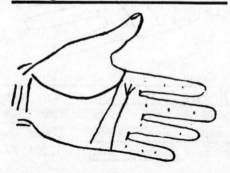

(without a fork)—Sensuality but no true, family affection.

Forked at the start, at the edge of the Mount of Jupiter, especially if there are three prongs all well into the Mount— Good fortune.

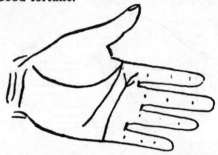

Forked at the start, at the edge of the Mount of Jupiter, one prong going up the Mount—Happy in love. Adding a cross on the Mount of Venus—An only love.

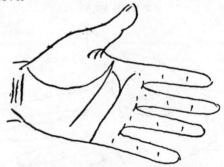

Forked at the start, one prong toward the Mount of Jupiter, the other toward (but not touching) the Line of Head—

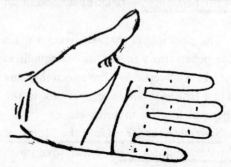

Self-deception (quite important).

Forked at the start, one prong to the Mount of Jupiter, the other to between the first and second fingers—A great home-loving nature, who will receive, in return, the same kind of affection and happiness.

I consider this the most satisfactory start for the Line of Heart.

Forked at the start, one prong ascending between the first and second fingers, the other prong just touching a good Mount of Jupiter, with an insignificant Mount of the Moon—Negative happiness. (See above.)

Resignation Due to Religious Belief.— All the fingers of the hand smooth and square tipped, except the first finger, which was very much pointed. The Line of Heart started with a much elongated fork, the prongs forming almost an island and united almost under the Mount of  the Sun. A star at the very beginning of the Line of Life.

"The subject had suffered from the consequences of a great family fatality occurring in his early childhood. He had finally placed his whole happiness in his faith in a higher and better world."

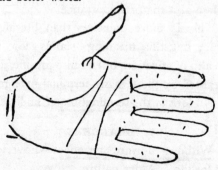

Forked at the start, with one prong to the Mount of Jupiter and the other to the Mount of Saturn—Fanaticism. More usually bad errors in the pursuit of happiness through love.

The idea of fanaticism is explained by the whole force of the subject's loving power being absorbed in the religious ideal represented by the Mount of Jupiter, but rendered gloomy and dangerous by the influence of the Mount of Saturn. The same Mount will also cause the failure of cherished love affairs.

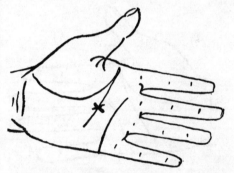

Short and starting from under the Mount of Saturn without forks—Premature death. Still more ominous if there is a cross at the center of a rather short Line of Head.

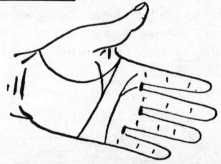

Forked at the start, with a fork from the Line of Head at its start reaching down into the Lower Mount of Mars— Separation resulting in marriage.

This peculiar reading, which I have verified three times lately, after borrowing it from a prominent English palmist, must be understood as follows: two people are deeply in love with each other; circumstances or dissatisfied parents separate them; their love instead of growing colder is increased tenfold by absence, so that they finally triumph over all obstacles.

IV. TERMINATION AND FORKS AT THE TERMINATION.

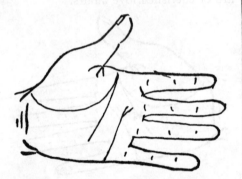

Extending around the Percussion, with a long, clear Line of Head and the upper Mount of Mars prominent—Daring spirit.

Remember that a fine Line of Heart gives you "a heart for any daring enterprise;" does not courage come from the Latin Cor, which means heart? In this

case it will give you coolness as well as bravery.

Completely encircling the Mount of Mercury at the termination—Singular aptitude for the occult sciences.

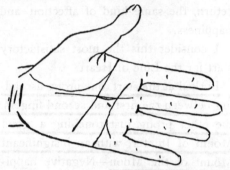

Forked at the Termination, with one prong deep into the Mount of Mercury and an island on the Line of Fate—A divorce, due to a guilty intrigue of the subject.

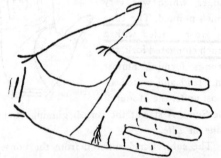

Very long and much frayed at the termination, or ending in a kind of tassel—For every little prong or branch a love affair of a minor importance.

This is more amusing than literally true; but this meaning stands for a wealth of affection, often quite prolific, as denoted by these many terminal prongs.

No fork at the termination—Childlessness.

V. BRANCHES.

Without upward branches—Poverty of feeling. A dry nature.

Very far apart from the Line of Head (especially in the middle) and both lines branchless—Life deprived of affections.

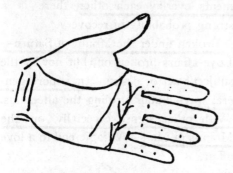

Downward branches—Disappointments caused by loved ones.

Lines dropping from the Line into the Quadrangle, if under the Mount of the Sun—Versatility seldom of much use to the subject. In any other place—Friends of the subject causing him trouble.

Very similar to preceding indication.

Hypertrophy of the Heart.—A number of minute perpendicular lines coming down from the Line of Heart and ending on or near the Line of Head.

"This serious heart trouble was discovered in the hand of a Chicago politician who died from it."

A straight branch, ending in a hook, entering the fourth finger—Accident crippling the subject.

A Wound Resulting in the Crippling of a Leg.—A line from the Line of Heart entering into the third phalanx of the fourth finger and ending there in a kind of hook. A good Mercury means agility—this line indicates lack of agility.

"A child was crippled in the leg by an accident."

A wavy branch down to the Mount of the Moon—Murderous disposition. (Extremely scarce.)

Two perpendicular lines dropping straight from a poor Line of Heart into the Mount of the Moon—Death by apoplexy.

The result of a defective circulation and an overwrought nervous system.

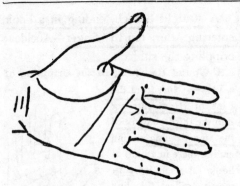

A straight upward branch reaching the Mount of Saturn, then turning back abruptly—Misplaced affection.

This is a clear indication of some trouble in one's career, due to a disastrous attachment.

VI. BREAKS.

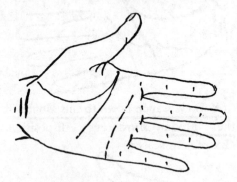

Much broken—Inconstancy; or hatred of the opposite sex.

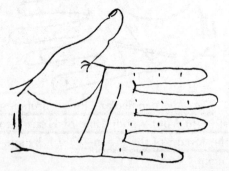

Broken under the Mount of Saturn in

both hands—Dangerous illness arising from defective circulation of the blood; aneurism; short life. If the two fragments overlay each other, there is a strong probability of recovery.

Broken under the Mount of Saturn—Love affairs broken off, but not by the subject's act or desire. In a more general way—Fatality ruling the affections. With other signs, especially on the Mounts of Mars—A tragic end to a love affair.

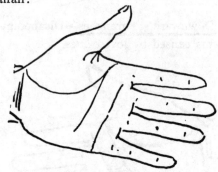

Broken under the Mount of the Sun—Love affair broken off through a caprice of the subject. (Artists are inconstant.) In a general way—Pride, often insane vanity, ruling the affections. In matters of health—A serious heart trouble; if found in both hands—This trouble will end fatally.

Heart Troubles of the Most Serious Character.—In the left hand a Line of Heart broken under the Mount of the Sun, then resumed weakly and forming an island by turning back in a curve after it reached the Mount of Mercury. A deep dot on the Line of Head. In the

right hand the <u>Lines of Life, Head and Heart were joined at the start.</u>

"Seen in the hands of a young man, a consumptive, who suffered, and died suddenly from a grave hypertrophy of the heart."

<u>Broken under the Mount of Mercury</u>—Love affair broken off on account of the avaricious disposition of the subject.

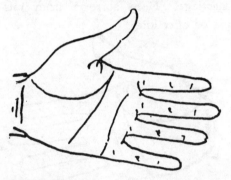

In a general way—Love of money ruling over the affections. <u>In matters of health</u> — Liver t r o u b l e s interfering gravely with the action of the heart.

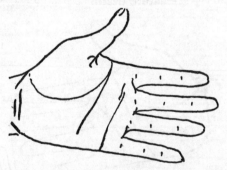

In the above observations, whenever, instead of a clean break or gap, <u>the two fragments are overlaying each other, the lovers shall be probably reunited, especially if the break exists only in one hand.</u>

VII. CONNECTED WITH THE MAIN LINES.

a. Directly.

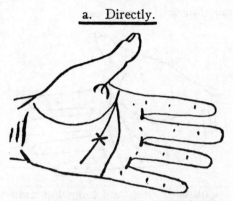

<u>Joined with the Lines of Head and Life at the start with (or without) a cross in the middle of the Line of Head—Sudden death (if repeated in both hands).</u>

This must not be read as "premature death," but simply as meaning that when death will come it will be "without warning." There is great chance, however, of its being accidental or violent death. The date is usually found on the Line of Life or on the Line of Fate.

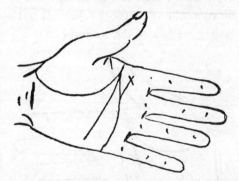

<u>Joined with the Lines of Life and Head at the start, with one prong of a fork of the Line forming a Saint Andrew's cross with a short bar on the Lower Mount of Jupiter</u>—A love affair bringing with it much sorrow, loss, **or** trouble, even unto death.

Take care not to mistake such a cross for the excellent cross of happy love affair, described on page 94.

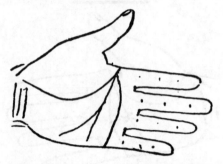

Unusually deep and long, but united at the start with the Lines of Life and Head, the latter terminating in a fork, one prong of which descends into the Mount of the Moon, while the other prong follows its natural course or joins the Line of Heart—Blind and fatal passion.

Imagination triumphs here over sound common sense; this is evidenced by the fork of the Line of Head. The depth of the Line is also an ominous indication of an intensity prejudicial to the lasting welfare of the subject.

Joined at its start with the Line of Head, under the Mount of Saturn—Disaster due to unreasoning passion. If repeated in both hands—Sudden death, often due to the same cause.

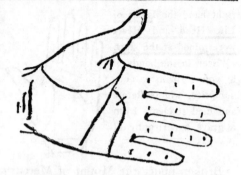

Joined to the Line of Head under Saturn with a bar across it—Wretched marriage. Deep sorrows from misplaced affection.

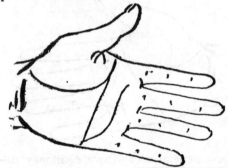

Joined in a wavy termination with the Line of Head, under the Mount of Mercury—Premature death.

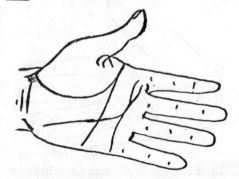

Starting from the Mount of Jupiter and connecting with a straight, clear Line of Fate arising from the Mount of the Moon, the said Line of Fate losing itself into the Line of Heart—Unexpected happiness, due to the intense devotion of the loved one.

The intensity of this affection generally prognosticates a fatal reaction coming.

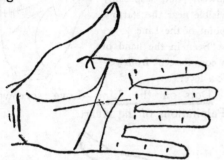

A line from the line to the Line of Fate, the latter being broken in its course—Widowhood or widowerhood or death of a dear one not a relative.

The place on the Line of Fate where the break occurs will give the date of the bereavement. It is supposed that the loss of the dear one has caused a serious, material change in the subject's prospects.

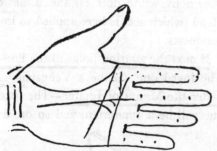

Branches from the Line of Fate ascending to the Line without touching it—Love affairs not ending in marriage. If they touch it—The unions are completed; if they cut it—The unions will be very unfortunate. (See final sub-heading in Chapter on the Line of Fate.)

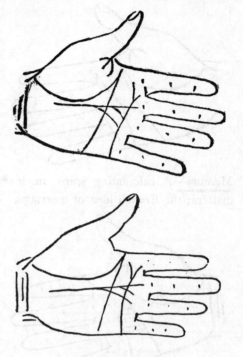

b. By Minor Lines.

Connecting Lines between the Line and the Line of Life—Illnesses caused

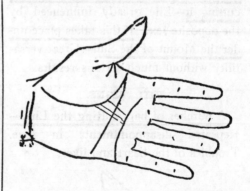

either by sorrows due to disappointed love or by a defective working of the heart.

Joined to the Line of Head by a Line starting from the latter—Fatal infatuation. If the hand shows no sensual tendency, but with a high Mount of

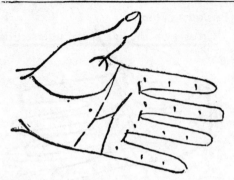

Mercury—A calculating spirit in love matters; the French idea of marriage.

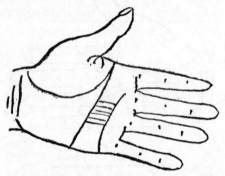

Lines from the Line downward reaching close to the Line of Head without cutting it—Life greatly influenced by the opposite sex. If this takes place under the Mount of the Sun—Great versatility without much serious results.

VIII. SIGNS.

A number of bars cutting the Line— Repeated disappointments in love. Troubles of the heart and liver.

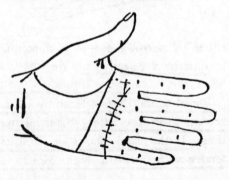

Oppression of the Heart Consequence of a Severe Liver Trouble.—The Line of Heart cut by a number of strong bars of a yellowish tint, especially visible near the starting point of the Line.

"Seen in the hand of a convalescent from yellow fever."

Dots on the Line—Love sorrows. Palpitations of the Heart.

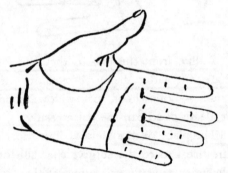

A white dot on the line—Success in love affairs.

That inventive, conquering genius shown by white dots on the Line of Head (which see) is here applied to love conquests.

If next the starting point of the line— The loved one will be a Venusian. If under the Mount of Jupiter—The loved one will be a Jupiterian, and so on, ac-

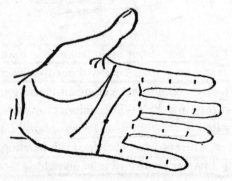

cording to the Mount above the white dot. (See pages 122-138, for any minute Description of Types.)

A deep dot on the Line under the Mount of the Sun—Love sorrow or trouble caused by some celebrated person and which is harmful to the subject's ambition.

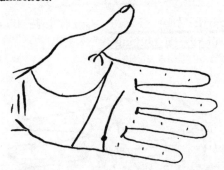

A deep dot on the Line under the Mount of Mercury—Love sorrow or trouble caused the subject by a doctor, scientist, or business man. With a poor, or wavy Line of Liver—Heart palpitation coming from a poor digestion.

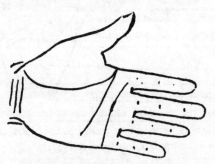

A long red scar (elongated dot) on the Line—Danger of apoplexy.

Black or bluish dots—Grave malarial fever. Seen also in hands of subjects threatened with inflammatory rheumatism.

Cut under the Mount of Mercury by a branch of a cross on that Mount—

Business failure.

Crosses on the line at the intersection

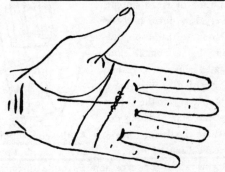

of the lines of Heart and Fate—Pecuniary troubles, due to love matters.

A star at the end of a branch of the Line going down into the Mount of the Moon—Hereditary madness of the erotic form.

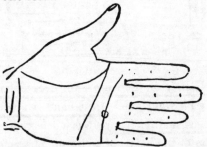

A circle on the Line—Weakness of the Heart. Under the Mount of the Sun —Trouble with the eyesight.

A square on or close to the Line—Preservation from physical harm, or love sorrow.

Curious **Square of Preservation.**—A strong Mount of Mars, a Line of Head sloping very low down into the Mount of the Moon, ending in two small elongated squares. A fine Line of Fate throwing a branch at 31 to the Mount of the Sun, a strong dot where this branch begins.

At the connection of the Lines of Fate and Heart, an angle thus formed that a square appears quite distinct. A cross on the Mount of Jupiter.

"A very bright servant girl who escaped almost miraculously the fatal clutches of Dumollard, the famous servant-girl murderer of Lyons, France. This terrible adventure marked by the dot was the source of her future fortune, as she made a comparatively brilliant marriage due to the notoriety she gained through the trial. She had headaches and presentiments, hence the slope of the Line of Head."

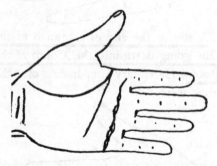

Islands on the Line—For every island a guilty intrigue. In a hand showing no sensual tendency—Very defective action of the heart, of a chronic character.

An island on the Line under the Mount of Saturn—A love affair which interferes very seriously with the subject's prospects; also, varicose veins.

An island on the Line with an island

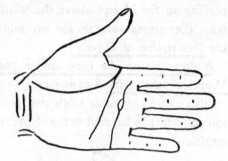

on the Line of Fate—Guilty love that will stop at nothing.

Serious Eye Trouble, Brought About by an Accident.—An island on the Line of Heart, under the Mount of the Sun. An exaggerate Mount of the Moon. A very thin palm.

"The subject was anæmic to a degree; a slight accident to one eye was rendered rapidly worse in its consequences by the poor quality of the blood, until complete blindness was the result."

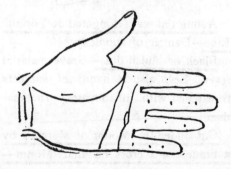

An island on the line under the Mount of the Sun—Very serious trouble with the eyesight.

SPECIAL OBSERVATIONS.

A double Line of Heart—Capacity for deep affection that will cause much sorrow to the subject.

This is to be a Sister Line of great length and evenness. Often read in that

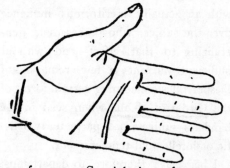

case for men—Special vigor; for women —Exemption from most female troubles.

THE GIRDLE OF VENUS.

In most of the books on Palmistry written in the English tongue, I have noticed a great reluctance on the part of the authors to call things by their names and to state facts with the bluntness that pertains to all scientific investigations. In fact, the tendency has been to soften down the terms in which to express the many unpleasant features that occur, naturally enough, in the examination of the average hand, thus debasing this noble science of Palmistry to the level of a puerile amusement to while away an idle hour. Now, if Palmistry is to be considered as nothing more than an ingenious form of recreation, I, for one, and, with me, all men and women who claim to be thinkers and prospectors in the realms of the unknown, we will beg permission to drop this child-play, here and now, and to turn our earnest attention to some more worthy problem within the boundaries of natural philosophy. But if, on the contrary—and as I, for one, firmly believe—the study and reading of the Hand bring us nearer the

solving of many complicated questions concerning the partially hidden temperament of man, physical, mental and moral, then, indeed, I claim the right for all teachers and students of Palmistry to face the symptoms just as they are— unpalatable though they may be—and to interpret them with the same unbiased and unveiled frankness that is found quite appropriate in the mouth of a surgeon facing his operating table.

This protest—which I have heard uttered many a time by faithful and undaunted searchers after truth—is particularly well timed, I think, just before presenting my reading of the Girdle of Venus, than which no line in the Hand has remained more wretchedly misunderstood, thanks to that very unscientific tendency of Modern Palmists— Desbarrolles excepted of course—to wrap up every disagreeable statement in terms so vague as to render it positively unintelligible.

A few among the more recent writers have even attempted to endow this line with an actually meritorious influence over the subject who possesses it, generalizing to that effect—and without sufficient warrant—a few remarks of Desbarrolles concerning certain forms of the Girdle of Venus when seen in the hands of subjects of a particularly artistic or intellectual temperament.

I beg leave, therefore, to depart most emphatically from this radically inaccurate and error-fostering method and to continue stating ungarbled and undoctored facts whenever I meet them in my regular chiromantic observations.

This book is not written for infants or for maidens kept purposely in ignorance of the nether side of human nature. Those who open it have doubtless realized, from the start, that all the maladies, physical, mental and moral, our sad race is heir to, are to be herein mentioned and expatiated upon in the language accepted by the medical profession, whenever, in the regular order of our studies, the examination of the hand brings us face to face with them.

This being stated as a necessary preface, I shall give at once the invariable interpretation accepted by Desbarrolles as the meaning of the Girdle of Venus.

It is understood by the Master to indicate those vicious habits generally developed—when they exist at all—at the time of puberty, and to which science gives the name of onanism. They have always been considered as arising from nervous, half hysterical troubles—concomitant with the transition from boyhood or girlhood to manhood or womanhood. To some extent—a very limited extent—the youth or maiden thus inclined is not to be held absolutely responsible for the outburst of this deplorable tendency; and most happily, under the watchful, intelligent care of the parents, it is, in many cases, eradicated almost at once from the subject's system. Certain hygienic measures, and the wholesome influence of the father or mother calling upon the tempted child to master the evil desire, very frequently conquer the vicious leaning. In that case, either the Girdle of Venus never shows itself in the hands, or it appears only in the Left Hand—a token of the temptation having triumphed for a time—and is not found in the Right Hand, the evidence of a well directed will-power having overcome mere animal instinct.

That the Girdle of Venus must, in all but a few very exceptional cases, be considered as the gauge, so to speak, of the gravest troubles the generative organs are made to suffer from through the evil thoughts of the human mind, is confirmed by the fact that its being double or triple or broken or starred is always accurately interpreted as denoting unnatural vices or syphilitic poisoning of the blood, or even erotic insanity of the worst character. The most indulgent reading of this line is that of hysteria, unaccompanied by any immoral acts, but accounted for, primarily, by some serious derangement of the generative functions.

Finally, even the exceptions to these most unpleasant readings only confirm them more strongly. As I stated in my

Chapter on the Line of Head, and earlier, in my Part III, on the Mounts, an exaggerate or much lined Mount of the Moon, as well as a Line of Head sloping deep into that Mount are not absolutely unfavorable symptoms, whenever the general temperament and tendencies of the subject are such as to reveal an especially gifted, artistic or poetical nature. In such beings' hands, the Girdle of Venus itself might be read—as the above markings would be—as the revelation of this most acutely delicate nervous sensibility which one expects to meet with in those rare and select geniuses that bring to the world its most exquisite delights in the guise of poem, song, painting, statuary. Then and then only, I repeat it, may the dreaded hysteria those indications so clearly denote be made to read as the extraordinary cerebral erethism indispensable to the conceiving and begetting of immortal masterpieces.

I. POSITION AND DIRECTION.

Normal: Starts from between the

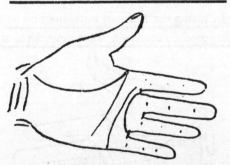

first and second fingers and ends between the third and fourth fingers. In a bad hand indicating a vicious disposition, that is, with a high or much rayed Mount

of Venus, an exaggerate Mount of the Moon and a red Line of Mars—Profligacy of the worst kind; must be especially watched in young people's hands.

II. CHARACTER.

Very deep and often red, and cutting through the Lines of Fate and the Sun as if to obliterate their best characteristics—The intellect of the subject is gravely impaired by his vicious tendencies and his career will suffer grievously from the same sad cause.

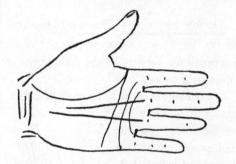

Very thin, and cut by—not cutting—strong and good Lines of Fate and the Sun—Wit, love and talent for literature, art, etc.; this supposes the hand in general to be a good one.

Hysterical Insanity.—A very short thumb. A Line of Head sloping deep into the Mount of the Moon, where it ends in a star. A big cross under that star. Another star on the same Mount connected by a forked line with the Line of Life. Straight and deep Lines of Fate

and Liver, the former entering into the second finger. A double girdle of Venus.

"A young woman suffering from the monomania of persecution visited Desbarrolles. She was wealthy and quite tenacious and sensible in money matters—this being a characteristic of such a Line of Liver—but intensely hysterical and gradually drifting to sheer insanity."

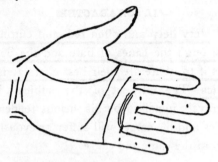

Double or Triple—The worst features of the Girdle are increased in the same proportion. Generally the indication of unnatural vices.

Sad Consequences of Continued Bad Habits.—A deep, black dot on the Line of Life at 18 and another at 23 connected by Lines of Influence with a black dot on the Line of Head, from there a very thin line went up into the Mount of Saturn, entering a triple Girdle of Venus.

"Seen in the hand of a very young man subject to frequent nervous fits and to increasing melancholia. He had lost all capacity for intellectual work and was constantly thinking of his wretched state of increasing weakness. Urged by Desbarrolles, he finally gave up the sad habits of his early youth, began a long trip on foot through the mountains of Switzerland, devoted himself to agricultural pursuits and, within a few years, was again a well man."

III. TERMINATION.

Terminating (or rather open at the termination) on the Mount of Mercury;

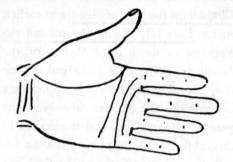

in an otherwise good hand—Unusual—though unhealthy—nervous energy and ardor in every undertaking. In a bad hand—The subject will add deceit to lasciviousness of the worst character.

IV. BREAKS.

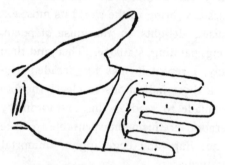

Broken—Sensuality at its worst.

V. CONNECTED WITH THE MAIN LINES.

Cutting the Lines of Fate, the Sun and Liver and seemingly shattering them at

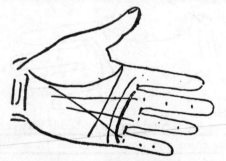

the intersecting points—Obstacles to success due to an inordinate pursuit of

sensual pleasure. (See above reading.)
Cutting a prolonged Line of Union—

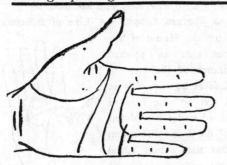

The hysterical temperament of the subject and his heartless selfishness is sure to destroy the happines of the one who loves him or her.

VI. SIGNS.
Cut by small lines, with the Mount of

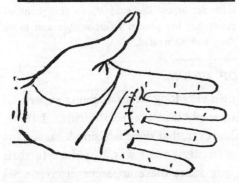

Venus and the Moon exaggerated—Hysteria of an erotic character.

Skepticism Struggling Against an Inclination Toward Convent Life.—High Mount of Jupiter; several vertical lines on the Mount of Saturn; a much chained Line of Heart. Spatulate fingers, a first finger as long as the second. A Line of Influence from

a star on the Mount of Venus cut the Line of Life at 20, ending under the Mount of Mercury, forming a large fork, with a sloping Line of Head. A double girdle of Venus.

"A young woman of 23, when she consulted Desbarrolles, suffered from intense hysterical excitement, due originally to a great sorrow from the death of a loved one, when she was 20. She had devoted herself to exaggerate religious practices, but her mind, which was quite intellectual and philosophically inclined, was constantly raising objections against the belief she tried to attach herself to. She was constantly hesitating between convent life and an impulse to throw aside all religious ideas."

Faintly marked in an otherwise good hand, but cut by a deep bar upon the

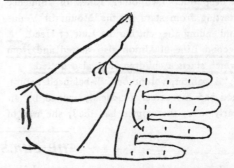

Mount of the Sun—Reverses due to women. In a bad hand—Loss of fortune due to extreme profligacy.

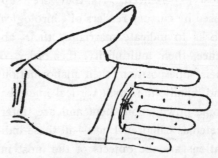

A star on the Girdle—especially if it is double or treble—A grave venereal disease from which the subject will never recover.

No person with such a sign in the hand ought ever to think of marrying.

Position in Life Ruined by a Woman.—
A Lunar and Mercurian type; a large Mount of Venus. A dot at the beginning of the Line of Life. A very long Line of Heart, from which starts under the Mount of Saturn a Line of Head drooping almost straight down the Triangle. A star on a strongly marked Girdle of Venus. A Line of Influence from the Mount of Venus ending on the Mount of Mercury, cut by a Line of Union, itself marked with a deep dot. Two other Lines of Influence starting from stars on the Mount of Venus and ending after cutting the Line of Head. A second Line of Union also dotted and from which starts a children line, also dotted.

"A painter, voluptuous, ill-balanced nature, had had his career practically ruined by an early love; the woman had died; she was of the Mercurian type, greedy and deceitful. Another woman he had loved had died. He had had a child from her, who had died."

A Modern Sappho.—A Line of Influence from the Mount of Venus cuts an upward branch of the Line of Life at 24 and ends in a star on the Line of Head under the Mount of the Sun. From that star rises a long island that ends in a star, on the Mount of the Sun, connecting with the end of a quadruple Girdle of Venus.

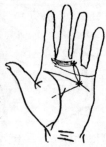

"A lady had divorced from her husband, receiving from him a large sum of money; this fortune had been squandered upon a lady friend, who had obtained the most detestable influence upon the subject, to the point of rendering her almost irresponsible and more than half demented."

THE LINES OF UNION.

I am now in the presence of the Lines that offer probably the greatest difficulties of all to every Palmist—even the most experienced. As they are supposed by cursory readers of Chirological works to indicate marriage, their absence, their multiplicity, the order of their superposition, their malformations and, finally, the small vertical lines that come down upon them and are interpreted as Children Lines—all these indications are the objects of the most intense curiosity to young and old, and, but too often, the causes of bitter disappointment or unwarranted satisfaction. They certainly are puzzling at times, and if the standing of Palmistry as a science depended on their infallibly correct reading, I am afraid it would not hold its own very long, at least among superficial or easily discouraged students. I think, however, that there is a simple, as well as a strictly honest way to reduce to their true value these apparent discrepancies between facts and Chiromantic indications as far as the Lines of Union are concerned; and that is to give to these markings the very modest place in the study of the hand that really belongs to them, and to search elsewhere for such revelations as had been supposed, for too long a time, to be confined to that very narrow space along the Percussion of the Mount of Mercury.

Although Desbarrolles has already insisted upon the principle that Unions in the hand are not to be understood as meaning only legal Unions, i. e., Marriages, it is to the better element of the British palmistic world that we owe the discovery of those Lines of Influence—from the Mount of the Moon generally—which indicate in connection with the Line of Fate—and sometimes the Line of the Sun—the most important among these Unions, be they marriages or not. I shall have occasion, in my very next chapter, to describe those Lines of Influence from the Mount of the Moon and to indicate their proper value in all such serious love affairs as affect one's existence.

Suffice it to say here, that the Lines of Union, on the Percussion of the Mount of Mercury, have been dethroned from their exclusive, prominent position as recorders of legal bonds, and are to be considered only as confirmations of what the Lines of Fate and the Sun and their Lines of Influence shall have previously revealed to us. As such they are decidedly useful, and I may add that, even by themselves, they are, by no means as error-breeding as it has become almost a fashion to believe them to be, especially if we are satisfied to read them as Lines of Attachment, not marriage.

However, in the following observations, the student will find much valuable and reliable information concerning those Lines, somewhat based on the old principles; but let it be understood that the interpretation therein given applies exclusively to very clearly marked Lines of Union. In fact, I am bound to admit that a long and deep Line of Union, in an otherwise excellent hand, is entitled

to a reading very similar to the old interpretation of Marriage. But remember, this must be, as far as possible, the confirmation of an event discovered elsewhere in the hand. And I add: this will be especially the case in women's hands. In men's hands, the Lines of Union often constitute the sole indications of attachments that really left their marks in the subject's brain—and consequently in his palm.

I. POSITION AND DIRECTION.

Normal: Cutting   the   Percussion

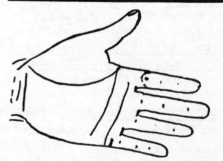

horizontally between the Line of Heart and the base of the Fourth Finger and penetrating (not very deep) into the Mount of Mercury.

Of course the design cannot show the exact position of the Lines of Union.

The longer the Line—The longer the Union, be it marriage or liaison. It is

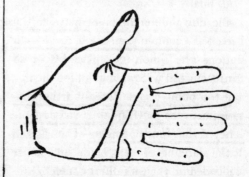

therefore customary to consider the long, deep lines as indications of legal Unions.

Sloping toward the Line of Heart— Widowhood or widowerhood. If the slope is very gradual—The last illness of the subject's spouse will be lingering.

Curving upwards—The subject will not marry.

I am still waiting for a confirmation of this curious reading.

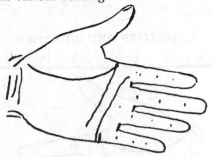

Close to the Line of Heart—The Union took place before 18 for maids and 21 years of age for men

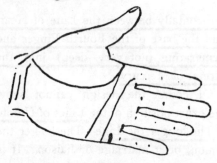

Close to the middle point between the Line of Heart and the base of the fourth finger—The Union took place before 28 for maids and widows and 35 for men.

At a point about three-fourths distance between the Line of Heart and the base of the fourth finger—The Union took place at about 38 for maids or widows and 45 years old for men.

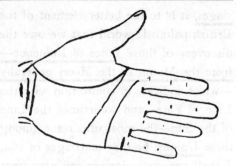

Above that point—The Union is dated between 45 and 70.

For a more accurate method of obtaining the date of such Unions as were legal Marriages, or amounted almost to the same thing, see Chapter on Lines of Influence (pp. 172-193) and the final section of the Chapter on the Line of Fate.

II. STARTING POINTS AND FORKS AT THE START.

Forked at the start, on the Percussion

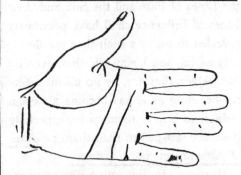

—Separation by the fault of the subject, not by that of the other party.

Of course this cannot be seen in this design of the inside palm.

I found, many a time, that this fork, at either end of a Line of Union, meant, not a legal separation or one brought about by the desire of either of the united parties to stay away from the other, but a separation de facto, as, for instance, a long sojourn of one of the united parties in a foreign country away from the other, such a period of separation having proved quite painful and left its mark on that account.

III. TERMINATION AND FORKS AT THE TERMINATION.

Terminating at the Line of the Sun;

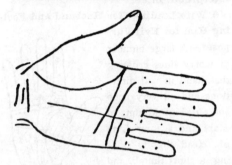

if it does not cut it—A union with a person either famous or very rich. If it cuts it—The union will be a mesalliance.

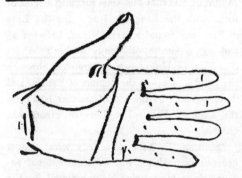

The Line forked at its termination—Separation not caused by the fault of the subject in whose hand the fork is found, but by the other party's fault.

The Line terminating in a fork, one prong of which droops toward the Line of Heart—Divorce in favor of the subject in whose hand the fork is found.

The Line drooping and terminating, deep and clear upon the Mount of

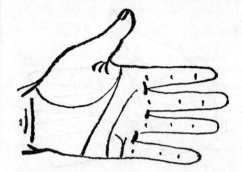

Venus, in the left hand only—Intended divorce; in both hands—The divorce has taken place.

Generally the same indication is marked in the hand when the Line of Influence from the Line of Life or the Mount of Venus comes up and merges into a drooping Line of Union. (See Lines of Influence, pp. 172-193.)

IV. BRANCHES.

An upward branch touching the

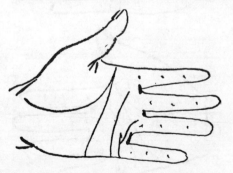

Mount of the Sun—A brilliant Union.

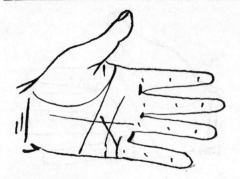

A downward branch cutting the Line of the Sun—A mesalliance.

Well traced but with capillary lines drooping from the Line to the Line of Heart—Troubles caused by the illness of the person with whom the subject is united.

I met this frequently in women's hands when the bread-winner of the family, having been ill for a long time, the circumstances of the wife had become much straitened.

V. BREAKS.

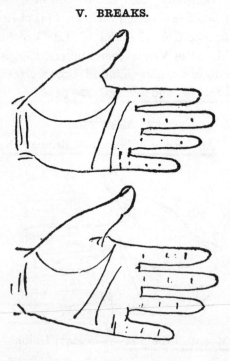

Broken—Separation or divorce.

Broken, but the two fragments overlaying each other—Separation followed by reunion; sometimes a second marriage between the same parties.

I observed this last reading in the hands of several people whose existence, very well known to me, confirmed this interpretation.

A Wife Leading Her Husband and Fooling Him for Evil Purposes.—A large number of worry lines crossing the hand in all directions and all very deep and red; high Mounts of Mars and a long Line of Head slightly sloping; a short thumb, and at about 29 the Line of  Life threw up a branch, which was crossed by a Line of Influence, ending under the Mount of Mercury and thus forming a kind of fork, with the Line of Head. On the Line of Fate was found a large island, between 25 and 29; a Girdle of Venus in both hands; one Line of Union, which stretched through the hand and up to the Mount of Saturn, and there was met by the top of another island on the Line of Fate. The Line of Heart was chained.

"Seen in the hand of a lady with a most nervous disposition, but with exceptional energy, these facts being demonstrated by the deep worry lines and the long Line of Head. At 29 she had a serious quarrel with her husband, probably on account of an intrigue indicated by the first island. The long Line of Union prolonged so far always indicates that the subject will obey his or her passion to any extent. The lady was also afflicted with palpitations of the heart, and the cross on the lower Mount of the Moon proved to be an indication of over-excited imagination and also of kidney troubles."

VI. CONNECTED WITH OTHER LINES.

Through Minor Lines.

A Line of Influence from the Mount

of Venus cutting the Lines of Life, Head, Heart and Marriage—Troubles connected with marriage, generally due to the interference of relatives.

A Line of Influence from the Mount of Venus cutting a small upward branch of the Line of Life and merging into (or cutting) a Line of Union—Legal separation.

Seduction by Married Man Causes Separation and Long Poverty. Finally Prosperity.—A star on a Line of Union connected with the Mount of Venus by a Line of Influence cutting an upward branch of the Line of Life at 25; islanded immediately afterward. A star on the

upper Mount of Mars, from which a Line of Influence merged into a fine Line of the Sun.

"A young English girl had been led astray by a married man. At 25 a separation between them had taken place, causing great trouble and sorrow to the subject. The man was a mixture of Martian and Mercurian type, a brilliant officer but a schemer and deceiver."

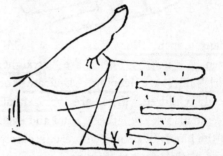

A Line of Influence from inside the Triangle cutting the Lines of Fate, Head and Heart and terminating after cutting a forked Line of Union—Divorce.

Whenever these Lines of Influence are islanded on the way, the trouble or divorce has a guilty intrigue (generally of the subject) as its real cause.

VII. SIGNS.

Cut by a line from the base of the

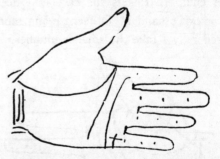

fourth finger—Opposition to the Union.

Upright lines coming down from the base of the fourth finger and touching (not cutting) the Line—Children; as

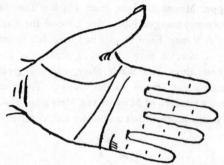

hood, or widowerhood.

many such lines as many children. Boys' lines are straight; girls' lines are leaning. Delicate (or dead) children, lines are very faint. Found also in the father's hand and even in the hands of people who are intensely fond of children not their own.

I always endeavor to find those children lines among a number of faint downward lines often found in that vicinity and very accurately read as chattering habits. Miscarriages, in the latter period of pregnancy, leave the same markings in women's hands. Often you will find marked a different number of children lines in each hand. I have found sometimes that you could add the two numbers and the total gave the total of children (this is the case in Queen Victoria's hands). Otherwise and more generally I take the smaller number.

An island on a children line—Delicacy of the child's health. If found at the termination of that children line— Death of the child.

A black spot or a star would supply the same reading. Of course all these indications are so minute that it is seldom that they are found available.

Cruel Death of a Child.—Upon a Line of Union descends a child line with a deep dot and a bar across before it touches the Line of Union.

"The child of a lady friend of Desbarrolles had died a violent death. The above signs were found in the mother's hand."

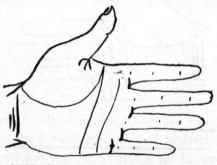

A black spot on the Line—Widow-

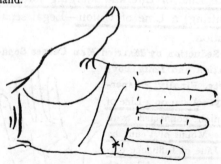

Drooping toward the Line of Heart, with a cross where the drooping begins—

The person to whom the subject is united will die suddenly.

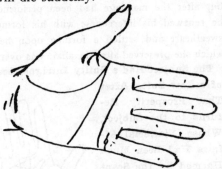

An island on the Line—Quarreling (or guilty intrigue).

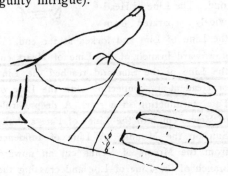

Full of little islands or downward branches—The subject not to marry.

This I repeatedly found correct. It indicates great dissipation resulting in impotency.

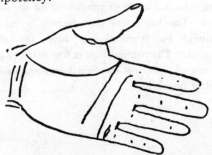

An island at the termination of the Line with another island at the base of the second phalanx of the thumb—A

union between near relatives.

Here again the island indicates the guilty nature of the affections.

SPECIAL OBSERVATION.

A clear, strong line, accompanied

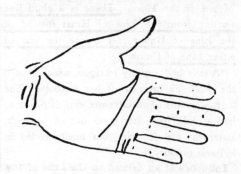

closely by a minute parallel line—The subject must have continued loving someone else since the union took place; in other words, an older attachment still survives.

I found quite often—especially in France, where such situations are very frequent—this minute parallel line to mean the influence of a parent over one of the united parties, overshadowing the new affection; I called it on that account, only half in jest, the mother-in-law line.

ADDITIONAL CASES.

Guilty Intrigue. Death of the Husband.—A Line of Head extending across the whole hand and separated from the Line of Life; a straight Line of Fate; a wavy Line of Heart; a double Girdle of Venus; two Lines of Union, the upper one starred; the Mounts of Venus and the lower Moon much rayed; a

Line of Influence starting from a star on the Mount of Venus and ending in a star on the Line of Fate; a small line from the Line of Head before it reaches the Line of Fate ends on the Line of Fate in the middle of the Quadrangle; from there starts downward a line ending in a star in the middle of the Mount of the Moon. <u>There is a child line starting from the Line of Heart instead of the Line of Union just before the end of either Line of Union.</u>

"A lady had a guilty intrigue, which caused the death by insanity of her husband. The lady, who was of an ultra-nervous disposition, had a child from her lover out of wedlock. Later she married him, but finally ended in hysteric insanity."

Influence of an Island on the Line of the Sun.—A good Line of Life, a fair Line of Head attached to the Line of Life, and <u>a Line of Heart crossing the whole hand,</u> leaving a very wide quadrangle. An Influence Line from the Mount of Venus cuts an upward branch of the Line of Life at 32 and connects on the Line of Head with the beginning of a large island on the Line of the Sun, extending clear through the quadrangle. The Line of the Sun extends very fine up to the top of the Mount.

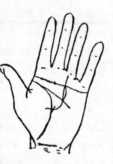

"A young woman came to consult Desbarrolles on a very important event. He predicted a separation to come off very soon, and **in fact the lady was separated from a lover** with whom she had lived several years; the gentleman had decided to marry someone else; but after the marriage had been performed he renewed his intercourse with his former sweetheart and settled a fortune upon her, which she preserved after the affair was over."

The Subject Had a Guilty Intrigue. Loss of a Law Suit. After That Prosperity Returns to the Subject, Whose Financial Affairs Had Been Much Harmed by the Scandal.—The third finger almost equal to the second. The Line of Head widely separated from the Line of Life and forked at the end. A downward branch of the Line of Heart cut <u>the Line of the Sun and reached the Line of Head at its connection with the Line of Fate,</u> terminating in a star. A deep Girdle of Venus cut into the Lines of Fate and the Sun on the Mounts. A Line of Influence from the Mount of Venus cut an upward branch of the Line of Life and crossing the island ended after crossing the Line of the Sun.

"A gentleman was partner in a firm whose head dragged it into a ruinous lawsuit through wild speculation. The partnership had been concocted by the wife of the speculating partner, who had an illicit attachment for the subject. The latter was thus financially ruined through his overwhelming love for that woman. The continuation in fine shape of the Lines of Fate and the Sun prognosticated a better future."

THE LINE OF FATE.

There are only two points I want to make clear to the student before beginning my readings of this Line. The first refers to its name, which is, in one respect, most unsatisfactory to me, since it seems to imply, to too great an extent, the existence of fatality as a ruling power over man's destiny. Now, the very basis of the system which I teach in these pages, in accordance with the great Masters at whose feet I humbly sat—in spirit at least—is that, within certain bounds which I do not pretend to delimit, freedom of action is left, or rather given, to man to mold his life as he sees fit. One of the essential differences between Palmistry and the various forms of fortune-telling—and I mean those forms that are not necessarily fradulent but have some sort of scientific foundation—consists therefore in this principle that hands reveal our tendencies, their working over us in the past, and their probable, logical consequences in the future, but that they also indicate whether or not we are endowed with such an amount of will-power as will help us conquer our weaknesses, physical, mental and moral, and save us from the worst possibilities delineated in our hands. Fatality ceases therefore to have any meaning in connection with Palmistic readings, and, I repeat it, the words Line of Fate are not to be understood as referring to it in the least.

Fate stands here for Career, Life-work, the Succession of Happenings, fortunate or otherwise, that form the running thread of our existence. On that Line, therefore, we expect to find such indications as will give us a fairly correct idea of all that is in store for us—health matters not included, if they are not to interfere with our occupations, ambitions, etc. Over some of these events we may have but little, if any control; but, as a rule, we shall soon discover by what means we may—if we care to—influence for the better the destiny thus outlined. So that, after all, the Line of Fate, in spite of its name, is the one marking in the hand that illustrates best the essential doctrine of free will.

The second statement that ought to find its place here relates to the close connection existing between the Line of Fate and the Line of the Sun. I consider them, in a great many respects, as equivalents and sister lines, as truly associated together as the Line of Mars is with the Line of Life. I wish the student to bear this in mind when perusing this chapter and the next, and to remember that Desbarrolles places the two lines on such an even level that he bases upon the existence, direction, etc., of either—when alone—the exact readings he would ascribe to the other. I now proceed with my examination of

THE LINE OF FATE.

I. POSITION AND DIRECTION.

Running straight to the Mount of Sat-

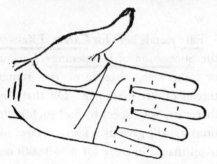

urn, into which it penetrates deeply—A life of exceptional good luck.

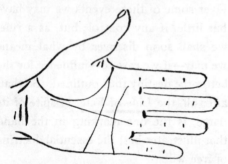

Running straight to the Mount of the Sun—Celebrity in fine art or literature.

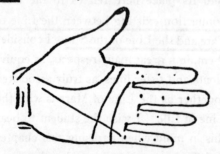

Straight to the Mount of Mercury—Great success in business.

Running straight to the Mount of Saturn and then curving toward the Mount of Jupiter, which it penetrates—Very extraordinary success in life; sometimes limited to a brilliant union.

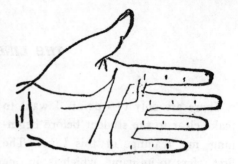

II. CHARACTER.

a. By itself.

1. Length.

Absent—Insignificant, eventless life.

Remember that the presence of a Line of the Sun should induce the student to read on that Line the life events of the subject.

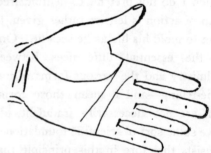

Straight and good, but only from the Line of Heart upwards—Good fortune in old age, generally due to success in science, or agriculture, i. e., some occupation that has no element of speculation or risk in it.

The influence of the Mount of Saturn is more visible in that portion of the Line, although we must bear in mind that it is exerted over the whole stretch of the Line of Fate.

2. Color: Width: Depth.

Of a deep red color, cutting through

the Mount of Saturn, and rising deep into the third phalanx of the second finger—Dishonorable death, or, at least,

prison. A still more threatening indication if there is added a star on the first phalanx of the second finger.

Unusually deep—Perseverance in an occupation not to the taste of the subject. Extreme nervous anxiety all through life. A strain of the will-power that often results in paralysis.

3. Malformations.

Chained or formed in crosses or zigzag at the start—Difficult childhood often due to losses of money or position

of the subject's parents.

Vocation Interfered With.—A Line of Influence starting from the second joint of the thumb cut a deep dot on the Line of Life at 18, and ended on the Mount of Mercury, after cutting every line. Good Mounts of Jupiter and the Sun ruling over an exaggerate Mount of the Sun. The beginning of a fine Line of Fate was cut up by a series of crosses.

"A famous actor of the Theatre Francais had had many troubles with his family, who would not allow him to adopt the stage as a profession. Left without money, he had been ill (at 18) from the privations he had to endure. His brilliant career was due to his telligence mastering his excess of imagination."

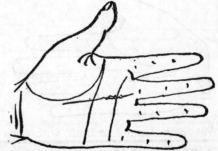

Chained when it crosses the Line of Heart—Troubles in love.

Poorly traced as it approaches the center of the hand—Troubles in middle life.

Remember that, in a normally shaped and lined hand, the Line of Fate crosses the Line of Head at 35 years old. (See pp. 150-51.)

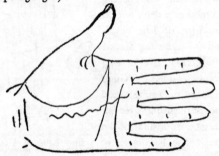

Wavy—A quarrelsome, changeable disposition; a very much checkered existence due to insufficient steadiness of purpose on the part of the subject.

b. In Connection with other indications.

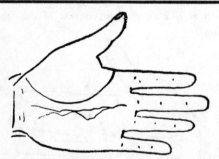

Wavy or chained or both, with a second line clinging to it (not a sister line, as such a line must not in any case touch the line it accompanies)—Unhappiness, generally due to the subject's unfortunate or hesitating way of ruling his life.

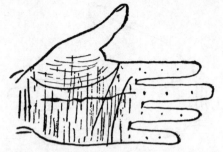

Deep and irregular, in a much rayed hand—Constant irritability; ultra-nervous disposition; the subject will be vexed at trifles, and his career will suffer much from this uneven temper.

III. STARTING POINTS AND FORKS AT THE START.

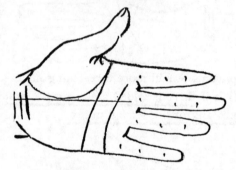

Starting from below the third bracelet of the Rascette—Some intense grief threatening the subject.

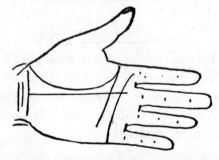

Starting from the first bracelet of the Rascette—Early responsibilities laid on the shoulders of the subject relating either to self or others.

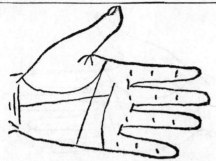

Starting from the first bracelet of the Rascette and ending at the Line of Heart—Serious love troubles all through life. Also in a bad hand confirming the symptoms—Heart disease.

Starting straight from the first bracelet of the Rascette and penetrating into the third phalanx of the second finger—An

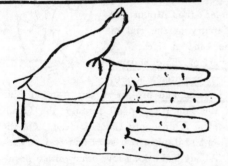

extraordinary destiny; whether for good or evil the other signs in the hands will tell. The strongest evidence of "fatality" in one's hand.

It is perhaps the only indication in the hand which the will-power of the subject seems incapable to triumph over.

Starting from the Line of Life—Success due to the subject's own efforts, but with a fair start from his own people. With the Mounts of Jupiter and Venus developed—A spirit of benevolence becoming the prime mover in the subject's life work.

Running close to the Line of Life for a while, but distinct from it—The subject's life is influenced by relatives, for the period during which the Line is so close to the Line of Life, said period measured and dated on the Line of Fate.

Starting inside the Mount of Venus—The family of the subject ruled his career.

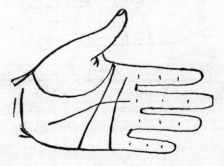

Starting from the Mount of the Moon and proceeding clear and uinterrupted to the Mount of Saturn, but not cutting the base of the second finger—Singular happiness in love; success due to the interest, love or caprice of the opposite sex.

Notice that from the Mount of Venus come the influences of our own people, parents, husband or wife, lover or mistress, and from the Mount of the Moon the influences of outsiders, not yet fully entered into our lives.

The same indication with the first and third fingers of good length and conically tipped—The gift of intuition, especially if the Line starts from the base of the Mount of the Moon.

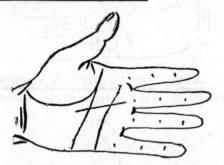

Rising from the center of the hand upward—Our destiny has really been shaped by ourselves without much helpful, or baneful, influence from insiders or outsiders.

If it cuts the base of the second finger —The same cause will bring about ill fortune.

Successive Unions with Two Prominent Men.—At 32 a Line of Influence from the Mount of Venus cutting an upward branch of the Line of Life and ending under the Mount of Mercury at the end of the Line of Heart. A Line of Fate starting from the lower Mount of  the Moon and broken at 32. A good Line of the Sun islanded all through the Quadrangle. A drooping Line of Head. On the Mount of Jupiter two stars and two crosses.

"A lady had a long love affair with a prominent man; it ended in separation at 32. Very shortly afterwards—before the death of that first lover—she married another man of fortune and family. The island of guilty intrigue lasts as long as the first man lived, although legally there was no wrongdoing in the case; but Unions in Palmistry have a broader meaning than in law."

Every upward line entering into the finger at its termination becomes an abnormal line and consequently has all its otherwise favorable indications annulled.

Starting from the Mount of the Moon with many horizontal lines crossing the Percussion of the Mount—Continual voyages.

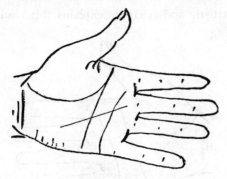

As we saw (page 112), these horizontal lines by themselves are already to be read thus.

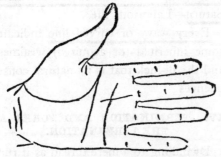

Starting from inside the Quadrangle—Great difficulties in middle life; sometimes (but rarely) a prognostic of imprisonment.

Forked at the start—Influence of a non-relative; if the line started low down in the hand—Often the sign of adoption in early life, especially if one prong goes deep into the Mount of Venus.

I have repeatedly met this fork low down in the hand in cases where there

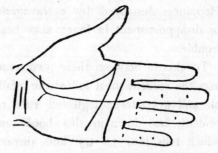

had been divorce or separation between the parents of the subject, resulting in a law suit for the possession of the child.

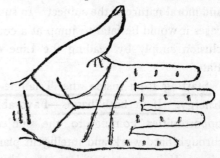

Forked quite widely at the start with one prong into the Mount of Venus and the other into the Mount of the Moon (in that case the Line starts at about 18 or 20 years old)—Struggle for success incited by some great love but handicapped by a wild imagination. If the Line is good and long—Everything will come out well. Otherwise, this fork will bring about disaster.

Starting from the Mount of the Moon

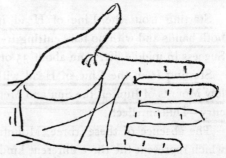

and terminating at the Line of Heart—

Happiness destroyed by extravagance or disappointment in love; also heart troubles.

To choose between these two readings the student must follow the infallible and never-to-be-neglected rule repeatedly laid down in this book, and which tells him to try and discern, through a close study of the Chirognomic Indications and by the examination of the Chief Lines what is the physical and moral nature of the subject. In such cases it would be fatal to jump at a conclusion simply by reading the Line of Fate.

Starting from inside the Triangle—Energy. If in both hands—Favorable opportunities coming to the subject through hard work and intelligent planning. If it penetrates into the third phalanx of the second finger—Painful, troubled life.

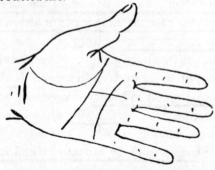

Starting from the Line of Head in both hands and with no bars cutting it—Success in middle life, from about 35 on.

Starting from the Line of Head with low Mounts of Jupiter, the Sun and Mercury—Dull intellect.

The absence of these three Mounts, which represent the three different kinds of intellectual developments, idealistic,

artistic and scientific explains this reading.

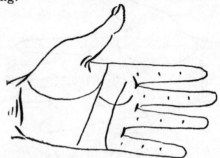

Starting from the Line of Head and coming up in a curve to the Mount of Saturn—Laborious life.

Every wavy or curved line indicates some inherited (or acquired) weakness and the ill-luck that is its natural consequences.

IV. TERMINATION AND FORKS AT THE TERMINATION.

Dwindling to a mere thread as it runs along the Line of Life, with a very high

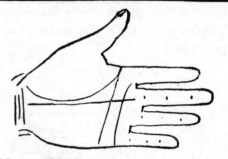

Mount of the Moon—Exaggerate senti-

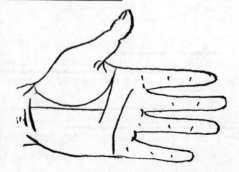

mentality; imagination interfering gravely with the possible success of the subject in his career.

Terminating abruptly at the Line of Head in both hands—Misfortunes through errors in judgment.

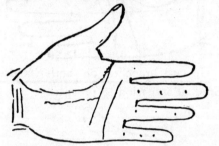

Poorly formed and Terminating at the Line of Head with a poor Line of Life— Misfortunes will be due to a deranged brain.

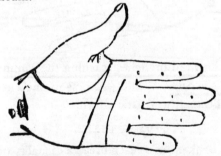

Terminating at the Line of Heart with an exaggerate or much lined Mount of Saturn—Persistent despondency caused by love troubles; will often culminate in insane morbidity.

Unfortunate Marriage of a Young Woman with an Old Man.—A Line of Influence from a star on the Mount of Venus to a star on the Line of Head. A Line of Fate stopping abruptly when it meets that Line.

"A young woman lost a husband much older

than herself and who died insane. Her whole existence was ruined by this marriage and his death, as she inherited nothing from him."

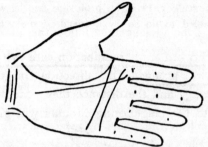

Terminating on the Mount of Jupiter, if the Line is good—Success in everything; often brilliant marriage.

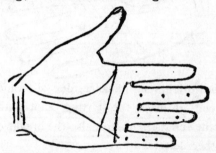

Terminating on the Mount of Mercury in both hands—Success in business.

Take care not to mistake a good Line of Liver for the above described Line of Fate, or vice versa.

Intestinal Trouble.—The medical stigmata on the Mount of Mercury crossed by a deep horizontal bar. A fine Line of Fate forked before reaching the Line of Head, both prongs stopped short. The Line of Head ended in a very large island. A Line of Influence—that might be called more justly a second Line of Fate—started from the Middle Mount of the Moon and went up to the Mount of Saturn, where it terminated in a fork.

"Seen in the hands of a physician whose

career was interrupted by a serious and persistent disease of the intestines. The trouble was finally conquered, but he had to start practically anew in his profession and he was enabled to do so by a friend of the other sex."

Forked at the termination with two or more prongs—The direction of the prongs and the distance they penetrate into the neighboring Mounts will give

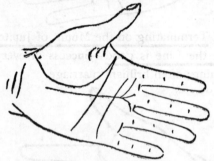

the fork its significance, due allowance being given for the starting point of the Line and its character; also the breaks or other defects, if any.

Thus a prong straight on (but not entering the third phalanx of the second finger), with a direct prong to the Mount of Jupiter and a third prong straight to the Mount of the Sun, would prove a most excellent combination, duplicating, so to speak, a fair proportion in length of the first, second and third fingers, i. e., ambition, prudence and brilliant intellect—a trio hard to beat.

V. BRANCHES.

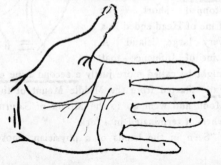

Downward branches—Material losses.

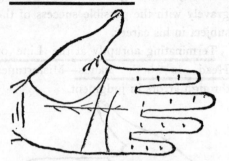

Upward branches on both hands—Gradual ascension to prosperity.

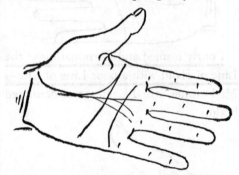

Upward branches reaching the Mount of the Sun—Wealth; success in one's intellectual or artistic efforts.

VI. BREAKS.

Broken—For each break a casuality or

a serious change in the subject's life; if one fragment overlays the other—A change not necessarily unfortunate.

Even if the break is a gap without any overlaying fragment, the events thus marked, although of an untoward nature

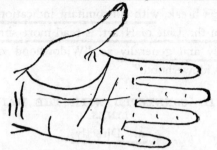

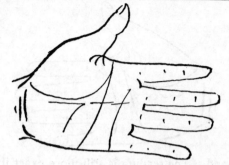

when they happen, may not prove fatal or even really disastrous for the subject.

Inheritance Through the Death of an Insane Relative.—The third finger abnormally long (not shown in the design). A Line of Fate, otherwise fine, entirely absent between 28 and 35. From a star on the Mount of Venus starts a Line of Influence, ending in a star at the connection of the Line of Head with a very fine Line of the Sun.

"The subject was an inveterate gambler. He had lost all he had, when the death of a relative, who was confined at the time in an insane asylum, placed in his possession at 35 another large fortune. From that time he dropped his bad habits and started on a prosperous, reputable career."

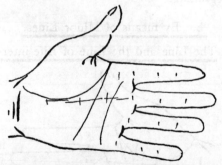

Broken and cut by many bars—Succession of unfortunate occurrences.

A very good Mount of Saturn and a well shaped second finger may cover up the deficiencies of the Line.

Forked, one prong arising from the Mount of the Moon, and the Line itself broken just where the fork ends—Danger of death by drowning or danger of unfaithfulness on the part of a loved one.

The Mount of the Moon is always compared by Desbarrolles to the briny deep with its constant changes and treacherous attractions.

Broken inside the Quadrangle, and starting again from the Line of Heart— A much compromised position or fortune will be retrieved, by the assistance of one of the opposite sex. Especially true if the hand contains a good Line of the Sun.

As told above, a good Line of the Sun corrects the defects of a poor Line of Fate.

Broken and wavy—Ill health from an abuse of some kind of pleasure, the nature of which is easily discovered in the

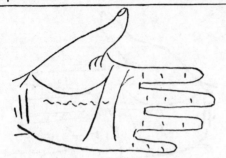

hand. The reading is still more exact if the Line is split lengthwise; this is not possible to show in the design.

I had occasion (when speaking of the Line of Head) to state how grave was the existence of such a split; it always indicates that the channel through which runs the vital fluid has become, so to speak, leaky and does not any longer perform its task in a satisfactory manner.

A decided break and a strong voyage line on the Mount of the Moon—The tenor of the subject's life will be radically changed and he will have to spend a great portion of it on the other side of the ocean, this sojourn abroad to begin at the date of the break.

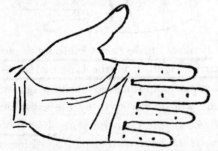

A break, and then the line terminating upon the Mount of Jupiter—A second (and brilliant) union of the subject at the date of the break.

That supposes generally that the existence, and date, of a previous union has been discovered in the hand, in fact,

this break, with concomitant indications on the Line of Heart, is read more simply and generally as "Widowhood or Widowerhood."

VII. CONNECTED WITH THE MAIN LINES.

a. Directly.

Starting from the Mount of the Moon and merging into a good Line of Heart, itself starting clearly from inside the Mount of Jupiter—A fairly certain indication of a brilliant marriage, or of an overpowering and successful passion.

It does not necessarily follow that the happiness will be lasting; in fact, there is a great chance of its being ephemeral just on account of the very intensity of its beginnings.

b. By means of Minor Lines.

The Line and the Line of Life inter-

sected by many short horizontal lines—

Family sorrows; as many lines of the kind, as many great sorrows.

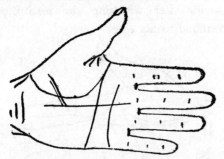

A deep line from the base of the Mount of Venus to the Line—Violent amorous passion. Should a second line act as a sister line to this one—Ungovernable passion reaching happiness over great obstacles; whether for a long time or not remains to be discovered elsewhere.

These two readings really belong to the Chapter on the Lines of Influence from the Mounts of Venus and the Line of Life. (pp. 172-193.)

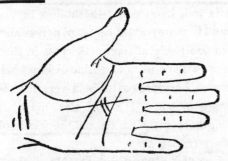

Deep lines from the Line of Heart cutting the Line—Painful love affairs will

injure the subject's worldly and financial prospects; very often read accurately as widowhood or widowerhood at the date the Line of Fate is cut, or at the date of a corresponding break in the Line.

Deep Lines from the Line of Head cutting the Line—Financial troubles due to lawsuits; or unsuccessful issue of one's artistic or literary efforts.

VIII. SIGNS.

Numerous bars crossing the Line on

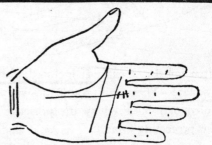

the Mount of Saturn—Obstacles constantly arising to mar the subject's life— If the Line has been good otherwise, those obstacles will only arise late in life.

Remember that many of these important readings have a general application and are not limited to the period of the subject's life inclosed within that portion of the Line. This is especially true of such indications as are found at the starting point of the Line of Life and the termination of the Lines of Fate and the

Sun. There, the ominous markings apply to the subject's life as a whole, not merely to his childhood or old age.

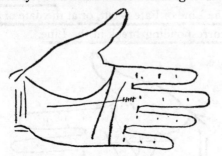

Numerous bars crossing the Line on the Mount of Saturn in ladderwise fashion—Succession of misfortunes and

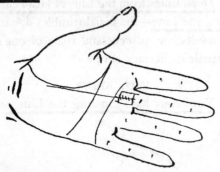

often imprisonment. If inclosed within a square—These evil prognostics are annuled or minimized by the presence of the protecting square.

A cross on the line at its termination,

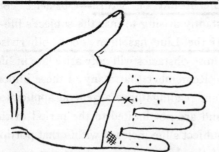

with a grille on the Mount of Mercury—Violent death, the consequence of some evil doing of the subject.

I saw this double sign quite recently in the hand of a banker who committed suicide after wrecking the institution confided to his care.

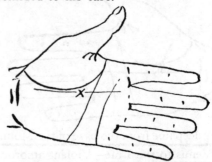

A cross on a break of the Line—A most critical change in the subject's existence. Without a break—A serious change of some kind. Always disastrous if found at the center of the Line.

This supposes the line to stretch from the Rascette to the upper part of the Mount of Saturn. It places therefore the cross inside the Plain of Mars. Now, it is well known that the hollow of the hand is an important center of nerves and but too easily affected. A cross in thât spot (with or without a Line of Fate) has always been proved to be a very threatening omen. I study this more at length in my Chapter on the Plain of Mars (which see).

Loss of Fortune of the Parents. Yellow Fever. Loss of Five Children. — Deep dots on the third finger. A deep dot on the Mount of Mercury. A large cross at the beginning of the Line of Fate, and one higher up on the Line at 25. A break on the Line shortly afterwards. The Lines of Fate and the Sun re-

sumed about the same time and ending finely. Two Lines of Influence cutting the Lines of Life, Fate, Head and the Sun.

"A man having suffered from yellow fever; he lost five children. His parents lost their fortune when he was quite young. Himself was ruined financially at 25, and suffered great losses at 23 and 25."

Adventurous Career in Wild Countries. Business Involving Many Risks.—Spatulate fingers; third finger almost as long as the second; exaggerate Mount of the Moon; sloping Line of Head; a cross on the Line of Fate before 20.

"A young man, after heavy losses at 20, begins a career of dangerous travels—many across the seas; visits wild regions and does business with savages; hates the humdrum of home, store or office."

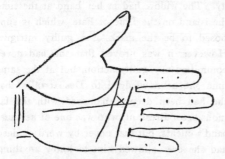

A cross attached to the Line inside the Quadrangle with smooth fingers and

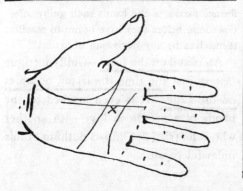

long, well developed first phalanges, especially the first phalanx of the first finger—Consolation derived from religious faith.

In general, a cross near the Line, between it and the Line of Life—An event that will affect a relative's life or comfort.

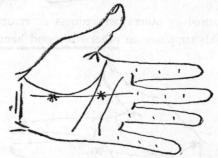

A star (or stars) on the Line—Danger and generally disaster at the date thus marked on the Line.

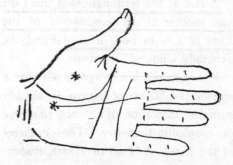

A star at the starting point of the Line —Loss of fortune or other great trouble happening to the parents of the subject when he was still a child. With another star on the Mount of Venus—One of the parents will have died about that time.

Of course the Line, in that case, is supposed to have started low down in the hand.

A star at the termination of the Line on the Mount of Saturn—Misfortune

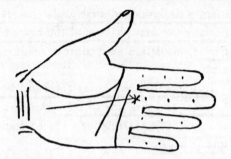

caused by others' wickedness or errors. This supposes an <u>otherwise good hand.</u>

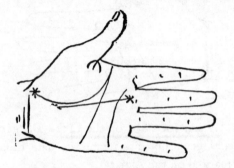

<u>A star at the termination of the Line and another at the termination of the Line of Life in both hands</u>—Paralysis, generally followed by paresis.

I have stated before (page 98) that a star on the Mount of Saturn is already sufficient indication of a strong paralytic or apoplectic tendency. The character of the Lines of Head or Heart, respectively, will indicate in what precise direction the danger lies.

<u>A star at the termination of the Line with another star on the Mount of the Moon</u>—Tendency to suicide.

Death of a Husband in a State of Insanity. Guilty Affair in Thought Only. — A good Line of Life and a good Line of Head; a fair Line of Heart; a Line of Influence starting from a star on the Mount of Venus and ending in a star on the Line of Head between

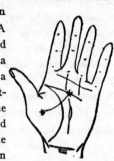

the Lines of Fate and the Sun; <u>a Line of Fate starting quite low islanded at 20, broken at 28, resumed at 40, ending on the Mount in good shape;</u> a Line of the Sun beginning in the Quadrangle at 38, ending on the Mount in good shape.

"The two stars indicate the death of the husband of the subject in a state of insanity. The widow had in her hand at the time the island on the Line of Fate, which is supposed to be the mark of a guilty intrigue. However, it was proved that she had never committed any guilty action, but at the same time she acknowledged to Desbarrolles that she had been deeply enamored with the famous actor Bressant, who was one of her husband's clients, but that never by word or deed had she ever allowed him to know anything of her infatuation. Desbarrolles insists upon this fact, which is confirmed by means of several other instances, that the nervous influence marks in the hands such guilty affections long before they have begun to manifest themselves by any beginning of action."

<u>An island on the Line</u>—Guilty intrigue lasting just <u>the time the island occupies on the Line.</u> It is even marked on the hands of a person in love with another who is married but knows nothing of this unlawful passion.

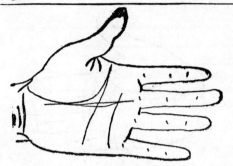

This is Desbarrolles' invariable reading, a great many illustrations of which are scattered through this work. I will admit, however—with many excellent British palmists—that this island on the Line of Fate is to be interpreted as heavy loss of money or position whenever the tout-ensemble of both hands and the general type of the subject protest against the very idea of his committing any breach of the seventh commandment.

Presentiments.—A Lunar Subject. A sloping Line of Head starred over a bluish spot just after it had crossed the Line of Fate. The said Line of Fate with a big island from 25 to 50, ending in a star at the connection of the Line of Heart and of a prolonged Line of Union. A fine Line of Intuition.

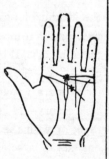

"A lady had felt an extraordinary, unexplainable antipathy for a man introduced to her by her husband. The latter had insisted that she should welcome his friend, and the latter had gradually obtained a sort of mesmeric influence over the woman, finally culminating in a guilty intrigue between them. This was bound to end fatally, and in fact she was deadly afraid of her lover, but dared not leave him; he had once attempted to poison her out of sheer jealousy. A strange example of the clearness and correctness of certain presentiments."

The Financial Ruin of Her Parents Causes a 17-Year-Old Young Girl to Lose Her Fiance.—A star at 17 on an otherwise fine Line of Fate. A Line of Influence starting from the Mount of Venus and reaching a straight Line of Union quite low down in the space between the Line of Heart and the third phalanx of the fourth finger.

"A lady of rank and wealth had been given up by a fiance she was much devoted to, because, when she was 17, her parents had lost their whole fortune."

Break of a Valued Love Affair Through the Discovery of Another Intrigue.—Two Lines of Influence from the Mount of Venus cut the Line of Life at five years' distance, uniting in a star on a Line of Fate which terminates right there.

"The discovery by a desirable and wealthy lover of the existence of another accepted admirer of his sweetheart brings about a break, which ruins the prospects of the lady whose hand contained the above markings."

An island at the starting point of the Line—A mystery connected with the

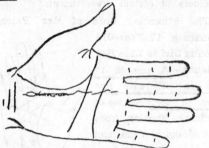

subject's birth. If the Line is very poor, this is a proof of illegitimacy.

Meaning, of course, that this stain on the innocent newcomer has marred his life prospects; which is unfortunately but too frequently the case.

Death of a Relative Breaking the Subject's Career. Love of Medicine. Separation from a Loved One.— A Line of Fate beginning late, broken inside the Quadrangle, then resumed to the Mount of Saturn. A Line of the Sun, much finer, starting low down, broken at

28, resumed in two fragments within the Quadrangle, the second very long and straight, going up the Mount of the Sun. Medical lines on the Mount of Mercury. A Line of Influence from the Mount of Venus, cutting the Line of Life at 45, goes straight to the Mount of the Moon, where it ends in an island.

"A young man, interrupted in his medical studies (at 28) by the death of a rich uncle, is obliged to adopt an entirely different profession (railroading). Succeeds fairly in it, until, at 45, the scandal of his liaison with a married woman obliges him to leave her and a favorite post and threatens his position. Finally he is returned to favor with his chiefs and is rapidly promoted."

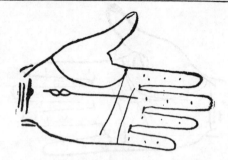

Two islands forming the figure 8 at the starting point of the Line—Gift of second sight, or at least somnambulism.

An island on the Line with a star on

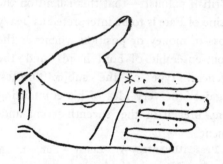

the Mount of Jupiter—Guilty love affair with one in a much higher position than the subject's. If the star is on the Mount of the Sun—The paramour will be an artist or literary man; if it is on the Mount of Mercury—He will be either a business man, or with the medical stigmata present also: a scientific man, a physician generally.

Two Lovers at the Same Time. The Younger Becomes Insane and Dies. The Older and Richer Pardons the Deceit.—Two stars on the Mount of Jupiter. A Line of Fate is marked with a deep, black dot at 30, and continues in a long island up to past 50. It is cut,

at the dot, by a Line of Influence starting from a star on the Mount of Venus and ending in a star at the connection of the Line of Head and the Line of the Sun. A Line of Influence from the lower Mount of the Moon merges into the Line of Fate at the black dot.

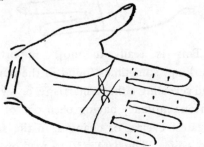

An island across the Line between the Mount of Venus and the Line of Heart, the island ending in a fork—Divorce, resulting from the fact of the subject leading astray an innocent girl.

A triangle between the Line and the Line of Life, touching the Line within

the Triangle with strongly marked Mounts of Mars—Fight or duel; or military success, at the date indicated.

Again the strange and powerful influence of the nervous center within the hollow of the hand shows itself most actively. This is studied in another chapter further on.

A square—Preservation from some

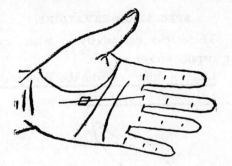

heavy financial loss, or other very serious disaster.

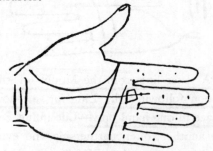

A square on a Line of Fate which enters into the third phalanx of the second finger—Again the square protects the subject from the disastrous possibilities indicated by the Line thus penetrating into the finger.

A square touching the Line within the Triangle; if on the side towards the Mount of Venus—Danger from an accident in home life. If on the side toward the Mount of the Moon—Danger from an accident in travel.

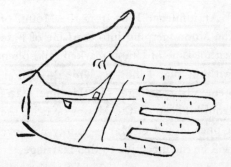

SPECIAL OBSERVATIONS.

These refer exclusively to what are generally known as

Lines of Influence from the Mounts of the Moon and Upper Mars.

A sister line from the Mount of the Moon following the Line for a short space in one hand only—Life influenced by another; often partnership and even marriage when the union benefited the subject's career. In both hands—Two careers followed simultaneously, or a regular career and some hobby besides.

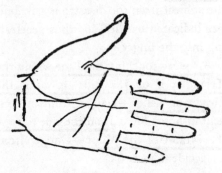

An influence Line from the Mount of the Moon merging into the Line of Fate with a Line of Union marked (and often without that Line of Union)—Union, generally marriage. If this line starts from high up on the Mount or from the Upper Mount of Mars—Vanity not love will be the incentive to this marriage.

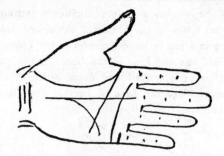

This is really a most important marking, sometimes found in the hands and revealing either a marriage, or a very serious intimacy having been one of the greatest events, or changes, in the subject's life. The date is to be read on the Line of Fate. Of course there may be several such lines in a hand.

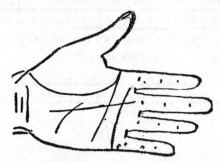

Should it not only touch the Line but cut it—Evil effect of imagination on the subject's life, culminating (with other indications) in actual insanity. As a marriage prognostic—It reveals a broken engagement and often means divorce, or at least an unhappy union.

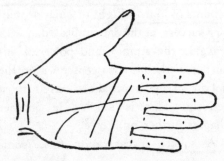

Should it rise toward the Line but not touch it—The love affair will not terminate in a marriage. Especially so if there is no Line of Union on the Percussion of the Mount of Mercury.

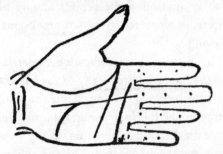

Should it be clearer and stronger than the Line of Fate in which it merges—The subject will be ruled over by the person he marries.

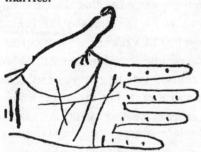

An influence Line from the Mount of the Moon merging into the Line, but cut, before it reaches the Line, by a Line of Influence from the Mount of Venus— Family opposition to the subject's marriage.

An island on a Line of Influence from the Mount of the Moon to the Line— Misfortune to the subject resulting from the union indicated by the Line of Influence.

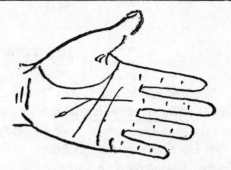

A branch from a Line of Influence from the Mount of the Moon to the Line of Fate, the said branch almost, or quite,

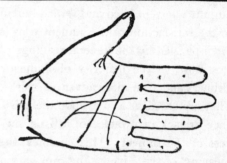

reaching the Mount of the Sun—A very fine indication of fame and fortune, resulting from the marriage thus prognosticated; especially so if there exist on the

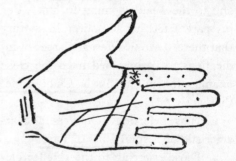

Mount of Jupiter of the same hand a cross and star, distinct and connected.

THE LINE OF THE SUN.

The general considerations concerning the Line of the Sun need occupy but a very little space, since I have already mentioned the fact that this Line is to be mainly considered as a sister line to the Line of Fate, or, even more comprehensively, as a second Line of Fate.

There is another point, however, that ought to be ventilated and settled herein to the satisfaction of the student who is often puzzled by the general readings of this Line, in the majority of Palmistic Primers and even more advanced works. They are based, as a rule, upon the existence or lack of promise of artistic success of the subject. This confines the meaning of the Line of the Sun within pretty narrow limits and leaves aside the other, infinitely more frequent, interpretations of the Line, those that refer to the fame or "good name" of the subject and to the wealth coming to him. For my part, I feel no hesitation in stating that there are four different classes of indications to be obtained from the close examination of the Sixth Chief Line; they are:

1. Those referring to its general characteristic of Second Line of Fate;

2. Those referring to the Intellectuality and the Artistic Aptitudes of the subject;

3. Those referring to the Reputation or Fame the subject may attain—meaning by the word reputation or fame, not only a high degree of celebrity, but everything that concerns the good name or fair reputation of the subject among his peers, to whatever social stratum he may belong;

4. Finally those indications referring to the Financial Prosperity of the subject; this is included, of course, in the readings under the first paragraph, but with this marked difference, that, in my opinion, the wealth in store for the subject, when indicated only on the Line of the Sun, is to come to him without actual work, i. e., by inheritance, or speculative venture (remember that the third finger —just above the Line—is the gambling finger), or as a reward for some great artistic or literary achievement; the latter, of course, entailing work, and often a good deal of it; but the work of genius, or at least unusual talent, not the commonplace labor of the everyday toiler.

I. POSITION AND DIRECTION.

Normal: Starts near the Rascette and

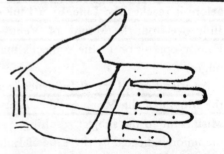

between the Mounts of Venus and the Moon, ending on the Mount of the Sun —Brilliant intellectuality. Fame and wealth.

II. CHARACTER.

a. By Itself.

1. Length.

Absent—Ill-success in projects and enterprises that would bring great riches and reputation if—they only succeeded.

With a particularly fine Line of Fate, this discouraging prognostic would be materially minimized. However, I must admit, that the total absence of a Line of the Sun, in an otherwise excellent hand, is generally an omen of very modest success, out of proportion with one's ambition and hopes.

Long and uncrossed—Riches. Unsullied reputation. Sometimes fame.

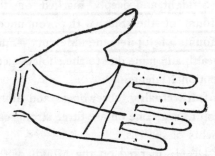

Straight and especially strong on the Mount of the Sun—Celebrity as an artist; protection of the great; calm security in the knowledge of one's own talents.

These readings are not often cumulative; they have to be read each for a different subject and with other indications, mostly chiromantic or resulting from the study of the Mounts.

Well formed in both hands—Success of the most complete kind.

Wavy—Lack of concentrative power. Often bad taste.

2. Color: Width: Depth.

Quite red, if straight and long—Strong artistic vocation.

Very broad—Lack of power of concentration.

Pale or simply poorly colored—Artistic aptitudes, but insufficient powers of execution; the "Art Amateur's Line."

Very deep, especially in Artistic Hands—Exaggeration in the output of vital force in the practice of one's talents. This will infallibly lead to paralysis or serious, probably fatal, heart trouble.

3. Malformation.

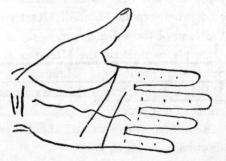

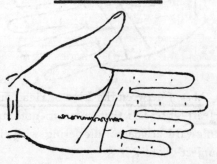

<u>Chained</u>—Poor success in the conquest of fame or fortune.

b. In Connection with Other Indications.

1. Length.

<u>Absent but with a good Line of Fate in the Hand</u>—The good luck shown by the Line of Fate much reduced if not wiped out by the absence of the Line. (See above.)

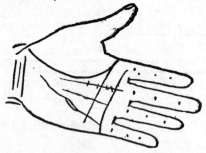

<u>Absent or badly traced, with an island on the Line of Liver and a Line of Fate cut up by small lines</u>—Bankruptcy.

Here again we find evidence of the business meaning of the Line of Liver. The absence of the Line of the Sun is indication of a mental capacity so poor as to be unable to devise the means to overcome threatening losses.

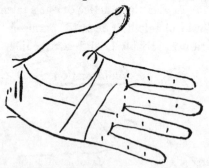

<u>Absent between the Line of Head and Heart</u>—Projects that come to nothing; untoward accidents interfering with the subject's career.

Of course this leaves the subject without the services to be obtained from his best brain power between the age of 35 to 50, which is usually the time in life when men get rich, if ever.

<u>Clear and straight in both hands, with a single star on the Mount of the Sun</u>—Celebrity due to talent.

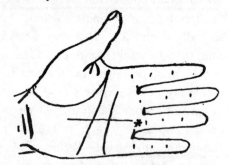

<u>Straight and deeply marked on the Mount of the Sun with pronounced Mounts of Jupiter and Mercury</u>—Sure wealth and fame due to the subject's exceptional talents.

Intellectuality, shrewdness and ambition to urge one on are three strong elements of success.

<u>Deeply marked on the Mount of the Sun, with pronounced Mounts of Venus and the Moon</u>—Aptitude for fine literary work.

Notice that this reading is to be applied to the greater portion of the subject's life, not only to that stretch included between the Line of Heart and the base of the third finger.

<u>Deeply marked on the Mount of the Sun with pronounced Mount of the Moon and short nails</u>—Literary or art critics of distinction

Remember what was said about these short nails on pages 39-40.

A good Line with a good Line of Fate and a high Mount of Jupiter—The combination of a bright mind and a combative nature. Ambition satisfied.

Deeply traced, with a Mount of Jupiter high in both hands—Friendship of people in high position. Lofty domineering spirit. The type of a Louis XIV. of France, majestic and fond of outward pomp.

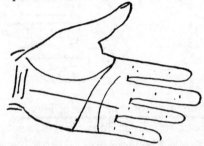

A good Line with a long Line of Head and a very long third finger—Talents absorbed in the acquisition of wealth by speculation.

I discovered these same characteristics in the hands of travelers in wild countries, especially in the Tropics.

Found in both hands, with a sloping Line of Head and a third finger almost, if not quite, as long as the second—Gambling propensities.

The sloping Line of Head denotes the mastery of imagination over reason,

which is the perdition of the born gambler, be he in front of the green cloth or around the wheat pit of the Board of Trade.

A fairly good line in a hollow hand—It ceases to be effective in helping the subject to fame and fortune.

An abnormally low Palm Proper is a grievous sign of persistent ill-luck. It means great, inborn discouragement incapable of "fighting to a finish" the battle of life. (See page 39.)

A straight line with a hollow palm and twisted fingers—Talents used for an evil purpose, but with miserable failure as the inevitable end.

Clever schemers will show such malformations. To the fairly conversant palmist such "crooks" are harmless, as he reads their true natures in an instant.

III. STARTING POINTS.

Starting from the Line of Life in both hands—Success in art or literature; bril-

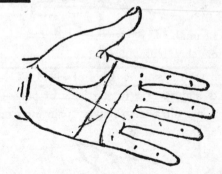

liant fortune. The assistance of relatives has helped the subjct considerably. Still truer if the Line starts inside of the Mount of Venus—The inspiration of love will guide the artist.

This depends, of course, on the other—especially chirognomic—revelations. Notice that, of the three vertical Chief Lines, the Line of Liver is the only one that is not benefited by a contact with the Line of Life at the start.

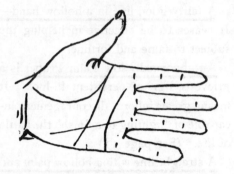

Starting from the Mount of the Moon and rising straight into the Mount of the Sun—Success due to influential outside protection, generally of the opposite sex.

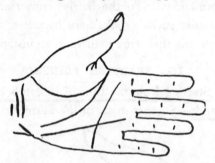

Starting from the Mount of the Moon and with a sloping Line of Head—Talents and success in the Line of poetry, fiction, ultra-imaginative painting, or Wagnerian music.

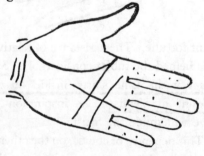

Starting from inside the Triangle—Success after serious struggles, and due to the subject's unaided efforts.

Starting from the Line of Head—The subject will owe his success to no other assistance than that of his own brains.

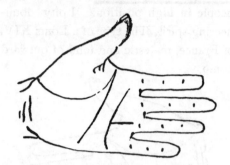

Starting from the Line of Heart—The love of art, music, literature, etc., will be influenced, seldom favorably, by some very serious love affair of the subject. The most frequent reading, however, is "financial sufficiency in old age;" this reading fits almost all types of hands; while the first reading requires the usual chirognomic corroborations.

Special Characteristics of a Famous Painter.—A thin hand. A high Mount of the Sun cut by a deep vertical line; a very long but low Mount of the Moon (a sign of weakness of the Mount's special qualities); rather long and square-tipped fingers.

"Seen in the hands of a well-known Parisian landscape painter especially famous for the accuracy of his drawings and the truth of his coloring. A man who took great pains to do well and was more of an artisan than an artist; he had none of the wild habits of his craft and lacked the quick wit and boisterous spirit for which his guild is famous the world over."

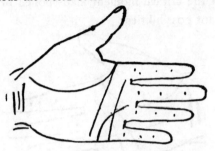

Starting from inside the Upper Mount of Mars—Aggressiveness in the conquest of fame or fortune.

Fatal Only Love.—A long and deep cross on the Mount of Venus.
Also a star on the same Mount, from which starts a deep Line of Influence, crossing the whole hand and forming on the Mount of the Moon a cross with a sloping Line of Head. Another Line of Influence, starting from the same star, reaches  deep into the Mount of Mercury, forming a cross between the Mounts of the Sun and Mercury, with a curved line from the Percussion of Mars to the Mount of the Sun. The Line of the Sun stopped by and at this second Line of Influence. A Line of Heart forked on the Mount of Jupiter and ending quite straight around the Percussion.

"A gentleman had grieved greatly on account of the death of a lady (a Mercurian) whom he had passionately loved (his only love). The second cross indicates that this sorrow had thrown him into mysticism, even to exaggeration (sloping Line of Head, cut by the first Line of Influence) and even danger of insanity. His whole career was practically stopped, wrecked by the death of the loved one."

IV. TERMINATION AND FORKS AT THE TERMINATION.

Narrow, deep and straight and termi-

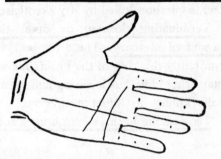

nating up the Mount of the Sun, uncrossed in both hands—Success. To be read as a Line of Fate with the addition of such other characteristics as pertain to the Mount of the Sun and the third finger.

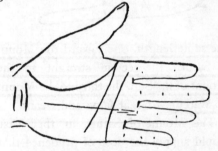

Terminating in a series of small lines when it reaches the Mount of the Sun—Failure, the nature of which is determined by other indications. In an artistic, literary, etc., hand—A sign of unsustained efforts toward success.

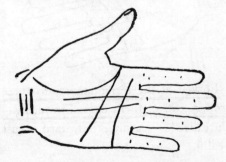

Terminating close to or upon the Mount of Saturn—The artistic talents of the subject will assume a gloomy character; inspiration killed by dry skepticism.

Terminating close to or upon the Mount of Mercury—The artist will be constantly thinking of the profits his art may bring him, thus lowering and eventually killing his loftier aspirations.

Terminating in three even branches of

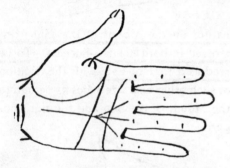

the same length, one toward the Mount of Saturn, the second straight to the Mount of the Sun, the third to the Mount of Mercury—Great fame and wealth.

The Mount of Saturn in that case would supply the dose of prudence that will render the success lasting and the wealth permanent.

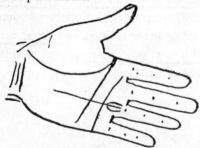

Forked at the termination into three prongs, two of them curved inwardly—Unrealized yearnings toward vast wealth.

These curved lines always indicate failure, as if a weakening of the subject, at the critical moment, had spoiled brilliant possibilities.

Forked at the termination with both prongs of even length—Equal influence of two different aspirations (or talents) upon the subject; they result in the annulation of actual results.

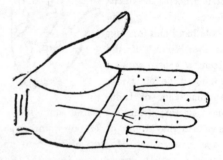

Forked at the termination into a pointed trident, starting above the Line of Heart—Fame, riches, all due to personal merit.

A rather curious marking which is an unconfirmed Desbarrolles reading.

V. BRANCHES.

Two or three branches rising from the Line, but irregular, uneven or broken or crossed by many bars—Failure in intellectual or artistic work through lack of concentration.

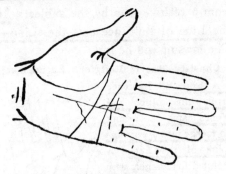

VI. BREAKS.

Broken repeatedly—Versatility that

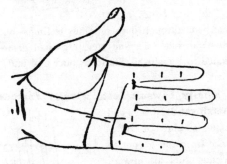

brings neither money nor fame to the subject.

This is the characteristics of the "Jack-of-all-trades," met with in all professions.

Broken inside the Quadrangle, generally connected with the Mount of Venus by an Influence Line, cutting it— Series of misfortunes (often due to one's own people) in the struggle for recognition; but final success, if the second fragment of the Line rises straight,

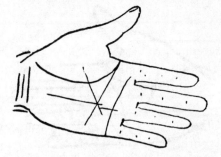

strong and clear to the top of the Mount of the Sun.

Broken at the Line of Head and resumed only from the Line of Heart— Chances of success or of acquiring wealth very small indeed.

VII. CONNECTED WITH THE MAIN LINES.

a. Directly.

Cut by a Line of Union—Loss of po-

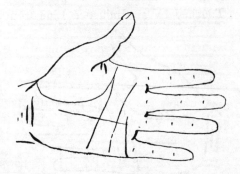

sition due to unsuitable marriage, or to a disgraceful entanglement.

The good name of the subject is under a cloud.

b. By Minor Lines.

Touched but not cut by an Influence Line from the Mount of Venus—Success after many struggles; money coming; generally through the subject's own people.

If the Line is cut by the Influence Line

—Ill-success; loss of money, generally through a relative.

Touched by an Influence Line from

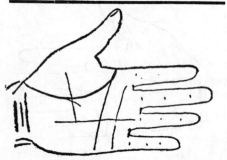

the Mount of Venus, cutting an upward branch of the Line of Life—Lawsuit

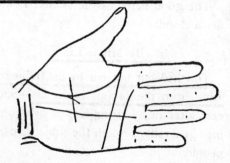

from a relative won by the subject. If the Line of Influence cuts the Line— The lawsuit will be lost.

Chastity Due to Religious Enthusiasm. —A Line of Influence from the Mount of Venus came up curving to merge into a very fine Line of the Sun. A pointed first finger, with a well-developed Mount of Jupiter, and a rayed hand.

"In the hand of a man who through deep religious feelings—not fanatical, but quiet and elevating—had determined to remain his life long pure and undefiled."

Family Lawsuit Lost. Finally Fortune Retrieved.—In a good hand, a Line of Influence from the Mount of Venus cuts an upward branch of the Line of Life, at 28, and ends at a star on a very fine Line of the Sun. This line continues unimpaired.

"A Russian lady suffered heavy financial losses through the loss of a lawsuit instigated by relatives. But her impaired fortune soon became more brilliant than ever."

Death of a Father Causes the Financial Ruin of His Children (Minors) on Account of a Guilty Understanding Between His Widow and Her Lover.— A good Line of Life; a Line of Head widely separated from the Line of Life and somewhat drooping at the end; a star on the Mount of Venus, from which

starts a Line of Influence, which is islanded before the Line reaches the Line of Head. From that island the Line continues until it cuts the Line of the Sun and the Line of Heart.

"A wife, after the death of her husband, had misused most of the fortune of her young children for the benefit of her lover."

A Line or branch from the Line of Head to the Line, not cutting it—Pecuniary success due to the subject's intelligence. If the Line cuts the Line of the Sun—Pecuniary loss through a blunder of the subject.

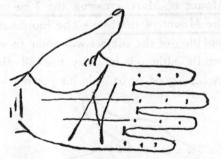

A Line or branch from the Line of

Fate touching (not cutting) the Line—Partnership that will prove successful. If the Line or branch cuts the Line of

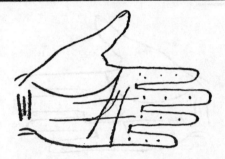

the Sun—Partnership that will prove disastrous.

A Line or branch from the Line of

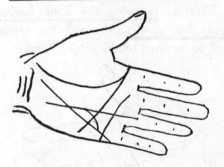

Liver touching (not cutting) the Line—The artistic career of the subject much assisted by his business ability. If this

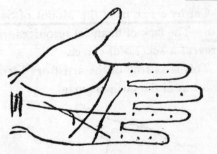

Line or branch cuts the Line of the Sun—The cupidity of the subject will interfere with his artistic career. Generally loss of prestige, and probably money also.

VIII. SIGNS.

Many bars that cut the Line horizontally—Artistic career hindered by envi-

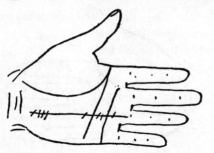

ous rivals; if mostly found at the beginning of the Line—Loss of fortune of the subject's parents during his youth.

This is, provided the Line begins quite low down; otherwise the losses will be incurred by the subject himself.

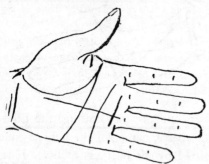

Cut by a line from the Mount of Saturn—The lack of financial resources will prevent a successful career.

This is as true of the artist or "literateur" as of the business man.

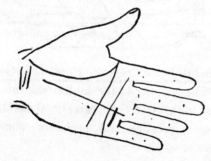

Cut by a line from the Mount of Mercury—Success prevented by fickleness in the disposition of the subject. If the Mount of Mercury be exaggerate or badly marked—The crookedness of the subject destroyed his chances.

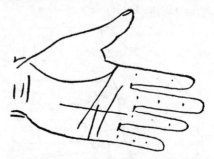

Cut by a cross line from the Upper Mount of Mars—Money losses coming to the subject through an enemy.

Cut by a curved Line from the Upper Mount of Mars, crossing the Line on the Mount of the Sun—The inordinate ambition of the subject will come to no results, although he may use all the means—good or bad—in his power.

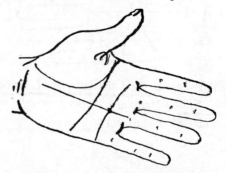

A deep or black spot at the connection of the Line and the Line of Heart—Imminent danger of blindness.

A cross touching the Line toward the Mount of Mercury—Poor business capacity to assist artistic efforts to success.

A cross touching the Line toward the

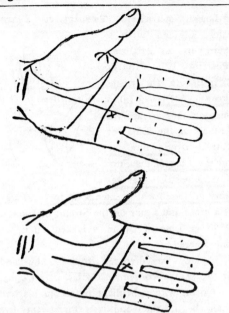

A star on the Line, within the Quadrangle—Catastrophe, followed, if the rest of the Line be good, by favorable events.

Disaster Due to the Marriage of the Subject's Lover, But Repaired by the Return of the Lover.—On the Mount of Jupiter there was both a cross and a star, one ray of the latter joining across the hand a deep Line of Union. At 30 a Line of Influence from the

Mount of Venus cut an upward branch of the Line of Life, ending in a star on the Line of the Sun, at the same age; from there arose an island lasting up to 40 years old. Then the Line of the Sun rose clear and straight to the end. Excellent Line of Fate from 30 up.

"The subject, a lady, lost a rich and generous lover through his marriage to another woman. He came back to her very soon, however, and her short-lived trouble ceased."

Mount of Saturn—Pious disposition.

A cross touching the Line, if the Mount of Saturn and the Moon are bad and the Line of Head slopes deeply— Danger of insanity of the religious kind.

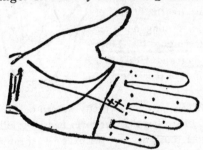

More alarming still if there are two crosses there instead of one.

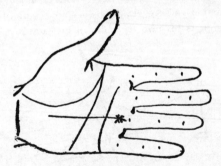

A star at the termination of the Line— Success due to the assistance and good will of others.

For these readings of crosses and stars I refer you to page 102, although there the signs are not supposed to touch the Line. Still those readings are worth comparing.

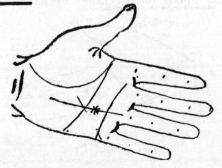

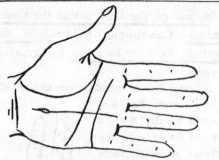

An island at the starting point of the Line—Success helped by a guilty love. Brilliant future for the illegitimate child of people in high position. This supposes an otherwise long and straight Line.

A Death Bringing About a Happy Event.—A Line of Influence starting from a star on the Mount of Venus, and ending in an island just touching the beginning of an excellent Line of the Sun; a good Line of Fate.

"The death of the only child of a lady's admirer—a very wealthy man—induces him to adopt as his own the child of his lady love."

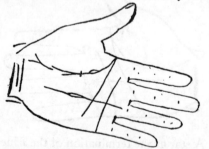

An island on the Line with indications of illness on the Line of Life—Disease of the eyes.

This is read more generally (as it would be on the Line of Fate)—Guilty intrigue, or, in an excellent hand—heavy financial loss.

Legal Separation. Twenty-five Years' Close Liaison with a Man in a Brilliant Position, Who Finally Dies Before His Sweetheart.—A Line of Influence cutting an upward branch of the Line of Life at 30 ends in a star on the Line of the Sun. Just above that star begins an island, which extends up to 55. There is a cross and a star on the Mount of Jupiter. A lower Line of Union is forked, an upper one starred.

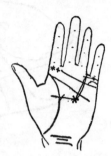

"A lady was divorced from her husband at 30, as the consequence of a catastrophy. A liaison with a brilliant officer (a married man) begins then and lasts for twenty-five years, when he dies."

Found Out.—A sloping Line of Head; a Line of Influence from a star on the Mount of Venus cutting the Line of Life and then islanded clear to the Line of Head, turning up after that, cutting the Lines of Sun and Heart and ending on the Mount of Mercury.

"A very young and pretty woman confessed to Desbarrolles that her lover had been killed by her husband on discovering them together, and that she had lost both reputation and fortune through that scandal."

A square on the Line—Preservation

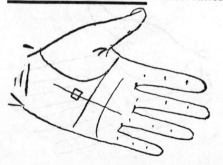

or rescue from attack against the sub-ject's reputation; also against great money loss.

Let me repeat here again, quite em-phatically, that all the readings I gave concerning the Line of Fate apply to the Line of the Sun, if the Line of Fate be absent or insignificant; and that most of these readings apply anyhow to the Line of the Sun.

SPECIAL OBSERVATIONS.

Two deep parallel lines, one at either side of a straight and deep Line of the

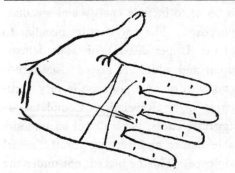

Sun—Glory; untold fortune. These are the Lines of Reputation. (See page 102.)

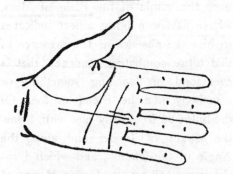

A good Line, but with two wavy, ir-regular sister Lines of the Sun—Mis-directed genius.

Lines of Influence running for a while along the Line but not touching it—

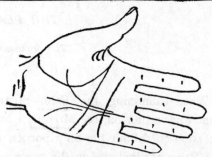

Legacies. If the Line of Influence starts on the Mount of the Moon—Expected Legacies. If it starts from above the Mount of the Moon—Unexpected lega-cies. If it starts from the Mount of Ve-nus—The legacy comes from a relative.

I generally apply to the Line of the Sun all the readings of the Lines of In-fluence in connection with the Line of Fate. (See page   .)

A Peculiar Square of Preservation.—A straight Line of Fate stopping within the Quadrangle. A short Line of the Sun starting up from the Line of Head. Two Lines of Influence at five years' distance, both starting from stars on the Mount of Venus. The upper  one cuts the Line of Head at its connection with the Line of Fate, and cuts also the Line of the Sun; the lower one cuts the Line of Fate and then the Line of Head just where the Line of the Sun starts. This combina-tion forms a perfect square.

"At five years' distance two large legacies had restored the compromised fortune of the subject, finally saving him from bankruptcy."

THE PLAIN OF MARS.

The Quadrangle—The Triangle.

When examining the Palm of the hand and farther on, the Mounts, I had occasion to delimit the only portion of the Palm not included in the space occupied by the Mounts and to give it its various names and its subdivision.

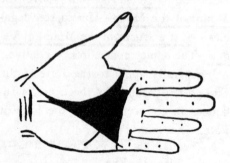

The Hollow of the Hand, The Palm Proper, is more scientifically designated as the Plain of Mars, as it connects at both ends with those Upper and Lower Mounts of Mars, concerning which there has been so much discussion and dissension among Modern Palmists, dissensions which the rather confusing and contradictory statements of Desbarrolles have not helped to settle. I shall try now to harmonize these warring elements and to get at the inward thought of the Master on the subject.

Desbarrolles never acknowledged, it is true, the existence of two Mounts of Mars, one expressing active courage—aggressiveness; the other, passive courage—resistance; or to apply the readings to more current circumstances: energy and resignation. After limiting the meaning of his only Mount of Mars—the one between the Mount of Mercury and the Mount of the Moon—to passive courage and resistance, he soon forgets this narrow interpretation and extends it so as to include energy and steadfast purposes. The only feature peculiar to of the Upper Mount of Mars I insist upon and which he placed elsewhere—and even on that point he is very vacillating in his Révélations Complètes—is aggressiveness, generally of an undesirable nature and verging toward actual violence. This he placed, not under the Mount of Jupiter, as the London Chirological Society insists on doing, but over the whole of the Plain of Mars, whose flat or bulging aspect indicated to him the absence or the presence of that ultra combative tendency that is ever fond of "spoiling something or somebody," be he friend or foe. Of the bulge so frequently met with, below the Mount of Jupiter and along the Angle of the Thumb, and which I insist upon calling the Lower Mount of Mars—not a single word in Desbarrolles' books, and, in his readings of cases, this portion of the Palm is invariably included within the Mount of Venus.

Now I feel no hesitation to admit that the Plain of Mars has to be studied closely in connection with aggressive courage whenever, instead of forming a more or less marked hollow, it bulges in what might be justly called a threatening fashion. I already called your attention to the fact that anatomically this portion of the Palm contains a radiating center of nervous fibres and numerous Pacinian Corpuscles. It is therefore a very excitable spot in the hand and the Ancient Chiromants had shrewdly discovered its peculiarities when they gave the name of Cross of Battle to the large cross met occasionally at the very middle of the Palm. But this admission on my part does not in any way modify my definitions of both Mounts of Mars, the Upper One so naturally placed between the clever Mount of Mercury and the dreamy Mount of the Moon, to help the first in its conquest of worldly influence, to protect the second against the excess of its langorous laziness; the Lower One, between the Mount of Jupiter, whose ambition it strengthens by this secret of success: Perseverance, and the Mount of Venus, whose loving instincts it completes by the gift of Constancy. If logic is ever to be listened to in the study of the hand, I think this is the time to give it the right of way and to accept its clear dicta, which are not in any way contrary to the intelligent reading of Desbarrolles' declarations on the subject. I understand that this question of the Mounts of Mars is the shibo-leth that admits or rejects candidacy to the honors of Membership or Fellowship in the London Chirological Society; but in spite of the terrible fate in store for those who decline to thus bow before the new-fangled Gessler's Cap, I thought I would have my straightforward say on the matter, advienne que pourra, especially since the best of modern French Palmists, Dr. Papus, Madame de Thebes, Marius Decrespe, etc., do me the honor of agreeing with me on this point.

As space is somewhat valuable in this volume and I see no necessity for uselessly repeating myself, I must refer you for the general Chirognomical observations concerning the Plain of Mars or Palm Proper to the Sixth Subhead in my Chapter on the Hand as a Whole, page 39; in fact there are many details concerning it included in the statements contained in pp. 37 to 39 included. I shall assume that those have been carefully studied and remembered, and introduce to you my readings of

THE QUADRANGLE.

I. POSITION.

Normal:

It occupies the space between the Line of Head and the Line of Heart, both being normal, and between the Mount of Jupiter and the Upper Mount of Mars, neither of these Mounts included.

Well formed, smooth and free from lines—A calm, steady, loyal disposition.

By "lines" I mean a number of these

tiny wrinkles, the presence of which is always the indication of an ultra-nervous and worrying nature.

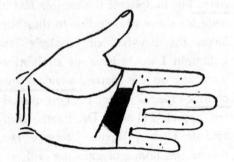

Well formed and wider toward the Percussion—Straight forwardness.

In a normally lined hand the Line of Heart rises and the Line of Head droops—both slightly—when they reach the Mount of the Sun.

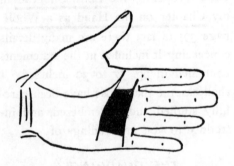

Too wide throughout—Independent disposition, even to folly; a very serious indication which no other favorable observation in the hand is sufficient to counterbalance.

This supposes a Line of Heart running too high (extreme jealously and sensuality) and a Line of Head running too low (ill-balanced reasoning power).

Wider under the Mount of Saturn than under the Mount of the Sun—The subject is careless about his reputation.

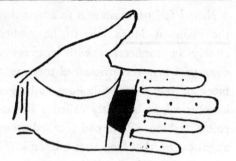

You will find just the opposite shape in every normally lined hand. Here the Mount of the Sun is taken in its meaning of "revealer of good or bad fame" in store for the subject.

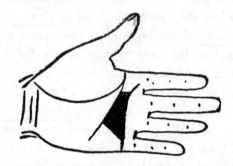

Wider under the Mount of the Sun than under the Mount of Saturn—Exaggerate sensitiveness about other people's opinions.

This, of course, supposes that the width is decidedly abnormal. By being

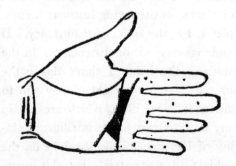

placed more closely under the influence of the Mount of Saturn, the subject will be more morbidly inclined than it is desirable he should be.

Narrow on account of the Line of Head rising toward the Line of Heart— Narrowmindedness. The feelings dominate over reason and often cloud it.

Narrow through the lowering of the Line of Heart toward the Line of Head —Meanness; no generosity. The head rules over the feelings.

Badly traced, almost invisible at its normal extremities—A weak or at least a very ordinary intellect, and a malignant or at least a very cold disposition.

This can occur only when the Lines of Head and Heart are very poorly traced —in itself an indication of a weak constitution, and, as a rule, with a wretched health goes a wretched temper.

II. CHARACTER.

a. By Itself.

Bulging and well shaped—Fecundity. Love of money for the sake of spending it generously.

Flat, i. e., level with the Mounts—Saving disposition.

Hollow—Miserly disposition.

Hard—Plenty of animal spirits.

Soft—Laziness; physical weakness.

b. In Connection with Other Indications.

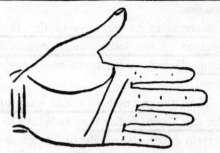

Wide, with a good Line of Head and a well-formed second phalanx of the thumb —Broadmindedness.

Reasoning is here at its best; and truly intelligent people can understand and appreciate almost anything.

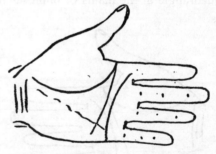

Narrow and with a poor Line of Liver —Asthma, Hay-fever.

The indication of some painful oppression; the character of these troubles is, as yet, imperfectly accounted for by medical experts.

Narrow, with fingers bending inside the palm—Stiffness in all intercourse

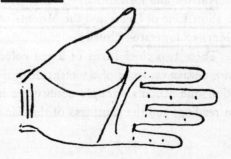

with one's fellow creatures; miserly disposition.

Narrow in its center, with the third phalanx of the fourth finger relatively long—Deceit. Also mind easily prejudiced.

Then, the narrowness would occur under the Mount of the Sun, reducing to a certain extent the intellectual brightness of the subject.

Narrow, with an excessive Mount of Jupiter—Extreme religious ideas; asceticism.

Again, narrowmindedness has here full sway. One would expect such a Quadrangle in the hands of blind fanatics.

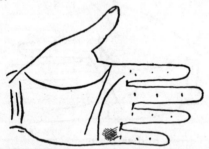

Very narrow in both hands, with an exaggerate or badly lined Mount of Mercury—Lying instincts.

Narrow, with exaggerate Mounts of Mars and Mercury—Unfairness. Another consequence of narrowmindedness.

Narrow and formed by red lines, with a short Line of Heart and the Mounts of Mars exaggerate—Cruelty.

These two chief Lines of a red color are always evidence of a violent disposition; the Mounts strongly confirm such a reading, and the shortness of the Line

of Heart is a token of a lack of kindly feelings.

III. SIGNS.

Furrowed by many lines in a large

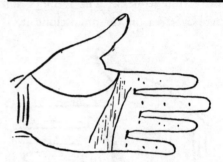

hand, with a long palm and short, smooth fingers—Weak understanding, often through physical weakness of the brain; hence restlessness; irritability.

These short fingers, in a hand not otherwise well endowed, are characteristic of a lack of judgment; the fluid rushes through too quick to be of any great use; and no knots to stop it on its way, giving the subject time to reason out the situations.

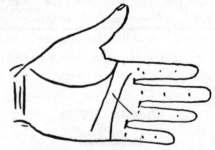

A line from inside the Quadrangle to the Mount of the Sun—Success due to the protection of the great.

A forked line inside the Quadrangle—An ill-balanced mind, altogether acting inopportunely.

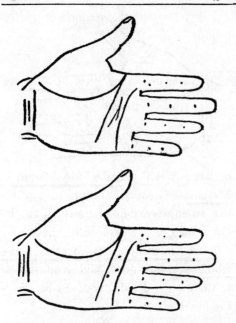

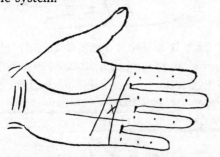

Red dots.—Murder or serious wound. The general character of the Hand will tell whether the subject is to be the guilty party or the victim.

White Dots—General weakening of the system.

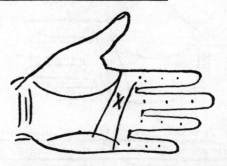

A cross in the Quadrangle touching the Line of Heart—Influence of the opposite sex on the subject. Will be favorable if the cross does not touch either the Line of Fate or the Line of the Sun.

A cross in the Quadrangle touching the Line of Head—The subject will exert in the matters of love or friendship more influence on the other person than

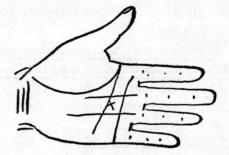

the said person will exert on him. The influence will be for good if the cross does not extend to either the Line of Fate or the Line of the Sun.

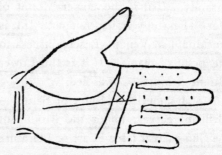

A finely shaped St. Andrew's cross in the Quadrangle beneath the Mount of Saturn, touching no main Line and with a clear, correct Line of Intuition—Aptitude for occult sciences. This is the "Mystic Cross."

This cross must be absolutely distinct and independent from any main line or branch of main lines. It must be a beautifully designed marking all by itself. Hence it is extremely rare, although many insignificant crosses are mistaken for it.

A cross in the Quadrangle under the Mount of Saturn and touching the Line of Fate—Fortunate life due to religion; found in the hands of great prelates and church dignitaries.

I always consider this as a sort of minor Mystic Cross.

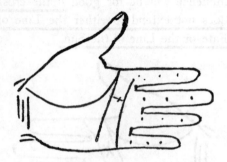

A poorly formed cross in the Quadrangle under the Mount of Saturn; if found in both hands—An unfavorable indication; drives to excess any unhealthy disposition shown by the Mount most prominent in the hand. If it is the Mount of Jupiter—Extravagant ambition. If it is the Mount of Saturn—Morbid disposition. If it is the Mount of the Sun—Excessive vanity and avarice. If it is the Mount of Mercury—Deceiving and even thieving instincts. If it is the Mount of the Moon—Coming Insanity. If it is the Upper Mount of Mars—Fearfully violent temper. If it is the Mount of Venus—Lasciviousness to the point of mania. If it is the Lower Mount of Mars—Cowardice.

A star under the Mount of Saturn—Brilliant career; under the Mount of the Sun—Great fame in art or literature

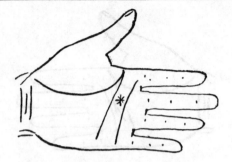

or large wealth; under the Mount of Mercury—Great reputation as a scientist, an engineer; also renown as an eloquent man or success as a business man.

A well-formed star (with other signs, which see)—A good and true subject at the mercy of a dearly-loved person of the other sex.

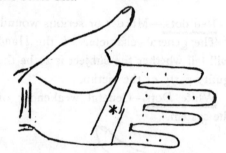

This is a sign I have frequently observed and found to be located generally between the Line of Life and the Line of Fate. It is often accompanied by a broken Line of Heart.

A Triangle—Aptitude for the study of the deepest sciences.

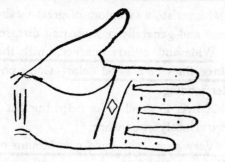

A square—Extremely quick temper, but a kind heart, if the Quadrangle is normally shaped.

If it touches one of the Main Lines, this square is to be read as a protection against the imperfection of that particular line.

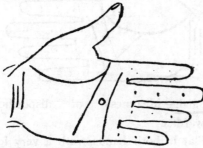

A circle—Eye troubles.

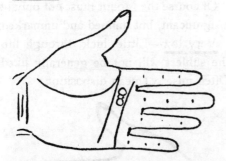

Three circles joined together under the Mount of Saturn—Epilepsy.

A Grille.—Raving madness (with other indications).

I should expect in this case a very wide Quadrangle, and very exaggerate Mounts of Mars.

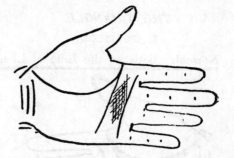

Should the Line of Heart run too high through the Mounts, or the Line of Head slope down, or rise in a curve out of its normal position, the student must at once reconstitute in his mind's

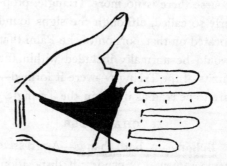

eye, the Quadrangle as it ought to be, and read accordingly the various indications—such as signs, etc., therein contained.

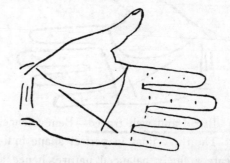

Total absence of a Quadrangle; if it is due to the non-existence of a Line of Heart—cold, hard nature; or, in a good hand—Poor action of the Heart.

THE TRIANGLE.

I. POSITION.

Normal: Between the Line of Life,

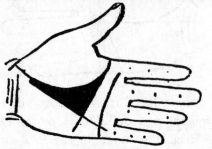

the Line of Head and the Line of Liver.

If any of these lines are missing, of course there is no more Triangle, properly so called, although the signs found located on that portion of the Palm that would be normally included within the limits of the Triangle—were it formed—are to be read as if within the Triangle.

II. CHARACTER.

Bulging in both hands—Aggressive temperament. Spendthrift disposition.

Bulging in one hand only—Bravery. Generosity.

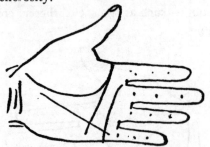

Broad and well traced—Benevolence.

The three lines in perfect shape indicate a finely balanced nature, hence a kindly one.

Large and well traced and of a healthy color—Good luck, long life, courage.

The Palm Proper is but too often red

and feverish, a symptom of great weakness and generally of a wasting disease.

Wide and clearly marked, with the three lines of a good color—Good understanding.

A liver in good order helps the brain marvelously in its work.

Very large, with developed Mounts of Mars—Audacity.

As stated above, the whole Plain of Mars is dominated by the idea of energy, pluck, etc.

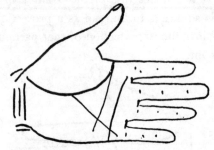

Small—Meanness of disposition. Cowardice

Flat in both hands, with a very low Mount of Saturn—Insignificant life.

Of course the Mount must not only be insignificant, but unlined and unmarked.

Very low—Little luck through life; the subject will not be generally liked. Often miserly, mean disposition.

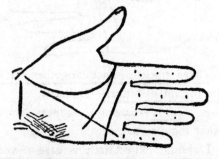

Low, with an exaggerate Mount of the Moon and only one bracelet well traced—Catalepsy.

A nervous trouble bringing about temporary suspension of animation.

Very low in both hands, with a short and broad Line of Heart—Lethargy.

Here, the circulation of the blood, not the nervous system, is at fault.

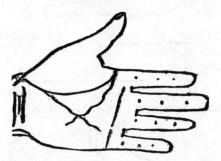

Narrow through a poor Line of Head inclining toward a poor Line of Liver—Business failure.

Heavy and pale, with a large, flabby palm, a short thumb and thick set fingers, the third phalanges puffed up inside—Material tastes.

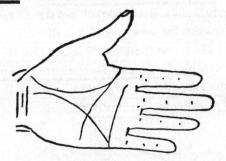

Poorly formed, the Lines of Head and Liver being curved inwards—Cowardice, meanness, miserly disposition.

Abnormally curved Lines always indicate a weakness of some sort, physical, mental or moral.

Developing gradually and more and more clearly— Improvement in the health of the subject.

Of course we can follow this development only in our hands or in those of close friends whose hands are constantly under our examination.

With the skin rough and hard—Contempt of physical pain.

Here again the idea of courage associated with the Triangle is made apparent.

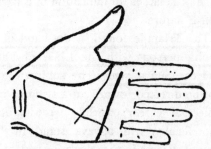

Badly formed and with a Line of Heart straight as a bar into the Percussion—Miserly habits.

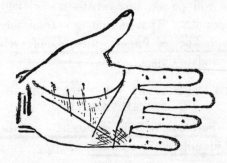

Much lined and with exaggerate Mounts of Mercury and Mars—Impatient, fretful disposition, easily aroused to anger.

An exagerate Mount of Jupiter would add to this characteristic an inordinate vanity wounded by imaginary slights.

Well formed, with a Line of Heart forked at its termination—Generosity.

Remember that a branchless, broken

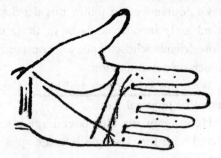

Line of Heart is an indication of a hard, selfish nature.

The Triangle found in the hand of a young person, with the Lines of Fate and the Sun absent—The subject must not be directed toward an artistic or intellectual career; worldly wisdom and superficiality will always stand in the way of success in that direction.

In other words, the existence of the three main lines gives assurance of fair health, good practical ability and plenty of will power, but reveals no brilliant aptitudes. That would go admirably with knotted fingers, square and even spatulate tipped.

III. THE FIRST (OR UPPER OR SUPREME) ANGLE.

Formed by the connection of the Lines of Life and Head.

Sharply pointed and well marked— Refined mind; more generally strong common sense.

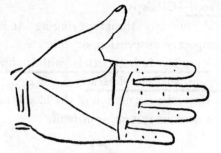

Blunt and short—Slow, dull intellect; rude instincts.

That goes with a short Line of Head and the various Chirognomical indications, to which I refer the reader.

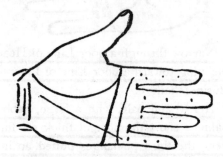

Exaggerate in its bluntness—Miserly habits from fear of poverty; little concern for other people's welfare.

That bluntness is obtained, in this case, by the Line of Head rising toward the Line of Heart and thus reducing the Quadrangle; hence the reading.

Blunt through the Line of Head being more or less separated from the Line of Life at the start—Independent disposition, amounting (if the space separating the Lines is very wide) to dangerous recklessness.

Exaggerate in its sharpness—Shrewd, malignant, envious disposition.

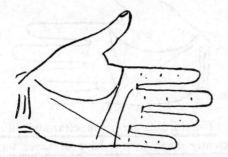

If this exaggerate sharpness is due to the Lines of Life and Head being connected too long at the start—Extreme diffidence and even cowardice.

IV. THE SECOND (OR INNER) ANGLE.

Formed by the connection of the Lines of Head and Liver.

The second Angle clear and well made—Longevity; bright intellect.

Due to the excellence of the Line of Liver.

The second Angle broad and heavy with a poor Line of Heart and a narrow Quadrangle—Uncharitableness.

The second Angle very sharp—Ill-health; nervousness; teasing disposition.

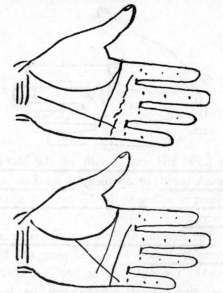

The Second Angle obtuse—Ultra nervous disposition.

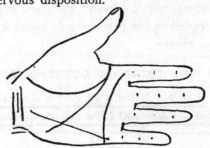

Due to the Line of Head drooping and the Line of Liver starting on the Mount of the Moon too near the Percussion.

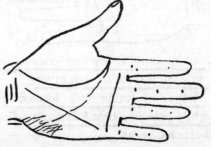

The Second Angle formed on the Mount of the Moon—Catarrh; even epilepsy, or paralysis if the Line of Head

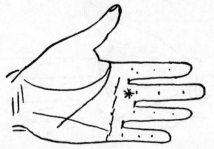

is poor and the Mount of the Moon much rayed; or apoplexy if the Line of Heart is poor and the Mount of Saturn starred.

The Second Angle found defective in a child's hand—The child must not be pushed too quick in his, or her, studies; the mental growth will be too quick, especially the imaginative faculties, and physical health will have to be attended to first; in a word: health before studies.

V. THE THIRD (OR OUTER) ANGLE.

It is not in truth an Angle since the Lines of Life and Liver, which are sup-

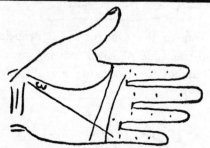

posed to form it, do not connect but simply come close to each other.

The Third Angle well formed and slightly open in a broad Triangle—Good all-around health.

The Third Angle well cut and narrow, and slightly open, with a well developed Mount of Mercury—Wit.

A perfect Line of Liver is apt to increase the quick mental faculties of the subject.

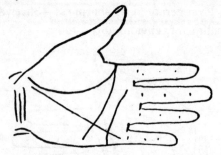

The third Angle broad, clear and sufficiently open, with a Line of Liver terminating high on the Mount of Mercury —Longevity; generosity; success in business.

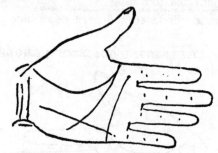

The Third Angle very obtuse, with the first phalanx of the thumb weak and the Mount of Venus exaggerate—Faithlessness.

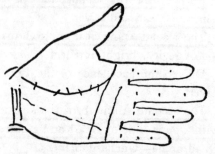

The Third Angle poorly formed, with small lines cutting the Line of Life— Neuralgia.

The Angle will be either too widely opened, with poor Lines of Head and Liver; or the Line of Liver will connect at the start with the Line of Life—always a sign of neuralgia or even palpitation of the heart and fainting fits (with a bad Line of Heart).

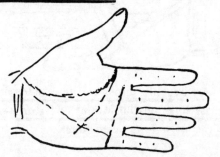

The Third Angle formed of lines much broken—Bad nature, both rough and incurably lazy.

I am inclined to think that this applies only to the Line of Liver.

VI. SIGNS.

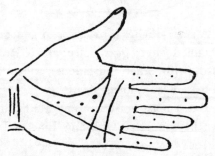

Red spots—Tradition says that it indicates pregnancy.

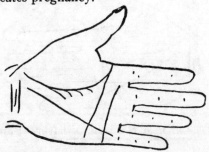

White spots—Anæmia; tendency to fainting fits.

Upward branches from the Line of Life terminating inside the Triangle—Riches and honors coming to the subject after many struggles.

Remember that in matters of success, the Plain of Mars represents our own unaided efforts.

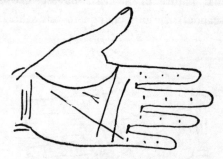

A short, forked line—General weakening of the system.

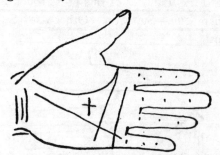

A cross, especially in the center—Troubles from others brought about by the quarrelsome disposition of the subject.

This is an attenuated form of the famous "Cross of Battle."

If in both hands and with other markings—One of the strongest indications of murder.

Many crosses—Continued bad luck.

A cross inside the Upper Angle of the Triangle—Law-suit (generally of a crim-

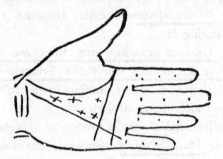

inal nature or at least having caused scandal); serious change in one's life.

If the branches of this cross touch no <u>main Line—Suit won.</u> <u>Otherwise</u>—Suit lost.

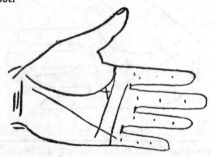

<u>A cross in the Triangle under the Mount of Saturn with long fingers and</u>

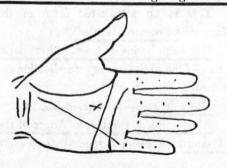

the first knots strongly marked— Skepticism. (See Chapter on Fingers, pp. 42-50.)

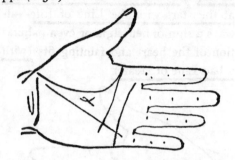

<u>An irregular cross in the center with cross lines on the Mount of Saturn</u>—A series of serious misfortunes.

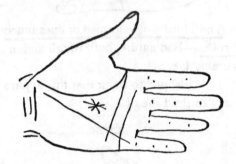

<u>A star</u>—Riches (or success in general) obtained after great struggles. Read also (with other indications), when in both hands—Violent death.

But it must not touch any Main Line nor be connected with any Line of Influence.

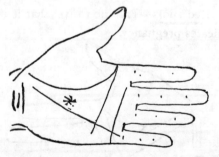

<u>A star near the Line of Liver</u>—Blindness.

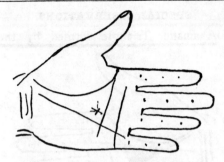

A badly formed solitary star—Troubles in love, resulting from some act of violence.

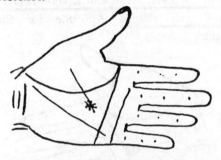

A star in the Triangle at the termination of a line of Influence from the Mount of Venus—A great sorrow. If the line

started from a star on the Mount of Venus—The sorrow arises from the death of a relative or close friend. (See Chapter on Lines of Influence, pp. 172-193.)

A circle—Troubles from a person of the other sex; with an exaggerate Mount of the Moon—Captiousness.

Over-excited imagination induces the

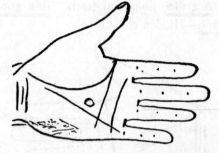

quick-tempered subject to constantly find fault and to resent violently imaginary offenses.

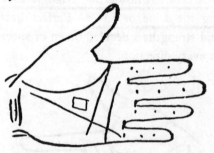

Square (if not touching any Main Line —A most serious warning of danger.

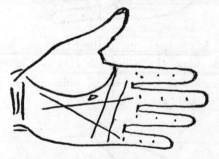

A Triangle between the Lines of Life and Fate—Military renown.

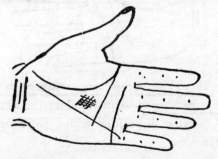

A grille—Shameful death. <u>In a good hand</u>—Hidden enemies.

A crescent inside the Triangle touch-ing the Line of Liver—Perfect health and strength; a decided omen of success in every direction.

A crescent inside the Triangle and touching the Line of Head—Violent death due to a fault of judgment or a foolhardy act of the subject.

The Third Angle very obtuse with a crescent inside—Unfaithfulness. Often a bullying disposition added to incon-stancy.

SPECIAL OBSERVATIONS.

A smaller Triangle formed by the

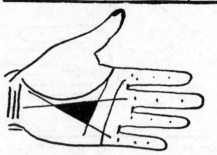

Lines of Fate, Head and Liver—If clear and well shaped—Aptitude for the occult sciences.

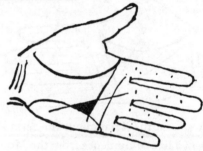

A smaller Triangle formed by the Line of Fate, the Line of Head and the Line of Intuition—An aptitude for the occult sciences that almost amounts to a gift of divination.

Much lined and with much lined Mounts of Mercury and the Moon. A very harmful disposition to worry. <u>If the Line of Head droops deeply</u>—Dan-ger of insanity.

LINES AND SIGNS ON THUMB AND FINGERS.

The student will find it profitable before perusing this chapter to turn back to pp. 45-46 and read over carefully my Chirognomical Observations concerning the Phalanges of the Fingers; also my readings concerning the Phalanges of the Thumb on pp. 53-55. In the indications I am about expatiating upon, he will find many statements that are simple confirmations of the great principles therein, laid down by me, after d'Arpentigny, Desbarrolles and the more recent Palmists, Papus, Decrespe, etc. The majority of these indications are, however, of a traditional or at least an empirical nature, and it is not easy to connect them logically with what I like to call "the laws of Modern Palmistry." They are gathered mostly from reputable authors of the old school and deserve respectful study solely on that account. Although met with but seldom, the rather complete enumeration I give of them may prove of use occasionally, and, without deserving to be memorized, they are valuable for reference purposes, as I never found them collected before in such large numbers.

I divide these observations between six headings, referring respectively to Lines and Signs: 1. On the Thumb; 2. On All the Fingers; 3. On the First Finger; 4. On the Second Finger; 5. On the Third Finger; 6. On the Fourth Finger, with subheadings for each phalanx of each finger.

I. ON THE THUMB.

1. On the First Phalanx.

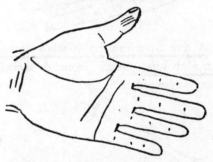

Downward lines—Will power more clearly marked, up to three lines; more

lines—Scattering of will power minimizing results.

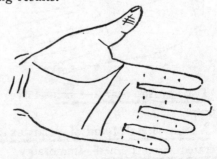

These lines crossed, or cross lines by themselves—Great obstacles to success.

Small, short lines near the nail—Legacies.

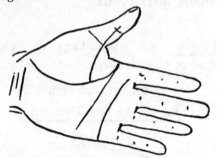

A line from the first phalanx to the Line of Life—Death from a metallic weapon (sword or dagger).

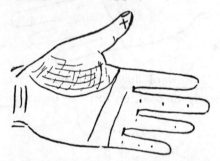

A cross near the nail with an exaggerate or much rayed Mount of Venus—Unchastity.

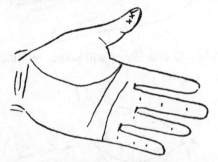

Two crosses near the nail—Love of luxury.

A star, with a Mount of Venus exaggerated or much lined—Immorality.

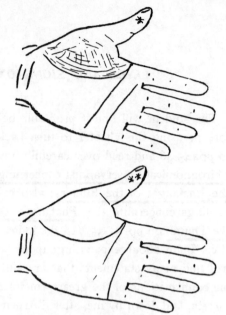

Two stars near the nail—Captiousness; constant fault-finding.

A triangle—The will power of the subject is concentrated on scientific labors.

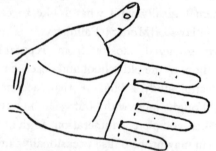

A circle—A great triumph for the subject, due to his steadfast will.

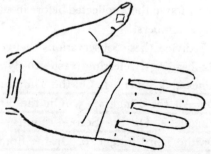

A square—The will-power is concentrated in one direction only. Often tyrannic disposition.

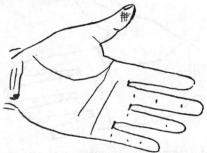

A grille near the nail (with other confirmatory signs)—A husband (or wife) in danger of death by said wife or husband.

2. On the Second Phalanx.

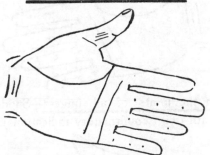

Downward lines, if not too many—Clear, sound reasoning power.

Cross lines—False reasoning; lack of common sense.

A forked line—Hesitating ways.

A cross—An easily influenced nature.

One or two stars—A nature easily led

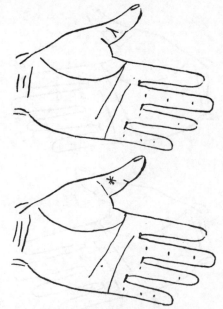

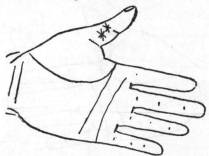

in the worst direction, but endowed with an amiable disposition.

A triangle—Deep scientific or philosophical talents.

A square—Logic not easily shaken; with bad indications—Blind stubbornness.

II. ON ALL THE FINGERS.

Little balls on the inside tips of fingers

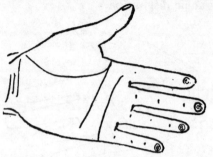

—Extreme sensitiveness, tact and taste.
One short vertical line deeply traced

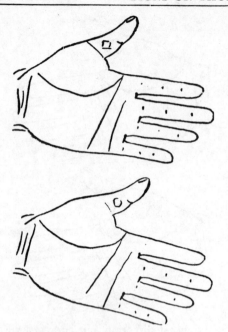

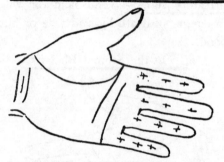

A circle—The triumph of reason.

on the joints of all fingers—Sudden
death (with confirmatory indications).

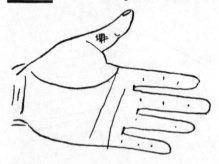

A grille—A lack of moral sense and
honest reasoning methods.

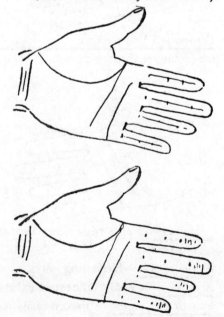

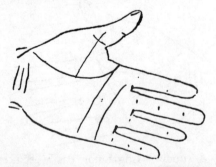

A line from the second phalanx to the
Line of Life—Troubles in married life.

One deep line running down the entire length of all fingers—A strong sense of honor.

Many cross lines on the first phalanx of all fingers—Bad general health.

Wavy, cross lines on the first phalanx of all fingers—Danger ahead; especially danger of drowning (with other confirmatory indications).

Triangles on the second joints of fingers—Tendency to sickness and physical weakness.

III. ON THE FIRST FINGER.

1. On the First Phalanx.

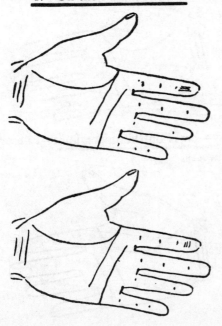

Downward lines—Religious exaltation.

Cross lines—Religious insanity.

A cross—Dangerous insanity due to visions, etc., often one of the signs of sudden death.

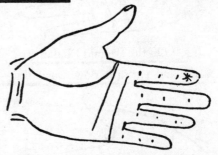

A star—A most serious event in the subject's life, generally fortunate.

A triangle—Aptitude for Theology, Ancient Magic, the Occult Sciences.

A circle—Triumph of faith over reason in the subject's mind.

A grille—Prison; convent life; the characteristic of the persecuting fanatics.

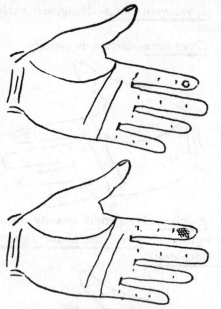

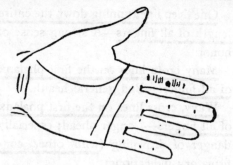

Cross lines on this and the Third phalanges—Envious and deceiving instincts.

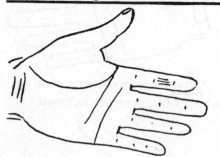

2. On the Second Phalanx.

Clear and straight downward lines—

A forked line—Ill-success.

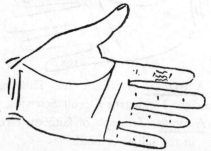

The noble ambition of the subject will receive assistance.

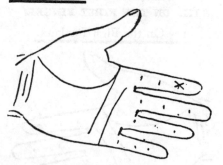

A cross on the upper joint—Literary success.

Confused or wavy downward lines— The ambition will be of an unworthy character.

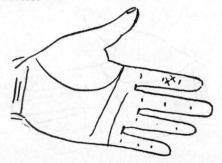

One or two crosses—The protection of the great.

A star, with straight downward lines from the first phalanx—Chastity.

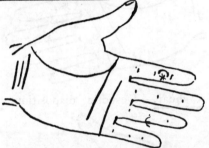

A star with a curved line next to it—Immodesty.

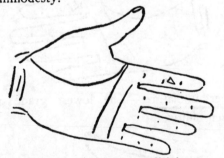

A triangle—An astute politician.

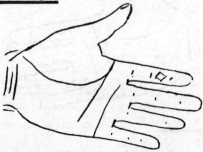

A square—Tenacity of purpose.

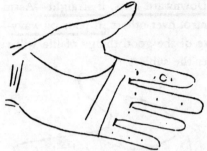

A circle—Crowned ambition.

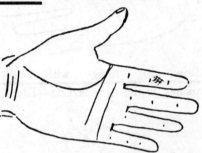

A grille—Perfidious instincts; ill-success.

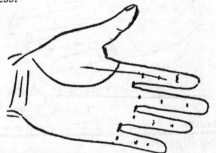

A single line from the Mount of Venus to the second phalanx—Nobility of character; great honors.

3.   On the Third Phalanx.

Downward lines, if straight—Assured control over others; if poor or wavy—A love of the good things of life will rule over the subject.

Downward lines, with upward branches on the Line of Life—Riches.

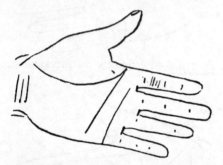

Cross lines—Legacies; also obstacles to the exercise of power; also in certain natures, revealed by other indications—Poor digestive organs.

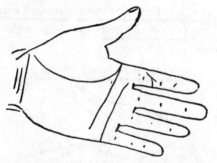

A forked line—Projects gone wrong.
A cross—The worst and grossest instincts and habits.
A star—Immodesty.

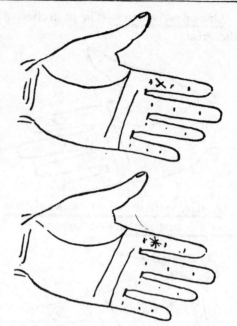

A square—Despotic disposition; in

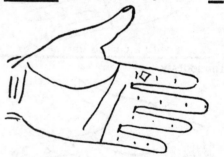

certain natures—The lowest grade of sensuality.

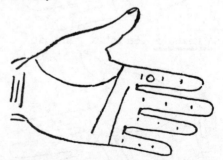

A circle—Success in one's pet ambition.
A grille—A thoroughly corrupt na-

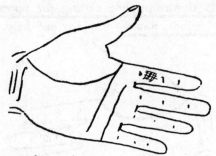

ture; often prison.

A single line from the Mount of Venus

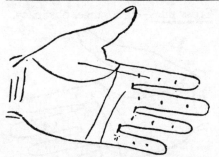

to the third phalanx—Violent death (with confirmatory indications).

IV. ON THE SECOND FINGER.

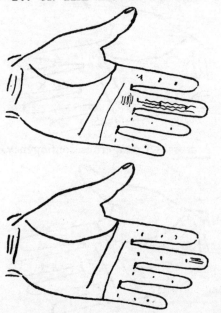

Downward, wavy lines down the whole

finger, with cross bars on the Mount of Saturn—Succession of fatal happenings.

1. On the First Phalanx.

Downward lines—Suicide.

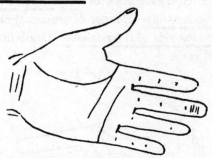

Cross lines—Suicidal insanity.

A black spot—Ague, chronic malaria.

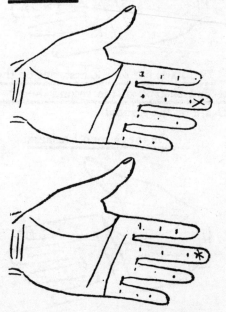

A cross—Superstition often amounting to insanity; frequently it reveals a tendency to crime or suicide.

A star—A most extraordinary existence, either for good or evil; if repeated in both hands—Danger of assassination; if on the side of the phalanx—Death in a just cause.

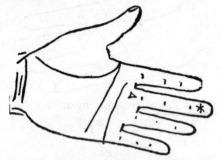

A star with a triangle on the Mount of Saturn—Depravity.

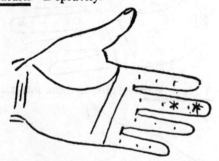

Two stars, one on the first, one on the second phalanx of the second finger—Death on the scaffold.

2. On the Second Phalanx.

A downward line cutting the upper and middle joints—Stupidity and folly.

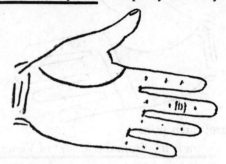

Cross lines—Ignorance, obstinacy.

A thick cross line—Death by poison.

A cross—A dangerous contingency.

A star—A catastrophy, probably a

crime, generally unavoidable. One of the few signs of fatality recognized by Modern Palmists.

A square—Another indication of an unavoidable fatality.

A triangle—Special aptitudes for the occult sciences.

A circle—Great success in one's researches into the occult sciences.

A grille—Ill-luck; indication of the class of diseases generally marked on the Mount of Saturn (nerves, legs, ears, etc.).

3. On the Third Phalanx.

One or two downward lines from the second to the third phalanx—Wisdom.

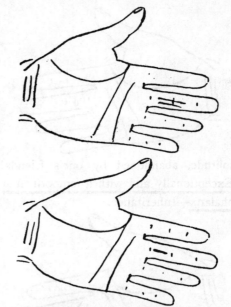

One straight, downward line not entering the Mount of Saturn—Military

success. If oblique—Death in battle.

Many downward lines, if perfect—A fortune in mining; otherwise—Extreme melancholia.

Many cross lines—A wretched life in

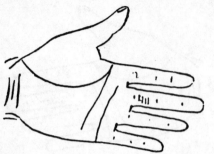

solitude, abandoned by one's friends. Exceptionally and with a <u>smooth first phalanx</u>—Inheritance.

<u>A forked line</u>—An unfortunate nature, hating other people's society and generally disliked.

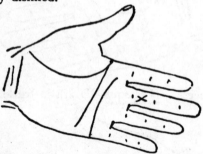

<u>A cross (in a woman)</u>—Sterility.

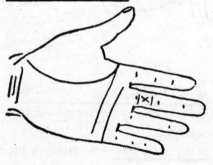

<u>A cross and two cross lines</u>—Thieving disposition.

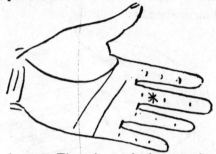

<u>A star</u>—The sign of the murderer (with other indications), <u>or in a good hand</u>—Of the possible victim of a murder.

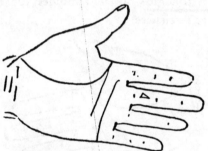

<u>A triangle</u>—A wicked nature threatened with ill-luck.

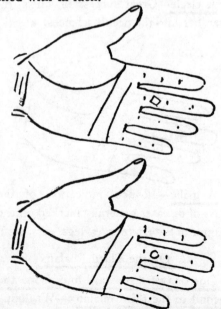

A square—Merciless, miserly disposition.

A circle—Great proficiency in the study of natural philosophy.

A grille—The insanity peculiar to misers.

V. ON THE THIRD FINGER.

1. On the First Phalanx.

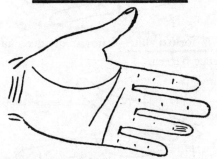

Downward lines—Artistic genius turning into insanity.

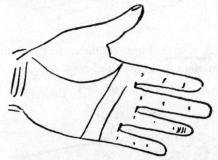

Cross lines—Obstacles to the artistic career, causing insanity.

A cross—Extraordinary chastity; the artist wedded to his art. Often insanity

due to the over-excitement of the artistic tendencies.

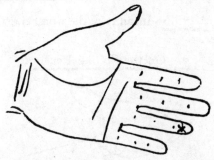

A star—When insanity is not superinduced by the above cause, the subject's genius bursts into splendor.

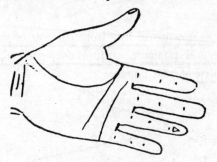

A triangle—Science of the beautiful.

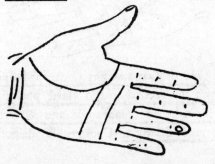

A circle—Most superb, if unexpected, success.

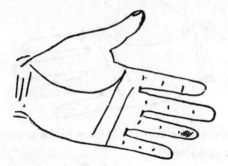

A grille—Insanity of the worst character.

2. On the Second Phalanx.

A downward line from the top of the second phalanx, cutting deep into the third—Great fame.

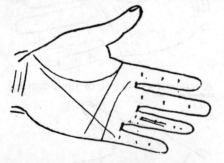

One or two straight downward lines from the second to the third phalanx, with a broad Quadrangle and a well-formed Triangle—Changeable disposition.

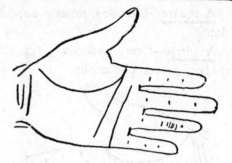

Cross lines—Lack of talent; jealousy.

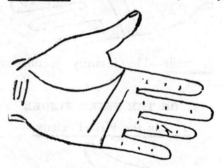

A forked line—Efforts divided and hence barren.

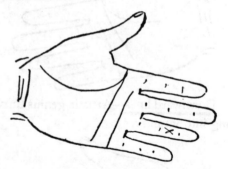

A cross—The venomous envy of the impotent and conceited competitor.

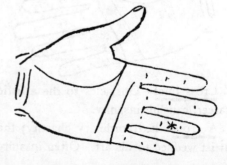

A star—Exceptional talents.

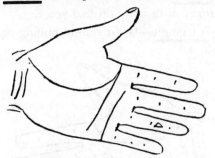

A triangle—The science of art, penetrating its divine mysteries.

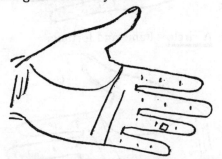

A square—A talent restricted within certain specialties.

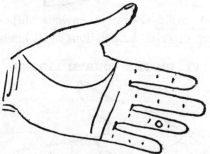

A circle—Great success.

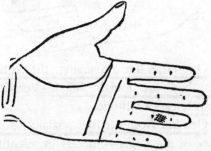

A grille—Most envious disposition.

3. On the Third Phalanx.

Several downward lines from the joint

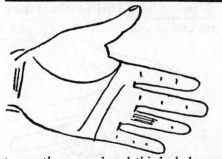

between the second and third phalanges to the base of the finger—Reverses due to persons of the other sex.

One single line not beginning so high and not reaching so low—Happiness.

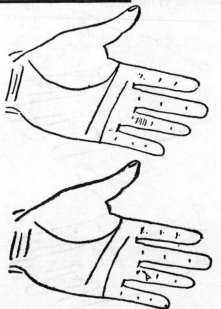

Cross lines—Constant ill-luck and persistent poverty.

A forked line—Useless efforts toward fame and wealth.

A semicircle—Unhappiness.

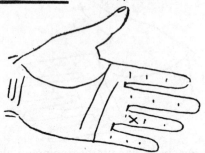

A cross—Vocation interfered with, ambition crushed.

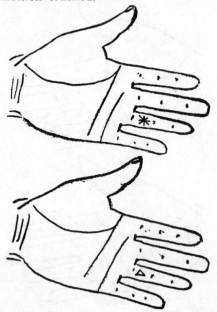

A star—Extravagant love for praise; danger of insanity on that score.

A triangle—Great skill in puffing one-self.

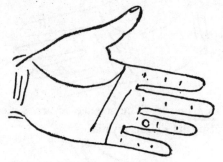

A circle—Fame and fortune.

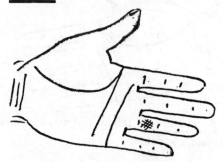

A grille—Poverty; envious disposition; deserved humiliations of all kinds.

VI. ON THE FOURTH FINGER.

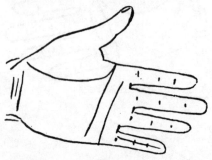

One clear line traversing the entire length of the fourth finger—Veracity. Two lines—Rectitude.

One line from the first phalanx to the base of the finger—Success in scientific pursuits.

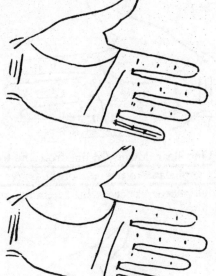

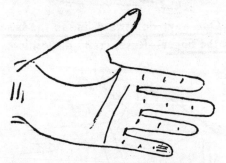

1. On the First Phalanx.

Downward lines—Meddlesome nature; sometimes the insanity of gigantic

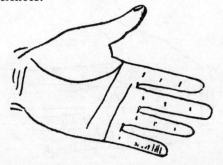

enterprises. In a very good hand—Eloquence, or aptitude for the occult sciences.

Cross lines—An incessant and empty talker; often a liar and a thief.

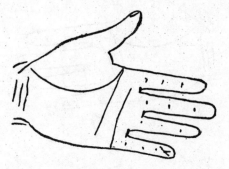

A forked line—Poor success in business.

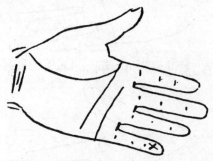

A cross, in a good hand—Prophetic instincts; in a bad hand—A theft or robbery that will cause its author great trouble.

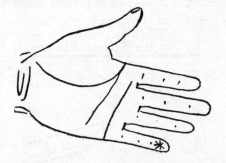

A star—Success as a speaker; no success in money-making.

A triangle—Aptitude for occult sciences, even to evocation of the dead.

A square—Commercial genius.

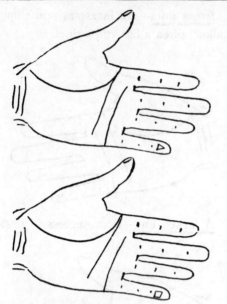

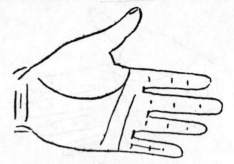

One clear downward line from the top of the phalanx to the base of the finger—Intelligence. Success in scientific researches.

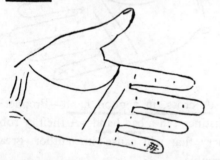

A <u>grille</u>—Stuttering; black magic;

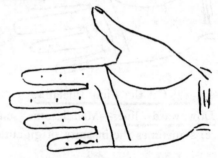

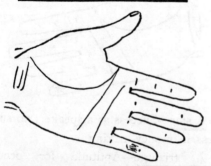

<u>One wavy downward line to the base of the finger</u>—Ruse; crafty disposition.

thieving instincts; all the worst features of the Mount of Mercury.

2. On the Second Phalanx.

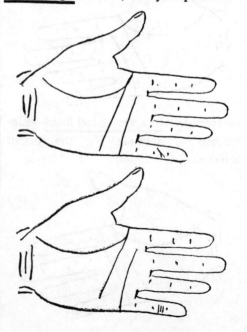

<u>Confused downward lines</u>—Deceiving instincts.

A forked line—The lack of order handicaps all possible success.

Cross lines—A much checkered career.

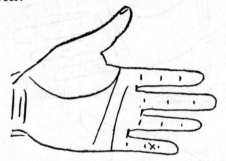

A cross—Great difficulties; often prison.

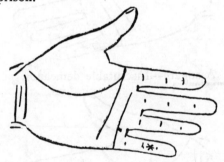

A star—Notoriety obtained through the worst features of the Mount of Mercury.

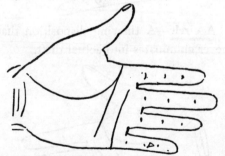

A triangle—Success in the practice of occult science.

A square—Hinders the quick versatility that belongs to the Mount of Mercury. Often means prison.

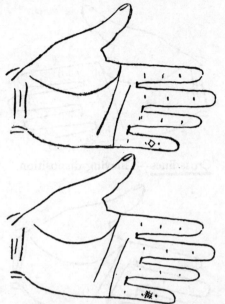

A grille—Prison also; silliness in the conduct of one's affairs.

3. On the Third Phalanx.

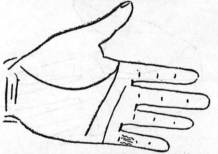

Wavy or confused downward lines—Thieving disposition.

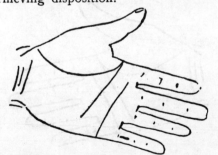

A thick downward line—Thieving disposition.

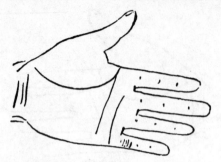

Cross lines—Thieving disposition.

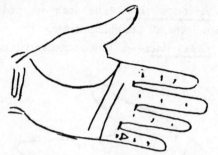

A triangle—Diplomatic ability.

A cross—Thieving disposition.

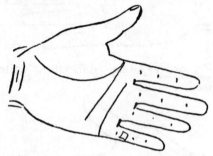

A square—Inscrutable demeanor.

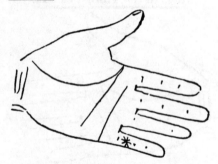

A star—Eloquence; wit.

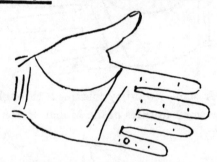

A circle—A thieving disposition that never culminates into actual theft.

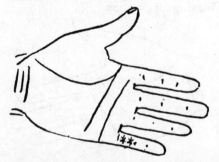

Two stars—Dishonorable death as the consequence of thefts.

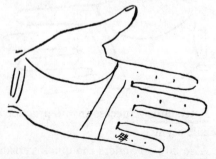

A grille—Stupidity of the fifth-rate thief; sometimes stupidity of the victim.

PART FIFTH

Additional Cases

These cases, as well as those disseminated through the other Parts of this book, are—many of them—borrowed from Desbarrolles' *magnum opus*, "Révélations Complètes." They have never been translated into the English language and their careful study constitutes, in my opinion, the very best of practice for the student of Palmistry. He finds combined in them many indications scattered through these pages, and he is taught how to *generalize* the information obtained and to apply it intelligibly. Book definitions are bound to be narrow and on that account somewhat misleading. By broadening them, not recklessly but in moderation, a well trained intelligence will soon know how to give them their full inward meaning. This study of "cases" ought really to precede the examination of "living hands."

PART FIFTH

Additional Cases

ADDITIONAL CASES.

Art and Science Happily Blended.—All the Chief Lines were perfect and the chirognomic indications of the very best as far as intellectuality was concerned. A curved line connected the Mounts of the Sun and Mercury without cutting either the Lines of the Sun or the Line of Liver.

"This curious marking was noticed in the hands of two famous Parisian professional men; one a barrister, the other a surgeon. The design shows simply this peculiar ring and does not give the other indications peculiar to each of these two subjects."

An Extravagant Yearning Toward Notoriety.—A rather short Line of Head; a similar Line of Fate, not bad, however. A very long and rather straight Line of Heart; as distinctive marking, a Line from the Upper Mount of Mars deep into the Mount of the Sun.

"Seen in the hand of a common village conjurer and pseudo-doctor, whose assurance and vanity were beyond description. He used to secure the attention of his rural admirers by the extraordinary lies he told them about his family, his talents, his career. He managed finally to run away with a rich farmer's daughter, who believed in his fables. Success at any cost, and boundless vanity, with half developed brains, are the type herein represented."

Monomania of Persecution.—A Double Girdle of Venus; a very poor Line of Heart; a Line of Head very widely separated from the Line of Life at the start and forming a broad island from the Mount of Jupiter to under the Mount of Saturn, where it stops short. A deep cross in the space between the Lines of Head and Life.

"The subject suffered from a monomania consisting in his believing that government agents were constantly after him and tortured him by means of hidden electrical batteries. He was a pronounced Saturnian; the first phalanx of his thumb was as small as that of a congenital idiot. His Mount of Jupiter was displaced toward a high Mount of Saturn; his Mount of the Moon was also exaggerate; all signs of sure insanity."

Dangerous Fall from Horseback.—A Line of Life broken at 35, the two fragments overlaying each other and joined to a cross bar from a dot on the inside fragment, the latter above the break, for the space of five years. Fine Lines of Fate and the Sun.

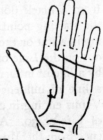

"A gentleman, otherwise in **very** happy and fortunate circumstances, was thrown from his horse at 35 and suffered from the consequences of this accident for over 5 years; finally he recovered completely. His very strong Mount of Jupiter pointed toward that particular kind of accident. The markings were similar in both hands."

A Child Crippled by the Act of a Cruel Relative.—A Line of Head broken under the Mount of Saturn; a Line of Influence from the Mount of Venus ends in a deep dot on the Line of Head on the Mount of Saturn. Otherwise a good, intelligent hand.

"A young girl, as early as 10 years old, had been roughly knocked down by an ugly tempered female relative, in whose charge she had been left after her parents' death; in consequence of this fall she had lost the use of a leg. The child was remarkably bright and studious."

A Three Time Repeated Trouble With the Legs Ends in Caries of the Bone.—A particularly bulging Mount of the Moon, a good Mount of Venus and a strong Mount of Saturn. A Line of Influence from a black dot on

the starting point of a Line of Life ending in a star on the Line of Head Another dot on the Line of Life at 18 connecting by a line of influence with the same star; a line of influence from the Mount of Venus ending in a black dot on the Line of Life at 30. Another Line of Influence from the Mount of Venus ending in a star on the Line at 35. From that time

on the Line of Life is formed or rather indicated by a succession of laddered small bars.

"A flower gardener—bad teeth, Saturnian type—suffered from a trouble of the brain at 18, caused by an accident; same illness again at 30, and returned at 35; the caries or necrosis of the bones of one of his legs then set in and rendered his life most precarious."

Epilepsy.—A very poor Line of Heart; A Line of Head drooping deep into the Mount of the Moon. In the Quadrangle, under the Mount of Saturn, three circles of unequal size touching each other.

"Seen in the hands of a very thin, ultra-nervous woman who had suffered all her life from epileptic fits. She was intelligent, however, and managed to do her housework very satisfactorily between the attacks of this terrible disease."

One and the Same Divorce Marked Twice in the Hand.—A fine cross on the Mount of Jupiter. From a dot on the second joint of the Thumb start two Lines of Influence cutting upward branches of the Line of Life, respectively, at 25 and 35 years of age.

"A young lady had made a love marriage at 25; at that date already, and, in fact, before the marriage was settled upon, the above indications were in the hand. The divorce took place at 35. She had these two warnings instead of one; she was duly notified but did not heed them."

A Fortunate Life in Spite of Repeated Rebuffs.—Square, knotty fingers; a Line of Fate, somewhat chained at the start, but fine up to 35; then broken; a fragment runs from the Line of Head to the Line of Heart; a second frag-

ment from the Line of Heart to the top of the Mount of Saturn. A fine star on the Mount of Jupiter; a beautiful Line of Intuition.

"Seen in the hand of a Jewish banker who lost his fortune at 35 and again at 50; but he retrieved his losses each time on the speculative market, by means of his extraordinary intuition."

A Lady Financially Ruined and then Deserted by Her Lover.—A fair Line of Life; a Line of Head widely separated from the Line of Life at the start and drooping at once into the Mount of the Moon. A Girdle of Venus. A Line

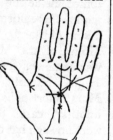

of Heart beginning, branchless, under the Mount of Saturn. A Line of Fate starred at 23, broken at 25; starred again at the connection with a Line of Influence from the Mount of Venus, the latter islanded and ending near the Mount of Mercury. A Line of Union cutting the Lines of the Sun and Head.

"At 23, a lady had been led astray by a man who had devoured her fortune and later had abandoned her and their two children to marry a rich girl. The lovers had lived together for 20 years when the desertion took place. But although the lady's life seemed irremediably ruined, she recovered from the shock and losses and the rest of her life was prosperous."

Hemorrhoids.—From a dark dot on the Line of Life at 32, started a Line of Influence, ending in a star on the upper Mount of Mars. From that star a line crossed over to a Mount of Saturn, much rayed by vertical lines and ended there in a star.

"The man who suffered since he was 32 of an aggravated case of hemorrhoids, was distinctly a mixture of the Mars and Saturn types."

Two Lovers at the Same Time.—A very strong fork at the termination of a good Line of Head. At about 28, two Lines of Influence started from the same point on the Line of Life and ended, one inside the Upper Mount of

Mars, the other at the end of a drooping prong of the forked Line of Head.

"A young unmarried woman acknowledged in court that she had, at the time, two simultaneous love affairs, which her talent for deceit had kept perfectly secret."

Series of Deaths in the Family.—A chained Line of Heart. At the lower part of the second phalanx of the second finger—toward the first finger—a clearly marked star. A drooping Line of Head terminating in

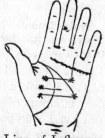

a star at the end of a Line of Influence on the Mount of Venus, beginning in a star. Above that, another Line of Influence from a star on the Mount, ending inside the Triangle; above that another Line of Influence from a star on the Mount, ending in a star inside the Quadrangle at the start of a fair Line of the Sun.

"Two similar cases are combined in this outline. In both cases, the star on the second finger was there. The two subjects (women) lost, successively, close relations, two of whom died insane."

Insanity Revealed by the Colors of the Lines.—A very badly chained Line of Heart; a Line of Head terminating in a star; a Line of Influence from a star on the Mount of Venus cuts the Line of Life at 38 and comes up in a curve to the Mount of Mercury. All the Lines were of a deep chocolate color.

"A lady came to Desbarrolles complaining that there were people on the floor above her flat piercing holes through their floor and trying to poison her by means of noxious fumes. Her monomania, on that point, was unconquerable. The Master discovered that she had lost a dearly loved son and that the sorrow had determined a severe liver trouble, which was then affecting her brain."

Brain Trouble Resulting from a Grave Disorder of the Lower Organs.—A very poor Line of Heart; a Line of Head broken under the Mount of Saturn and drooping suddenly to the bottom of a much rayed Mount of the Moon, where it ends in a star. A star above it

on the same Mount.

"In repeated cases, Desbarrolles discovered that chronic troubles of the womb, bladder or kidneys determined gradually a weakening of the cerebral faculties, especially so if the break and droop of the Line of Head indicated such tendencies."

Asthma.—A very narrow Quadrangle due to the abnormal curving down of the Line of Heart. A dot on the Line of Head under the Mount of Saturn. A deep bar cut the Line of Life at 25; from it started, on either side, curved branches, which joined inside the Triangle, there forming a kind of island. The Mount of the Moon was somewhat rayed. High Mounts of Mars; short nails. In another case there were no such bar and island, but the same formation of the Quadrangle and a deep black dot therein.

"I had occasion to repeatedly verify—with very slight modifications—these two readings of the Master, concerning Asthma. In the first case the subject was hot tempered and sanguine."

Deafness.—A Venus-Saturnian type; on the third phalanx of the second finger a number of downward lines. A big island, under the Mount of Saturn, on a Line of Head that begins to droop immediately afterward.

"Seen in the hand of a young man who

had grown deaf, quite early in life, and who was more and more under the influence of morbidity and strange superstitions; Saturn had him entirely under its influence."

Constant Oppressions Amounting to Monomania.—A poor Line of Heart; a drooping Line of Head islanded under the Mount of the Sun. A Line of Influence from a star on the Mount of Venus cut the Line of  Life at 38 and ended at the beginning of the above mentioned island. The first phalanges of the first, second and third fingers were abnormally large; the second finger especially long.

"At 38, the subject had lost his wife, of whom he was very fond. He had devoted himself to religious practices until he was constantly under the influence of hallucinations, hearing voices at all hours and unable to silence them. A severe brain fever had coincided with the date of his wife's death, and the shape of his fingers predisposed him to an extraordinary influx of vital fluid, without sufficient health to utilize it."

A Poisoning Case.—A Girdle of Venus starred under the Mount of Saturn. A short Line of Heart terminating as it reaches the Line of the Sun. A Line of Influence from a star on the Line of Life at 16 terminates at a  deep black dot on the Line of Heart.

"A talented Parisian actress had suffered from a great love sorrow when she was hardly more than 16 years old; she had poisoned herself out of jealousy and despair on being deserted by the loved one. The poisoning is indicated in this case (Desbarrolles says) by the star on the Girdle, at that particular place."

A Profitable Meeting at a Fashionable Seaside Resort.—No star on a very prominent Mount of Jupiter, but one at the termination of a fine Line of the Sun inside the Quadrangle. From that star a line  ran up straight to a well-formed Mount of Mercury at the usual place for Lines of Union. The Line of the Sun itself starts from a clear Voyage line on the Percussion of the Mount of the Moon.

"A French 'lady of leisure' met at Ostende—the fashionable seaside resort —a royal personage; he was attracted by her beauty and wit. A short-lived 'liaison' was the result of this meeting; it swelled materially the 'lady's' bank account and enriched her jewel-case."

Double Guilty Intrigue.—A Line of Fate much crossed up to 23 years old, then opening in the shape of a large island, extending to 30 or 35, but not quite closed at the top.  The left "branch" of the Line islanded again between 32 and 37; after that the Line continues straight and fine. A Line of Head widely separated from the Line of Life and forked at the termination. A fine Line of the Sun coming up to the Mount in a curve from the Lower part of the Mount of the Moon. A very long third finger. A Girdle of Venus strongly marked.

"Seen in the hand of a lady about 40 years old who belonged to the Jupiter-Mercury type. She had been quite successful in business, although disposed to take many risks. Until 23 she had great financial difficulties to meet; then she had accepted the protection of a wealthy married man, whose assistance had made her fortune. She had left him at 30 to marry another lover of hers. The second island had lasted as long as the first protector lived, as, according to palmistry, this second union, during the life of the first lover, is considered adultery. The lady was very shrewd but somewhat hysterical."

Insane Husband, Death of.—From a star on the Mount of Venus close to the second phalanx of thumb comes a Line of Influence, which cuts the Line of Life at 28 years of age  and ends in a star near the end of the Line of Head. A clear star upon a Line of Union.

"A lady visitor of Desbarrolles lost her husband after having been obliged to keep him for several years in an insane asylum. He died a raving maniac when the subject was 28."

Intestinal Cancer.—A drooping and forked Line of Head; upon this Line, just before the fork begins, a star; another star at the end of the lower prong of the fork. From the first  star drops a perpendicular line, which forms a square, with a horizontal line and another vertical drooping from the end of the upper prong of the above men-tioned Line of Head. An independent star in the lower part of this square. There were deep dots on the corner of the square.

"These very interesting markings were found in the hand of a lady who suffered for years from an intestinal cancer, but whom a successful operation finally cured."

Troubles of the Respiratory Organs.—On the Line of Head, under the Mount of Saturn, a clear star. A Line of Influence from the Mount of Venus cut an upward branch of  the Line of Life, and after crossing the above mentioned star ends in another star on the Upper Mount of Mars. The hand much rayed and the large Mount of Jupiter with Lines on the Middle Mount of the Moon revealing tendencies to gout.

"Excessive good living had first determined an over-production of uric acid, then gout, then finally a trouble of the brain. Later consumption set in. The sign on Upper Mars was in the Right Hand, and the Left Lung was the one attacked by tuberculosis. This crosswise influence of the brain upon diseases is observed in most cases."

Prolonged Fainting Fits.—In the Left hand a star at the termination of the Line of Heart. A bluish streak toward 60 on the Line of Life. The same indications found in the  Right hand, but there the star was inclosed within a square. Very short thumbs. Short nails. Square tipped fingers.

"The subject, a civil engineer by profession, suffered repeatedly all through his very active life of very unexplainable fainting fits, so long in duration as to amount almost to a state of lethargy. His nature was very nervous and there was evidently a lack of harmonious distribution of the vital fluid."

„Extraordinary Escape from Death.— A very poor Line of Heart. At the termination of an otherwise fine Line of Fate a break surrounded by a large square, occupying almost the whole of the Mount of Saturn.

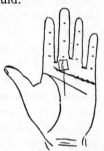

"A workingman, a house painter by trade, suffered frequently from dizziness, due to lead-poisoning. In one of these fits he fell from a very high scaffolding, but landed into a passing wagon loaded with tan bark, thus escaping what seemed to the bystanders a certain and cruel death."

Repeated Cases of Strange Preservation. —A star on both hands on the Mount of Saturn, with a square constituted by the Line of Heart, two perpendicular Lines from between the first and second, and the second and third fingers, respectively, and the line forming the base of the second finger. A ray from that star cut deeply the Line of Heart, connecting with a cross on the Upper Mount of Mars. There were two other crosses in the Quadrangle. The Line of the Sun, although starting rather high up (at 28), was very fine to the end.

"A lady from Tyrol, met at Baden, had escaped assassination at the hands of a disappointed lover. Another time, in childhood, she had fallen out of a third-story window and suffered nothing from the accident."

Wretched Childhood; Extreme Ambition. — In both hands a clear, deep Line curving up from the Upper Mount of Mars to the Mount of the Sun. Until 30 years old, the Line of Fate, afterward very fine up to the Mount of Saturn, was cut up into small fragments. Just where the Line ceased to be bad, there merged into it a fine Influence Line from the Mount of the Moon. A Line of Influence from the Line of Life at 10 years old cut the Line of the Sun on the Mount of that name.

"The lady, whose chirognomic markings revealed her as having real aptitudes for the dramatic profession, had been in very poor circumstances until 30 (her parents having lost their all when she was about 8), when an inheritance from a former admirer enriched her."

The Founder of a New Religion.— The subject was a Saturnian - Martian, with spatulate fingers and first knot strongly marked. In both hands a finely shaped "Mystic Cross" cut the Line of Fate. Another Cross, the "Cross of Battle," was found in the center of the Triangle.

"He was a man of great intellect and a natural antagonist of all known creeds. He broke away from the Church he had entered as a minister and decided to found his own independent religion."

A Man Poisoned by His Wife, Who Had Led Him a Terrible Life.—A black dot on the Line of Head under the Mount of Saturn. A very deep and very red Line of Union.

"The man had been very unhappy in his married life. The character of the Line of Union indicates always a bad temper in the person with whom the subject is united."

The Hand of a Favorite of a Royal Prince.—On a high Mount of Jupiter a cross and a star. A Line of Head widely separated from the Line of Life. A much rayed hand and a high Mount of Mercury. A beautiful Line of the Sun; a soft palm. Spatulate, smooth fingers with a short thumb. Two Lines of Influence starting from stars on the Mount of Venus and ending at the Line of the Sun, cutting it. A star on the lower prong of a fork ending the Line of Head. Two superposed islands at the beginning of the Line of Liver. An elongated island from 18 to 35 on the Line of Fate. A long Line of Influence from the Line of Life (just below a black dot at 16), cutting an upward branch of the Line and ending on the Mount of Mercury. High Mounts of Venus and the Moon.

"A lady, quite famous as an opera singer, was for years the protegée of a Royal Prince, himself married; before that liaison, she had had many adventures and had lost, by death,

two very dear friends; sorrow had rendered her insane for a while. She remained nervously excitable and almost clairvoyant at times. Her first sweetheart had abandoned her when she was barely 17; she had been very ill at 16. Altogether her life had been most miserable until she met the prince, who remained attached to her for over twenty years and left her a large fortune."

Flow of Blood. Hemorrhoids.—A rather excessive Upper Mount of Mars; a Line of Liver rising ladderwise in broken fragments and ending there. From a long bluish indentation on the Line of Life stretching from 24 to 40 years of age came a Line of Influence ending in a star at the connection of the Line of Head and Liver. The Line of Head, otherwise good, ended in a square-like design.

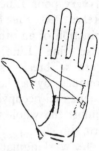

"Found in the hand of a man who suffered severely for over 16 years from a very severe case of hemorrhoids, with frequent loss of blood."

Aggravated Case of Catarrh.—The Upper Mount of Mars and the upper part of the Mount of the Moon much rayed and cross-rayed.

"The subject—a decided Mercurian — was suffering from a catarrh of the stomach that rendered digestion of solid food almost impossible, so that he really underwent the pangs of hunger."

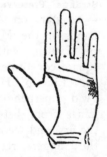

PART SIXTH

Phrenology and Palmistry Compared

The discoverers and exponents of *Phrenology* were two German scientists: Franz Joseph *Gall*, born in the Grand Duchy of Baden, March 9, 1758, who began lecturing on craniology in Vienna in 1796, meeting with great opposition and even persecution on account of his belief in the influence of the brain upon the contours of the skull. He died in 1828. His pupil and associate, Johann Caspar *Spurzheim*, was born at Longrich on the Moselle, December 31, 1776. Their first great book, *Anatomie et Physiologie du Système Nerveux et du Cerveau en Particulier*, came out in Paris in 1810-19; later, Spurzheim, who had settled in London, published *The Physiognomical System of Drs. Gall and Spurzheim, based on an anatomical and physiological examination of the Nervous System and the Brain in Particular* (London: 1814).

In 1835 W. Lewis translated from the French Dr. Gall's classical work on the subject: *On the Functions of the Brain and of Each of its Parts* (6 vols).

PHRENOLOGY AND PALMISTRY COMPARED.

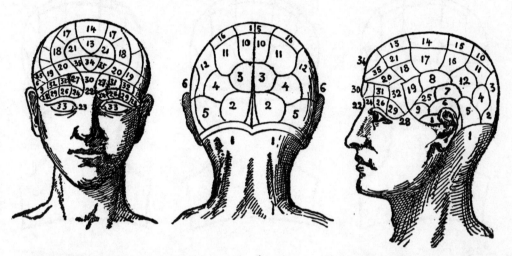

Phrenology needs no defender; its discoverers and their many worthy continuators have conquered for it the full and respectful consideration to which it is entitled. Their success in that direction is a pleasant, reassuring omen as to what awaits, within a few short years, orthodox, honest, accurate Palmistry. It is enough to say that the scientific world has finally given a verdict—not unanimous, but widely endorsed—in favor of the verity of Phrenology, both in theory and in practice. In these pages we have not to undertake to present any plea in its behalf. But we are glad to assist in its triumph by demonstrating how accurately Palmistic markings "dovetail"—if I may use such homely language—with Phrenological revelations. Desbarrolles, whose broad mind embraced every element of truth and caused it to do its

work in the good cause, has gathered thousands of observations that guarantee the correctness of this series of comparative statements. I have simply given them, after personal revision, the succinct form acceptable to English-speaking readers.

I propose to do so later with the indications of Physiognomy—the admirable science that sprang, full-armed, from the brain of Lavater. And finally Graphology, or the Reading of human nature through handwriting, will also be called upon to confirm the statements solidly established on the triple foundation of Palmistry, Phrenology, Physiognomy.

The disciples of Desbarrolles, believing, as he did himself so thoroughly, that Phrenology—although of comparatively recent date—verifies every one of the principles laid down by the ancient and

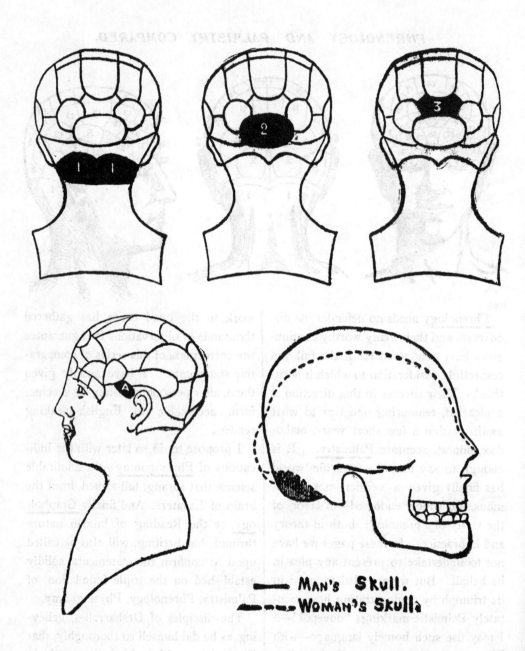

MAN'S SKULL.
WOMAN'S SKULL.

modern Chiromants or Palmists, follow their master in his very simple examination of phrenological signs, using not their fingers, but their eyes, to discover the more or less prominence of this or that organ. Touch is not indispensable to locate 26 out of the 36 Functions or Faculties recognized by the founders of Phrenology, Messrs. Gall and Spurzheim. The following ten organs, however, can not be surveyed without the help of the fingers:

(1) Amativeness,

(2) Parental Love,

(3) Inhabitiveness.

(4) Friendship.

These four occupy the back part of the head. Laterally placed are:

(12) Cautiousness,

(16) Conscientiousness,

(17) Hope,

and behind the ears are located:

(5) Combativeness,

(6) Destructiveness,

(7) Secretiveness.

It is quite reassuring, however, to know that the ten organs thus hidden from the view are all so clearly represented in the hands that the qualities or defects they represent are available even at a cursory glance.

I will now proceed to give clear equivalents—or corresponding marks in the hands—for almost every one of the 36 organs recognized by the fathers of Phrenology; there are only five among them that are not fully represented in the hands.

A. ALIMENTIVENESS.

[Hunger; gratification of the taste for good food and drink.]

The third phalanx of each finger very bulging inside; an exaggerate Mount of Jupiter; smooth and often pointed fingers; a comparatively short but straight Line of Head; a fairly long Line of Heart; a straight and good Line of Liver; a Mount of the Moon very prominent and a thumb short and broad; Mounts of Mars conspicuous, as the Martians are great drinkers.

(1) AMATIVENESS.

[Mating instinct, life-sustaining faculty; constancy.]

Represented by the more or less prominent development of the Mount of Venus and by its being more or less rayed and cross-rayed; the Girdle of Venus imperfect, broken and duplicated is indication of immoral habits, or at least immoral tendencies that may never be developed.

(2) PARENTAL LOVE.

Indicated by a large development of the Mount of Mercury toward the Percussion where the children lines are marked; also well formed Mount of Venus without many lines or cross-lines.

(3) INHABITIVENESS.

[Love for home and country.]

More particularly indicated by the absence of any lines of voyage or travel and by the absence of the Line of the Sun; also by a soft hand with fingers that are never spatulate, and above all by short nails, which give a love of ruling one's home. The Mount that will be most prominent will be Jupiter, as the Jupiterians are good livers and are fond of giv-

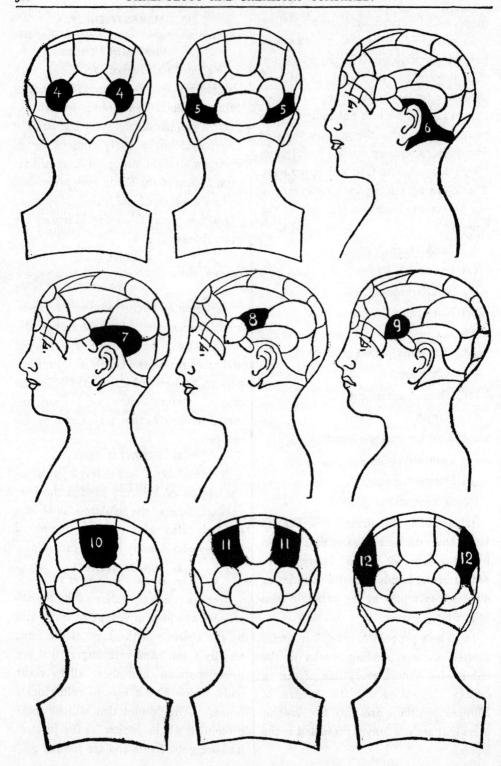

ing dinners and parties and of adorning their homes in every possible way.

(4) FRIENDSHIP.
[Fondness for social intercourse.]

Characterized by developed Mounts of Venus and Jupiter, a good Line of the Sun, a short thumb, square, smooth fingers, a Line of Heart long and forked at the start and a Line of Head slightly sloping towards the Mount of the Moon. The presence of the Line of the Sun will add to the feeling a poetical tendency and a generous heart.

(5) COMBATIVENESS.

Both Mounts of Mars fully developed but not rayed; the Mount of the Moon will be smooth, and the nails generally short.

(6) DESTRUCTIVENESS.

Represented by the Mounts of Mars and the Moon exaggerate; few lines in the hands; the Line of Heart very deep and red and running like a straight bar from one side of the hand to the other; often a "clubbed" first phalanx of the thumb.

(7) SECRETIVENESS.

The Line of Head will be very narrow and straight, cutting the whole hand; the Mount of Mercury fully developed; both knots on all fingers quite pronounced and the fingers long; the Line of Heart thin and short.

(8) ACQUISITIVENESS.
[Selfishness; the sense of ownership.]

A very prominent Mount of Mercury; a Line of Head forked at the termination, one prong normal, the other going up to the Mount of Mercury; knotted, spatulate fingers, often crooked; a very red

Line of Heart; a good Line of the Sun; a long thumb; often the Saturnian type.

(9) CONSTRUCTIVENESS.
[Skilled fingers, quick, inventive brain.]

Spatulate fingers with little balls inside the first phlanges of each finger. (Phrenology is more satisfactory than Palmistry in the discovery of this aptitude.)

(10) SELF-ESTEEM.
[Love of freedom; self respect.]

A prominent Mount of Jupiter; a Mount of Saturn, either prominent or much rayed; a Line of Head quite separate from the Line of Life; long, knotty, very spatulate fingers; enormous thumb; the Mounts of Mars very prominent, as the Mounts of Mars and Saturn combined always mean audacity, great pride and the spirit of revolt.

(11) APPROBATIVENESS.
[Sensitiveness; love of praise.]

A very long first finger, almost as long as the second finger, pointed and smooth; a developed Mount of Venus; conspicuous Mounts of Mercury and the Sun.

(12) CAUTIOUSNESS.
[Diffidence; hesitation.]

This represents the pure Saturnian type with very long and knotty fingers; the Line of Head is connected for a long space with the Line of Life and is straight and very long; a very long thumb; a narrow Mount of the Moon; insignificant Mounts of Mars.

(13) BENEVOLENCE.

A well developed Mount of Venus but with few rays or cross-rays; a beautiful Mount of Jupiter; a very fine Line of Heart with forks on Jupiter; a long Line of Head drooping slightly towards the

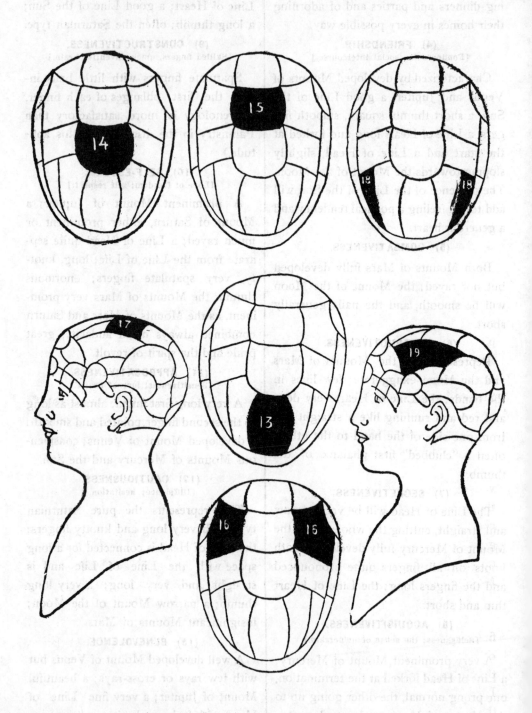

Mount of the Moon; the Mounts of Mars and the Moon developed but not rayed; the fingers smooth.

(14) VENERATION.
[Respect of God, virtue and law.]

The fingers very long and smooth, the tips square with large nails; the first finger is quite long but somewhat pointed and without first knot; little or no Mount of Mars; the Mystic Cross in the Quadrangle; the Mount of the Moon is developed but not rayed; a little of the Mount of Saturn indicating a fear of troubles to come after life.

(15) FIRMNESS.

A straight Line of Head, sometimes crossing the whole hand; long and square fingers, the inside of the third phalanges rather lean; the thumb long and broad but without excess; well developed Mounts of Mars; the Line of the Sun well traced; very little Mount of the Moon; a full Mount of Jupiter, not rayed.

(16) CONSCIENTIOUSNESS.
[Love of fair play; integrity.]

Fingers very square; the knots are not very visible; the nails are rather short; the Line of Head straight without excess; a strong Mount of Venus and a good Mount of Jupiter, with the Mounts of Mars visible but not rayed, and the Mount of Mercury quite insignificant.

(17) HOPE.

A much developed Mount of Jupiter; fingers pointed and smooth; a thin Line of Head drooping towards the Mount of the Moon and ending in a fork; a long Line of Heart; the Mounts of Venus and the Moon quite prominent; slight Mounts of Saturn and Mercury; a short, pointed thumb. The Line of Head is usually separated from the Line of Life. Often the third finger is almost as long as the second.

(18) SPIRITUALITY.
[Credulity; superstitition.]

The hands are very soft and very much rayed; the fingers are pointed and smooth; the thumb is short; the Line of Intuition is clearly marked. In the hands of people of action, like Cromwell and Joan of Arc, the Mounts of Mars are very developed, and their special intuitive faculties are confirmed by a beautiful Line of the Sun; the Mount of the Moon is decidedly exaggerate, and the Line of Head droops down almost to the Rascette; the Girdle of Venus is only feebly marked, as the nerves here are not the ruling power.

Another form of intuitive instinct, quite natural and in fact quite material in its origin is manifested by a treble Girdle of Venus; it generally corresponds with a diseased state of the organs of generation in woman, a state of health that is found very generally in the female clairvoyants who have been studied, in the hospitals. It is generally accompanied by a chained Line of Heart and by a star at the end of a much sloping Line of Head. It has been found, again and again, that when the female troubles are cured the clairvoyant state vanishes; the phenomenon may be studied during (and after) pregnancy, as temporary clairvoyance, due to such causes, invariably ceases after child-birth.

(19) IDEALITY.
[Sublimity, love of the beautiful]

The Mount of the Sun very prominent;

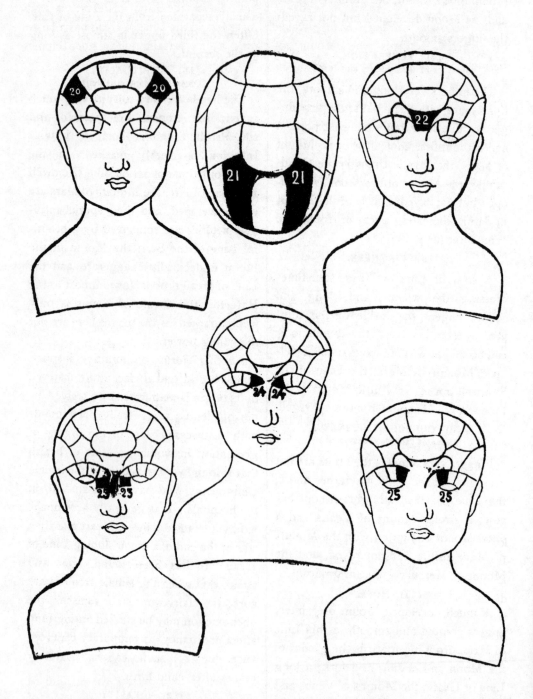

the Line of the Sun is superb, at least on the Mount itself, which often leans towards the Mount of Mercury. The fingers are smooth and slightly square; they are sometimes pointed, when the poetical enthusiasm is only temporary; the thumb is indifferent; all the Mounts under the fingers are full and unrayed; the Line of Head is long, drooping towards the Mount of the Moon which is itself very prominent and rayed, at the base, by a number of confused lines. Often a line starts from the lower Mount of the Moon along the Percussion and goes straight up to the Mount of Mercury being a form of the Line of Intuition. The third finger is long and is the only one in the hand slightly spatulate; it is furrowed inside by a number of lines from the third to the second phalanx. The nail of the third finger is often fluted—an indication of abundance of fluid; the type of the subject will be the Sun type somewhat mixed with that of the Moon.

(20) MIRTHFULNESS
[Mocking wit; quick combining quality.]

Very short nails; well developed Mounts of Mars and Mercury; pretty long fingers; a cross in the Triangle; the Line of Head separated from the Line of Life; a short Line of Heart, and a fairly developed Mount of the Moon; often a well developed Jupiter. The Mounts of Mars and Venus will give the gift of witty raillery.

(21) IMITATION.

A well developed Mount of Mercury; the fingers are smooth and mixed in type; the Mount of Venus is prominent; the Mount and the Line of the Sun are both there; the Line of Heart is well marked and the Line of Head has a large fork at its termination; a good Upper Mount of Mars is necessary.

(22) INDIVIDUALITY.
[The investigating and classifying faculty]

A well developed Mount of Mercury; the fingers very long, smooth (knotted with the classifiers) and quite spatulate; the Mount of the Moon is in evidence. The hands are soft, the nails short, and the Line of Head quite long, rising slightly at its termination towards the Mount of Mercury; there is a Line of Intuition and a good Mount of Jupiter.

(23) FORM.
[Good judgment and memory of shapes and faces.]

The Line of Life curving somewhat abnormally inside the hand, thus giving an unusual development to the Mount of Venus. A beautiful Line of the Sun and smooth fingers, square without excess. Whenever fingers are square the artistic tendency lies entirely towards the classical, and a painter or sculptor with that characteristic will never be able to do anything without a model.

(24) SIZE.
[Good judgment and memory of dimensions.]

Desbarrolles states that this organ has no equivalent in Palmistry.

(25) WEIGHT.
[Excellent sense of touch; perfect equilibrium.]

Spatulate fingers, endowed on their inside tips with round, ball-like developments.

(26) COLOR.

Is clearly indicated by the breadth of the Upper Mount of Mars, modified as follows by the other Mounts: The Upper Mount of Mars alone prominent,

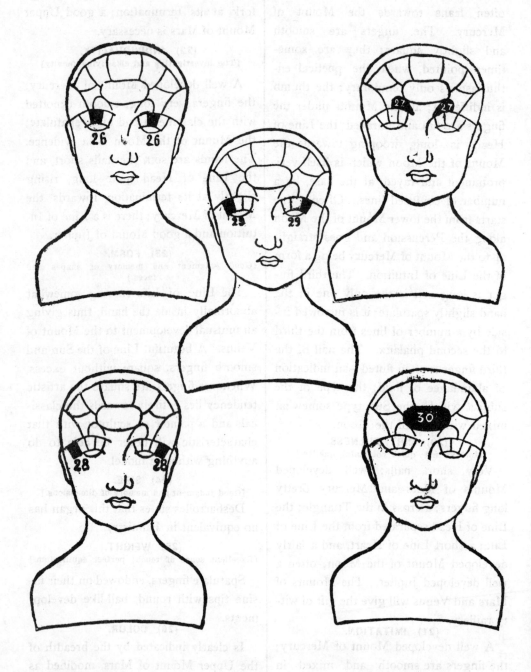

gives a love for red, the color of blood; it is well known that iron which is the attribute of Mars enters into the composition of blood. With the Mount of Mars, the Mount of Jupiter gives also a preference for very bright colors; the Mount of Saturn for dark colors; the Mount of the Sun secures the gift of true coloring; the Mount of Mercury indicates a taste for weak coloring, the Mount of the Moon loves a silver blonde coloring, and the Mount of Venus all pinkish tints.

(27) LOCALITY.
[A strong taste for traveling; a need of change.]

The Line of the Sun and the Mount of the Moon strongly developed, indicating respectively journeys by land and voyages by sea; cross lines on the Percussion along the Mount of the Moon and upward lines from the Rascette. Accidents during travels or voyages are marked by islands, crosses or stars on these lines.

(28) CALCULATION.

Very square fingers; both knots quite marked; a long thumb and a straight Line of Head; the Mount of Jupiter prominent, in the hands of great merchants and bankers; the Mounts of Mercury and (sometimes) Saturn especially marked in the hands of employees having dealings with money, like cashiers, collectors, etc.

(29) ORDER.
Long fingers strongly knotted and square tipped; short nails; Jupiter is generally predominent.

(30) EVENTUALITY.
[Taste for and memory of events.]
This organ is not well marked in the hand. It generally corresponds with a well marked Mount of Mercury with Mounts of Jupiter, Moon and Venus.

(31) TIME.
No equivalent in Palmistry; the markings referring to Eventuality (30), would fairly apply to this organ.

(32) TUNE.
[Love and talent for music.]

To point out at once, as Phrenology does, people with special musical aptitudes, Palmistry is powerless; but once those aptitudes discovered or acknowledged, Palmistry can supply accurate and minute distinctions which are entirely unknown to Phrenology. Harmony (or scientific music) is indicated by a strong Mount of the Moon, while Melody (or tuneful music) belongs to a strong Mount of Venus; with the former we shall have also knotty fingers, and with the latter smooth fingers. Counterpoint is sometimes intuitively understood by the smooth fingers, otherwise it is simply the result of close calculation. To a strong Jupiter belong noisy brass instrumental music, also solemn and religious music; to the Mount of Saturn belong the dead marches and dirges, and to the Mount of the Sun the simple and pure melodies, in direct imitation of nature. A strong Mount of Mercury denotes a talent for instrumental and orchestral music, while good Mounts of Mars call for military marches. Long fingers indicate a gift for complicated variations, trills, etc., while short fingers, with a well traced Line of the Sun, follow the text closely and are satisfied with expressing it in all its beauty.

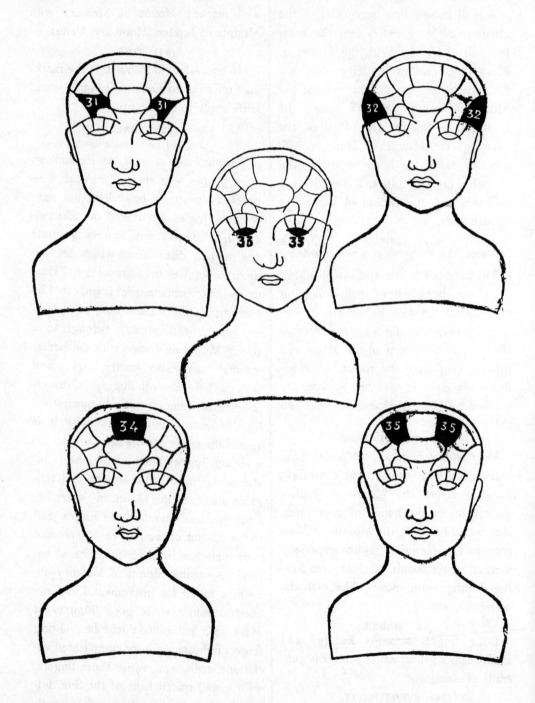

(33) LANGUAGE.
[An easy flow of words, spoken or written.]

The Line of Head is very long, with a Mount of the Moon developed, the indication of a wide memory; add to this a strong Mount of Mars supplying the necessary energy, finally a well marked Mount of Venus that will conquer all hearts. True eloquence is always indicated by the Mounts of Mars, Mercury and Venus; a strong Mount of the Moon will make a man fluent in words but not eloquent; the Mount of the Sun will make him grandiloquent, not convincing.

(34) COMPARISON.
[Gift of analysis and classification.]

This is expressed by the Mount of the Sun perfectly formed and with a beautiful Line of the Sun and the Mount of Mercury leaning towards the Mount of the Sun. To this are added form and imagination given by the Mounts of Venus and the Moon. The Line of Heart is long and well shaped; so is the Line of Head, which droops somewhat towards the Mount of the Moon.

(35) CAUSALITY.
[A love and aptitude for philosophical researches.]

All by itself it is represented by long, knotty and spatulate fingers, with soft hands and short nails. The Mount of the Moon is very prominent, and a forked Line of Head droops towards it; there is little or no Mount of the Sun. But when Causality is lighted up by a fine Mount of the Sun, the Mount of Mercury is prominent, the Line of Head is straight and long, the fingers are smooth and the nails short, whilst the Line of the Sun is very beautiful. In this case inspiration illumines dry, abtruse reasoning, and often reaches astounding results "by a short cut."

I have covered now the 36 Functions and Faculties determined and enumerated in the original works of Gall and Spurzheim. Two more distinctive organs can be added to the list and are discoverable both on the head and in the hands; I'll call them B and C.

B. MEMORY OF LANGUAGE.

Its marking in Phrenology consists in a swelling of the orbicular bone, just below the eye.

In Palmistry, this organ is indicated by the prominence of the Mount of the Moon.

C. CONCENTRATIVENESS.
[The faculty of close attention fully developed]

This organ (which I do not find marked in most works on Phrenology) was located by the Spaniard Cubi e Soler who places it between the organs of Inhabitiveness and Self-esteem.

The fingers are square, the thumb of an average length but broad, the Line of Head narrow, straight and long; the Mount of Mercury inclines towards the Mount of the Sun, and the Line of the Sun is well marked on the Mount. The Upper Mount of Mars and the Mount of the Moon, whose union in even heights gives aversion to being disturbed and a sufficient domination over one's self, are here just one Mount without rays The hand is sensitive but not rayed; the Mount of Jupiter is apparent but not so strong that it dominates over the Mounts of Mercury and the Sun.

PART SEVENTH

Palmistic Dictionary

Containing, besides
  A Complete Index of this Work, and necessary *Cross-References*,
new matter referring to
  All Prominent Chiromants and Defenders of Chiromancy in the Past;
  All Works on Palmistry that have been published since the invention of printing [such as came
under the author's notice];
  All Definitions of Scientific Words connected with the Science;
  All Readings of Importance concerning Mental and Moral Characteristics, Health and Life
Events; in other words: *Every Palmistic Discovery and Statement* concerning a Human existence
from Birth to Dying Day.

PALMISTIC DICTIONARY.

The readings inserted in this Dictionary are not all taken verbatim from the context of this work. They have been much simplified and, in a few instances, added to for the purpose of elucidation. The reader would not be fully benefited by referring to them, unless he had made himself fully conversant with the contents of Parts I to VI inclusive.

The Indexing refers only to the Various Headings and Sub-headings of the Twenty-three Chapters composing the body of this work. There are, however, over 4,500 indications contained in this Dictionary, and they will doubtless be found sufficient for all practical purposes. To extend this Part Seventh any further could only have been done at the expense of the clearness and uniformity of purpose which have never ceased to hold foremost place in the author's mind.

Abscess in the Head.—Case: 190.

Abscess, Intestinal.—Case: 113.

Absence of One of the Five Main Lines. —Always means a fatality, especially if repeated in both hands. In the general meaning of the missing Line one must look for the interpretation of the coming illness or unfortunate event.

Accident Destroying Agility.—A lentil-like black spot low down on the percussion of the Mount of Mercury.

Accidents from Quadrupeds or Vehicles. —A Line of Influence from the Mount of Venus or Line of Life to the Mount of Saturn.

Accidents, Liability to.—A cross on the Mount of Saturn; crosses or (worse) stars in the Plain of Mars.

Accident, Very Serious.—A cross on the Line of Head under the Mount of Saturn or the Sun.

Activity at Its Best.—Hand proper shorter than fingers, with square tips. Elastic Hand. Fine Mounts of Mercury and Mars. Strong first Phalanx of the Thumb. Long Line of the Head.

Activity, Exaggerate, Without Much Results.—Hand proper longer than fingers, with spatulate tips. Much rayed hand. Exaggerate Mounts of Mars. Line of Head crossing the Hand like a bar. Exaggerate first Phalanx of the Thumb.

Actors, Painstaking.—Hand proper shorter than fingers, with moderately conical tips. Fine Mount of the Sun. Good Fourth Finger and Mount of Mercury. A long Line of Head clearly forked at the termination.

Adept, An; an Englishman; author of "Hand Reading" (London: 1894).

Adultery.—See Guilty Intrigue.

Adventurous Career.—Case: 287.

Agrippa, Cornelius; a German (1486-1535); wrote "La Philosophie Occulte." The Hague: 1727. German edition of his works (1856).

Ambition, Lack of.—Soft Hands. Short fingers. Abnormally short First Phalanx of the Thumb, and first finger below normal. Insignificant Mounts, in general, except those which indicate the subject's type. Poor, feeble lines, especially Lines of Head, Fate and the

Sun. Total lack of Mounts of Mars. and a low Plain of Mars, especially the Triangle.

Ambition, Successful.—Well proportioned Hand and Thumb. Line of Life starting into the Mount of Jupiter or throwing branches into it. Same start of the Line of Head. A fine line running from tip to base along the first finger. Well shaped and long Lines of Fate and the Sun; good Line of Liver. Mounts of the Sun, Mercury and Mars excellent. Sometimes the Line of Fate ends on the Mount of Jupiter.

Amorous Nature, Very.—Hand thick and medium hard. Pronounced Mount of Venus much rayed. Girdle of Venus quite distinct. Often high Mount of the Moon, with drooping Line of Head. Line of Heart beginning branchless under the Mount of Saturn.

Albertus Magnus; a German; probable author of "Geheime Cheiromant-Belustigungen (1205-1280), Kunst aus der Hand Wahrzusagen" (republished in Leipsic: 1807).

Alchemists.—16. The name was given to the searchers after the "Philosopher's Stone," that mysterious substance that was to transform ("transmute" is the technical word) all low metals into gold. All through the Middle Ages and up to the XVIII. century great scientists devoted their lives to these researches, which, incidentally, brought to light marvelous chemical discoveries.

Ambition, Boundless. — Exaggerate Mount of Jupiter. First finger abnormally long in proportion to other fingers. An upward line or branch from either the Line of Life or the Line of Head. A Line of Head separate from the Line of Life and crossing the whole hand like a bar. Often absence of the Line of Heart. Exaggerate Mount of the Sun. A Line from the Upper Mount of Mars to the Mount of the Sun.

Ambition, Extreme; Wretched Childhood.—Case: 352.

Anæmia.—A state of the blood in which there is a poverty of red corpuscles; hence, general debility of the system; a very pale palm; short and pale nails. The lower part of the Mount of the Moon exaggerate or much lined.

Analytical View of Things—Aptitude for Details.—Large hands. Long, knotty fingers. Strong Thumb Knot and second Phalanx of the Thumb. Second Phalanges of all fingers rather above normal size.

Andrieu, Jules; a Frenchman; author of "Chiromancie; Etude sur la Main, le Crâne, la Face" (Paris: 1882).

Aneurism Caused by Gout.—Case: 112.

Aneurism (Dilatation of an Artery).— Exaggerate or much lined Mount of the Sun. Line of Heart broken under the Mount of Saturn.

Anger, Short-lived.—Well shaped nails, pink on the outer edge. Mounts of Mars above normal, but fine Mount of Venus and healthy Line of Heart.

Animals, Love of.—Strong Mounts of Venus and the Sun. A fine and long Line of Heart. First Phalanges of Fingers a trifle below normal.

Anonymous; American; "Dick's Mysteries of the Hand" (New York: 1884).

Anonymous; English; author of "How to Read Hands" (London: 1892).

Anonymous; English; "The Hand Phrenologically Considered" (London: 1848).

Anonymous; French; "La Chiromantie Universelle Représentée en plusieurs centaines de figures, contenue en LXXXVIII. tableaux (Paris: 1682).

Anonymous; French; "Les Petits Mystères de la Destinée" (Paris: 1861).

Anonymous; French; "La Science curieuse, ou Traité de la Chiromancie" (1667).

Anonymous; German; "Die Chiromantie, nach Astronomischen Lehrsaet-
zen Lehrende" (Frankfort: 1742).

Apollo, The Line of.—The Line of the
Sun: 30.

Apoplexy, Danger of.—Very red skin.
Plain of Mars hollow toward Head.
Exaggerate or much lined Mount of
Jupiter. A sprig on Mount of Jupiter.
A grille and a star on the Mount of
the Moon. Line of Liver very uneven
and red where it crosses Line of Heart.
Long red scar on the Line of Heart.
Two perpendicular lines from the Line
of Heart to the Mount of the Moon.

Apoplexy, Two Strokes of.—Case: 244.

Architecture, Aptitude for.—Square-
tipped fingers, inclined to Spatulate.
Long square nails. Long second Phalanx of Thumb. Mounts of Venus
and the Sun (for art), of Mercury (for
calculation). Good Line of Head.

Aristotle; a Greek (B. C. 384-322); pre-
sumed author of "Chyromantia Aris-
totelis cum figuris" (Ulm: 1490). Mentions Chiromancy in his "De Coelo et
Mundi Causa" and other leading
works. See the complete edition of
his works published in Paris (1539)
in Latin. Quoted: 16; 19; 20; 22.

Arm, Broken.—Case: 240.

Arm, Wound on Either.—Capillary
cross lines on the Mount of the Sun.
See Accident Affecting Agility.

Arpentigny, Casimir Stanislas d'; the
great chirognomist (1798-?). Wrote
La Chirognomonie (1839); La Science
de la Main (1865). His Biography—
33. Quoted: 19; 20; 22; 23; etc.

Art and Money-making United.—
Square-tipped fingers. Line of the
Sun ending on the Mount of Mer-
cury. A straight Line of Head and a
Mount of Mercury at least equal to
the Mount of the Sun.

Art and Science Blended.—Fingertips
inclining to the square type; second
knot. The Mount of the Sun thrown
toward the Mount of Mercury. A tri-

angle on the Mount of the Sun. Sometimes a Line of the Sun ending between the third and fourth fingers or
even on the Mount of Mercury.
Often a Line of the Sun triple forked
at the termination, throwing a prong
toward the Mount of Mercury and one
toward the Mount of Saturn.

Art and Science Happily Blended.—
Case: 347.

Art, Extraordinary Success in.—With
the usual characteristics of an exceptionally well endowed artistic nature.
(See above.) Line of Fate terminating on the Mount of the Sun and a
line (or branch) straight from the Line
of Head to the same Mount. The
Line of the Sun starting from the Line
of Life.

Art, Failure In.—Poor Mounts of the
Sun and Venus. A Line of the Sun
either broken or triplicated, or formed
of confused fragments. Lack of persistency shown in poor Line of Head
and insufficient first Phalanx of the
Thumb. Mounts of Jupiter and the
Sun often exaggerate, indicating envious disposition without real talent.

Art (Painting, Sculpture), Aptitude for.
—Conicaly tipped fingers (especially
the third one) for Painting; square-
tipped for Sculpture. In both cases
strong Mounts of Venus and the Sun.
If the artist is imaginative and not an
imitator, strong Mount of the Moon,
with half soft hands and a slightly
drooping Line of Head.

Aspir; the "inhalation"—so to speak—
of the vital fluid.

Assassination, Danger of.—In a good
hand: a cross or star on the upper
Mount of Mars, also a large cross in
the center of the Triangle, also a star
on the third Phalanx of the Second
Finger. A line from the Quadrangle
under the Mount of Saturn, cutting
deep into a Girdle of Venus.

Asthma.—Poorly traced Line of Liver,
with narrow Quadrangle due to Line
of Heart curving down to Line of

Head. With the same indications, a black spot inside the Quadrangle.

Asthma.—Case: 169. Case: 350.

Astrologers.—16. Ancient scientists who claimed to read in the stars the destiny of man. The art is still practiced. It is based on fixed rules, necessitating the working out, in each case, of difficult astronomical problems.

Astronomy, Aptitude for.—Long and knotted fingers, square and even spatulate tips, with hard, bony palms. Mounts of Saturn and Mercury prominent. Line of Head clear and long. Second Phalanges of Fingers and Thumb above normal.

Atheistic Tendencies, Physician with.—Case: 105.

Audacity.—Spatulate, smooth fingers. Long first Phalanx of the Thumb; Lines of Life and Head separated at the start. Upper Mount of Mars and Mount of Jupiter prominent. Bulging and wide Plain of Mars. Straight and fine Lines of Head and Heart; no Line of Liver or a very good one.

Aura.—The imponderable atmosphere that surrounds us, penetrates us and radiates back from us.

Avarice.—Fingers bent forward, square-tipped (especially the third one) and knotted. Thin, hard hand. Narrow Quadrangle. Line of Head crossing the whole hand like a bar. Often no Line of Heart. Thumb inclining toward the hand. Mount of the Sun prominent, but, more generally, all mounts, so to speak, "dried up." When the Line of Heart is present it often terminates on the Mount of Mercury.

Bad Habits, Sad Consequences of.—Case: 262.

Bain, Dr. Alexander; an Englishman; author of "Mind and Body, the Theories of Their Relation" (London: 1883).

Balzac, Honoré de; the great French novelist (1799-1850); devoted many a page to Chiromancy, in which he had implicit faith. See especially his "Physiologie du Mariage," his "Cousin Pons," his "Louis Lambert."

Bankruptcy.—A poor Line of the Sun (sometimes absent); a poor Mount of the Sun covered with confused lines. The Mount of Mercury insignificant. An island on the Line of Liver. Often a bad break on Line of Fate, when the bankruptcy really ruined the subject's life prospects; or the Line of Fate stops abruptly at the date of the disaster.

Baughan, Rosa; an Englishwoman; author of "Character Indicated in Handwriting" (London: 1886); also "Hand Book of Palmistry" (London); also "Chirognomancy" (London: 1884).

Beamish, Richard; an Englishman; author of "The Psychonomy of the Hand" (London: 1865).

Bell, Sir Charles; a Scotchman (1774-1842); author of "The Hand, Its Mechanism and Vital Endowments" (London: 1832).

Bello, Paul; an Englishman; author of "Character and Fortune Revealed" (London: 1894).

Belot, The Rev. Jean; author of "Oeuvres de Jean Belot Contenant la Chiromence, etc." (Rouen: 1640).

Benevolence.—Half soft hands, with long nails, rather brittle. Fine Mounts of Jupiter and Venus. A wide Quadrangle and a specially good Line of Heart, starting, forked, from inside the Mount of Jupiter. Sometimes the Line of Fate, starting inside the Mount of Venus, is read in this wise.

Bent.—Of Fingers: 43. Of Thumb: 53.

Bernstein, Julius; a German (1839-?); author of "Die elektrischen Ströme der Nerven."

Bichat; a famous French physician (1771-1802); author of "Anatomie Générale" (1801) and of "Recherches

Philosophiques dar la Vie et la Mort" (Paris: 1820). 20.

Biliousness.—Yellow-hued palm; cold, sometimes clammy, skin. Exaggerate or much lined Mount of Mercury.

Birth, Illegitimate.—An island at the starting point of an otherwise poor Line of Fate. Sometimes confirmed by an island at the starting point of the Line of Life. Seen it marked by a Children Line, reaching down to the Line of Heart on the Mount of Mercury close to the Percussion.

Birth, Mystery at.—Same markings as for Birth, Illegitimate (which see).

Bladder Troubles.—Lower part of Mount of the Moon exaggerate or much lined.

Bladder Trouble.—Case: 115.

Bladder Troubles, Specialist for.—Case: 214.

Blindness.—Of one eye: One circle on Line of Life; of both eyes: two circles. A cross on the upper part of the Line of Liver and a circle on Line of Heart. Same cross with a break of the Lines of Head or Heart under the Mount of the Sun. A star in the Triangle close to the Line of Liver.

Blood, Circulation of the, Defective.— Numerous white spots on the nails. Line of Heart broken under Mount of Saturn. See Heart Troubles.

Blood, Downward Flux of.—Exaggerate or much lined Mount of Saturn.

Blood, Flow of.—Case: 354.

Blood Poisoning.—Black or bluish spots on the nails.

Blood, Superabundance of.—Red skin. Red nails. Red lines. Exaggerate Mounts of Mars and Jupiter. Line of Mars deeply marked.

Blood to the Head, Rush of.—Exaggerate or much lined Mount of Jupiter. See also Heart Trouble.

Blood, Troubles with the.—Exaggerate or much lined Upper Mount of Mars. See also Heart Trouble.

Bohemian, Unconventional Ways.— Very small hands. Soft Palm. All first phalanges flexible, and that of the thumb thrown back. In a bad meaning: abnormal shortness of the First Finger and exaggerate Mounts of Venus and the Moon.

Boldness.—In a good sense, see Courage. In a bad sense: Lines of Life and Head widely separated at the start. Exaggerate Mounts of Jupiter and Upper Mars. Abnormally long third finger.

Bone, Caries of the.—Case: 348.

Breast, Wound on.—Capillary cross lines on Mount of Saturn.

Brain Fever.—Deep Line of Liver entirely absent in the Quadrangle. Same Line ending at Line of Head, with many bars cutting Line of Life (often turns to melancholia). Line of Head quite close to Line of Life for a while.

Brain of Man.—The gray matter contained within the cavity of the skull; its connection with the various parts of the body—24. Illustration, 25.

Brain Trouble.—Plain of Mars hollow toward Head. An Influence Line from the Mount of Venus cutting Line of Head. A star on the Line of Head at the end of a Line of Influence. Line of Head wavy and inclining toward a wavy Line of Liver. A break of the Line of Head. Pale and wide Line of Head with black spots on it and Line of Life forked at the start. Line of Head starred, or crossed, by a deep bar, or badly broken, or sloping into an exaggerate, much rayed or starred Mount of the Moon.

Brain Trouble, Constitutional.—Absence of the Line of Head. Island at the starting point of the Line of Head (if the trouble is inherited).

Brain Trouble Due to Guilty Intrigue.— Island on Line of Influence ending in a star or black dot on Line of Head.

Brain Trouble from Disorder of Lower Organs.—Case: 350.

Brain Troubles.—Case: 191.

Brain Trouble, Temporary.—Thinness of a small portion of Line of Head.

Brain, Threatened Softening of the.—Case: 239.

Brilliancy, The Line of.—The Line of the Sun, 30.

Broad Ideas.—Well proportioned Palm and fingers. Square tips the best. Excellent thumb. Finely shaped Quadrangle. Line of Head long, slightly separated from the Line of Life at the start and slightly forked at the termination. Mounts of Jupiter and Venus the most prominent, though not exaggerate.

Bronchitis.—Exaggerate or much lined Upper Mount of Mars. Cross lines (especially if deep or forked) from the Percussion into the Upper Mount of Mars.

Brute Animality, Instincts Verging to.—Thick, very hard hand. Thick, claw-like nails overrun by flesh or skin. Much hair and a naturally rough and red skin. Characterless tips; short, smooth fingers. Clubbed first Phalanx of the Thumb. Insignificant Mounts, except exaggerate Mounts of Mars and Venus. Only the three chief lines; generally short, especially the Lines of Head and Heart. A cross in the middle of the Triangle.

Bulwer, John; an Englishman; author of "Chirologia, or the Natural Language of the Hand" (London: 1644).

Burglar, The.—Heavy, thick, elementary hand. Smooth, short fingers. Clubbed first Phalanx of Thumb. Mounts of Mars and Venus abnormal. Often exaggerate Mount of the Moon, square shaped at its lower part. Only the three chief lines, short and red. A star and often a grille on the Mount of Mercury, and similar signs on the Upper Mount of Mars. A cross in the Triangle.

Business, Aptitude for.—Elastic Palm. Fingers longer than Palm, with second knot marked and square tips. Strong first Phalanx of the Thumb and good Line of Head. Mount of Mercury most prominent, with the fourth finger above average length. A line from the Rascette to the Mount of Mercury. Lines or Branches from the Line of Head to the Mount of Mercury. An excellent Line of Liver. At least fair Lines of Fate and the Sun. (These indications prognosticate not only aptitude, but success.)

Business Failure.—See Bankruptcy.

Campbell, Robert Allen; an American; author of "Philosophic Chiromancy" (St. Louis: 1879).

Cancer, Recovery from Intestinal.—Case: 353.

Cardano, Girolamo; a famous Italian physician; author of "De rerum Varietate" (Basle: 1557).

Card Sharpers.—Long, thin fingers, often crooked. The Mount of Mercury predominant and often crossed or starred. No characteristics of the gambler, as they take no risks. Lower part of Mount of the Moon high, as in most criminals' hands.

Career Broken by Death of Relative.—Case: 290.

Carpus or Carpia Bones.—35; the eight Bones forming the wrist.

Catalepsy.—Case: 170.

Catarrh.—Case: 354.

Catarrh of the Stomach.—See Intestinal Troubles.

Catastrophe Caused by Guilty Intrigue, Terrible.—Case: 188.

Catastrophe Ending a Love Intrigue, Threatened.—Case: 179.

Celebrity.—See Fame and Success.

Celibacy.—A cross on the first Phalanx of the first Finger. A Line of Union turned up at the termination (if there is only one Line of Union in either hand).

Cerebral, The.—The Line of Head—30.

Chaldean Shepherds.—16. See Astrologers.

Chance, The Line of.—The Line of Fate —30.

Chapman, M. G.; an Englishman; author of "Palmistry Made Easy" (London: 1893).

Charity.—See Benevolence.

Chastity Inspired by Religion.—A fine Mount of Jupiter, with a pointed first Finger. A cross on the first Phalanx of the Third Finger. A very smooth, thin hand, with the Mounts quite insignificant, outside of Jupiter.

Chatterjie, Roman Kristo; a Hindoo writer on Palmistry. His work on "Indian Palmistry" was noticed in the "Palmist" for August, 1897.

Cheiro; an Irishman; author of "The Book of the Hand" (London: 1891); also "The Language of the Hand" (London and New York: 1897).

Chemistry and Physics, Aptitude for.— Second Finger and Mount of Saturn finely shaped and prominent, though not exaggerate. Long knotted fingers; half thin hands. The medical stigmata (which see) are found on the Mount of Mercury.

Childhood, Wretched.—Line of Fate starting low down and much broken, crossed or twisted in its first part.

Childhood, Delicate.—Case: 156.

Childbearing, Difficulties in (or after).— The Line of Life too close to the second Phalanx of the Thumb. An Influence Line direct from the Mount of Venus to the Mount of Saturn. First Bracelet of the Rascette convex in shape.

Children, Death or Illness of.—Bars, dots, stars or islands spoiling the Lines of Children (which see).

Children; How Marked.—Perpendicular Lines on the Percussion from the base of the Fourth Finger to the Line of Union with which they correspond. The eldest child farthest around Percussion.

Chirognomic Observations—33. Concern the shape of the hand.

Chirognomy in Every Day Life—76. How to discover by a cursory glance at people's hands how to impress them favorably, i. e., in accordance with their hidden idiosyncrasies.

Chirognomy or Cheirognomy.—The art of discerning the character and physical temperament from the outward shape of the hand. From the Greek words "Cheir," the hand, and "Gnomon," one who knows. D'Arpentigny and Desbarrolles used at first the word "Chirognomony" to express the same idea; but this uncouth form was soon abandoned.

Chirology or Cheirology.—Language of the Hand. From the Greek words "Cheir," hand, and "Logs," word, language.

Chiromancy or Cheiromancy.—The art of discovering the disposition of a person and of foretelling events by inspecting the lines and lineaments of the hand. From the Greek words "Cheir," the hand, and "Manteia," power of divination.

Chiromantic Observations—139. Concern the Lines and markings in the inside of the Hand.

Chirometry or Cheirometry.—A new word, which purposes to indicate the measuring of man's impressions through hand reading.

Chirosophy or Cheirosophy.—Knowledge acquired through the hand. From the Greek words "Cheir," the hand, and "Sophia," wisdom.

Clairvoyance.—A soft hand, with short, smooth fingers and often a small thumb. The Mounts of Saturn, Mercury, and especially the Moon, quite prominent or rayed. A good many minor cross lines. A drooping and often fragmentary Line of Head and a poor Line of Heart (defect in circulation). A clear Line of Intuition, often islanded at the start. A Line of Liver, also islanded at the start, is read in the same way in the absence of a Line of Intuition proper.

Cocles, Bartholomeus; an Italian, and one of the leading Chiromants of his century; author of "Physionomiæ et Chyromantiæ Compendium" and of a number of other works published in Latin, German, French, from 1525 until long after his death, a Rouen edition coming out in 1698.

Combativeness.—Square palm; short, smooth fingers; often spatulate tipped; broad, short nails; plenty of hair. Upper Mount of Mars predominant. Lines rather redder than Normal. A large cross in the Triangle. (This reading applies to an otherwise good hand.)

Common Sense.—Average sized hands. Nails large (broad and long) and rounded at the base.

Complaint (Hereditary).—An island at the beginning of the Line of Life.

Composer of Music.—(See Music, Aptitude for.) Add to it a strong Mount of Mercury (for calculation) and put square fingers instead of pointed or conical. There will be less Mount of Venus than Mount of the Moon.

Concentration, Lack of.—A weak, short Thumb. Short, smooth Fingers with a soft Palm. Mounts of Jupiter, Mercury and Mars absent or insignificant. The Mounts of the Moon, and sometimes the Sun, are generally exaggerate. Poor, drooping Line of Head. Often confused and even cross lines on the Mount of the Sun.

Concentration, Power of.—Strong, long thumb. Long, knotted fingers. Fine Mounts of Jupiter, Mercury and Lower Mars. Long and straight Line of Head. Insignificant Mount of the Moon.

Consistency of Hand, How to Judge.— 37. Its importance in the diagnosis of Disposition and Health. See Hand Proper and Palm Combined.

Constancy.—A strong first Phalanx of the Thumb and a dominant Lower Mount of Mars. Line of Heart beginning forked into the Mount of Jupiter, the latter quite prominent. A long, straight Line of Head. Mount of Venus visible but not very strong. Very little, if any, Mount of the Moon. Few, if any, worry lines.

Constitution, Weak.—Hand, thin, narrow and meager. Nails long, thin and brittle. Line of Life chained or linked. A number of downward branches on the Line of Life. Very poor Line of Liver. The state of the Lines of Head and Heart and the nature of the markings on the Mounts (generally very low) will tell the cause of the weakness.

Constitution, Well Balanced.—Pink and mottled skin. Perfect nails. Elastic, medium thick palm. The three chief Lines long and clear, hardly redder than the skin. No worry lines. The Mounts clear of any untoward markings, but slightly bulging and very firm under touch. An excellent Line of Liver is considered essential to secure perfect health.

Consumption, Tendency to.—Very thin Palm, with long, knotty fingers. Nails long, thin, brittle, convex and fluted. Exaggerate or much lined Mount of Jupiter. Many islands on the Line of Liver. Many islands on the Line of Head. The Line of Life is sure to show many weak points if the consumptive tendency assumes fatal proportions.

Contents, Table of—7.

Continuity in Thought or Action, Lack of.—Case: 228.

Conventionality, Excess of.—Hair on two lower phalanges of fingers. Stiff fingers, close together and sometimes slightly bent forward. Stiff, rather long first phalanx of the Thumb. The Lines of Life and Head connected for quite a while. Narrow Quadrangle, due to Line of Heart curving down abnormally toward Line of Head.

Corruption, Early.—A very strong (often double) Girdle of Venus in both hands, with crooked fingers, even as a child, and a wavy or starred Line of Heart. Often a very short, fragmentary Line of Head.

Corvus, Andreas; an Italian; author of "L'art de Chyromance," first published in Latin (Venice: 1500).

Cotton, Louise; an Englishwoman; author of "Palmistry and Its Practical Uses" (London: 1892).

Courage.—(From cor: heart in Latin.) A long Line of Heart, starting deep and high into the Mount of Jupiter, with large and firm Mounts and Plain of Mars. The First Phalanx of the Thumb is above normal and the Line of Head straight and clear. Line of Liver excellent or absent. All the lines a trifle redder than usual, indicating a generous blood. Mounts of Venus and Jupiter very fine. The Palm firm and the fingers usually long. This is not, however, an absolute indication.

Cowardice.—In a man: Hands without any hair. Hand thick and flabby. Nails long, thin and narrow. Fingers bent forward. Mounts of Mars and Jupiter (often Venus) insignificant. The Mounts of Saturn and the Moon (fear) and Mercury (self interest) exaggerate or badly rayed. The Triangle small and formed of lines much curved inwards.

Craig, A. R.; an Englishman; author of "The Book of the Hand" (London: 1867), and "Your Luck's in Your Hand" (London and New York: 1884).

Cringle, Tom; an Englishman; author of "The Hand and the Physiognomy of the Human Form" (Melbourne: 1868).

Crippled by Cruel Relative, Child.—Case: 348.

Crippled Through Womb Troubles.—Case: 240.

Critic, The Born.—Short nails with soft palm. Fingers spatulate or square, with strong first knot. Second phalanges of all fingers and thumbs above normal. The Mount of Mercury predominant. Some Upper Mount of Mars and often a cross in the Plain of Mars.

Cruelty, Instincts of Slow.—Very small hands; hairy hands (in woman). Very long, thin fingers, with a small palm. The Mounts of Saturn and the Moon strangely developed. Surprisingly insignificant Mount of Mars. Mount of Venus and Line of Heart often absent. Mounts of Mercury (ruse) and the Sun (envy) exaggerate or badly lined. Drooping Line of Head. Often a very bad Line of Liver. Very narrow Quadrangle whenever the Line of Heart happens to be there.

Cruelty, Violent.—See Brute Animality.

Cureau de la Chambre; a Frenchman; author of "Discours sur les Principes de la Chiromancie" (Paris: 1653).

Curiosity.—Straggling fingers, very flexible and showing light between; short nails. Mounts of the Sun, Mercury and the Moon predominant. Many worry lines. Lines of Head and Life often separated at the start.

Dale, I. B.; an Englishwoman; author of "Indian Palmistry" (London: 1896).

Deaf and Dumb.—Case: 170.

Deafness.—Dots and often island on Line of Head under the Mount of Saturn, with a rather bulging Mount of Venus. An exaggerate or much rayed Mount of Saturn.

Deafness.—Case: 97. Case: 235. Case: 350.

Death Bringing About Happy Events. —Case: 306.

Death by Apoplexy.—Two parallel lines from Line of Heart low down into Mount of the Moon.

Death, Disastrous.—Case: 193.

Death, Early.—A short Line of Life in both hands. The Lines of Head and Heart stopping short before reaching the Line of Fate. The Line of Head coming up wavy to the Line of Heart under the Mount of Mercury.

Death, Extraordinary Escape from.— Case: 352.

Death of a Child, Cruel.—Case: 270.

Death of Husband in a State of Insanity.—Case: 184. Case: 353.

Death on Battle Field.—In a good hand with fine Mount of Jupiter and Plain of Mars, a star on the Upper Mount of Mars. A Line from the Upper Mount of Mars to the Mount of Saturn.

Death, Sudden, Often Violent.—Line of Life ending in a deep spot or bar. Line of Life terminating abruptly with a few short parallel lines. Lines of Life, Head and Heart joined at the start in both hands. One short downward line on the joints of all the fingers. A cross on the Middle of the Line of Head. Violent death often marked (in a good hand) by a grille on the Upper Mount of Mars. See also Scaffold, Death on.

Deaths, Series of.—Case: 349.

Deceitful Disposition.—Short and pale nails. Long, thin fingers. Fourth finger often crooked, or at least too long. Mounts of Mercury and the Moon predominant, the former with a distinct cross or many cross lines. A drooping, widely forked Line of Head.

Decrespe, Marius; a Frenchman; author of "La Main et ses Mystères" (Paris: 1894); "Matière des Oeuvres Magiques" (Paris: 1893).

Dedication.—To Mlle. Emma Calvé. Her Photograph and Autograph. Frontispiece.

Delicacy of Mind.—Small hands—36.

Delirium Tremens.—See Alcoholic Insanity.

Denunciator, Perfidious.—Case: 224.

Depravity, Moral.—Thin hands with long fingers. No Mount of Jupiter or the Sun to speak of. Mounts of Mercury and the Moon dominant, with a much rayed and cross-rayed Mount of Venus. A double or triple Girdle of Venus. A Line of Heart starting forkless under the Mount of Saturn. A drooping, widely forked Line of Head.

Desbarrolles, Adrien Adolphe, the great chiromant (1801-1886); wrote "Les Mystères de la Main" (Paris: 1859); "Révélations Completes" (Paris: 1879); His biography—138. His Introduction to this book—18. There are no English translations of his works and this volume contains all out of them that is of practical use.

Destiny, A Great.—For good or evil. A long Line of Fate starting from the Rascette and penetrating into the third phalanx of the second finger. The other indications will give this marking its full significance.

Details, Love of.—Long Fingers, generally knotted, especially the second knot. Long second phalanx of the thumb. Mount of Jupiter and Mercury (sometimes Saturn) dominant. Long and straight Line of Head. Little or no Mount of the Moon.

Diabetes.—Many confused and crossed lines at the bottom of the Mount of the Moon. A cross at the same place on the Mount.

Diabetes.—Case: 115.

Defamer of Character, The.—Thin, long hands. Pointed, crooked Fingers. Excessive Mounts of Jupiter and the Sun (Vanity). Mount of Mercury predominant and crossed. A prong of the Line of Head runs deep into a heavy Mount of the Moon.

Digestion; Impaired in Old Age.—Thick and short Line of Liver.

Disappointments in Ambition.—A Line or branch from the Lines of Life or Head entering deep into the Mount of Jupiter and there barred and crossed; many cross lines on the Mounts of Saturn or the Sun at the end of fine Lines of Fate and the Sun. Downward branches of the Lines of Life, Fate and the Sun.

Disappointments in Love.—The Line of Heart barred or crossed or starred almost at the start. Many downward branches on the Line of Heart. Line or branch from the Line of Fate cutting the Line of Heart. Influence Lines from the Mount of Venus or the Line of Life cutting the Line of Heart.

Disappointments in Money Matters.—See Financial Losses.

Disaster Due to Interrupted Love Affair.—Case: 305.

Discontent, Chronic.—A thin palm, with short, smooth fingers and a small first phalanx of the Thumb. A poor Line of Life and wretched Lines of Heart and Liver. Many worry Lines. The Mount of the Moon predominant or much rayed. See Misanthropy.

Discoverers in Dangerous Countries.—Hand proper shorter than fingers with spatulate tips. Strong, hard palm. Third finger much above average. Mounts of Mars, Jupiter and the Moon predominant, with a large Mount of the Sun. Line of Head slightly drooping.

Discovery of an Intrigue.—Case: 289.

Dishonesty.—Fourth Finger crooked. Mount of Mercury starred.

Dishonorable Instincts.—Fingers crooked, especially First and Fourth.

Divorce.—Most complete indication: A Line of Influence from the Mount of Venus cutting an upward branch of the Line of Life and ending under or on the Mount of Mercury; clearer still if it cuts a Line of Union. A Line of Influence from the Mount of Venus ending in a fork as it reaches the Line of Heart.

Divorce Against the Subject.—A fork at the start of the Line of Union, especially when accompanied by the indications marked above.

Divorce in Favor of Subject.—A Line of Union terminating in a fork, especially with the indications marked under the heading Divorce.

Divorce; Lawsuit; Loss.—Case: 189.

Divorce Twice Announced in the Hand.—Case: 348.

Dizziness, Fits of.—Line of Head terminating at the Line of Heart under Mount of Mercury.

Domestic Troubles.—Plain of Mars hollow toward Life. Lines of Influence from the Mount of Venus or the Line of Life cutting the other Main Lines. (For each kind of trouble see separate headings.)

Dreamer, The.—Long, slender, pointed Fingers; thin, elongated palm. Prominent Mounts of the Moon, Venus and sometimes Saturn (if the dreams are tinged with sadness). Very drooping Line of Head. A line of Intuition, often islanded at the start. A cross close to the Line of the Sun. (Religious ecstasy.)

Dreaming, Useless.—Hand proper longer than fingers with pointed tips. Hand thick and soft. Exaggerate Mounts of the Moon and drooping Line of Head. No Mounts of Mars and very little other Mounts.

Dramatic Profession, Aptitude for.—Square fingers with no knots, or only the second knot. Good first phalanx of the thumb. High Mounts of Jupiter, Sun and Mercury, and some Mounts of Venus and the Moon. The Lines of Life and Head separated at the start, the latter with a moderate fork at the termination.

Dropsy.—The lower part of the Mount of the Moon exaggerate or much lined A star in the same place on the mount.

Dropsy.—Case: 114.

Dropsy of the Heart.—Case: 240.

Drowning, Danger from.—An angle or a star on the Mount of the Moon, especially if found on a voyage line from the Percussion. Wavy cross Lines on first phalanges of all fingers. Lines arising also from inside the Rascette and ending in a star on the Mount of the Moon.

Drowning, Saved from.—Case: 116.

Drunkenness.—A line or branch from the Mount of Venus or the Lines of Life or Mars terminating in a star on the Mount of the Moon. An upward line from the third angle of the Triangle ending about the center of the Mount of the Moon. See Delirium Tremens.

Du Moulin, Antoine; a Frenchman; author of "Chiromance et Physiognomie par le regard des Membres de l'Homme" (1556).

Ears, Trouble with the.—See Deafness.

Easter-Henderson, Eliza; an American; author of "A Guide to Palmistry" (Boston: 1895).

Effeminacy.—In a man: hands without any hair. Hand thick and flabby; or ultra thin and pale and soft. Absence of the Mounts of Mars, Jupiter and often Venus. The Mounts of the Moon and Mercury predominant.

Egotism, Unbounded.—A large first phalanx of the thumb and the Mounts of Jupiter and the Sun exaggerate. The Lines very stiff and rather too highly colored. Often no Line of Heart and a Line of Head crossing the hand like a bar. Even a grille on the Mount of Jupiter.

Egyptian Priests—16. (See Kabbala.)

Eloquence, The Gift of.—Lines of Life and Head separated at the start. Fine Mounts of Jupiter (the statesman), of the Sun (the golden mouthed), of Mercury (the clear, practical politician). They may not all be there in the same hand. Line of Heart and Mount of Venus in good shape if the orator feels deeply what he says and speaks in defense of some noble cause. Line of Head long and forked at the termination; slightly sloping. This slope and the Mount of the Moon will infuse in the speech more poetry than common sense.

Embezzler, The.—Thin, soft hand. Fingers long and knotty. Third finger

above normal in length and fourth finger crooked. Mount of Mercury predominant, with a star or even grille clearly marked on it. Widely forked Line of Head, one prong drooping in an exaggerate Mount of the Moon. Many worry Lines. Often exaggerate Mounts of Jupiter and the Sun (excessive vanity).

Embezzler, Husband an.—Case: 106.

Empiricism—24. Scientific practice depending purely on experiments, not theories.

Engineering, Aptitude for.—Large, square palm. Long, knotty, spatulate fingers, the second finger and the Mount of Saturn often predominant. Scientific markings on the Mount of Mercury. Large Mounts of Mars and fine, straight Line of Head.

Energy.—In a man: hands slightly hairy. Hand thick and medium hard. Short nails. First phalanx of Thumb and Mounts of Mars and Jupiter predominant, with long Lines of Head often somewhat separated from the Line of Life at the start.

Engagement Broken, An.—(Also applies to all sorts of attachments much more serious than "Engagements"). Line of Heart broken; under the Mount of Saturn; circumstances, not the subject, broke the tie; under the Mount of the Sun; the subject's caprice did it; under the Mount of Mercury; love of money was the cause.

Ennemoser, Joseph; a German; author of "Geschichte der Magie" (Leipsic: 1844).

Enthusiasm for Highest Ideal.—Thin, soft hands with pointed (or at least strongly conical) fingers. The First Finger and the Mount of Jupiter especially fine. A drooping Line of Head and High Mount of the Moon. If enthusiasm purely "artistic" the Mounts of the Sun and the Moon are predominant.

Envy.—An exaggerate or much lined Mount of the Sun, with a poor fragmentary Line of the Sun. Cross lines on the third phalanx of the third finger. Sometimes a kind of ring on the Mount of the Sun surrounding the base of the finger.

Epilepsy.—Line of Head sloping and broken in small fragments, with a large cross (the rays of which terminate in spots) in the Triangle.

Epilepsy.—Case: 229. Case: 348.

Eugenie, Empress.—Her hands examined by Desbarrolles—80.

Extravagance.—The Thumb set very low down and with its first phalanx thrown very much backward. Flexibility of the fingers. Often a wide space between the Lines of Life and Head at the start, and a sloping Line of Head. A poor Mount and Line of the Sun and a Line of Fate stopping early in life.

Eyes, Trouble with the.—Exaggerate or much lined Mount of the Sun. An ill-formed circle on the Mount of the Sun, with a poor Line of the Sun. White Dot on Line of Life. A Line of Influence from the Mount of Venus, ending in a black dot or a star at the connection of the Lines of Head and the Sun. Broken Line of Head under the Mount of Saturn or the Sun. A circle on the Line of Heart under the Mount of the Sun.

Eyes, Trouble with the.—Case: 189.

Eye Trouble, Serious, Accidental.—Case: 258.

Eye, Wound in the.—Case: 164.

Eyesight, Diseased.—Case: 156.

Fabricius, Johann Albert (1668-1736); a German; author of "Gedanken von der Erkenntniss der Gemuether aus der Temperamenten der Chiromantie und Physiognomie" (Jena: 1735).

Failure in Life.—A very hollow Plain of Mars.

Fainting Fits.—Line of Liver connected at the start with Line of Life. Line of Heart chained or curving down to Line of Head.

Fainting Fits, Strange.—Case: 353.

Faithlessness.—See Inconstancy.

Fall from Horseback, Dangerous.—Case: 347.

Fame and Success.—A star on the Mount of Jupiter and another star at the end of a fine line of the Sun. A clear Line of Fate from Rascette to Mount of Saturn, or, better still, terminating either on the Mount of Jupiter or on the Mount of the Sun. A perfect Line of Liver. Two straight sister lines to the Line of the Sun on the Mount of that name. The Lines of Head and Heart normal and especially long. All the Mounts, except Saturn and the Moon, very much in evidence. For intellectual or artistic people only, a fine Mount of the Moon desirable.

Fame and Success, Due to Love Sorrow.—Case: 187.

Fanaticism.—Long, thin, smooth fingers, especialy the first. A line or branch from the Line of Head reaching the Mount of Jupiter, then turning and ending on the Mount of Saturn. If the fanaticism has a persecuting tendency the second finger, in its exaggerate first phalanx, shows the baneful influence of Saturn.

Farming Life, Taste for a.—Insignificant tips or often spatulate. Long, thick nails. Ordinary thumb. Mount of Saturn quite marked. Insignificant lines outside of the three chief lines. Strong Mounts of Mars if the farmer loves hunting.

Farwell, Eveline Mitchell; an Englishwoman; author of "Fingers and Fortune" (London: 1892).

Fatalities, Two Great.—Case: 190.

Fatality, Not the Arbiter of Humanity—27.

Fatal Love, Object of a.—Case: 178.

Fate, The Line of.—273. 1. Position and Direction—274. 2. Character: a. By Itself—274; b. In Combination with Other Indications—276. 3. Starting Points and Forks at the Start—276. 4. Termination and Forks at the Termination—280. 5. Branches—282. 6. Breaks—282. 7. Connected with the Main Lines: a. Directly—284; b. By Minor Lines—284. 8. Signs—285. Special Observations (Influence Lines from the Mount of the Moon)—292.

Fault-finding.—Long, knotty fingers, especially with first knots; often spatulate. Short nails. Two stars near thumb nails. A narrow Quadrangle. A poor Line of Liver running rather close to the Percussion. Mounts of Mars exaggerate and very little Mount of Venus. A poor Line of Heart.

Female Troubles.—Plain of Mars hollow toward Moon. The lower part of the Mount of the Moon exaggerate or much lined. A cross in the same place on the Mount. The Line of Life after a short normal run starting toward bottom of Mount of the Moon.

Female Troubles, Exemption of.—A Double Line of Heart.

Fever, Bilious.—Line of Liver thin and red as it crosses Line of Head, especially with an island on the latter. See Biliousness and Liver Troubles.

Fever, Malarial, Typhoidal.—Bluish dot on Line of Life. Very narrow, highly colored, often broken Line of Liver, with dark dots on Line of Head. Black or bluish dots on Line of Heart.

Fever, Tendency to.—Dry skin. Red dots on Line of Life. In general, red lines.

Fiancé, Loss of a.—Case: 289.

Finger, The First.—Or Finger of Jupiter, or "Index"—42. Alignment—42. Leaning—42. Space between it and next Fingers—43. Length: a. By Itself—44; b. Compared to the other Fingers—44. Its Phalanxes taken separately—45. Meanings of its Tip —50. Its Nail—41. Lines and Signs —329.

Finger, The Fourth.—Or Finger of Mercury, or "Auricularius"—42. Alignment—42. Leaning—43. Space between it and the next Fingers—43. Length: a. By Itself—44; b. Compared to the other Fingers—45. Its Phalanxes taken separately—45. Meanings of its Tip—50. Lines and Signs—340.

Finger, The Second.—Or Finger of Saturn, or "Medius"—42. Alignment—42. Leaning—43. Space between it and next Fingers—43. Length: a. By Itself—44; b. Compared to the other Fingers—44. Its Phalanxes taken separately—45. Meanings of its Tip 50. Its nail—39. Lines and Signs —333.

Finger, the Third.—Or Finger of Apollo, or "Annularius"—42. Alignment—42. Leaning—43. Space between it and next Fingers—43. Length: a. By Itself—44; b. Compared to the other Fingers—45. Its Phalanxes taken separately—45. Meanings of its Tip—50. Lines and Signs—337.

Fingers; being Points, attract vital fluid; send it up to the brain; return it to the source of all life; hence the Lines —20. Exhaustive Study—42. 1. Position: a. Alignment of Bases; b. Leaning toward each other; c. Closeness; d. Spaces between; e. Bent and Flexibility. 2. Length: a. Of all Fingers; b. Of each; c. Compared with each other; d. Of Phalanges taken separately. 3. Shape: a. Outside of Tips and Knots; b. The Types; c. Tips; d. Knots; e. Comparison Types (Tips and Knots Combined): The Pointed, The Conical, The Square, The Spatulate; f. Each tip by Itself. 4. Lines and Signs on them— 325.

Financial Losses—Breaks, crosses, stars and downward branches on the Line of Fate or the Sun. Lines of Influence from the Mount of Venus cutting the Line of the Sun. A cross on the Mount of Mercury, one arm of which cuts the Line of Heart. An island on the Line of Liver.

Financial Ruin of Minors Through Mother's Misconduct.—Case: 302.

Financial Ruin of Parents—Case: 289.

Financial Success After Fatality—Case: 185.

Financially Ruined and Deserted, Lady —Case: 349.

Fire, Life Saved in a.—Case: 102.

Flexibility—Of Fingers—43. Of Thumb —53.

Forces, Diminishing.—A large downward branch of the Line of Life.

Forger, The.—Long, slender, crooked fingers. The Mount of Mercury exaggerate; also the Mount of Venus (gift of form), and, if very clever, the Mount of the Sun. Star on the Mount of Mercury. Heavy lower part of the Mount of the Moon. Widely forked but rather straight Line of Head. No Mount of Jupiter.

Fortune by Inheritance.—A star on the first bracelet of the Rascette. Also a cross within an Angle or Triangle at the same place. A long Sister Line to the Line of Head. See also Legacies.

Fortune, by Unaided Efforts.—The Lines of Fate and the Sun starting from inside a well formed Triangle. Long First Phalanx of the Thumb. Fine, straight Line of Head and Mounts of the Sun and Mercury predominant, with well marked Mounts of Mars. Often branches of the Line of Fate ending on the Mount of the Sun or the same Line terminating on the Mount of Mercury in excellent shape.

Fortune of the Parents, Loss of.—Case: —286.

Fortune, The Line of.—The Line of the Sun—30.

Found Out.—Case: 306.

Friendship of the Great.—Line of Fate terminating either on the Mount of Jupiter or on the Mount of the Sun.

Mounts of Jupiter and the Sun predominant. A Line from the Quadrangle to the Mount of Mercury. One or two crosses on the second phalanx of the first finger.

Frith, Henry, and Heron-Allen, Edward; Englishmen; authors of "Chiromancy, or the Science of Palmistry" (London: 1883).

Frivolity.—Second Finger too short and often more pointed than the others. A weak first phalanx of the Thumb. A poor Line of Head. A very fragmentary Line of the Sun. Insignificant (or absent) Lower Mount of Mars.

Future Written in the Hand.—Why and when—27.

Galen, Claud; the famous Greek physician (103-193); author of "Secundum Hippocratem Medicorum Principia" (Edition of 1528, Paris).

Gambler, The Born.—Soft hand; short, smooth fingers; the third finger equal to the second, if not longer. A large Mount of the Moon and a very drooping Line of Head.

Gautier, Jules; a Frenchman; author of La Chirognomie et la Phrénologie" (Paris: 1867), and "Chiromancie et Chirognomomie" (Paris: 1885).

Generative Organs, Troubles of the.— (For Women, see Female Troubles.) Exaggerate or badly marked Mount of Venus. First Bracelet of the Rascette very convex. A star at the connection of the Lines of Head and Lover.

Generosity.—Space (wide) between base of First Finger and Thumb.

Georget; a Frenchman; author of "Physiologie du Système Nerveux" (Paris: 1821).

Gessmann, Gustav W.; a German; author of "Katechismus der Handlesekunst" (Berlin: 1893) (a reprint by Laird & Lee, Chicago, 1898, with Preface by Comte de Saint-Germain); "Katechismus des Gesichtlesekunst" (Berlin: 1894); and other works in

German on "Phrenology," "Astrology," "Graphology," etc., all plentifully illustrated and quite clear and modern in their deductions.

Girdle of Venus, The.—259. 1. Position and Direction—261. 2. Character—261. 3. Termination—262. 4. Breaks—262. 5. Connected with the Main Lines—262. 6. Signs—263.

Girl-Mother Deserted.—Case: 119.

Goclenio, Rudolphus; author of "Aphorismorum Chiromanticorum Tractatus" (Leipsic: 1597), and numerous other works on Palmistry.

Gout.—"Satin Skin." Exaggerate or much lined Mount of Jupiter. The middle part of the Mount of the Moon exaggerate or much lined. A downward line, often crossed, on the middle part of the Mount of the Moon. The Line of Life forked and red at its termination.

Gowers, W. R.; an Englishman; author of "Epilepsy and Other Chronic Convulsive Diseases" (London: 1881).

Greed.—See Avarice.

Grief Ending in Insanity.—Case: 190.

Guilty Intrigue.—An island on the Line of Fate. An island on the Line of Heart. An island on a Line of Union. Independent island inside the Mount of Venus. An island on a Line of Influence from the Mount of Venus or the Line of Life to any other part of the hand, but especially true if it cuts the Line of Heart and also a Line of Union.

Guilty Intrigue. Death of Husband.—Case: 271.

Guilty Intrigue, Double.—Case: 353.

Guilty Intrigue, Fatal.—Some one of the above indications and also stars or bad breaks on the Line of Fate. A Line of Influence from the Mount of Venus and one from the Mount of the Moon, both cutting Line of Fate at the same place.

Guilty Intrigue in Thought Only.—Case: 288.

Guilty Intrigue. Lawsuit Lost.—Case: 272.

Guilty Intrigue, Projected.—Case: 236.

Guilty Love; Death, Lawsuits.—Case: 183.

Hand as a Whole.—35; measured on back from wrist to tip. Size—36. Hair—36. Illustration—37.

Hand Proper.—Measured on back from wrist to first knuckle. Longer than Finger—37. The same length—37. Shorter than Fingers—37.

Hand Proper and Palm Combined.—1. Thick and very hard—37. 2. Thick and hard—37. 3. Thick and Medium Hard—38. 4. Thick and Medium Soft—38. 5. Thick and Soft—38. 6. Thick and Very Soft—38. 7. Thin and Very Hard—38. 8. Thin and Hard—38. 9. Thin, Narrow and Meager—38. 10. Thin and Soft—38. 11. Thin and Very Soft—38. 12. Transparent—38.

Hand; the "Organ of Organs"—Aristotle, 19.

Happiness, Perfect and Durable.—A harmonious blending of all the best Chirognomic and Chiromantic Indications to be found in this book wherever they do not contradict the particular type the subject is found to belong to.

Hartlieb, Johann; a German; author of "Die Kunst Ciromantia" (Augsburg: 1745); this work was written at the end of the XV. Century, and is one of the old standards.

Haunted by Ghosts.—Case: 112.

Hay Fever.—Poor Line of Liver with a narrow Quadrangle, due to Line of Heart curving down to Line of Head.

Headaches, Chronic.—Line of Liver red at its termination. Chained Line of Head. Short Line of Head and irregular Line of Liver. Bars cutting Line of Head. Number of small breaks of the Line of Head. Line of

Head cut by many bars (especially if the Line is drooping).

Headaches, Serious.—Very large branch from starting point of Line of Life down to the Rascette. Drooping and much broken Line of Head. See also Biliousness and Liver Trouble.

Head, The Line of.—213. 1. Position and Direction: a. By Itself—213; b. In connection with other Indications —214. 2. Character: a. By Itself —215; b. In combination with other Indications—216. 3. Starting Points and Forks at the Start—218. 4. Termination and Forks at the Termination—220. 5. Branches—225. 6. Breaks—227. 7. Connected with the Main Lines: a. Directly—229. b. By Minor Lines—231. 8. Signs—233. Special Observation—239. Curious Cases—240.

Head, Wound on.—Capillary cross lines on Mount of Jupiter. A break of the Line of Head.

Health, The Line of.—The Line of Liver —30.

Heart, Hypertrophy of the.—Case: 251.

Heartless Disposition.—Hand thin and hard. Long Finger of Saturn. Line of Heart absent. Line of Head cutting the hand like a bar. The Mount of Venus insignificant.

Heart Oppression Due to Liver Trouble —Case: 256.

Heart Palpitations.—Line of Liver red at the start, especially if connected with Line of Life. Many dots on Line of Heart.

Heart Palpitations Due to Grief.—Case: 193.

Heart, The Line of.—241. 1. Position and Direction—241. 2. Character: a. By Itself—243; b. In combination with other Indications—245. 3. Starting Points and Forks at the Start —247. 4. Termination and Forks at the Termination—250. 5. Branches —250. 6. Breaks—252. 7. Con-

nected with the Main Lines: a. Directly—253; b. By Minor Lines—255. 8. Signs—256. Special Observation —259.

Heart Troubles.—Plain of Mars hollow toward Heart. Short, square shaped and bluish nails. Exaggerate or much lined Mount of the Sun. Line of Influence from Mount of Venus cutting Line of Heart. Chained Line of Heart. Line of Heart broken. Bars cutting Line of Heart.

Heart Trouble Due to Diseased Liver. —Lines of Life and Liver closely connected, with red or bluish spots on the former. Line of Heart broken under the Mount of Mercury.

Heart Troubles, Very Serious.—Case: 252.

Heart Weakness.—Short and square nails. Narrow, thin palm. Pale skin. Total absence of the Line of Heart, with poor Line of Head and wavy Line of Liver. Very pale and wide Line of Heart. A circle on Line of Heart.

Hebra, Heinrich; a German; author of "Untersuchung ueber der Nagel" (Vienna: 1880); a study on "Nails."

Hemorrhage.—A grille on the Upper Mount of Mars. The Line of Heart absent or very poor. Sometimes (in female cases) a star on the lower part of the Mount of the Moon.

Hemorrhoids.—Exaggerate or much lined Mount of Saturn. A Line of Influence from a dot on Line of Life, ending in Star on Upper Mount of Mars.

Hemorrhoids.—Case: 349.

Henze, Adolph; a German; author of "Die Chirogrammatomantie, oder Lehre der Charakter der Menschen aus der Handschrift zu erkennen" (Leipzic: 1862); the original discoverer of "Graphology," and the teacher of Desbarrolles.

Hepatica, The.—The Line of Liver.— 30.

Herder, Johann; a German (1744-1803); author of Ideen zur Philosophie der Geschichte der Menschheit" (1794).

Heron-Allen, Edward; an Englishman; author of "A Manual of Chirosophy," "Codex Chiromanticæ," etc. Translator of D'Arpentigny's "Science of the Hand." Now living in London; has visited America.

Highwayman, The—Thick, hard hands, with short, smooth, heavy fingers of the Elementary type. Only the Mounts of Mars and the lower part of the Mount of the Moon prominent. Only the three chief lines, very red in color. A star, or even a grille, on the Mount of Mercury.

Hindoo Brahmins—16. (See Dale and Chatterjee on Indian Palmistry.)

Hippocrates; a world renowned Greek Physician (B. C. 460-377); said "Phthisici ungues adunci," when speaking of the shape of the nail of the first finger in consumptives. His complete work issued in German (1847)—41.

Hoeping, Johann; a German; author of "Chiromantia Harmonica" (Jena: 1681), and of his large work, "Institutiones Chiromanticæ."

Hopeful Disposition.—Pink and mottled skin—38.

Housewife, The Gifted.—Palm and Fingers even; Palm elastic; Fingers square; the first knot quite marked. Nails short. Mounts moderate. Long Line of Heart starting deep into the Mount of Jupiter. Mounts of Venus and Mercury pronounced (kindness of heart and prudence in money matters). Very few lines outside of the Chief Lines. The Line of Head moderately long.

Humboldt, Alexander, Baron von; a German; author of "Kosmos" (1845-62)—20; 22.

Humphrey, George M.; an Englishman; author of "On the Human Foot and the Human Hand" (Cambridge: 1861).

Hydrophobia, Danger of.—Break of Line of Head under Mount of the Sun —228.

Hypochondriac, The.—(Thinks himself ill.) The Medical Stigmata (which see) clearly marked, with an exaggerate Mount of the Moon, into which droops the Line of Head.

Hysterical Insanity.—Case: 261.

Hysteria.—Second Finger crooked. A star on the Mount of the Moon connected by a Line of Influence with the Mount of Venus. Double or Triple Girdle of Venus. A Girdle of Venus cut by many bars.

Hysteria Destroying Conjugal Happiness.—Girdle of Venus cutting a prolonged Line of Union.

Idealism.—Hand proper shorter than fingers, with pointed tips. Slender Palm. Almond shaped nails. Mounts of Jupiter very prominent, with the first phalanx of the first finger above normal.

Idiocy.—A very ill-shaped hand, with dwarfed, very high up Thumb and half formed fingers. The Mount of the Moon, and often the Mounts of Mars, are the only ones bulging. Drooping, broken, twisted Line of Head. Generally a very poor Line of Heart. Often one of the Main Lines missing.

Idiocy, Congenital.—Case: 154.

Ill-health, Continuous.—Thin Palm. A wide and pale Line of Life. A Line of Life formed of small ladderlike fragments. Line of Liver connected with Line of Life at the start. A number of dots on Line of Life.

Ill-health in Childhood.—Line of Life chained or Linked in its first part. If this ill-health is to influence the whole career, Line of Fate twisted or much crossed at the start.

Ill-health in Old Age.—Faint, poorly formed star on Mount of Saturn. Lines of Life and Fate connected by confused lines at bottom of Triangle. Cross near termination of Line of Life. Short and broad Line of Liver.

Ill-health, Temporary.—A portion of the Line of Life thin or chained.

Illness Caused by Love Sorrows.— Lines connecting Lines of Life and Heart.

Illness, Not Very Serious.—A bar cutting Line of Life. A bar cutting Line of Liver.

Illness, Sudden, Grave.—A semicircular line cutting Line of Life—175.

Illness, Very Serious.—A break or cross, or star or black dot on the Line of Life. The same signs on Line of Liver. An island is a still worse indication.

Imagination at Its Best.—Hand proper soft and shorter than fingers; the latter smooth, with pointed tips. First phalanges of all fingers longer than normal, especially those of the first and third fingers. Almond shaped nails. Mounts of Jupiter and the Sun excellent. Finely developed Mounts of the Moon and Venus. A broad, perfect Triangle.

Imagination Blended with Practical Ideas.—Hand about same size as fingers, with conical tips. A rather elastic palm. Second knot marked. The Mounts of the Sun and Mercury blended into one. Very little droop of the Line of Head and moderate Mounts of the Moon ano Venus.

Imagination, Diseased.—Thin (even transparent) and very soft hand. The sign of the Moon on an exaggerate Mount of the Moon. Very drooping and widely forked Line of Head. Strong Girdle of Venus.

Imprudence.—Smooth, short fingers. Short first phalanx of the thumb. Lines of Life and Head widely separated at the start. Very little, if any, Mount of Saturn, and the second finger more conical than the others.

Impulsiveness.—See Imprudence. Add: Fingers thrown backward naturally and often flexible.

Inconstancy.—Soft hands; conically tipped, smooth fingers. First phalanx of the Thumb below normal. A short Line of Head and a chained Line of Heart. Cross lines on the Lower Mount of Mars. A crescent inside the third angle of the Triangle.

Incurable Disease.—A star on the Mount of Saturn. A cross cut by a downward branch of the Line of Life.

Indagine, Johann; a German, and one of the leading Chiromants of all times; Author of "Introductiones Apostlesmaticæ Elegantes in Chyromantiam, etc." (Strasburg: 1522). This, and his "Chiromantia, Physiognomia Periaxiomata de Faciebus Signorum" (1534), had a number of editions in Latin, German, French and English, the latter published in 1651 under the title of "The Book of Palmistry and Physiognomy."

Independence, Great Spirit of.—First Finger leaning toward Thumb. Wide space between bases of First and Second Fingers. Spatulate tipped, knotted fingers. Short nails. Long first phalanx of the thumb. Mount of Jupiter predominant. Separation between Lines of Life and Head at the start. Long Line of Head. Plain and Mounts of Mars quite marked.

Indifference to All Things Beautiful.— Hard Palm. Spatulate fingers. Third finger too short. Mount of the Sun absent. No Mount of the Moon to speak of (except in health meanings). Poor Line of Heart and stiff Line of Head.

Indigestion, Chronic.—A wavy Line of Liver and an islanded Line of Life. Irregular or wavy Line of Liver, with poor Line of Head.

Influence, E x t e r n a l.—Transmitted through the nerves; quotation Charles Bonnet—19.

Influence Over Others, Great.—Long Fourth Finger.

Ingeber, Johann; a German; author of "Chiromantia, Metoposcopia, et Physiognomia practica" (Frankfurt: 1724).

Inheritance.—Case: 186.

Inheritance, Double.—Case: 185.

Inheritance Through Death of Insane Relative.—Case: 283.

Initié, Un; a Frenchman; author of "Les Mystères des Sciences Occultes" (Paris: 1894).

Inquisitiveness.—See Curiosity.

Insanity.—The Sign of the Moon on the Mount of Saturn. Many confused lines on a bulging Mount of the Moon, with a sloping, starred or chained Line of Head. The Sign of the Moon on the Mount of the Moon. Line of Head sloping to bottom of Mount of the Moon, with a star on second phalanx of second finger. Wavy Line of Head rising close to Line of Heart under Mounts of the Sun or Mercury. Line of Head sloping deeply and broken. Line of Head merging into Line of Liver, the Line of Life being forked at the start. A split Line of Head.

Insanity, Alcoholic.—Line of Mars very red, ending in a fork, one prong ending in a star on Mount of the Moon, with a black dot on Line of Head.

Insanity Caused by Love, Temporary.—Case: 237.

Insanity, Hereditary, Erotic.—A star at the end of a branch of Line of Heart drooping into Mount of the Moon.

Insanity of a Materialistic Philosopher.—Case: 240.

Insanity of an Erotic Character.—A star on the Mount of the Moon connected by a Line of Influence with the Mount of Venus. A star at the end of a branch of the Line of Heart drooping into the Mount of the Moon.

Insanity, Religious.—The Sign of Saturn on the Mount of the Moon. Two crosses close to the Line of the Sun on the Mount of the Sun.

Insanity, Senile.—Line of Life tasseled at its termination, one prong deep into the Mount of the Moon.

Insanity Shown in the Colors of the Lines.—Case: 350.

Insanity, Temporary.—Case: 186.

Insanity, Violent.—The Sign of the Moon on Upper Mount of Mars. The Sign of Mars on the Mount of the Moon. The Line of Life of a livid color. All Lines very red and the Mounts of Mars and the Moon exaggerate.

Intellectual Power.—Fingers longer than palm, slightly conical, especially the first and fourth fingers, and knotted (for deep students). Mounts of the Sun, Jupiter and Mercury predominant. Superb Line of Head. Long Line of Heart starting from deep into the Mount of Jupiter and just a trifle forked and sloping at the termination. Excellent Lines of Sun and Liver.

Intestinal Troubles.—A strong red line between the first and second fingers. Much lined lower part of the Upper Mount of Mars and upper part of the Mount of the Moon. Large island at termination of Line of Head.

Intestinal Trouble.—Case: 281.

Intrepidity.—Square palm. Smooth, spatulate fingers, with square, strong nails. Third finger above normal. Rather short thumb, with first phalanx longer than second. Mounts and Plain of Mars predominant, with .fine Mount of Mercury. A Fine Line of Heart.

Introducing the Introduction—13.

Intuition, Gift of.—Thin and very soft hands. Short nails. Short, smooth, conical Fingers. The first phalanges of all fingers above average. A short, but conical, first phalanx of the Thumb. The Mounts of the Moon and Mercury predominant. Sometimes the Mount of Saturn strongly marked. A clear Line of Intuition; or, if it is not there, a clear Line of the Liver running closer to the Percussion than normal. A fine Triangle. A Line of Fate rising from low down into the Mount of the Moon. Often a drooping Line of Head. A triangle on the Mount of the Moon.

Intuition, The Line of.—210. 1. Position and Direction—210. 2. Character—210. 3. Starting Point—211. 4. Termination—211. 5. Branches—211.—6. Breaks—211. 7. Connected with the Main Lines: a. Directly—211; b. By Minor Lines—211 8. Signs—212.

Invention and Method United.—Case: 116.

Inventive Genius, Practical.—Elastic Palm. Short nails. Long, knotted fingers; the fourth finger above normal. A long Thumb. The Mounts of Mercury and the Sun predominant, the former with one or more downward lines. A fine Line of Head slightly drooping; often with a fine triple fork at the end.

Inventive Genius, Unpractical.—The above signs, except that the knot will be absent, at least the second knot. The Line of Head will droop too much down the Mount of the Moon; the latter above normal. Confused downward lines on the Mounts of the Sun and Mercury.

Irony.—Short nails, with soft palm. Mount of Mercury (sometimes Saturn) predominant. A poor Line of Heart.

Irreligion.—See Skepticism.

Island on Line of the Sun, Influence of. —Case: 272.

Jaundice.—Exaggerate or much lined Mount of Mercury. A spot or a star on the Mount of the Moon.

Jaundice.—Case: 208.

Judgment, Sound.—See Common Sense.

Jupiter, Mount of.—1. Position—84. 2. Meanings—85. 3. Displacements—86. 4. Revealing Illnesses—89. 5. Revealing Mode of Suicide—90. 6. Signs—93. 7. Signature: a. Physical Peculiarities—122; b. Health Peculiarities—124; c. Mental and Moral Peculiarities—124. 8. In connection with another prominent Mount—137.

Kabbala.—15; 17; 22. In its more modern meaning, a book written sometime in the XIII. century and containing a Jewish interpretation of occultism in its essence and manifestations. It is claimed to have come to the Jews through the Egyptian priesthood, and to go back to prehistorical times.

Kidney Troubles.—The lower part of the Mount of the Moon exaggerate or much lined. A cross at the same place on the Mount. A long Line of Voyage reaching almost to the Line of Life and forked at the termination.

Knot.—Marked bulge of one (or both) of the Finger Joints. Upper Knot called "Philosophical Knot." Lower Knot called "Knot of Material Order" —48. Only one Knot on the Thumb: the "Philosophical Knot"—54.

Kollmann, Arthur; a German; author of "Der Tast-Apparat der Hand der Menschlichen Rassen und der Affen in Seines Entwickelung und Gliederung" (Leipsic: 1883).

La Chambre, Dr. de; a famous French physician; author of "L'Art de connaître les hommes" (Paris: 1662).

Langridge, M. C.; English author of "The Key to Palmistry" (London: 1894).

Languor.—Line of Liver forked at termination.

Lavater, J. Caspar; a Swiss; author of the modern theory of Physiognomy, described in his books, "Etudes sur la Physionomie" (The Hague: 1783), and "L'Art de Connaître les Hommes par la Physionomie" (Paris: 1806).

Lawyer, Aptitude to Be a.—Short nails. Fourth Finger predominant. Long second phalanx of the Thumb. Large Mounts of Mercury and Mars. Line of Head separated from Line of Life at the start and distinctly forked at the termination.

Lawsuit.—A Line of Influence cutting an upward branch of the Line of Life and merging (or cutting) the Line of the Sun. In the first case, the lawsuit is won, in the second it is lost. Crosses in the First Angle of the Triangle.

Lawsuit Lost, Family.—Case: 302.

Laziness.—Hand proper longer than fingers. Hand thick and soft. Very short, conical fingers. Mounts of the Moon, Venus and (sometimes) the Sun predominant. Drooping Line of Head, with short first Phalanx of the Thumb. The Second Angle broad and poorly marked.

Ledos, Eugène; a Frenchman; author of "Traité de la Physionomie Humaine" (Paris: 1895), and of other works on sister sciences.

Legacies.—An angle or star on the middle of the First Bracelet of the Rascette. A Line of Influence from a star on the Mount of Venus merging into the Line of the Sun. Lines of Influence from the Mount of the Moon running alongside the Line of the Sun without touching it. See Inheritance.

Leg Crippled.—Case: 251.

Leg, Wound on.—Capillary cross lines on the Mount of Mercury. A lentil-like dark spot low down on the Mount of Mercury.

Legs, Deprivation of the Use of.—Case: 171.

Legs, Troubles with the.—Exaggerate or much lined Mount of Saturn. Line of Head broken under the Mount of Saturn.

Lethargy.—Very poor Lines of Life and Heart; a single uncrossed Bracelet of the Rascette. A very low Plain of Mars.

Lethargy.—Case: 170.

Levi, Eliphas; a Frenchman; author of "Dogme et Rituel de la Haute Magie" (Paris: 1850).

Liar, The.—Fourth finger crooked. Mounts of Mercury and the Moon exaggerate and rayed. A cross on the former. No Mount of Jupiter. The Line of Head drooping and widely forked at the termination.

Life, A Short.—Short Line of Life (especially in both hands).

Life in Convent.—A square at the lower part of the Mount of Venus. A grille on the Mount of Jupiter in an otherwise excellent hand.

Life Ruined by Imprudence.—Widely separated Lines of Life and Head. A Second finger below normal, and a Third finger longer than the Second. A Line of Fate from the Mount of the Moon stopping abruptly at the Line of Head, the latter drooping into an exaggerate Mount of the Moon.

Life Ruined by Love.—A Line of Fate merging into a broken or starred Line of Heart under the Mount of Saturn. A wavy Line of Head running at the termination toward the Line of Heart, which it cuts. Poor, or starred Lines of Fate and the Sun. A double Line of Heart.

Life Ruined by Our Own People.—Lines of Influence from the Mount of Venus cutting Lines of Fate, Head and Heart, also the Line of the Sun.

Life, The Line of—Exhaustive Study.—153. 1. Position and Direction—153. 2. Character: a. By Itself—154; b. In combination with other Indications—157. 3. Starting Points and Forks at the start—157. 4. Termination and Forks at the Termination—159. 5. Branches—161. 6. Breaks—162. 7. Connected with the Main Lines: a. Directly—163; b. By means of Minor Lines—166. 8. Bars, Capillaries and Signs—166.

Life, Uneventful.—No Line of Fate.

Line of Heart starting from between the first and second finger. The Mounts insignificant.

Lines in General.—141. Main Lines, 14 in number. Preliminary study—141. 1. Grouping: Six Divisions, each under a Principal Main Line. Chief Lines: Life, Head, Heart. 2. Meaning. 3. Character: a. Color; b. Length; c. Depth. 4. Malformation (illustration: a. Broken; b. Split; c. Chained or Linked; d. Islanded. The Lines are also: a. Forked (at the extremities); b. Branched, either upward or downward; c. Tasseled.

Lines of Influence from the Mounts of Venus or Lower Mars or the Line of Life.—172. 1. Inside the Mounts: A. Concentric to the Line of Life—74. C. Cross Lines—174. 2. From the Mounts or the Line: A. Ending inside the Triangle but cutting no Main Line—174; B. Terminating upon any of the other Mounts—175; C. Merging into or cutting Main Lines—179; D. Starting from a sign—183; E. Ending in a sign—187; Starting and ending in a sign—190.

Lines of Influence in General.—172. Either Sister Lines or Cross Lines. From the Mounts of Venus or Lower Mars or the Line of Life—173. From the Mount of the Moon—292. From the Upper Mount of Mars—307.

Lines, Vanishing of the.—An admirable instance of such disappearance, translated from Desbarrolles—147.

Lion Killer, A Famous.—Case: 230.

Literary Man; Special Nature—Case: 220.

Literature, Aptitude for.—Long First and Fourth Fingers, often conical. Mounts of Mercury and the Sun predominant, with the Mounts of Venus and the Moon indispensable for writers of Poetry or Fiction. A slightly drooping Line of Head, somewhat forked at the Termination; often white dots on it. Small downward line on the first joint of the first finger. A

line from the Rascette straight to the Mount of the Sun.

Liver, The Line of.—200. 1. Position and Direction—201. 2. Character: a. By Itself—201; b. In combination with other Indications—202. 3. Starting Points—204. 4. Termination and Forks at the Termination—204. 5. Branches—205. 6. Breaks—205. 7. Connected with the Main Lines—205. 8. Signs—206.

Liver Trouble, Very Serious.—Damp skin, especially if clammy cold. Exaggerate and much lined Mount of Mercury. Yellow colored Lines, especially Line of Liver. Line of Liver formed in ladder-like fragments. Dark spots on the Mount of the Moon.

Logic, the Ruling Principle of Modern Palmistry.—32.

Longevity.—Very long and good Line of Fate, especially if it comes out in a great circle. Long and clear Line of Liver, if not connected at the start with Line of Life. A complete Rascette. Lines of Head and Heart in a healthy condition.

Longevity, Great.—Case: 165.

Loss of Blood from the Bowels.—Case: 191.

Loss of Fortune by Parents.—Case: 181.

Loss of Money, Repeated.—A very Hollow Plain of Mars. Breaks, Bars, Stars or Islands on the Line of the Sun. Islands on the Line of Liver. An Island on the Line of Fate in a hand that denotes no immoral instincts.

Love Affair Broken Off.—Case: 289.

Love Affairs, Two Simultaneous.— Case: 188.

Love, Disappointment in.—Plain of Mars hollow toward Heart. The Line of Heart cut by a bar near the start. Line of Head running close to the Line of Head. Line of Fate chained when crossing Line of Heart. Badly formed star in the Triangle.

Love, Capacity for.—A large Mount of

Venus in a hand generally soft. A fine clear Line of Heart. Via Lasciva as Sister Line to Line of Liver. A fine Line of Mars.

Love, Extreme Passion in.—A thick, soft hand. Exaggerate Mounts of Venus and the Moon. Line of Heart starting forkless under Mount of Saturn. Often Chief Lines quite red, with strong Mounts and Plain of Mars. Clear, red Line of Mars.

Love, Fatal.—See Life Ruined by Love.

Love, Fatal Only.—Case: 299.

Love for a Near Relative.—An island on a Line of Union.

Love, Ideal.—A finely forked Line of Heart starting high inside the Mount of Jupiter.

Love Not Ending in Marriage.—A Line of Influence from the Mount of the Moon terminating just before it reaches the Line of Fate.

Love, Troubles in.—See Love, Disappointments in.

Lovers at the Same Time, Two.—Case: 290. Case: 349.

Lucas, Louis; a Frenchman; author of "Chimie Nouvelle," and "Acoustique Nouvelle," published between 1855 and 1860.

Luck, The Line of.—The Line of Fate —30.

Luna, The Line of.—The Line of Intuition—30.

Lymphatic Disposition.—See Anœmia, which is its most dangerous form.

Map of the Hand.—29. Illustration— 31. "Back of the Hand:" 1. Hand Proper; 2. Fingers; 3. Thumb; 4. Tips; 5. Knots; 6. Nails; 7. Hair. "Inside of the Hand:" 1. Mounts (Jupiter, Saturn, Sun, Mercury, Upper Mars, Moon, Venus, Lower Mars); 2. Palm Proper or Plain of Mars; 3. Main Lines (Life, Head, Heart, Fate, Sun, Liver, Via Lasciva, Intuition, Mars, Girdle of Venus, Ras-

cette, Union); 4. Minor Lines; 5. Signs.

Marriage.—(See Union.)

Marriage, Ill-fated.—Case: 184.

Marriage, Unfortunate.—Case: 281.

Marriage, Unfortunate.—Case: 180.

Mars, Lower Mount of.—1. Position— 85. 2. Meanings—87. 3. Displacements—89. 4. Revealing Illnesses— 90. 5. Revealing Mode of Suicide—90. 6. Signs—121. Signature (in common with Upper Mount of Mars); a. Physical Peculiarities—131; b. Health Peculiarities—132; c. Mental and Moral Peculiarities—132. 8. In combination with another prominent Mount—137.

Mars, The Line of.—194. 1. Position and Direction—194. 2. Character— 194. 3. Starting Points and Forks at the Termination—195. 4. Breaks and Signs—195. 5. Special Observations —195.

Mars, Upper Mount of.—1. Position— 84. 2. Meanings—86. 3. Displacements—89. 4. Revealing Illnesses— 89. 5. Revealing Mode of Suicide— 90. 6. Signs—108. 7. Signature (in common with Lower Mount of Mars): a. Physical Peculiarities—131; b. Health Peculiarities—132; c. Mental and Moral Peculiarities—132. 8. In combination with another prominent Mount—137.

Mathematics, Higher, Aptitude for.— Dry, hard palm. Long, knotted fingers. The Fourth Finger above normal. The Mounts of Mercury and (sometimes) Saturn predominant. Second phalanges of Fingers and Thumb above normal. Very straight Line of Head. Mounts of the Moon and (often) the Sun absent.

May de Francoine, Phillipe; a Frenchman; author of "La Chiromancie Medicinale" (The Hague: 1665).

Meanness.—Thin, hard palm. Fingers close together and bent forward. Very narrow Quadrangle, due to Line of

Heart curving abnormally toward Line of Head.

Mechanical Parts of Fine Arts, Aptitude for.—Hand proper longer than fingers, the latter with square tips and Second Knots marked. Mount of Mercury thrown toward Mount of the Sun. Straight Line of Head.

Medical Stigmata.—Four to seven clear downward lines on the Mount of Mercury denote the scientist, espcially the physician or surgeon.

Medium, Extra Lucid.—Case: 212.

Melancholia.—A grille on the Mount of the Moon. Exaggerate or much lined Mount of Saturn. Drooping Line of Head. No Mounts of the Sun or Jupiter. Wavy downward lines on third phalanx of Second Finger.

Melton, John; an Englishman; author of "Astrologaster, or the Figure Caster" (London: 1620).

Memory, Gift of.—Remarkably fine, straight Lines of Head and Liver, with First and Fourth Fingers markedly conical.

Memory, Loss of.—A much broken up Line of Head. A wavy or fragmentary Line of Liver.

Mensal, The.—The Line of Heart—30.

Mercenary Spirit in Intellectual or Artistic Work.—Hard palm; square tipped fingers. Third Finger leaning toward Fourth. Third Finger too short. Line of Head very straight and stiff. Mount of the Moon insignificant. Line of the Sun terminating on Mount of Mercury.

Mercury, Mount of.—1. Position—84. 2. Meanings—86. 3. Displacements —89. 4. Revealing Illnesses—89. 5. Revealing Mode of Suicide—90. 6. Signs—104. 7. Signature: a. Physical Peculiarities—129; b. Health Peculiarities—129; c. Mental and Moral Peculiarities—130. 8. In combination with another prominent Mount—137.

Mesalliance, A.—A Line of Union cut-ting the Line of the Sun.

Metacarpus or Metacarpal Bones.—35. The five bones forming the "body of the hand."

Meticulous, Teasing, Tormenting Disposition.—See Fault-Finding.

Metoposcopy.—The study of physiognomy. From the Greek words "metopon," the forehead, and "Scopein," to view.

Meyens, Dr. Philipp; a German; author of "Chiromantia Medica" (1667).

Middle Ages.—16. The historical period that extends from the Fall of the Roman Empire (476) to the Conquest of Constantinople by the Turks (1453).

Military.—Hand proper longer than fingers, with square fingers. Mounts and Plain of Mars predominant. Strong Mounts of Venus and Jupiter. Often the three Chief Lines only. Triangles on Upper Mount of Mars and Plain of Mars. One deep line on third phalanx of second finger.

Milky Way, The.—The Via Lasciva—30.

Ministry, Aptitude for the.—Pointed First Finger. Short nails. Moderate Mount of Venus. Good Lines of Head and Heart. A cross in the Quadrangle under the Mount of Saturn.

Misanthrope, The.—Long, knotty, often spatulate, Fingers. A very pronounced or badly marked Mount of Saturn. Absence of the Mounts of the Sun and Venus. Short Line of Heart.

Miserly Disposition.—Hand thin and hard. Thumb close to first finger. Fingers bent inward. Line of Head cutting Hand like a bar. Line of Heart often absent, or, if there, forming a very narrow Quadrangle.

Misuse of Artistic or Intellectual Talents.—Third Finger crooked. Mount of the Sun thrown toward a very bad Mount of Mercury. Exaggerate Mount of the Moon. No Mount of Jupiter. Often an exaggerate or much lined Mount of Saturn.

Monomania of Persecution.—Case: 347.

Montaigne, Michel de; a Frenchman (1533-1602); author of "Essais." Long and curious passage concerning Palmistry in the Paris edition of his works (1854), II., p. 282.

Moon, Mount of the.—1. Position—84. 2. Meanings—86. 3. Displacements —89. 4. Revealing Illness—90. 5. Revealing Mode of Suicide—90. 6. Signs—111. 7. Signature: a. Physical Peculiarities—133; b. Health Peculiarities—133; c. Mental and Moral Peculiarities—134. 7. In combination with another prominent Mount—137.

Moral Nature, Ill-Balanced.—Damp skin, especially if clammy cold—39.

Morbid Disposition.—Yellow-hued and soft palm. Second Finger too long, especially the first phalanx. Mount of Saturn exaggerate, often covered with confused lines. Lines yellow and weak. Line of Head drooping into a light Mount of the Moon. Line of Liver wavy or fragmentary.

Morbid Instincts, Disastrous.—Third Finger very much shorter than Second. See above indications.

Moreau, Adèle; a Frenchwoman and a pupil of the famous Mlle. Le Normand; author of "L'Avenir dévoilé; Chiromancie Nouvelle, Etude des Deux Mains" (Paris: 1869).

Mother Died When the Subject Was Born.—Case: 95.

Mother-in-Law Influence.—A Sister Line closely accompanying a strongly marked Line of Union.

Mounts, Lines and Signs on the.—91. 1. On the Mount of Jupiter—91. 2. On the Mount of Saturn—97. 3 On the Mount of the Sun—101. 4. On the Mount of Mercury—104. 5. On the Upper Mount of Mars—108. 6. On the Mount of the Moon—111. 7. On the Mount of Venus—117. 8. On the Lower Mount of Mars—121.

Mounts of the Hand.—81. Elevations in the Palm of the hand that surround the "Palm Proper" or "Plain of Mars" Eight in number: 1—of Jupiter—85, 2—of Saturn—86, 3—of the Sun—86, 4—of Mercury—86, 5—of Upper Mars—86, 6—of the Moon—86, 7—of Venus—87, 8—of Lower Mars—87). Position—84. Meanings—85. Displacements—87. As they reveal Illnesses—89. As they indicate Suicidal Tendencies—90.

Mounts, Signatures of the.—Definition: A Mount towering over all the others in both hands is considered as corresponding with a definite Physical, Mental and Moral Type—122. 1. The Jupiterian—123. 2. The Saturnian—124. 3. The Solar Subject—126. 4. The Mercurian—129. 5. The Martian—131. 6. The Lunar Subject —133. 7.The Venusian—134. Combinations of the two most prominent Mounts—136.

Mueller, Johann; a German (1801-1858); author of "Handbuch der Physiologie des Menschen" (1841); we read the French translation published in Paris by Jourdan (1854)—20—23.

Murderer, The Slow.—Long, thin hands; knotty fingers. The Mount of Saturn exaggerate or much rayed. Stars on the second finger. Mount of the Sun exaggerate (envy); Mount of Mercury heavily marked with cross lines (deceit). The lower part of the Mount of the Moon much rayed and with a drooping prong from the Line of Head. Short Line of Life if he is to die on scaffold.

Murderer, The Violent.—Thick, hard hands. Spatulate fingers. Clubbed Thumb. The three Chief Lines very red and no others. Exaggerate Mounts of Mars and Venus (in this case vicious instincts, not love). The Lines of Heart and Head are short, also Line of Life if destined to die on scaffold. Stars on the Second Fingers. Large cross in the Triangle.

Music, Great Aptitude for.—A moderately soft hand and conical, smooth fingers. Mounts of the Sun, the

Moon and Venus well developed. A slightly drooping Line of Head. This applies to natural aptitudes, not to merely cultivated, artificial talents.

Musical Instrumentists and Composers.
—Hand proper shorter than fingers, with square tips. Slight knots (especially the second) frequently visible. The above indications as to the Mounts obtain here, with the addition of a strong Mount of Mercury and the essential difference that the Line of Head is apt to be separated from the Line of Life at the start and normally directed to the end.

Mystic Cross, The.—A well formed
cross in the Quadrangle under the Mount of Saturn. The token of exceptional occult powers—313.

Nails.—1. Short—39; 2. Short, hard,
covered with skin—39; 3. Short, with soft palm—39; 4. Short on second finger—39; 5. Short and pale—40; 6. Short, square, bluish—40; 7. Short, square, broad—40; 8. Short, triangular—40; 9. Short, narrow, curved—40; 10. Large, broad, long—40; 11. Long, thin, brittle—40; 12. Long, thin, curved—40; 13. Long, thin, narrow—40; 14. Moderately thin and narrow—40; 15. Almond shaped—40; 16. Pink on outer edge—41; 17. Ridges on certain nail—41; 18. Cross Ridges—41; 19. Hippocrates' nail—41; 20. White spots—41; 21. Black and bluish spots—41.

Napoleon III.'s Hands Examined by
Desbarrolles—80.

Narrow-mindedness.—See Meanness.
In this case, however, the Line of Heart may be a trifle more normal. The fingers are often both smooth and square tipped.

Naurath, Ludwig von; a German; author
of "De Manuum Morphologia et Physiologia" (Berlin: 1833).

Naval Profession, Aptitude for the.—
Long, knotty fingers, especially the Third finger, which is much above

average. A large Mount of the Moon, much lined along the Percussion. Fine Mounts and Plain of Mars. With a large first phalanx of the Thumb. Line of Head often separated from the Line of Life at the start and drooping at the termination.

Nerve System of Man.—Illustration—
21.

Nervous Disorder Left by Some Disease.
—A downward branch starting from a black spot on Line of Life.

Nervous Nature, Ultra.—Case: 158.

Nervous Trouble.—Plain of Mars hol-
low toward Moon. Flat First Phalanx of the Thumb. Exaggerate or much lined Mount of Saturn. A large spot or dot on the lower part of the Mount of the Moon. Line of Life chained or linked.

Nervous, Worrying Nature.—A num-
ber of minor cross lines. See Lines of Influence from the Mount of Venus. A large or much rayed Mount of the Moon.

Neuralgia, Severe.—Deep, colorless in-
dentation (sometimes many dots) on Line of Head. An island on the same Line.

Nurse, The Good.—Elastic Palm. Long
knotty fingers (especially the second knot). A fine Mount of Mercury, with the Medical Stigmata (which see). Fine Mounts of Venus and Jupiter. Healthy Lines of Head and Heart. No worry lines.

Obstinacy.—Hard palm. Spatulate, or
at least square fingers, with first knot marked and short, but abnormally broad nails. Short but very flat first phalanx of the Thumb. Line of Head starting from under the Mount of Saturn and rather short. The Mounts of Mars (especially the Lower one) exaggerate.

Occult Sciences, Aptitudes for the.—
Thin palm, long, smooth fingers, especially the first phalanges. Mounts of the Moon, Mercury and Saturn pre-

dominant. Drooping Line of Head. Line of Intuition. A cross in the Quadrangle. (See Mystic Cross). A Triangle on the Mount of the Moon. The Small Triangle well formed.

Only Love.—A large cross on the Mount of Venus, with a clear cross on the Mount of Jupiter.

Only Love.—Case: 164.

Onychomancy.—Divination of future events by the markings on the nails— 41. From the Greek "Onuchos," finger nail, and "Manteia," divination.

Opera Singers.—Hand proper longer than fingers, the latter with conical tips. Lines of Life and Head widely separated at the start, the latter forked at the termination. See Music, Aptitudes for.

Order in Every Day Life.—Strong second knot on all fingers. See Knot. Generally square tipped fingers.

Order in Ideas.—Strong first knot on all fingers. See Knot. Often spatulate tipped fingers.

Order Wanting in Ideas or Actions.— Very small, smooth hands, with a soft palm and insignificant first phalanx of the thumb.

Oppressions Causing Monomania.— Case: 351.

Outdoor Life and Sports, Love for.— Large, hard hand. Spatulate finger tips. Third finger longer than normal. Second finger good size. Lines of Life and Head separate at the start. No worry lines. Often very low Mounts (except Mars) and only the three Chief Lines.

Overwork or Dissipation, Signs of.—A much islanded Line of Head.

Owen, Sir Richard; an Englishman (1804); author of "On the Nature of Limbs" (London: 1849).

Oxenford, Ina; an Englishwoman; author of "The New Chirology" (London: 1895); also of "Life Studies in

Palmistry" (London: 1897); in collaboration with Miss Anna M. Cosgrave.

Pacini, Filipo; an Italian (1812-1883); discoverer of the termination of nerves below the epidermis, and of Pacinian Corpuscles (which see).

Pacinian Corpuscles.—Agglomerations of nervous matter found only in mankind and gathered in the palm of the hand, mostly inside the Mounts under the fingers and the Plain of Mars— 19; 24.

Pain in the Side, Unexplained.—Case: 210.

Painter, Famous German.—Case: 225.

Painter, Special Characteristics of a Famous.—Case: 298.

Palm.—Measured inside, from wrist to finger base—35. "Size and Shape:" 1. Narrow—38; 2. Wide—38; 3. Too Wide—38; 4. Square—38. "Color and Skin Character:" 1. Very pale— 38; 2. Yellow—38; 3. Pink and Mottled—38; 4. Red—38; 5. Very Red— 38; 6. Satin Skin—39; 7. Dry Skin— 39; 8. Damp Skin—39.

Palm Proper.—Inside hand, not including the Mounts—35. 1. Flat but high —39; 2. Flat but low—39; 3. Hollow —39.

Palmist and Chirological Review; a Monthly published since 1892 by the Roxburgh Press, 15 Victoria St., Westminster, London; edited by Mrs. Katherine St. Hill and Mr. Charles F. Rideal.

Palmistry.—The art or science of reading one's nature and fate in the lines and lineaments of the hand. Lately it has been made to combine Chirognomy and Chiromancy into one homogeneous science. The word is unknown in the Latin, German, French and Italian works on Palmistry, both ancient and modern. With them "Chiromancy" is made to apply to the whole of the science.

Papus, Doctor; a Frenchman; author of "Traité de Magie pratique" (Paris:

1885); also "Traité Méthodique de Science Occulte" (Paris: 1891).

Paracelsus; a German-Swiss; author of "Philosophia Sagax" (1493-1541).

Paralysis.—Nails short and triangular shaped. Exaggerate or much lined Mount of Saturn. A star on the Mount of Saturn. A grille and a star on the Mount of the Moon. Main Lines all poorly marked (after the attack).

Paralysis.—Case: 99. Case: 182.

Passion.—See Love, Extreme Passion in.

Passionate Disposition; Easily Angered. —Hair on all phalanges. Dark colored hair on hand. Thick, hard palm. Red skin. Short, broad and red nails, the base overrun by flesh or skin. Exaggerate Mounts and Plain of Mars. Red skin. A deeply colored Line of Mars.

Past Written in the Hand.—How and when—26.

Pecuniary Losses.—See Bankruptcy and Financial Losses.

Perfidy.—See Traitor, The.

Perseverance.—Elastic Palm. Square, Knotted Fingers. Strong first Phalanx of the Thumb. Lower Mount of Mars predominant. A long, straight Line of Head. The Mount of Mercury and the Fourth Finger well developed.

Peruchio; an Italian and a prominent chiromant; author of "La Chiromance, La Physionomie et la Geomance" (Paris: 1636).

Phalanges (singular: phalanx).—35; the small bones of the fingers; three for each finger, two for the thumb. The "Nailed" phalanx is called "First;" the "Middle" one, "Second;" the "Lower" one, "Third." Normal size —46. Illustration—47. Phalanges taken separately—45.

Philosophy, Aptitude for the Study of.— Thin, hard palm. Very long and knotted fingers, especially the first

knot. Often spatulate fingers, but with the first and fourth finger tips decidedly less spatulate and almost, or quite, conical.

Phrenology and Palmistry Compared.— A. Alimentiveness: 1. Amativeness; 2. Parental Love; 3. Inhabitiveness; 4. Friendship; 5. Combativeness; 6. Destructiveness; 7. Secretiveness; 8. Acquisitiveness; 9. Constructiveness; 10. Self Esteem; 11. Approbativeness; 12. Cautiousness; 13. Benevolence; 14. Veneration; 15. Firmness; 16. Conscientiousness; 17. Hope; 18. Spirituality; 19. Ideality; 20. Mirthfulness; 21. Imitation; 22. Individuality; 23. Form; 24. Size; 25. Weight; 26. Color; 27. Locality; 28. Calculation; 29. Order; 30. Eventuality; 31. Time; 32. Tune; 33. Language; 34. Comparison; 35. Causality. B. Memory of Language. C. Concentrativeness—355.

Physician, Aptitude to be a.—The Medical stigmata on the Mount of Mercury (which see) in a large elastic hand with square tipped, knotted fingers.

Pickpocket, The.—Thin, narrow palm. Long, thin, crooked Fingers, especially the Fourth Finger. An exaggerate Mount of Mercury, or one much cross lined. The lower part of the Mount of the Moon exaggerate. A poor, drooping Line of Head.

Plain of Mars, The.—308. The space on the Palm unoccupied by the Mounts. 1. The Quadrangle: a. Position—309. b. Character—311. c. Signs—312. 2. The Triangle: a. Position—316; b. Character—316; c. The First Angle—318; d. The Second Angle—319; e. The Third Angle— 320; f. Signs—321; g. Special Observations (The Small Triangle)—324.

Pleasure, Love of; Without Excess.— Hand thick and medium soft. Well developed (but not exaggerate) Mounts of Jupiter and Venus. No worry lines.

Pleurisy.—See Respiratory Organs.

Poetical Aspirations.—Pointed (or at

least conical) Fingers. A long, thin first phalanx of the thumb. A thin, soft palm. Mounts of the Sun, the Moon and Venus very prominent. A drooping Line of Head. Often a Line of Heart much chained and islanded.

Poisoner, The.—See Murderer, The Slow.

Poisoning Case.—Case: 354.

Politics, Aptitude for.—Statesman revealed by fine Mounts of Jupiter, the Sun and Mercury. With a Line of Head beginning high on the Mount of Jupiter and slightly forked at the end, and with fine Mounts and Plain of Mars. The bar-room Politician shows but little Mount of Jupiter, but an exaggerate and badly marked Mount of Mercury. The Line of Head will be drooping and the Upper Mount of Mars much lined, showing aggressive brutal instincts.

Pompeius, Nicolaus; a German; author of "Figuræ Chiromanticæ" (Hamburg: 1682), and "Præcepta Chiromantica" (Hamburg: 1682).

Prætorius, Johann; a German; author of "Cheiroscopia et Metoposcopia" (Jena: 1659), and other noted works on the subject.

Preface-to-Be-Read.—9.

Preliminaries.—13.

Presentiments.—Case: 289.

Preservation, Curious Square of.—Case: 258.

Preservation, Repeated Instances of.—Case: 352.

Pride, Indomitable.—Exaggerate Mounts of Jupiter and Mounts and Plain of Mars. A grille on the Mount of Jupiter. Often a number of Lines or branches from the Lines of Life or Head running high up into the Mount of Jupiter. Often exaggerate Mount of the Sun.

Primitive Nature.—See Elementary Hand—66.

Prison.—A square on the lower part of the Mount of Venus. A grille on the Mount of Saturn.

Profitable Meeting at a Watering Place. —Case: 351.

Profligacy.—See Love, Extreme Passion. Add to those indications a much rayed Mount of Venus; a star near the thumb nail; a star on third phalanx of first finger.

Protection from Disaster.—Case: 188.

Prudence.—A fine Second Finger and a well formed Mount of Saturn. A second Phalanx of the Thumb above Normal. Finger tips square and second knots marked. Line of Head attached quite a space to the Line of Life. A fine Lower Mount of Mars and a Mount of Mercury fully developed, with Fourth Finger slightly above average.

Pythagoras.—A famous Greek philosopher (B. C. 560-500)—16.

Quadrangle, The.—309. (See Plain of Mars.)

Quain's "Elements of Anatomy" (London: 1876).

Quarrelsome Disposition.—See Violent Nature.

Rascette, The.—196. 1. Position and Direction—196. 2. Character—197. 3. Connected with the Mounts—197. 4. Breaks—198. 5. Connected with the Lines—198. 6. Signs—198.

Reading, Love of.—The more or less conical shape of the First Finger, in combination with the indications concerning the Palm, the other finger Tips, the Knots, the Mounts, will indicate—with a fine Line of Head in all cases—in what direction the subject's Love of Reading will find its satisfaction.

Reason Lost Through Love Sorrow.— Case: 237.

Recklessness.—See Imprudence. Just increase untoward indications therein enumerated.

Recovery from Serious Illness.—The overlaying fragments of a Line of Life connected by a bar. Similar fragments encased within a square. Around all evil signs on the Hand to be interpreted as serious illnesses the presence of a square is reassuring. Wanting that, the fact that the bad indications are not repeated in both hands is a promise of recovery.

Religion, Change of.—Case: 244.

Religion, Founder of a New.—Case: 352.

Religion, Resignation Due to.—Case: 249.

Religious Enthusiasm Determining Absolute Chastity.—Case: 302.

Religious Veneration.—Slender, soft palm; smooth, pointed fingers, especially the First. A fine Mount of Jupiter.

Requeno, Vincenzo; an Italian; author of "Scoperta della Chironomia" (Parma: 1797).

Respir.—24. The "exhalation"—so to speak—of the vital fluid.

Respiratory Organs, Disease of.—Thin Palm. Long, brittle, curved or fluted nails. Pale lines. Mount of Jupiter exaggerate. Many islands on the Line of Head. A Line of Influence ending in an island on the Mount of Jupiter.

Respiratory Organs, Severe Trouble of. —Case: 351.

Responsibility, Dislike of.—First Finger too short. Lines of Head attached too long to the Line of Life at the start. Insignificant (or absent) Mounts of Mars. First Phalanx of Thumb below normal.

Revengeful Enemy, Ambition Interfered with by.—Case: 95.

Rheumatism.—"Satin" skin. Exaggerate or much lined Mount of Saturn. The Midle part of the Mount of the Mount of the Moon exaggerate or much lined. A line down the Middle part of the Mount of the Moon, especially if crossed. Line of Life widely forked and red at the termination. Cross Lines from the Line of Life to the Mount of Saturn.

Rheumatism, Hereditary.—Several lines crossing the Mount of Saturn and the Line of Heart.

Rheumatism, Inflammatory.—With other indications of Rheumatism (which see), black, bluish or red dots on the Line of Heart.

Riches.—See Financial Success.

Ronphile; a Frenchman; author of "La Chyromantie naturelle" (Lyons: 1653).

Rothmann, Johann; a German; author of "Chiromantiæ Theorica Practica" (Erfurt: 1595). English translation by Wharton (London: 1652).

Royal Personage, Favorite of a.—Case: 354.

Ruined by a Woman, Position.—Case: 264.

Ruined, Minor Children Financially.— Case: 178.

Sadness, Superstitious.—Second Finger leaning toward First. Exaggerate Second Finger (especially first phalanx) and Mount of Saturn. Drooping Line of Head, with exaggerate Mount of the Moon.

Sahn, Frank; a German; author of "Die Chiromantie der Alten" (Berlin: 1856).

St. Germain, Comte C. de; a Frenchman (1846—); author of "Hand Book of Palmistry" (New York: 1883); "Practical Palmistry" (Chicago: 1897); "The Practice of Palmistry for Professional Purposes" (2 vols. 1,250 ill.; Chicago: 1897-98); editor of the monthly, "American Journal of Palmistry" (Chicago: 1897, 1898—).

Sanders, Richard; the leading English chiromant of the XVII. Century; author of "Physiognomie, Chiromancie, Metoposcopie," etc., Handled with Their Natural Predictive Significations" (London: 1653); also of "Palmistry; the Secrets Thereof Disclosed" (London: 1664).

Sappho, a Modern.—Case: 264.

Saturnian, The.—The Line of Fate—30.

Saturn, Mount of.—1. Position—84. 2. Meanings—86. 3. Displacements—88. 4. Revealing Illnesses—89. 5. Revealing Mode of Suicide—90. 6. Signs—97. 7. Signature: a. Physical Peculiarities—124; b. Health Peculiarities—125; c. Mental and Moral Peculiarities—125. 8. In combination with another prominent Mount—137.

Saturn, The Ring of.—The Girdle of Venus—30. There is, however, a Ring of Saturn, just encircling the base of the Finger, on the Mount, the meaning of which—Extraordinary Magic (or Occult) Powers.

Scaffold, Death on the.—Line of Head broken under the Mount of Saturn. A cross in the Plain of Mars and stars on the second finger. The Line of Life terminating abruptly and generally with a deep bar at the date of the execution.

Schalitz, Christian; a German; author of "Die von Aberglauben, Vanitaeten und Teuscherei gereinigte Chiromantia, etc." (Frankfort: 1729).

Seduction by Married Man.—Case: 179.

Seduction by Married Man.—Case: 269.

Seers and Saints.—Transparent hand. Almond shaped nails. Very pointed, smooth fingers, especially the first finger. Often high Mount of the Moon. Line of Intuition and Mystic Cross (which see) in both hands.

Selfishness, Excessive.—Hand thick and flabby. Very pale Palm and Lines. Short, smooth fingers, somewhat conical, with thick third phalanges. Exaggerate Mounts of Venus and the Moon. Often absence of the Line of Heart; if it is there it is poor and much branched downward.

Sensitiveness to Criticism, Extreme.—

Short nail on Second Finger, the other almond shaped. Lines of Life and Head attached too long at the start. An exaggerate Mount of the Sun (envy) and an exaggerate Mount of the Moon. Many Worry Lines.

Sensual Instincts.—See Love, Extreme Passion in.

Separation, Ending Happily, Cruel.—Case: 193.

Separation; Fatal Journey.—Case: 182.

Separation from a Loved One.—Case: 290.

Separation, Legal.—Case: 306.

Separation (Not Divorce).—The forks at the starting point or termination of Lines of Union are often accurately read as separation of some duration, due not to quarreling or such causes, but to the necessities of existence.

Shipwreck, Danger of.—A star or island on a short Line of Voyage along the Percussion of the Mount of the Moon.

Sider, A.; a Frenchman; author of "La Chiromancie Royale et Nouvelle" (Lyons: 1666).

Signs and Lines on Thumb and Fingers. —325. 1. On Thumb—325. 2. On all the Fingers—328. 3. On First Finger—329. 4. On Second Finger —333. 5. On Third Finger—337. 6. On Fourth Finger—340.

Signs in General.—91. Sixteen in Number. Illustration—91. 1. The Spot or Dot. 2. The Cross. 3. The Star. 4. The Circle. 5. The Square. 6. The Triangle. 7. The Angle. 8. The Island. 9. The Grille, or Gridiron. 10. The Sign of Jupiter. 11. The Sign of Saturn. 12. The Sign of the Sun. 13. The Sign of Mercury. 14. The Sign of Mars. 15. The Sign of the Moon. 16. The Sign of Venus.

Skeleton of Hand, Illustration of.—35.

Skepticism "versus" Convent Life.—Case: 263.

Skill, Practical.—Long, knotted fingers. Especially well shaped (square) second finger and good Mount of Mercury.

Skin Disease.—Case: 156.

Somnambulism.—An island at the starting point of a Line of Liver that runs close to the Percussion. Still stronger if that island is found at the start of a Line of Intuition.

Somnambulism.—Case: 208. Case: 212.

Sorrow from Death of Loved One, Extreme.—A Line of Influence from a star on the Mount of Venus, and ending in a dot or star on the Line of Heart.

Spadoni; an Italian; author of "Studio di Curiosita nel quale tratta di Fisionomia, Chiromantia e Metoposcopia" (Venice: 1675).

Spark, J. J.; an Englishman; author of "Scientific and Intuitional Palmistry" (London: 1895).

Speculative Business, Talent for.— Slightly conical finger tips, especially the Fourth Finger. No knots. Third Finger above normal. Mounts and Plain of Mars and Mercury finely developed. Long Line of Head slightly drooping at the termination.

Spendthrift Disposition.—Very Flexible Fingers, with a third Finger often above normal. A first phalanx of the thumb much thrown backward and flexible. High Mounts of Jupiter and the Sun. The Line of Head separated from the Line of Life and drooping somewhat in a high Mount of the Moon.

Sphinx Die; German Periodical; Vols I., II., IV. and V.

Spinal Troubles.—Nails short, narrow and curved. A star on the Mount of Saturn. A drooping Line of Life often starred or broken under Saturn. A much rayed and often starred Mount of the Moon.

Spleen, Disease of.—Case: 169.

Square of Preservation, Peculiar.—Case: 307.

St. Hill, Katherine; an Englishwoman; author of "The Grammar of Palmistry" (London: 1892); also "Hands of Celebrities" (London: 1895).

Sterility.—A cross on the Mount of Saturn—98. The Line of Life lying too close to the Second Phalanx of the Thumb—153. A star at the connection of the Line of Head and Liver— 171. Weak and poor Line of Heart terminating forkless—244.

Sterility.—Case: 207. Case: 208.

Stocker, R. D.; an Englishman; author of "A Concordance of Graphology and Physiognomy" (London: 1895).

Stone, The; Disease of.—The lower part of the Mount of the Moon exaggerate or much lined.

Stubbornness.—See Obstinacy.

Success.—Bases of the fingers on a fair alignment. Strong Thumb. Fine Mounts of Jupiter, the Sun and Mercury. Straight, long Line of Head. Fine Line of Fate, ending on either the Mount of Jupiter or the Mount of the Sun. Long Line of the Sun. Clear Line of Liver. See Ambition Successful; Art, Extraordinary Success in; Fortune.

Success After Repeated Rebuffs, Final. —Case: 349.

Success (Late in Life).—The Lines of Fate or the Line of the Sun, or both, starting from the Line of Heart and running deep into the Mounts unbarred and unstarred.

Suicidal Tendencies.—Stars on the Mounts of Saturn and the Moon, the latter Mount quite prominent. Drooping Line of Head. A Line of Head merging into Line of Liver, with poor Line of Fate and numerous bars on the Line of Life. For Modes of Suicide see page 90.

Suicide, Attempted.—Case: 351.

Sun, Mount of the.—1. Position—84. 2. Meanings—86. 3. Displacements —89. 4. Revealing Illnesses—89. 5. Revealing Mode of Suicide—90. 6.

Signs—101. 7. Signature: a. Physical Peculiarities—127; b. Health Peculiarities—127; c. Mental and Moral Peculiarities—128. 8. In combination with another prominent Mount—137.

Sun, The Line of the.—294. 1. Position and Direction—294. 2. Character: a. By Itself—295; b. In combination with other Indications—296. 3. Starting Points and Forks at the Start—297. 4. Termination and Forks at the Termination—299. 5. Branches—300. 6. Breaks—301. 7. Connected with the Main Lines: a. Directly—301; b. By Minor Lines—301. 8. Signs—304. Special Observations—307.

Superstition.—Exaggeration of the Second Finger and Mount of Saturn. Often exaggeration of the Mount of the Moon and drooping of the Line of Head.

Surgeon, The.—See Physician, The; also Medical Stigmata. Add to these indications: Hard Palm. Long, spatulate, knotted fingers. Excellent Mounts and Plain of Mars.

Swindler, The.—Long hand. Crooked fingers, especially the Fourth Finger. Wretched Mounts. The Mount of Mercury either exaggerate or marked by confused lines, a cross and even a star. Line of Head deeply forked. Professional swindlers have a Mount of the Moon very heavy in its lower part.

Synovia in Knee Joints, Lack of.—Case: 242.

Synthetical View of Things; Aptitude for Understanding the Whole Better than the Details.—Small hands. Short, smooth fingers.

Tact.—Long fingers, with little balls on the inside of first phalanges. Second knots well marked. Mount of Mercury predominant, with a long, shapely second finger. Excellent Line of Heart. A triangle on or near the termination of the Line of Life. Good Line of Liver. Fine Plain of Mars.

Tact, Lack of.—Short, square, smooth fingers. Short nails. Mounts of Mars exaggerate. Lines of Life and Head separated at the start. Sometimes no Line of Heart; otherwise a very poor one. Fourth Finger and Mount of Mercury far below Normal.

Taylor, Langdon; an Englishman; author of "A Handy Guide to Palmistry" (London: 1895).

Teaching, Aptitude for.—Square, tipped, knotted fingers. Long, well shaped Thumb. Mounts of Mercury and Mars predominant. Mounts of Jupiter and Venus well marked. If intellect remarkable: fine Mount of the Sun. Lines of Head and Life slightly separate at the start. Fine Lines of Head and Heart.

Teeth, Trouble with the.—Exaggerate or much lined Mount of Saturn. Long and wavy Line of Liver, with similar Line of Fate, and second phalanges of all fingers abnormally long.

Thickness of Hand and How to Judge.—37. Its importance in the diagnosis of Disposition and Health. (See Hand Proper and Palm combined.)

Thief, The.—Heavy, elementary hand. Crooked fingers, especially the fourth one. Mount of Mercury very much exaggerate and much crossed and even starred. Lower part of the Mount of the Moon very bulging. No Mount of Jupiter at all. Few lines. See Burglar, The; Pickpocket, The, etc.

Thigh Bone, Dislocation of the.—Case: 106.

Thoughtless Disposition.—Wide space between base of Second and Third Fingers. A wide space between the Lines of Life and Head. High Mount of the Moon. Very little, if any, Mount of Mercury.

Throat, Sore.—Exaggerate or much lined Upper Mount of Mars. Cross lines (especially if deep or forked) from the Percussion of the Upper Mount of Mars.

Thumb.—What distinguishes Man from lower animals. Exhaustive Study—51. In Idiots, Infants, Epileptics, Criminals. 1. Position. 2. Size. 3 Shape. 4. First Phalanx: a. Size; b. Shape. 5. Knot. 6. Second Phalanx: a. Size; b. Shape. No third Phalanx. 7. Combination of Phalanges. 8. Lines and Signs—325.

Tibertus, Antiochus; a German; author of various works on Chiromancy, published in 1494 and 1541 in Bonn and Mayence.

Time in the Hand, How to Reckon.—148. Illustrations—149, 151. On Line of Life—148. On Line of Fate—150. On Line of the Sun—152. On the Percussion—152. On the Mount of Jupiter—152. On Line of Heart—413. On Line of Head—413. On Line of Liver—413.

Timidity.—Thin, soft palm. Long, knotted fingers, inward bent. Low (if any) Mounts of Mars, Mercury and Jupiter. The Line of Head attached too long to the Line of Life at the start. Narrow Quadrangle.

Tips of Fingers.—Shape of extremity of nailed Phalanx. Four leading types of Tips: Pointed; Conical; Square; Spatulate—46.

Tobaco Heart, The.—Case: 245.

Todd, R. B.; an Englishman; author of "Cyclopædia of Anatomy and Physiology" (London: 1839).

Touch, Sense of; the most indispensable of the five senses—19.

Traitor, The.—Crooked Fingers, especially the fourth finger. Short and pale nails. Absence of the Line of Heart.

Travel (or Voyage) for a Loved One's Sake.—A Line of Voyage coming from the Percussion of the Mount of the Moon and merging into the Line of Heart under the Mount of Mercury. Often: Line of Head merging into the Line of Heart under the same Mount.

Traveler, The Born.—Square palm; thick, elastic hand. Short, spatulate fingers; very rarely knotted. A pronounced Third finger if dangerous voyages are projected; also fine Mounts of the Sun and the Moon; with a deep, straight Line of Head. Little of the other Mounts or Lines except the essential ones.

Travel, Successful.—A Line from the Rascette straight to the Mount of Jupiter.

Triangle, The.—316. (See Plain of Mars.)

Triangle, The Small.—324. (See Plain of Mars.)

Tricasso; an Italian and a leading Chiromant of the XVI. Century; author of "Chyromantia Novamente revista e con Somma diligentia corretta e stampata" (1534). Excellent French translation issued in Paris in 1552.

Types of Hands, Leading.—1. The Psychic (or Pointed)—57. 2. The Artistic (or Conical)—59. 3. The Useful (or Square)—61. 4. The Necessary (or Spatulate)—63. 5. The Philosophical (or Knotted)—65. 6. The Elementary—66. 7. The Artistic-Elementary—67. 8. The Murderer's—68. 9. The Idiot's—69. 10, 11, 12. Mixed Hands—70. 13. The Woman's—72. Types of Woman's Types: a. The Dreamer; b. The Emotional; c. The Globe Trotter; d. The Busybody; e. The Drudge; f. The Quicktempered.

Tyrannical Disposition.—First Finger too long. Long, hard nails. First phalanx of the Thumb exaggerate. Exaggerate Mount of Jupiter. Deep, straight Line of Head crossing the hand like a bar. The Line of Heart often absent.

Unconventionality.—Thick, soft palm. All fingers falling apart easily. Fingers bent backward, smooth and conical. Thumb set very low and curved backward. Lines of Head and Life often separated at the start. **Mounts**

of the Sun, the Moon and Venus predominant.

Ungodliness.—See Skepticism.

Union.—Short, horizontal Line on the Percussion of the Mount of Mercury. Cross on the Mount of Jupiter. Line of Influence from the Upper Mount of Mars or the Mount of the Moon to the Line of Fate (sometimes to the Line of the Sun). Marked sometimes by a break on Lines of Fate or the Sun, indicating a great change in the subject's life.

Union, a Brilliant.—A cross and a star united on the Mount of Jupiter. A fine Line of Fate ending on the Mount of Jupiter. A Line of Fate merging into an extremely good Line of Heart.

Union, A Love.—A long, fine Line of Union. A clear cross on the Mount of Jupiter. A Line of Influence from the Mount of the Moon blending with the Line of Fate, or running alongside of it for a space—never cutting it. A branch of the Line of Fate merging into the Line of Heart.

Union, A Mercenary.—A prominent Mount of Mercury. A Line of Influence from the Mount of Mars touching the Line of Fate (often "cutting" it, if the Union is to be unfortunate).

Union, Lines of.—264. 1. Position and Direction—265. 2. Starting Points and Forks at the Start—266. 3. Termination and Forks at the Termination—267. 4. Branches—267. 5. Breaks—268. 6. Connected with the Main Lines—269. 7. Signs—269. Special Observation—271. Additional Cases—271.

Union, Mismated.—A deep, red Line of Union. A Line of Influence from the Mounts of the Moon or Upper Mars cutting the Line of Fate. A broken Line of Heart. A poor Line of Fate from the date corresponding with the Union. A Line from the Line of Heart ending in a crook on the Mount of Saturn. Deep bar, cutting the Line of Heart. A branch of the Line of Fate cutting the Line of Heart.

Union Prevented by Death.—A sharp break on a Line of Union.

Unions, Successive.—Case: 278.

Unselfishness.—See Benevolence.

Useless Details, Mania for.—Very large hands. Exaggerate second knots. See also Fault-finding.

Vacillation.—Soft Palm. Fingers smooth and spatulate. First Phalanx of Thumb below normal. Insignificant Mount of Jupiter. Line of Head attached too long to the Line of Life and short. Plain of Mars low. Lines of Fate and the Sun both forked and accompanied by wavy, short sister lines, especially on the Mounts of Saturn and the Sun.

Vanity.—Exaggerate Mounts of Jupiter and the Sun, with abnormally long third finger. Often exaggerate Mounts of Venus and the Moon. The Line of Life forked at the start, one prong entering the third phalanx of the first finger. Sometimes a similar prong of the Line of Head ends at the same place.

Vanity, Morbid.—Third Finger leaning toward Second. Exaggerate Mount of Jupiter displaced toward the Mount of Saturn. A prong of a fork of the Line of Head going up deep into the Mount of Jupiter, then turning and terminating on the Mount of Saturn.

Venereal Disease.—Case: 163.

Venereal Disease, Grave.—A star on a double Girdle of Venus. A black spot on the Mount of Venus.

Venus, Mount of.—1. Position—85. 2. Meanings—87. 3. Displacements—89. 4. Revealing Illnesses—90. 5. Revealing Mode of Suicide—90. 6. Signs—117. 7. Signature: a. Physical Peculiarities—135; b. Health Peculiarities—135; c. Mental and Moral Peculiarities—136. 7. In combination with another prominent Mount—137.

Versatility.—Hand proper shorter than supple fingers with conical tips. Fine, long Third and Fourth Fingers. Beautiful Mounts of the Sun and Mercury. Line of the Sun exceptionally good. This supposes the Versatility to be of a useful character as far as the career of the subject is concerned.

Via Lasciva, The.—209. 1. Position and Character—209. 2. Termination and Forks at the Termination—209. 3. Breaks and Branches—209. 4. Connected with the Main Lines: a. Directly—209; b. By Minor Lines—209. 5. Signs—210.

Vice, Worst Consequences of Sensual.— Exaggerate or much lined Mounts of Saturn and Venus. Triple Girdle of Venus. A pale, wide Line of Heart.

Vindictiveness.—The Mounts and Plain of Mars very exaggerate; also the Mount of the Sun (envy). A very narrow Quadrangle, due to the abnormal lowering of the Line of Heart. Often Line of Heart entirely absent, with a Line of Head crossing the hand like a bar.

Violent Nature.—Very hairy hands (in a man). Reddish colored hair. Hand thick and hard. Nails long, thick and curved clawlike. Exaggerate Mounts and Plain of Mars. Red lines, especially a deep and Long Line of Mars.

Violent Temper.—Case: 225.

Violinist, Brilliant Girl.—Case: 214.

Vocation Interfered with.—Case: 275.

Voyages (Lucky).—Line from the Rascette to the Mount of Jupiter. Horizontal Lines along the Percussion of the Mount of the Moon, when not broken or badly marked.

Voyages, Unlucky.—Broken, crossed, starred, islanded Horizontal Lines along the Percussion of the Mount of the Moon. Two lines from the Rascette to the Mount of Saturn, crossing each other there.

Warren, Claud; an Englishman; author of "Life Size Outlines of the Hands of Twenty-two Celebrated Persons" (London: 1882).

Weakening of the System, General.— Line of Life forked at the Termination—159.

Wealth.—See Success; Inheritance, etc.

Wearing-out of the System.—Very deep Lines. Line of Life tasseled or ending in a series of crosses. Capillary lines drooping from or attached to Line of Life. See Languor.

Widowerhood.—Case: 183.

Widowhood.—Case: 185.

Wife, A Deceiving.—Case: 268.

Woman, The New.—Square palm; long, knotty fingers. Very short nails. Lines red and deep. The hand furrowed by cross lines. Line of Life and Head widely separated at the start. Excessive Mounts of Jupiter and the Sun (Love of notoriety). Mount of Mercury in evidence, with a strong Mount of the Moon and a much drooping Line of Head. Line of Heart and Mount of Venus insignificant.

Womb Displacement.—Case: 171.

Womb Troubles.—Case: 154.

Woods, Joseph; an Englishman; author of "Scientific Palmistry and Its Use" (London: 1897).

Worry Lines.—Those Lines of Influence from the Mounts of Venus or Lower Mars or the Line of Life that cross the hand for a little distance only and are not clear enough to be especially read in accordance with the rules set down in pp. 172-193.

Worlds of the Kabbala, The Three.—15. According to Desbarrolles they represent the three elements in the hand: "The Inspirational," the "Mental," the "Material." A whole, most curious system is found deducted from these principles in "Les Mystères de la Main" (Paris: 1859). Also in the works of Eliphas Levi, Dr. Papus, M. Decrespe, etc. Without denying the marvelous logic of the Master's reasonings, it has been found preferable to leave them out of a purely practical work of this kind.

Wound, Dangerous.—A black dot on Line of Life. Lines from the first phalanx of the Thumb to the Line of Life.

Wound in the Leg.—Case: 97.

Wound, Mortal.—Stars or breaks of Lines of Life, Head or Heart when repeated in both hands and with an accompanying break or ominous sign on the Line of Fate.

Yearning Toward Notoriety, Extravagant.—Case: 347.

Yellow Fever.—Case: 286.

PROCESS FOR MAKING PRINTS OF THE HANDS.

First. Use a paper about the consistency of that used for typewriting purposes.

Second. Procure some gum camphor. Take only a very small piece of it and place it in a plate.

Third. Light it up with a match, and pass the sheet of paper rapidly over the flame until it becomes a deep black, taking care not to burn the paper or to make it turn yellow by exposing it too long to the flame.

Fourth. Prepare a small cushion, made of tissue paper, elastic under pressure, without being too soft.

Fifth. Place under the top sheet a small oval-shaped pad made of a certain number of extra sheets of paper, and the purpose of which is to fill the hollow of the palm.

Sixth. Place upon this cushion the prepared sheet of paper, and ascertain where the small pad is. Then place the hand, with fingers stretched, upon the sheet, and press softly, but firmly.

Seventh. Before lifting the hand, pass a well-sharpened pencil around the palm and fingers so as to clearly mark their shape.

Eighth. Lift the hand quickly, so as to avoid any rubbing.

Ninth. To preserve this print it will be well to use a Fixatif, which can be procured from any art store. The Fixatif is to be sprayed upon the picture at a distance by means of a blow-pipe or vaporizer.

Tenth. Take an impression of both hands, and see that they are clear, repeating the operation until you get good impressions, showing all the lines, and not having any black spots covering any important features.

APPENDIX

READING OF DATES ON HORIZONTAL LINES.

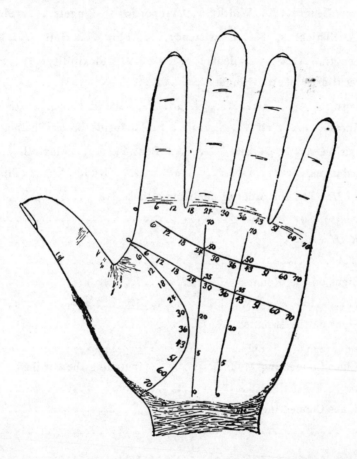

Mr. H. C. Christensen, a resident of Chicago, of Danish parentage, has given lately a great deal of his time to the close study of Modern Palmistry. Following indications obtained from a distinguished English Palmist, he has prepared a most interesting drawing, containing Date-Markings on Normally placed Lines of Head and Heart. I understand that this additional method of securing time measurements has been verified in numberless cases as proving extremely useful and accurate. I have, therefore, no hesitation in presenting it to my readers, requesting those among them who are competent to discuss such a difficult topic to furnish me with their criticisms, even should they be entirely unfavorable to the proposed scales. I may add, that, very lately—in fact, during the month of December, 1897—Miss Ina Oxenford, the excellent London palmist, honored me with a communication on a similar subject wherein she states that she has reached recently a much closer calculation of dates than has ever been realized—or even attempted by Desbarrolles, Papus, Heron-Allen or even herself or her teacher, Mrs. Kathryn St. Hill. In the meantime, here is Mr. Christensen's Table for the Measurement of Dates on five Chief Lines, which I insert without further explanations, as it needs none.

Comte C. de Saint-Germain's

MODEL CHART FOR COMPLETE HAND-READING.

L. H.—Left Hand.   R. H.—Right Hand

HAND PROPER   Length......Width......Proportion to Fingers......Shape......
AND PALM.   Thickness......Consistency......Skin.....Hair......Nails.....

FINGERS.   Length............Bent.................Flexibility...............

Peculiarity of Any Finger.......................................

Tips..........1st...........2d.........3d.........4th.........

Knots........1st.........2d........Inside Lower Phalanges.......

THUMB.   Position..........Size..........Bent.........Flexibility.........

Phalanges.........1st.........2d........Knot........Tip.........

MOUNTS.   *L. H.*   [In the order of their importance.]......................

....

R. H....

....

Signs on the Mounts.   *L. H.*.....................................

....

Signs on the Mounts.   *R. H.*.....................................

....

Lines Connecting Mounts.   *L. H.*   [Including the Girdle.]...........

....

Lines Connecting Mounts.   *R. H.*.................................

....

LIFE.   *L. H.*..

....

Lines of Influence..

....

R. H....

....

Lines of Influence..

....

....

HEAD. *L. H*...

....

R. H..

....

HEART. *L. H*...

....

R. H..

....

FATE. *L. H*..

....

Lines of Influence...

....

....

R. H..

....

Lines of Influence..

....

....

SUN. *L. H*...

....

Lines of Influence..

....

....

R. H...

....

Lines of Influence ....

....

....

LIVER. *L. H*..

....

R. H...

....

UNION. *L. H.* ....

....

....

    R. H. ....

....

....

QUADRANGLE. *L. H.* ....

....

    R. H. ....

....

TRIANGLE. *L. H.* ....

....

    R. H. ....

....

ON FINGERS AND THUMB. *L. H.* ....

....

    R. H. ....

....

RASCETTE. *L. H.* ....

....

    R. H. ....

....

SUNDRY INDICATIONS. *L. H.* ....

....

....

    R. H. ....

....

....